Thomas Claverhill Jerdon

The Birds of India

: being a natural history of all the birds known to inhabit continental India, with

descriptions of the species, genera, families, tribes, and orders, and a brief notice

of such families as are not found in India.

Thomas Claverhill Jerdon

The Birds of India
: being a natural history of all the birds known to inhabit continental India, with descriptions
of the species, genera, families, tribes, and orders, and a brief notice of such families as are
not found in India.

ISBN/EAN: 9783337222116

Printed in Europe, USA, Canada, Australia, Japan

Cover: Foto ©Andreas Hilbeck / pixelio.de

More available books at **www.hansebooks.com**

THE

BIRDS OF INDIA;

BEING

A NATURAL HISTORY

OF ALL

THE BIRDS KNOWN TO INHABIT CONTINENTAL INDIA:

WITH

Descriptions of the Species, Genera, Families, Tribes, and Orders, and a
Brief Notice of such Families as are not found in India,

MAKING IT A

MANUAL OF ORNITHOLOGY

SPECIALLY ADAPTED FOR INDIA.

BY

T. C. JERDON,

SURGEON MAJOR, MADRAS ARMY,

Author of " Illustrations of Indian Ornithology."

In Two Volumes.

VOL. II.—PART I.

Calcutta:
PRINTED FOR THE AUTHOR BY THE MILITARY ORPHAN PRESS,
6, BANKSHALL STREET.

1863.

PREFACE.

In consequence of the time that the careful compilation of an Index will take, and other circumstances, the Author has been induced to issue the Second Volume in two parts. This will be attended with great additional expense to the Author; but, in consideration of the numerous observers, now fortunately scattered over the country, who are anxious for the early appearance of the Work, the Author has not grudged it.

The concluding part will, he hopes, be issued in a few months.

CONTENTS OF VOL. II, PART I.

CONTENTS

THE BIRDS OF INDIA.

Sub-fam. TIMALINÆ, Babbling Thrushes.

Syn. *Crateropodinæ*, Swains.—*Timalidæ*, Bonap.—*Liotrichidæ*, Caban., and Van Hoeven (in part).

Legs and feet stout and large ; bill various in form and length, almost always compressed, usually notched ; wings short and rounded ; tail largish, graduated : plumage often lax.

This family presents a large assemblage of birds of diverse and varied aspect ; some with short and thick bills ; a few with long and curved beaks ; others with this organ moderate and Thrush-like. In fact, we have represented here, as far as the beak is concerned, Thrushes, Shrikes, Jays, Finches, Titmice, and Tree-creepers. Their most characteristic features are their strong legs and feet, combined with a short rounded wing, and a compressed bill. Their colors are usually plain and sombre, in one group varied with some richer tints. Their habits correspond with their structural details. They are mostly social, or even gregarious ; they are a good deal on the ground, on which they hop vigorously, or climb with facility through tangled thickets or reeds ; and their food is both insects, fruits, and grain. The majority of those, with whose habits we are familiar, lay blue eggs. The sexes rarely differ, if at all, and the young are clothed much as the parent birds, only somewhat duller. The greater number of the species, as at present recognized, are Asiatic, chiefly from India and Malayana ; and it is only of late years that most of them have been made known to science. They extend through the Eastern Isles to Australia and New Zealand ; several are African ; and possibly many birds of the New Continent may be found to associate naturally with the birds of this group.

Swainson was the first naturalist who seized on their peculiarities of structure, and named them *Crateropodinæ*, a name which perhaps ought to be retained. Bonaparte, in his Conspectus,

A

separated them, some of them being placed as a sub-family,
Timalinæ, of his *Maluridæ*; and others in the *Ptilorhynchinæ*, a
sub-family of the *Garrulidæ*, or Jays. Latterly, however, he fully
recognized the extent of the group, so far as to locate in his
family, *Timalidæ*, most of the birds now usually placed here;
but he included in it many of the short-legged Thrushes,
Brachypodinæ; and, with more justice, I consider, the group
of Mocking-birds, or American short-winged Thrushes. Blyth,
in his Catalogue, also classed them much as the Prince
formerly did; but now nearly adopts the group as defined by
Gray and Horsfield, with some additions. This naturalist also
is inclined to place the diminutive, short-winged warblers, such
as *Drymoica, Prinia*, &c., with the Babblers; but I prefer class-
ing them as a type of the *Sylviadæ*.

Taking all their characters and habits into consideration, I fully
agree with Gray and Horsfield in their views as to the extent of
this family; but I believe that many other forms, not usually
associated with this family, also belong here, some of which will
be pointed out in the proper place. As we approach the limits
of the group on either side, there are of course a few forms whose
place is not so clear or marked; and one or more have been placed
in the next family, the *Brachypodidæ*; and this we can easily understand (as the two groups approach each other, if they do not actually unite,) without agreeing with the Prince of Canino, and placing
the short-legged Thrushes, of strict arboreal habits, with these
strong-legged and active clamberers, and ground birds. A few of
this family also approach the *Myiotherinæ*, and several of the smaller
members of the *Timalia* section were classed by Temminck under
his somewhat heterogeneous *Myiothera*. Some of the forms of
this family also approach the *Leiotrichinæ*; they are classed
together by certain foreign Ornithologists; and one, or more genera
have been bandied between the two groups by other writers.

Bonaparte divides the *Timalidæ* (excluding the Bulbuls) into
Liotrichinæ, Garrulacinæ, Crateropodinæ, Miminæ, and *Timalinæ*.
I shall divide them, without bestowing any distinct name, or
defining the limits of each very closely, into the following sections:
1*st*, the thick billed, or Finch-thrushes; 2*nd*, the Jay-thrushes

and Shrike-babblers; *3rd*, the Quaker and Wren-babblers; *4th*, the Creeper-thrushes; 5th, the Laughing-thrushes; 6th, the true Babblers; and lastly, the Reed-thrushes.

Although the series, as here given, is not unbroken, I think that it presents the affinities, *inter se*, of the various sections pretty closely; and the two most abnormal groups are here placed each on the confines of the family. With regard to their external relations, I think, that whilst they perhaps join the Tits, and *Liotrichinæ*, through *Suthora* and the *Alcippe* group, on the other side they are undoubtedly connected to the Warblers through some of the Reed-thrushes, such as *Eurycercus* and *Schœnicola*, and they join the true Thrushes by the Mocking Thrushes of America.

1*st*. The thick-billed, or Finch-thrushes, (*Paradoxornithinæ*, Gray.)

There has been considerable difference of opinion as to the affinities of these very curious birds. Mr. Gould, who founded the typical genus, contents himself with calling it a paradoxical bird. Gray places the smaller forms with the *Parinæ*, and the larger in the *Fringillidæ*, next *Phytotoma*. Bonaparte, likewise, in his Conspectus, classed them among the Finches, but subsequently admitted their alliance with the *Timalinæ*, associating them with *Leiothrix*, and thus formed the sub-family, *Liotrichinæ*, in which, moreover, he placed *Conostoma*. Hodgson considered the larger ones nearly allied to *Conostoma*, an undoubted member of this family; and Blyth, whilst placing them in the *Paridæ* (as does Horsfield), also admitted the relationship to *Conostoma*; and he is now inclined to class them near the *Timalinæ*. Tickell does not allow their affinities for this family, and calls them Fringillideous. Putting aside the bill, the structure in every other respect is quite Crateropodine. The strong legs and feet, the rounded wing, the long graduated tail, the lax plumage, all agree with the characters of this family; whilst the bill, (on which so much stress is laid by some, to the exclusion of every other feature,) as already noticed, varies greatly in this family; and here it is reduced to a minimum in shortness, and a maximum in depth and width. *Conostoma*, *Pyctoris*, and some other genera, foreign to India, approach it in these points, and make an easy transition to the more ordinary form of beak.

Gen. PARADOXORNIS, Gould.

Syn. *Bathyrhynchus*, McLell.—*Heteromorpha*, Hodgson (partly).

Char.—Bill short, stout, as high at the base as long; culmen much curved, compressed on the sides, blunt, sinuated on the margin; nostrils small, round, concealed by setaceous feathers; rictus with a few slender bristles; wings feeble, rounded, the 6th quill longest, the four first graduated; tail long, firm, graduated; legs and feet very stout; tarsus nearly entire; lateral toes equal; hind toe and claw large; claws all freely curved; the middle toe not much elongated; plumage soft and lax.

The birds composing this curious genus differ somewhat in the form of the bill and wing, and one of them has been classed separately by Gray; but I think that, with the exception perhaps of *Heteromorpha*, they range better together than if each peculiarity is made to constitute a sub-genus. The present genus is characterized by the deep sinuation of the tomiæ of the mandibles.

373. Paradoxornis flavirostris, GOULD.

P. Z. S., 1836, 17—HORSF., Cat. 609—GOULD, Icones, pl. 1.—Birds of Asia, Part VI., pl. 8.—Bathyrhynchus brevirostris, McLELLAND.

THE YELLOW-BILLED FINCH-THRUSH.

Descr.—Above, the head and hind neck pale rufous; back, wings, and tail, dull olive-brown; cheeks and throat white, with small black spots; ear-coverts and a gular band, black; beneath, pale earthy rufescent. One (female) specimen wants the black gular band, and has the white of the lower parts rufescent-white, with some brown spots on the throat and breast.

Bill bright yellow; legs plumbeous; irides red brown. Length 8½ inches; wing 3¼; tail 3¾; bill at front ½, nearly as deep at the base; tarsus 1₁₀.

I have only procured this very interesting bird on the Khasia hills, at an elevation of above 5,000 feet, in a pine wood, and found that it had partaken of various seeds. There were two or three young birds in company with the parents, one of which I also shot, and found that it closely resembled the old birds in plumage. They were rather shy, though they did not conceal themselves in the manner of the *Garrulax* group, but flew from tree to tree. McLelland obtained his only specimen in Assam, very probably on the Khasia hills; and Hodgson has also procured it in the Sikhim Terai, and Nepal.

374. **Paradoxornis gularis,** Horsfield.

Horsfield, MSS.—Gray. Genera of birds, pl. 94, f. 2—Gould, Birds of Asia, Part VI., pl. 10.—P. caniceps, Blyth—Heteromorpha, apud Blyth, Cat. 528—Horsf., Cat. 612—*Chongto-phep-pho*, Lepch.

The Hoary-headed Finch-thrush.

Descr.—Above rufescent brown; head pure grey, with a black superciliary line, commencing with the nostrils; beneath white, with the chin black.

Bill yellow; legs and feet plumbeous; the claws pale; irides light brown. Length 6 inches; wing 3½; tail 3; bill at front ½ inch nearly; tarsus 1. The wing in this species is proportionally longer, and the hind toe is very large.

I procured this bird at Darjeeling, where, however, it is rare, and it is found at from 3,000 to 6,000 feet of elevation. It has also been sent from Bootan.

375. **Paradoxornis ruficeps,** Blyth.

J. A. S., XI., 177, and XII., 1010, with a figure—Horsf., Cat. 611—Heteromorpha, apud Blyth, Cat. 527—Gray Genera of Birds, pl. 94, f. 1—Gould, Birds of Asia, Part VI., pl. 11.—*Chongto-phep-pho*, Lepch.

The Red-headed Finch-thrush.

Head, cheeks, ear-coverts, nape, and sides of neck, bright rufous; the rest of the upper plumage olive-brown, darker, and tinged with rufous on the wings; beneath, white, a little sullied with fulvescent on the neck and flanks.

Bill, with the upper mandible, horny brown, the lower one pale yellowish; legs plumbeous; irides red brown; orbitar skin pale blue. Length about 7½ inches; wing 3½; tail 3½; bill at front ½ inch, ⅜th deep; tarsus above 1 inch.

This species differs somewhat from the two last by its less compressed bill, which is also less sinuated at the margin ; and Blyth, at one time, classed it as a *Heteromorpha*. Gray, moreover, separates it from *Paradoxornis*, appropriating for it McLelland's name of *Bathychynchus*.

It is found in the hilly regions of Nepal, Sikhim, Bootan, the Khasia hills, extending into Arrakan. I have procured it both at Darjeeling, and on the Khasia hills, and found it in dense bamboo jungle, feeding on the seeds which ripened this year (1862) over a large extent of the hills. Whilst feeding on the bamboos, in small parties, it did not shun observation, but on being followed soon concealed itself. Tickell saw this bird at Ging, near Darjeeling, and found it feeding on grain, maize, rice, and buck-wheat. "It perches," says that naturalist, " on the top of high trees, as well as bushes, when off its feed, and in fact shows nothing, in its manners, of the thicket-loving, skulking habit of the *Crateropodines*." In the few opportunities I had of observing it, I saw nothing opposed to the view of its being placed in this family, and several undoubted members of the *Timalinæ*, viz., the *Malacocerci*, are great grain-eaters.

Gen. HETEROMORPHA, Hodgson.

Char.—Similar to the last, but the bill with the margin straight; the head crested.

This sub-genus, applied by Hodgson also to the other species of *Paradoxornis*, is retained as distinct by Gray for this species ; and from its form, and the mode of coloration, I am inclined to accept it.

376. Heteromorpha unicolor, HODGSON.

J. A. S., XII., 448, with figure—HORSF., Cat. 610—GOULD, Birds of Asia, Part VI., pl. 9—*Lho-ramnio-pho*, Lepch., *i. e.*, the Mountain Actinodura.

THE BROWN FINCH-THRUSH.

Descr.—Throughout of an ashy olive-brown, brightest on the head, wings, and tail ; head with full but short crest.

Bill orange-yellow; legs slaty-grey; irides brown. Length 7¾ inches; wing 3 7/16 : tail 4; bill at front 9/16; tarsus 1⅛.

This plainly-coloured Finch-thrush is not distantly allied to *Conostoma oemodium*. The Lepchas call both birds by the same name, and both are peculiar to the more elevated regions of the Himalayas, and have not been procured elsewhere.

Hodgson states that it is found in the higher regions of Nepal, dwelling in thick brushwood, frequently alighting on the ground, but also feeding on trees, on bugs and other insects, in small flocks, and not noisy. I procured a single specimen from Mount Tongloo, near Darjeeling, 10,000 feet high.

Gen. CHLEUASICUS, Blyth.

Char.—Bill much as in *Paradoxornis*, but shorter, wider, and more tumid on the sides.

This genus is now included by Blyth and Horsfield in *Suthora*; but I think that it is more allied to the last group than to the Tit-like members of that genus, and the sole species has very much the colors of *P. ruficeps*.

377. Chleuasicus ruficeps, BLYTH.

J. A., S. XIV., 178—BLYTH, Cat. 529—*Chongto-phep-pho*, Lepch.

THE RED-HEADED TIT-THRUSH.

Head and neck bright ferruginous; the rest of the upper plumage olive-brown, more or less inclining towards ferruginous, specially on the shoulder of the wing; entire under parts white.

Bill whitish horny; legs greenish plumbeous; irides red-brown. Length 5½ inches; wing 2⅝; tail 2¾; bill at front ⅜; tarsus ⅞.

This bird has only yet been procured in Sikhim. I got it at Darjeeling, but had no opportunity of observing its habits.

Gen. SUTHORA, Hodgson.

Syn.—*Temnoris and Hemirhynchus*, Hodgson (postea).

Char.—Bill very short and stout, as high and nearly as wide as long; ridge much curved; the sides slightly tumid; rictus smooth; nostrils concealed by plumes; wings short, rounded, 6th quill longest; tail rather long, graduated, feeble; tarsus long, smooth; toes short; nails compressed and acute, hind toe stout; outer toe slightly longer than the inner.

This remarkable group of small birds cannot, I think, be separated from the last series, as is done by Gray and others, for they are distinctly connected to *Paradoxornis* by *Chleuasicus*. Gray, Horsfield, and Blyth, however, agree in placing them among the *Parinæ*, near the long-tailed Tit-mouse and *Panurus biarmicus*, as does Hodgson, though he asserts their relationship with *Heteromorpha*, &c. But it appears to me questionable if the bearded Tit-mouse really belongs to the *Parinæ*, for it differs from them by its short wings, large legs and feet, short tumid bill, and dense plumage; and, in these points, certainly agrees with *Suthora*. Bonaparte, indeed, in his Conspectus, placed *Suthora* among his *Leiotrichinæ*, with *Paradoxornis* and *Conostoma*.

378. Suthora nipalensis, Hodgson.

Ind. Rev. 2, p. 32—BLYTH, Cat. 530—HORSF., Cat. 613.— Temnoris atrifrons, HODGS., P. Z. S., 1845—GOULD, Birds of Asia, pl. upper figure—*Suthora, Nipal.*

THE BLACK-FRONTED TIT-THRUSH.

Descr.—Crown bright fulvous, passing to duller fulvous on the back; forehead, and a broad streak over the eyes to the nape, black; lores and sides of the face, with the plumes growing from the base of the lower mandible, pure white; ear-coverts, and a spot behind the eye, below the black streak, bright fulvous; below the ear-coverts, and the sides of the neck, pure ash, paler on the breast, and passing to white on the abdomen; chin and throat black, with whitish margins; wings dark brown, the first two or three quills edged with white, the next two or three with rufous, and the remainder edged throughout their entire length with the same colour, but of a deeper hue; tail bright cinnamon brown, edged externally with rufous; the inner webs dusky.

Bill black, bluish at the base; legs fleshy white; irides brown. Length $4\frac{1}{4}$ inches; wing 2; tail $2\frac{1}{4}$; bill $\frac{1}{4}$; tarsus $\frac{3}{4}$.

Gould has figured two varieties, one with ashy crown and white cheeks, the other with rufous crown and ear-coverts. Are these the different sexes?

This bird inhabits the Central and Northern regions of Nepal and Sikim. It associates, says Hodgson, in small flocks; frequenting the brushwood and tall grass, and has the manners and food of *Parus*. I only obtained one specimen near Darjeeling.

379. Suthora poliotis, BLYTH.

J. A. S., XX., 122—HORSF., Cat. 615—S. Nipalensis, apud GOULD, Birds of Asia, pl. (the two lower figures).

THE ASH-EARED TIT-THRUSH.

Descr.—Crown of head, and back of neck, brownish grey; the ear-coverts and sides of the neck grey; face, and superciliary stripe, white, bounded above by a broad black line; rest of the upper plumage rusty red; wings as in the last; beneath, the chin barred with black and rust colour, the rest of the lower plumage uniform rusty.

Bill blackish; legs fleshy. Dimensions of the last.

The Ash-eared Tit-thrush has been found in Nepal, and also in the Khasia hills.

380. Suthora fulvifrons, HODGSON.

J. A.S., XV., 579—BLYTH, Cat. 531—HORSF., Cat. 614—Temnoris Nipalensis, HODGSON, J. A. S., XIII., 450, with figure—GOULD, Birds of Asia, pl. 61.

THE FULVOUS-FRONTED TIT-THRUSH.

Upper parts light rufescent brown, inclining to fulvous on the forehead, throat, and breast; a pale dusky streak on each sinciput; secondaries, and the base of the caudals, broadly margined with bright chesnut-fulvous; the belly and flanks albescent greyish.

Bill pale; legs light brown. Length 5 inches; wing $2\frac{1}{8}$; tail $2\frac{1}{2}$; bill at front $\frac{1}{4}$; tarsus $\frac{3}{4}$.

This bird has hitherto only been sent from Nepal. In it the bill is reduced to its minimum in this group, and it might easily be

mistaken for a thick-billed Tit-mouse. Another species of this
genus from China has lately been figured by Gould in his Birds of
Asia, as *Suthora Webbiana.*

I agree with Mr. Blyth in considering that *Struthidea* of Australia belongs to this family, and probably to this group ; as perhaps
also *Sphenostoma,* and *Xerophila* of Gould, which, indeed, I see
Bonaparte includes in his *Timaliæ,* placing them after the *Paradoxornis* group, in a sub-family with *Psophodes* and *Melanochlora,*
which latter, however, I look on as a true Tit. Near this group
perhaps should come the genus *Pyctorhis,* but as its affinities
for the *Alcippe* and *Timalia* section, are perhaps stronger, I shall
bring it into the system along with the latter series, and go on to the
Jay-thrushes.

Gen. CONOSTOMA, Hodgson.

Char.—Bill short, stout, compressed, arched, with the culmen
broad and rounded ; nostrils round, concealed ; rictus with a few
short bristles ; wings short, feeble, much rounded, 6th, 7th, and 8th
quills being about equal and longest ; tail moderately lengthened,
rounded, broad ; feet large and strong ; tarsus long, nearly smooth ;
the outer toe longer than the inner ; hind toe very large ; nails
long, slender, and moderately curved.

This genus, of which there is only one representative, was considered by its founder to belong to the *Glaucopinæ,* or Tree-crows
of Swainson, with analogies for the *Timaliæ,* and *Crateropi,* of the
lower regions; and Gray agrees with this view of its affinities. Blyth
classes it with the *Paradoxornis* group, as do Bonaparte and
Horsfield, who had previously placed it near the *Garrulax* series.

Taking into consideration its short wing, strong legs, and lax
plumage, I have no hesitation in placing it near *Heteromorpha,*
at the same time leading, through the next form, towards *Garrulax*
and its allines.

381. Conostoma œmodium, HODGSON.

J. A. S., X., 857, with figure.—BLYTH, Cat. 526—HORSF., Cat.
309, and 612 bis—GOULD, Birds of Asia, pl. 84.—*Lho-ramnio-pho,*
Lepch.

The Red-billed Jay-thrush.

Descr.—Head, neck, and body above, dull olive-brown, clearest on the secondaries, and most rufescent on the wings ; the outer edge of the first three primaries pale rufescent or vinous; beneath paler, and passing into dusky slaty blue, all the feathers at their base being of that tint.

Bill dull orange; legs slaty grey; irides brown. Length $11\frac{1}{2}$ inches; wing 5 ; tail $4\frac{3}{8}$; tarsus $1\frac{11}{16}$; bill at front $\frac{7}{8}$th, nearly $\frac{1}{2}$ inch deep.

This bird has hitherto been only procured in Nepal and Sikhim. I got one specimen from Mt. Tongloo, close to the Nepal frontier. Hodgson says that its habits are terrene and rasorial.

" It is," says he, " a shy forester, adhering to the wilds, and tenanting the skirts of forests, where brush-wood as well as trees abound. Five or six of these birds are usually found together, chattering, hopping and feeding on the ground, and resorting to the trees and shrubs for shelter. Their food is principally insects in summer, but in winter, doubtless, they take some vegetable food. They inhabit the northern region of Nepal, close to the snows."

The next genus, though somewhat allied in form, differs in its longer and less deep bill, in the apert nostrils, and shorter claws. Like the last, it is composed but of a single species, which was by some considered congeneric with a New Zealand bird, but has lately been separated from it.*

Gen. Grammatoptila, Reich.

Syn. *Turnagra*, apud Blyth—*Keropia*, Gray.

Char.—Bill short, stout, moderately compressed, gently curving from the base, slightly hooked and notched; nostrils obliquely oval, exposed ; a few thin rictal bristles ; wings short, rounded, 5th and 6th quills longest; tarsus strong ; feet stout; lateral toes slightly unequal, claws moderate, broad. Crested.

382. Grammatoptila striata, Vigors.

Garrulus, apud Vigors, P. Z. S., 1830—Gould, Century, pl. 37—Blyth, Cat. 480—Horsf. Cat. 301—*Nampiok-pho*, Lepch—*Kopiam*, Bhot.

---

* The New Zealand bird, *Keropia crassirostris*, appears to me related to the Bower-birds of Australia.

THE STRIATED JAY-THRUSH.

Descr.—Above light wood-brown, tinged with umber brown on the head, and rufescent on the wings; the tail almost chesnut brown; the outer edge of the outermost primaries tinged with hoary; beneath, brown slightly paler than above; all the body feathers, both above and below, striated longitudinally with yellowish white; the streaks on the abdomen wide, and longer than those on the back.

Bill black; legs dusky plumbeous; irides red brown. Length 12 inches; wing 5¼; tail 5¼; bill at front nearly 1, ⅜th deep; tarsus 1½.

This bird has a remarkably strong and Jay-like bill, and was originally described as a Jay by Vigors. In its mode of coloration it approaches some of the *Garrulax* series, *viz. Trochalopteron lineatum*, and *T. imbricatum*. The striated Jay-thrush is a very common bird about Darjeeling, from about 6,000 feet to 9,000 feet, but is more often heard than seen. It frequents the densest thickets, in pairs, or in small and scattered parties. It has some very peculiar calls, one of them not unlike the clucking of a hen which has just laid an egg. I found both fruit and insects in the stomach of those which I examined, chiefly the latter. It extends from Bootan to Nepal, but I am not aware if it is found further to the west.

We next come to the Shrike-thrushes. These are disguised so completely as Shrikes that they have usually been classed as such; but, after a full consideration of all their characters, and noting their apparent affinities for some of the next group, many of which have strong Shrike-like bills, I think that their true place is in this family.

Gen. THAMNOCATAPHUS, Tickell.

Char.—Bill lengthened, compressed, high at the base, well hooked at the tip, and strongly notched; rictal vibrissæ small and few; wings short, much rounded, the 3rd to the 7th primaries about equal and longest; tail moderately long, nearly even; the outermost feathers slightly shorter; tarsus long; lateral toes unequal; feet strong; plumage soft, full, and puffy.

383. **Thamnocataphus picatus,** Tickell.

J. A. S., XVIII.—Blyth, Cat. 866.

The White-winged Shrike-thrush.

Descr.—Above dull greyish-black, deeper on the crown, and blackest on the lores and ear-coverts; a narrow white bar on the wing-coverts, continued along the margin of two of the first row; beneath, uniform rufescent-white, tinged with ferruginous on the flanks and lower tail-coverts.

Bill dusky; legs apparently plumbeous. Length 9 inches; wing $3\frac{3}{4}$; tail $3\frac{3}{4}$; tarsus $1\frac{1}{4}$; bill at front $\frac{7}{8}$th, depth at the base $\frac{3}{8}$.

This remarkable form differs from all the other members of this family (except *Sibia* and *Gampsorhynchus*) by its white wing-spot, assimilating it still further to the Shrikes, and indeed it is very similar, in its mode of coloration, to some of the African Shrikes. The general character of its plumage, however, combined with its elevated and strong tarsi and feet, its habitat in a region rich in varied forms of this family, and its near affinity for *Gampsorhynchus*, have influenced me in placing it here.

It has only been procured near Darjeeling by Major Tickell, and the specimen in the Museum of the Asiatic Society at Calcutta is, I believe, unique. Nothing is recorded of its habits.

Gen. Gampsorhynchus, Blyth.

Char.—Bill of moderate length, nearly equal to the head, rather wide at the base, deep, moderately compressed; culmen curved, strongly hooked at the tip, and notched; gape conspicuously armed with straight vibrissæ; nostrils oval, pierced in the front of the membrane; wings moderate, much rounded, 5th, 6th, and 7th quills about equal and longest; tail rather long, graduated; tarsus moderately long, strong; claws tolerably curved.

Major Tickell considered this form congeneric with the last, from which it differs chiefly by its shorter bill, graduated tail, and colours. Its mode of coloration allies it to some of the next group, and the Lepchas give it the same name as they apply to the species of *Paradoxornis* and *Chleuasicus*.

384. Gampsorhynchus rufulus, Blyth.

J. A. S., XII., 370—Garrulax, apud Gray—Blyth, Cat. 865—
Horsf., Cat. 225—Thamnocataphus senilis, Tickell—*Chongto-phep-pho*, Lepch.

The White headed Shrike-thrush.

Descr.—Above uniform olive-brown; head in adults white, in
the young bright ferruginous; beneath, white in adults, and more
or less ferruginous in younger specimens; shoulder of the wings
more or less white; under surface of the wings pale fulvescent;
the tail-feathers narrowly tipped with pale fulvescent or
whitish.

Bill dusky horny above, pale beneath; legs reddish horny; irides
orange yellow in some, straw yellow in others. Length 9 inches;
extent 11¼; wing 3½; tail 4¾; tarsus 1¹⁄₁₆.

This curious bird is found from Nepal through Sikhim and the
Khasia hills to Arrakan. In Sikhim it frequents the warmer valleys
up to 3,000 feet of elevation. I had not an opportunity of observing it myself, though I procured several specimens; but the
Shikarees assured me that it was found in small flocks in thick
bushy places. Those which I have examined had eaten grasshoppers and other insects.

The next group consists of the Quaker-thrushes and Wren-
babblers: a great many of them are clad in grey and russet
plumage, with more or less of white, and many of them
resemble each other so closely that they are only distinguished
specifically by the form of the bill, and the size. It is more developed in Malayana than in India, and appears to correspond to a
certain extent with the section *Cacopittæ* of Bonaparte. Some of
this series approach the *Paradoxornis* group; others the Shrike-
thrushes; and a few are close to the *Timaliæ*, with which, indeed,
most of them are usually placed; but I think that they form a
peculiar section, distinguished as well structurally, as by a particular mode of coloration.

I shall begin with one formerly alluded to, which is, however, by
no means a typical member of the group.

Gen. PYCTORHIS, Hodgson.

Syn. *Chrysomma*, Hodgs.

Char.—Bill rather short, strong, deep, arched, entire; rictus strongly bristled; orbit nude; wings rather short and feeble, 4th and 5th quills longest; tail long, graduated; legs and feet stout and large; claws large, moderately curved.

385. Pyctorhis sinensis, GMELIN.

Parus, apud GMELIN—BLYTH, Cat. 860—HORSF., Cat. 339—Timalia hypoleuca, FRANKLIN—JERDON, Cat. 95—T. Horsfieldii, JARD. and SELBY, Ill. Orn., pl. 111—Tim. bicolor, LAFRESN., Mag. Zool., pl. 39—*Gal-chasm* or *Bulul-chasm*, H. in the south.—*Bara-podna*, H. in the N. W. P.—*Yerra kali-jitta* Tel.—*Mullala*, Sindh.

THE YELLOW-EYED BABBLER.

Descr.—Above clear red brown, rufous or cinnamon color on the wings, and the tail obsoletely banded with dusky; lores, and all the lower plumage, white; lower surface of wings and tail dusky cinereous.

Bill black, with the nostrils deep yellow; legs orpiment yellow; irides dark brown, with an outer circle of buff; orbits bright orange. Length $6\frac{1}{2}$ inches; wing $2\frac{9}{10}$; tail $3\frac{1}{2}$; bill at front not quite $\frac{1}{2}$; tarsus $1\frac{1}{10}$.

This species of Babbler is universally spread throughout India, extending to Burmah, and, from the name, perhaps to China. It has been sent from Nepal by Hodgson; is not rare in Bengal and the N. W. P.; is said to be common in Sindh, and I have seen it in every part of the South of India. It is also found in Ceylon, and it is very common in Upper Burmah. It frequents low jungles, or the skirts of forests, long grass, hedge-rows, and even comes occasionally into gardens. Though sometimes to be met with singly, it is generally seen in small parties of five or six, flying from bush to bush before you, and trying to conceal itself in some thick clump. It has a low chattering note when at rest, and when flying from bush to bush, a loud sibilant whistle. I have, on several occasions, heard one, perched conspicuously on a high bush or

16

hedge-row, pour forth a remarkably sweet song. It feeds mostly on insects, often on ants and small coleoptera. Mr. Blyth remarks, that he possessed some of these birds alive, and noticed that they frequently placed one foot upon their food, while they pecked with the bill. Mr. Philipps states that, in the N. W. Provinces, this is the bird said by the natives " to support the heavens by its legs, lest they fall." In Southern India this is related of the common Plover, *Pluvianus Goernsis*. The same observer also says, that it generally builds on Banyan trees. I wish that he had described the eggs, which I have never been able to procure.

386. Pictorhis longirostris, Hodgson.

P. Z. S., 1854—Horsf., Cat. 669.

The larger Yellow-eyed Babbler.

Descr.—Above, rufous-brown, darkest on the crown, wings and tail, the last distinctly rayed; chin, throat, the middle of the belly, and vent, white; ear-coverts, sides of neck, and breast, pale rufescent, brightening on the flanks, thighs, and under tail-coverts.

Bill black, yellowish at the base beneath; legs pale horny. Length 8¼ inches; wing 2¾; tail 3¼; bill at front ⅝; tarsus 1.

This bird has been only recently described from specimens sent home from Nepal by Hodgson. It is probably the species noticed by Mr. Frith (J. A. S., XIII., 370), as being found in Bengal, which he states to differ from the common species, in being about half larger.

I discovered a third species of this genus at Thayet-myo in Upper Burmah, which I have described in the 4th vol. of the 'Ibis,' as *Chrysomma altirostre*. Its short deep bill approximates it to the *Paradoxornis* series.

Gen. Trichastoma, Blyth.

Syn. *Malacocincla*, Blyth.

Char.—Bill about equal to the head, straight, stout, high, much compressed; the tip hooked; nostrils large; wings moderate, 4th quill longest; tail somewhat short, weak, nearly even; tarsus moderate; feet large, the lateral toes slightly unequal; claws moderately curved, the middle and hind claw very long.

Plumage full and lax, with the coronal feathers slightly elongated.

This genus appears to have some affinities for *Pyctorhis*, but differs in its longer bill, shorter, nearly-even tail, and shorter tarsus.

387. **Trichastoma Abbotti**, BLYTH.

Malacocincla, apud BLYTH, J. A. S., XIV., 601—BLYTH, Cat. 838—HORSF., Cat. 662—Malacopteron, apud GRAY.

THE BROWN-BACKED TIT-BABBLER.

Descr.—Above, plain olive-brown, tinged with rufous on the rump and tail; under parts paler; the throat and the middle of the belly white; ear-coverts, sides of breast, and flanks, rufescent; lower tail-coverts pale ferruginous.

Bill horny, pale beneath. Length 6 inches; wing 3; tail $2\frac{1}{8}$; bill at front $\frac{1}{12}$.

This bird has been sent from Nepal by Hogdson, from Dacca by Tytler, and also from Arrakan. I have not had an opportunity of observing it.

Other recorded species of *Trichastoma* are *T. bicolor*, Less. (*ferruginosum*, Bl.); *T. rostratum*, Blyth; and *T. olivaceum*, Strickland, all from Malacca.

Gen. ALCIPPE, Blyth.

Syn.—*Setaria*, Blyth—*Siva*, postea *Ioropus*, Hodgs.

Char.—Bill short, moderately stout and compressed; culmen slightly curved, hooked and notched; nostrils slightly impended by some setæ; rictal bristles moderate; wings moderate, rounded, 4th and 5th quills equal; tail moderate or rather short, very slightly rounded; tarsus stout, moderate; lateral toes unequal; claws tolerably curved.

The birds of this genus are of small size, with plain colors, and, mostly, undefined markings; and, in their habit are less social, perhaps, and more silent, than most of the *Timaliæ*, with which however, they have undoubted affinities; and they exhibit distant relationship to some of the *Leiotrichinæ*; more than one species, now referred to this genus, having been described as *Brachypteryx*.

C

388. Alcippe nipalensis, Hodgson.

Siva, apud Hodgson, Ind. Rev., 1838—Ioropus, Hodgs., J. A. S., XIII., 937—Blyth, Cat. 848—Horsf., Cat. 330—*Samdayal-pho,* Lepch.

The Nepal Quaker-thrush

Descr.—Above, the head ashy brown; lores, ears, and sides of neck also ashy; back, wings, and tail, olivaceous brown; an inconspicuous dark brown line over the eyes, extending to the nape; beneath, the chin white, the rest of the lower parts albescent, mixed with earthy brown.

Bill horny yellow; feet pale fleshy brown; irides whitey brown. Length $5\frac{1}{2}$ inches; wing $2\frac{3}{4}$; tail $2\frac{1}{4}$; bill at front barely $\frac{3}{8}$; tarsus $\frac{7}{8}$.

This bird has been found in Nepal, Sikhim, the Khasia hills, and Burmah, as far as Tenasserim. It is very common about Darjeeling, frequenting trees, singly, or in small parties, and feeding chiefly on insects. I had the nest and eggs brought me by the Lepchas; the nest was loosely made with grass and bamboo leaves, and the eggs were white with a few reddish-brown spots.

389. Alcippe poiocephala, Jerdon.

Timalia, apud Jerdon, Suppl. Cat. 95 bis—Blyth, Cat. 850.

The Neilgherry Quaker-thrush.

Descr.—Head and nape dusky cinereous; back and rump greenish olive, inclining to rufous on the rump, darker and more ferruginous on the wings and tail; beneath, pale rufescent or fulvous, lightest and albescent on the chin and throat.

Bill horny, yellow at the gape and edges; legs pale fleshy; irides greenish-white; the very narrow orbits yellow. Length nearly 6 inches; wing $2\frac{8}{10}$; tail $2\frac{8}{10}$; bill at front $\frac{9}{20}$; tarsus $\frac{7}{8}$.

This is very similar to the last, but differs structurally in having the rictal bristles less elongated, and the feet shorter, with a more robust hind toe.

It is found in all the forests of Malabar, as high as North Canara, in Coorg, Wynaad, and the slopes of the Neilgherries, up about 5,000 feet, but it is not a common bird. It goes singly or in small flocks, flying from branch to branch of low trees; is silent, and lives chiefly on various insects.

390. Alcippe atriceps, JERDON.

Brachypteryx, apud JERDON, Cat. 78—BLYTH, Cat. 861.

THE BLACK-HEADED WREN-BABBLER.

Descr.—Head, cheeks, and nape, black; wings, tail, and under tail-coverts brownish olive, darkest on the tail and wings; beneath, white, with a tinge of olive-brown on the sides and towards the vent.

Bill horny-brown; legs plumbeous; irides pale orange or buff. Length $5\frac{1}{2}$ inches; wing $2\frac{5}{10}$; tail 2; bill at front $\frac{5}{10}$; tarsus $\frac{9}{10}$; extent 7.

The Black-headed Wren-babbler is found in the same localities as the last, but not ascending so high on the slopes of the hills, and being most abundant in the lower forests, contrary to the habits of the previous species.

It frequents the thickest underwood in dense and lofty jungles; lives in small flocks of five or six, and is continually hopping about the thick bushes with an incessant loud twittering note. It lives on various insects, small *mantidæ*, grass-hoppers, and the like.

In my Catalogue I placed it under *Brachypteryx* from its likeness to *B. Sepiaria* of Horsfield, which, I see, is now considered by some to be also an *Alcippe*, though Blyth says it is intermediate to this and *Malacopteron*. Perhaps this has led Gray to associate this genus with *Brachypteryx* in his *Myotherinæ*. A very closely allied species is *A. nigrifrons*, Blyth, from Ceylon; and *Brachypt. nigro-capitata*, Eyton, is probably another.

Though so similar in structure, I am by no means certain that these last-named species, *viz.*, *A. atriceps*, *nigrifrons*, *nigro-capitata*, and *sepiaria*, should not be classed apart from the more dingy-colored species first noticed. The habits of *A. atriceps*, as observed by myself, are more those of *Timalia*, or, at all events, of *Dumetia* and *Pellorneum*, than the more staid and quiet demeanour of *A. poiocephala* and *Nipalensis*.

Next to *Alcippe*, perhaps, should be placed the pre-eminently Malayan group of the Quaker-thrushes, named *Malacopteron* by

Eyton, and to which belong *Turdinus, Turdirostris, Macronous Trichixos*, and *Napothera*. Among the recorded species are *Malacopteron magnum*, Eyton; *M. major*, Blyth; *Macronous ptilosus*, J. and S. ; *Turdinus macrodactylus*, Strickland, *Turdirostris superciliaris*, Hay, &c. &c., from Malayana: *Turdinus crispifrons*, Bl., *T. brevicaudatus*, Bl., *T. guttatus*, Tickell, are from Tenasserim; and there is a new species of that genus from the Khasia hills. *Cacopitta*, Bonap., with a few species from the Islands, apparently belongs to this section of the *Timalinæ*. Some of the birds, however, described under these names are more nearly allied to the true *Timaliæ*. Although several species have been lately described, yet from their plain and sombre plumage, many are perhaps overlooked ; and Wallace states that he got some new species from Malacca, quite common there, but neglected by the bird-dealers. They vary a good deal in the form of their bill, some having this organ large, and much hooked; and others comparatively slender and slightly hooked. The last-named observer found that they feed chiefly on fruit, but also on insects. It appears to me (judging from the figures only, and the account of their habits) that *Phyllastrephus*, an African genus, belongs rather to this family than to the Bulbuls, or Warblers, and if so, it should be located in this section ; and *Alethe*, Cassin, also from Africa, is said to be near *Napothera*.

Close to the black-headed species of *Alcippe* should be placed the following group with which I would commence the series of Wren-babblers, and these nearly agree with Bonaparte's section *Timaleæ* of his *Timalinæ*.

Gen. STACHYRIS, Hodgson.

Char.—Bill somewhat long, high at the base, straight, compressed, tapering or conic, the tip very slightly bent downwards, and faintly notched ; nostrils nearly concealed ; rictus almost smooth ; wings short, rounded, 5th, 6th and 7th quills equal and longest ; tail rather short, slightly graduated ; tarsus moderately long, stout ; lateral toes nearly equal, claws moderately curved ; middle toe not elongated ; hind toe and claws very large. The head is usually crested or sub-crested, the feathers being semi-erect and divergent.

Blyth, Horsfield, and Gray locate this genus near *Pyctorhis* and *Timalia*, the latter, indeed, ranking them as *Timalia*. Bonaparte puts it among *Liotrichinæ*, and Hodgson considered it to have affinities for the *Brachypodinæ*, but leading to the Crateropodans, and with a tendency to pass into the *Leiotrichinæ*. He further compares its habits with those of *Zosterops*. It appears to me that there are two types of form in this genus, and that, whilst the more common species belong to this family, others, especially *S. chrysæa*, appear to have relations to *Myzornis, Erpornis, Zosterops*, and *Iora*, which in fact are the views of the founders of the genus.

391. Stachyris nigriceps, Hodgson.

J. A. S., XIII., 378—Blyth, Cat. 861—Horsf., Cat. 340.— *Sangriam-pho*, Lepch.

The black-throated Wren-Babbler.

Descr.—Above olive-brown; beneath paler and tinged rufescent; the crown, face, and throat, dusky black; the feathers of the crown edged with whitish grey; a white supercilium, and also a white moustache from the base of the lower mandible, and some white on the chin and throat.

Bill dusky horny above, paler beneath; legs pale horny green; irides pale yellow. Length $5\frac{1}{2}$ inches; extent 7; wing $2\frac{3}{8}$; tail 2; bill at front $\frac{9}{16}$; tarsus $\frac{3}{4}$.

This bird inhabits the S. E. Himalayas and the Khasia hills. It is very common about Darjeeling, from 5,000 feet to nearly 10,000 in summer; is quite arboreal, hunting among the upper foliage and flowers of trees, singly, or in small parties, and feeding chiefly on insects. Hodgson says that it builds a large globular nest, and lays four or five eggs of a pale fawn color, unspotted. A nest and eggs were brought to me at Darjeeling, said to be of this species; the nest was rather large, very loosely made of bamboo leaves and fibres, and the eggs were pale salmon color, with some faint darker spots.

392. Stachyris pyrrhops, Hodgson.

J. A. S., XIII., 378—Blyth, Cat. 862—Horsf., Cat. 341.

The Red-billed Wren-babbler.

Descr.—Above olivaceous-brown, with a tinge of rufous on the head; lores and chin black; a pale line impending the latter; below rufescent, more or less brown on the belly and flanks.

Bill sordid sanguine; legs pale fleshy-brown; irides blood-red. Length 4½ to 5 inches; wing 2; tail 2; bill at front $\frac{7}{10}$; tarsus ¾.

I did not procure this bird in Sikhim. It has been sent from Nepal, Mussooree, and Kussowlee, and it is probably the *Prinia*, No. 132, of Adams' List of Birds, said to be common on Apricot trees in the lower Himalayan ranges, in the N. W. Provinces.

393. **Stachyris ruficeps**, Blyth.

J. A. S., XVI., 452—Blyth, Cat. 863—Horsf., Cat. 670—
Syak-birang-pho, Lepch.

The Red-headed Wren-babbler.

Descr.—Crown of the head light ferruginous, the rest of the upper plumage plain olive; chin and the middle of the throat white, with faint black streaks; the rest of the lower parts whitish, with a fulvous tinge on the sides of the neck and breast, or, throughout of dull oil-yellow or pale ferruginous, darkest on the breast, and fading, and becoming dusky towards the vent.

Bill plumbeous above, reddish beneath; legs pale yellow brown; irides light brown. Length 4¾ inches; wing 2¼; tail 2⅛; bill at front $\frac{7}{10}$; tarsus ¾.

This bird, which, says Mr. Blyth, is allied in form and size to the last, is found in Nepal, Sikhim, and the Khasia hills. It is common at Darjeeling, frequenting high trees in small parties, searching the foliage for minute insects. A nest and eggs, said to be of this species, were brought to me at Darjeeling. The nest was a loose structure of grass and fibres, and contained two eggs of a greenish white color, with some rusty spots.

394. **Stachyris chrysæa**, Hodgson.

J. A. S., XIII., 379—Blyth, Cat. 864—Horsf., Cat. 342—
Syak-birang-pho, Lepch.

THE GOLDEN-HEADED WREN-BABBLER.

Descr.—Above yellow olivaceous; forehead and crown yellow, the latter with black streaks; lores black; wings and tail dusky, margined with olive; beneath bright yellow.

Bill plumbeous; legs pale brownish yellow; irides light brown. Length 4½ inches; wing 2¼; tail 2; bill at front nearly ½; tarsus 1⁄1.

The Golden-headed *Stachyris* is found in the S. E. Himalayas, the Khasia hills, and Arrakan, generally at a lower level than the last, from 3,000 to 5,000 feet or so. It frequents high trees generally, feeding on the minute insects that infest flowers and buds, and often has its forehead powdered with the pollen of flowers, as we see in *Zosterops* and other birds.

This species differ from its congeners in its mode of coloration, more pointed bill, and other points, and perhaps should be removed to a distinct genus near *Zosterops* or *Myzornis*.

Very probably some of the smaller *Timaliæ* of the Malayan Fauna should be placed in *Stachyris*. *Tim. poliocephala*, Temm., judging from the figure, has much of the character and plumage of *Stachyris*.

Gen. MIXORNIS, Hodgson.

Char.—Bill rather long, compressed, with a tendency to arch; tip blunt, barely notched; nostrils ovoid, advanced; wings moderate, rounded, the first four graduated, 5th and 6th sub-equal and longest; tail moderate or rather short; tarsus strong; toes rather short, laterals very unequal; hind toe large; nails well curved.

This genus is very closely allied to the last, inclining more towards *Timalia*. Hodgson says that it 'resembles *Iora*, but the bill is more meruline, inclining to the *Crateropodinæ*.'

395. Mixornis rubicapillus, TICKELL.

Motacilla, apud TICKELL, J. A. S., II., 575—BLYTH, Cat. 855—HORSF., Cat. 338.—M. chloris, HODGS.—M. ruficeps, HODGS.—M. gularis, HORSF.?

THE YELLOW-BREASTED WREN-BABBLER.

Descr.—Above dull olive-green, inclining to rufescent or brown; wings and tail rufescent brown; part of the forehead, supercilium, ears, and sides of the neck, yellowish-green, with some dusky streaks; crown of the head dull ferruginous; beneath pale yellow, fading to whitish on the lower abdomen, and olivaceous on the flanks and vent; the throat and upper part of the breast with some blackish streaks.

Bill horny; legs pale horny brown; irides reddish-hazel. Length 5¾ inches; wing 2⅜; tail 2; bill at front ⅝; tarsus 1⅝.

This bird, very similar in color to *Stachyris ruficeps*, has been found at the foot of the Nepal and Bootan Himalayas, and in part of Central India; but it appears to be rare, for I have never met with it. It will probably occur in the Sikhim Terai, at the foot of the Khasia hills, and in various parts of lower Bengal. Tickell says that it is found in thick under-wood, hollows, ravines, &c., and is lively and agile, with a frequent piping note, and occasional chatter. *M. gularis* of Java looks like a faded specimen of this bird; but is put as distinct by Horsfield. In this genus are placed several species from Sumatra, Java, and Borneo.

Gen. TIMALIA, Horsfield.

Char.—Bill strong, deep, much compressed, very gently arching throughout; nostrils oval, apert; strong rictal bristles; wings short, much rounded, 5th and 6th quills longest; tail moderate, rounded; tarsus stout; lateral toes unequal; hind toe, and especially the claw, large.

This genus, founded on the only species occurring in our province, was one of the first of this family separated from the old Linnæan *Turdus*, and, perhaps, on this account has been selected for the family name, though I do not consider it as one of the most typical forms.

396. Timalia pileata, HORSFIELD.

LIN., Trans. XIII., 151—HORSF., Zool. Res. Java, pl.—HORSF., Cat. 332—BLYTH, Cat. 856.

THE RED-CAPPED WREN-BABBLER.

Descr.—Forehead and ears white; top of the head bright rusty-red; the rest of the upper plumage olivaceous-brown, tinged with ashy on the sides of the neck and nape; wings and tail tinged with rusty brown; beneath, the chin, throat, neck, and part of the breast, pure white; the lower part of the neck with narrow black streaks, the shafts of each feather being shining black and prolonged; abdomen and vent pale ferruginous, tinged with olivaceous on the flanks, and the lower tail-coverts olive-brown.

Bill black; legs fleshy brown; irides dusky red. Length 6¾ inches; wing 2⅜; tail 2$\frac{9}{10}$; bill at front ⅝; tarsus nearly ⅞.

The Red-capped Babbler has been procured in Nepal, the Bengal Sunderbuns, Assam, and Arrakan, extending through Burmah and the Malayan peninsula to Java. It has thus the most extensive geographical distribution of any of this family. I have seen it in the grass jungles of Purneah, Rajmahal, Sylhet, and Cachar, as well as in Upper Burmah, where it is much more abundant than in Bengal, and less shy, affecting hedge-rows near villages, instead of the unfrequented grass jungles and thickets in which alone it is seen in Bengal. Horsfield says that it is common (in Java) in groves and woods; approaches villages, constructs its nest in hedges, and is one of the social birds which delight to dwell in the neighbourhood of cultivation. It has, he says, a pleasant note, which consists of a slow repetition of the five tones of the diatonic scale (C. D. E. F. G.), with perfect regularity, and at small intervals of time.

There are many other species of *Timalia* in Malayana, viz., *T. nigricollis*, T.—*T. erythroptera*, Bl.—*T. maculata*, T. (*pectoralis*, Bl.), from Malacca; and others from the islands.

Gen. DUMETIA, Blyth.

Syn. *Timalia*, apud Franklin.

Char.—Bill moderate, or rather short, compressed, pointed; culmen slightly curving from the base, and the commissure also slightly curved; a few small rictal bristles; wings short, rounded, 4th, 5th, and 6th quills nearly equal; tail moderate, rounded; tarsus stout; middle toe not elongate; lateral toes about equal, hind toe and claw moderately large.

This genus, instituted by Mr. Blyth for two small species confined to continental India, is barely separable from *Pellorneum*, with which at one time Mr. Blyth classed them; but it differs

D

in the bill being somewhat shorter, the middle toe less elongate, and in its distribution. The species have all the wandering habits of the *Malacocerci* and *Chatarhœa*, and in this they certainly differ from the *Drymoicœ* and *Priniœ*, which are only a little smaller than these birds.

397. Dumetia hyperythra, Franklin.

Thimalia, apud Franklin—Blyth, Cat. 787.

The Rufous-bellied Babbler.

Descr.—Above brownish olive, the tail obsoletely barred with dusky; forehead and whole body beneath rufous.

Bill horny; legs fleshy yellow; irides pale yellow-brown. Length $5\frac{1}{4}$ inches; wing $2\frac{1}{10}$; tail $2\frac{2}{10}$; tarsus $\frac{8}{10}$.

This bird is found in low jungle and brushwood, from Nagpoor northwards to Central India and Midnapore, but has not been obtained in Lower Bengal. It has similar habits to the next, with which I formerly confounded it; and Mr. Blyth remarks that its note is like that of *Chatarhœa caudata*, but proportionally weaker.

398. Dumetia albogularis, Blyth.

Pellorneum, apud Blyth, J. A. S., XXI.—Blyth, Cat 788—Horsf., Cat. 660—T. hyperythra, apud Jerdon, Cat. 69—*Pandijitta*, Tel, *i. e.*, Pig-bird.

The White-throated Wren-Babbler.

Descr.—Like the last, but with the chin and throat pure white. Length $5\frac{1}{2}$ inches; wing $2\frac{2}{10}$; tail $2\frac{1}{4}$; bill at front $\frac{4}{10}$; tarsus $\frac{17}{20}$.

This little Babbler is found throughout Southern India in suitable localities, in bushy jungle, ravines, thick hedge-rows, &c., but it is entirely absent in the forest districts of Malabar.

It always occurs in small parties, skulking along one after the other, under bushes or through them, rarely showing itself on the top; hence the Telugu name of Pig-bird given it by the Yanadees of Nellore. It feeds almost exclusively on small insects, and has a low chattering call.

Gen. **PELLORNEUM**, Swainson.

Syn. *Cinclidia*, Gould—*Hemipteron*, Hodgs.

Char.—Bill moderate, straight, compressed, very gently curving throughout, slightly hooked at the tip, and notched; rictal bristles feeble; wings much rounded, 5th, 6th, and 7th quills nearly equal; tail moderate, rounded; tarsus moderate; feet large; middle toe lengthened; laterals barely unequal; hind toe long; claws tolerably curved.

399. **Pellorneum ruficeps,** SWAINSON.

BLYTH, Cat. 823—HORSF., Cat. 323—Megalurus ruficeps, SYKES, Cat. 87—Motac. dumeticola, TICKELL—Cinclidia punctata, GOULD—P. olivaceum, JERDON, Cat. 86—*Adavi liku-jittu*, Tel.

THE SPOTTED WREN-BABBLER.

Descr.—Above olive-brown; crown and nape deep rusty colored, with a more or less marked white eye-brow from the forehead to the nape; ears dusky-white, or mixed brown and white, or entirely brown; beneath, white or fulvous white, with spots of dark olive on the sides of the breast and belly, olivaceous on the flanks and under tail-coverts.

Bill horny above, yellowish fleshy beneath; legs fleshy yellow; irides brick-red. Length 7 inches; extent 9; wing 3; tail 3; bill at front $\frac{9}{10}$; tarsus, $1\frac{1}{10}$.

This bird has a wide geographical distribution, only inferior, in this family, to that of *Tim. pileata*. It is found throughout Southern India, both on the east and west coasts; in Central India; in the South East Himalayas; the Khasia hills; and through Burmah to Tenasserim. It associates in small flocks, frequenting underwood and thickets in forest jungle, often descending to the ground, where it hops about in search of various insects, or climbing up the small branches of shrubs; it keeps up a continual chattering, and, occasionally, one of them, perched on a bough, elevating his head and neck, gives utterance to a sort of crowing laugh, not unlike that of *Trochalopteron cachinnans*. Col. Sykes's observation that it frequents the plains like a Lark, must have arisen from some mistaken identity.

Besides the affinity of *Pellorneum* for some of the last noticed group, there is also considerable similarity to at least one of the next birds mentioned, the *Pomatorhini*. Other species of *Pellorneum* recorded are *P. fuscocapillum*, Blyth, from Ceylon, formerly classed as *Drymocataphus; P. Tickelli*, Blyth, from Tenasserim; and a closely allied species from the Khasia hills.

At the end of this Section, Bonaparte places two Oceanic types, *Clitonyx*, Reich, and *Certhiparus*, Lafresn., with what justice I cannot say.

The next group is one which shows the extreme form from the species of this family first noticed ; for while in *Paradoxornis* and *Suthora*, the bill was reduced to its minimum in length and maximum depth, here it is extremely elongated, slender, and curved, varying of course in the different species.

Gen. POMATORHINUS, Horsf.

Char.—Bill long, compressed, pointed, much curved throughout, entire at the tip; nostrils barely apert, lengthened ; a few very small rictal bristles; wing short, rounded; 5th and 6th quills longest; tail long or moderate, rounded ; tarsi and feet long and stout; anterior toes not much elongate ; hind toe large ; claws large, moderately curved, somewhat blunt.

Bonaparte ranges this genus with the Babblers, his *Crateropodinæ;* but it is certainly more nearly allied both in plumage and habits to the *Garrulax* series. It is found in India and Malayana, extending to Australia, but of a somewhat different type. They hunt in pairs, and less in parties than many of this family, and their diet is exclusively insects, in seeking for which on the ground they are said to use their bills freely like *Upupa*, but I have not had an opportunity of observing them thus employed; and from the thick brushwood and tangled brakes they usually frequent, it is difficult to watch them closely. Though not habitually frequenting the open forests, they are never found away from a forest country. They nidificate in banks generally, and the eggs of those that are known are white.

The first species in our list is a slightly aberrant form ; its bill being shorter and less arched, and it has much resemblance to *Pellorneum ruficeps*.

400. **Pomatorhinus ruficollis,** HODGSON.

As. Res., XIX—BLYTH, Cat. 834—HORSF., Cat. 350.

THE RUFOUS-NECKED SCIMITAR-BABBLER.

Descr.—Above olive-green ; head and nape dusky ; back and sides of neck deep rusty ; lores and ear-coverts blackish ; a white supercilium from the brow to the nape; beneath, as above, but paler, and shaded with white on the breast and belly, merging into pure white on the chin and throat.

Bill yellow, dusky above ; legs plumbeous ; irides red or red-brown, (or sometimes hoary according to Hodgson). Length 8 inches; extent 9½ ; wing 3 ; tail 3¼ ; bill at front ¾ ; tarsus ¼.

This species is found in the S. E. Himalayas and the Khasia hills.

401. **Pomatorhinus ferruginosus,** BLYTH.

J. A. S., XIV., 597—BLYTH, Cat. 833—HORSF. Cat. 351— *Piong-kohut,* or *Poniong-hut,* Lepch.—*Bhotetet,* Bhot.

THE CORAL-BILLED SCIMITAR-BABBLER.

Descr.—Above greenish-olive brown, the cap black (in the males); lores and ears black ; a long white supercilium, tinged with rufous in front (in the male); beneath, the throat white, and the rest of the under-parts deep ferruginous, fading on the belly, and olivaceous on the flanks.

Bill coral-red; legs greenish brown ; irides red-brown. Length 8¼ inches; extent 11 ; wing 3½ ; tail 4 ; bill at front 1 ; tarsus, 1¼.

The Coral-billed Babbler has been found in the S. E. Himalayas, Nepal, and Sikhim, at from 3,000 to 6,000 feet of elevation. I procured it near Darjeeling, but know of nothing peculiar in its habits. A very nearly allied race, *P. Phayrei,* Blyth, is found in the hill regions of Assam and Arrakan, differing only in the crown being of the same color as the back ; and *P. albogularis,* Bl., also closely allied, is from the Tenasserim province of Burmah.

402. **Pomatorhinus schisticeps,** HODGSON.

As. Res., XIX.—BLYTH, Cat. 828—HORSF., Cat. 345—P. montanus, apud McLELLAND—*Pubdoa* Beng.

Phoyeum-pho, or *Pharreeum-pho.*, Lepch.

The Slaty-headed Scimitar-babbler.

Descr.—Above dark olive-green; crown, nape, and ear-coverts, dark slaty; a long white supercilium from the base of the bill to the shoulder; lores black; sides of the neck and body intense ochreous red; beneath, the chin, breast, and belly, pure white; lower part of abdomen, with the flanks, vent, thigh-coverts, and under tail-coverts, olive-green; tail faintly cross barred.

Bill orange-yellow, with the ridge dusky; legs fleshy-brown; irides hoary; orbitar skin slaty. Length 11 inches; extent $12\frac{1}{2}$; wing 4; tail $4\frac{1}{2}$; bill at front $1\frac{3}{8}$; tarsus $1\frac{1}{4}$.

This species of *Pomatorhinus* extends from Nepal, through Sikhim and Bootan, to Assam, Sylhet, and Arrakan. It is not rare near Darjeeling, at about 5,000 feet high, and goes generally in pairs, the male uttering a loud hooting call, answered by the female in a different tone. A nest made of moss and some fibres, and with four pure white eggs, was brought to me at Darjeeling as belonging to this bird.

403. **Pomatorhinus leucogaster**, Gould.

Blyth, Cat. 829—Horsf., Cat. 346—P. olivaceus, Blyth.

Gould's Scimitar-babbler.

Descr.—Above uniform dull olive; the head tinged with dusky-cinereous, and a faint rufescent tinge on the nape; lores and ear-coverts black; a long white supercilium, and a deep ferruginous spot behind the ear, continued on the sides of the neck and flanks; beneath, the throat, breast, middle of abdomen, white; flanks and lower tail-coverts olivaceous.

Bill yellow, dusky above; feet leaden brown. Length 9 inches; wing $3\frac{7}{8}$; tail 4; bill at front 1; tarsus $1\frac{1}{4}$.

This appears like a somewhat diminutive race of the last (*schisticeps*), and is widely spread from the N. W. Himalayas, through Nepal, to Assam, and as low as Tenasserim. I did not procure it at Darjeeling. It appears not to ascend the hills to any height.

404. **Pomatorhinus Horsfieldii,** SYKES.

Cat. 73—JERDON, Cat. 89—BLYTH, Cat. 831—HORSF., Cat. 347—*Namala-pitta,* or *Dasari-pitta,* Tel.

THE SOUTHERN SCIMITAR-BABBLER.

Descr.—Above deep olive-brown ; a white superciliary stripe ; neck in front, breast, and middle of abdomen, white ; the flanks, vent, and under tail-coverts olive-brown.

Bill yellow, dusky, above ; legs dusky green ; irides dark-red. Length $9\frac{1}{2}$ inches ; wing $3\frac{8}{10}$; tail 4 ; bill at front $1\frac{1}{10}$; tarsus $1\frac{3}{10}$.

This is the only species of *Pomatorhinus* we possess in the south of India, or indeed in any part of India except the Himalayas. It is found in all the forests and hill ranges of Southern India, especially in the more elevated districts such as Wynaad, Coorg, and the Neilgherries, up to above 6,000 feet ; also in the Eastern Ghâts, Goomsoor, &c. ; and in the heavy jungles of Central India. It frequents tangled under-wood, in forests, especially in swampy places, and bamboo jungles ; and it makes its way through the most dense and tangled bushes with great facility. It is very shy and wary, and speedily evades observation. It is usually in pairs, the male calling out, as well expressed by Col. Sykes, *hoot, hoot, hoot,* while the females answer *hooee.* Occasionally it is met in parties, keeping up a continual chattering call.

It feeds entirely on insects. I procured its nest near Nediwuttum on the Neilgherries, on a bank on the road side, made with moss and roots, and containing four white eggs of a very elongated form. A nearly allied species, *P. melanurus,* Bl., occurs in Ceylon ; and this, with the two last species, and *P. montanus,* Horsf., from Java, may be considered representative species.

405. **Pomatorhinus erythrogenys,** GOULD.

P. Z. S., 1831—GOULD, Cent. H. B., pl. 55—BLYTH, Cat. 827—HORSF., Cat. 345—P. ferrugilatus, HODGS.—*Ban-bukra,* at Mussooree—*Yongohut-pho,* Lepch.

THE RUSTY-CHEEKED SCIMITAR-BABBLER.

Descr.—Above light olive-brown; the forehead and sides of the head rusty; a hoary spot just before the eye, and a short faint dusky moustache; beneath, white, dashed on the top of the breast with dusky; and the sides of the body, the lining of the wings, thighs, and under tail-coverts, bright rusty.

Bill horny; legs fleshy-yellow; irides pale yellow (hoary according to Hodgson); orbitar skin slaty. Length $10\frac{1}{2}$ inches; extent $11\frac{1}{2}$; wing $3\frac{3}{4}$; tail $4\frac{1}{2}$; bill at front $1\frac{4}{10}$; tarsus $1\frac{1}{2}$.

The female is said to differ from the male in wanting the dark moustache.

This *Pomatorhinus* is found throughout the whole extent of the Himalayas, from Simla to Sikhim and Bootan. It is not rare at Darjeeling. Hutton says that it is "common in the N. W. Himalayas, from 3,000 to 10,000, and even 12,000 feet; always in pairs, turning up the dead leaves on copsewood-covered banks, uttering a loud whistle, answering and calling each other; it breeds in April, constructing a nest on the ground, of dry grasses and leaf stalks of walnut trees, and is covered with a dome-shaped roof, so nicely blended with the fallen leaves and withered grasses, among which it is placed, as to be almost undistinguishable from them. The eggs are three in number, and white, of ordinary oval shape. When disturbed the bird sprung along the ground with long bounding hops, so quickly, that from its motions and the appearance of the nest, I was led to believe it was a species of rat."

Somewhat allied in appearance and structure to this last species is *P. hypoleucos* of Blyth, from Arrakan, and a new species, lately found by me on the Khasia hills, *Pom. McLellandi*. The former species, originally described by Blyth from a young specimen, under the generic name of *Orthorhinus*, is still considered generically distinct by Tickell, who says that "the bill is soft in texture, and subcylindric in form, the sinciput flat, and the tail broad and fan-like."

Other *Pomatorhini* not previously noticed are *P. Isidorei*, Lesson, from New Guinea; *P. borneensis*, Cab., from Borneo; *P. musicus* and *P. stridulus*, Swinhoe, from China. The Australian

Pomatorhini have been recently separated as *Pomatostomus*; their habits appear very similar, but the nidification differs.

Gen. XIPHORAMPHUS, Blyth.

Syn. *Xiphorhynchus*, Blyth, olim.

Char.—Bill still more curved and more slender than in *Pomatorhinus*, much compressed; wings and tail as in that genus; claws longer, more slender, and very slightly curved.

This is simply an exaggerated form of *Pomatorhinus.*

406. **Xiphoramphus superciliaris,** BLYTH.

J. A. S., XI., 175—BLYTH, Cat. 856—HORSF., Cat. 353— JERDON, Ill. Ind. Orn., Pl. 49—*Karriok-tamveep*, Lepch.

THE SLENDER-BILLED SCIMITAR-BABBLER.

Descr.—Above uniform reddish brown; quills and tail dusky; crown, occiput, and sides of head, dark cinereous, with a narrow superciliary white line; under-parts dull rufo-ferruginous; throat whitish, streaked with dusky grey; the breast fainter rufous than the belly, and obscurely spotted with dusky; shoulders of wings and tibial feathers dark cinereous.

Bill dusky black, plumbeous at the tip; legs leaden brown; irides red-brown. Length 9 inches; wing 3; tail $4\frac{1}{2}$; bill at front $1\frac{7}{8}$; tarsus $1\frac{1}{4}$.

This very curious bird has hitherto been only procured in Sikhim. It is rare, and is found from 7,000 to 10,000 feet, and upwards. I know nothing of its habits, but I doubt its being known to any one as a pleasing songster, as Mr. Blyth was informed.

The next group, that of the Laughing Thrushes, *Garrulacinæ*, Bonaparte, is peculiarly a Himalayan and mountain tribe, only three having been found in Southern India; one or two in Ceylon; and a few more on the Khasia hills, and the upland forests of Burmah, extending northwards to China, but sparingly into Malayana. They have received several names. Swainson formed of them his genus *Crateropus*, which was formerly used by myself, but that name is now restricted to a peculiar African type; and Gould formed his *Ianthocincla* for some. *Garrulax* of Lesson is now generally adopted, but it has been sub-divided.

E

All the species of this group have a more or less Thrush-like bill, short rounded wings, a long and broad, graduated or rounded tail, and strong legs and feet. As introductory to this division of the *Timalinæ*, I extract some excellent general remarks by Hodgson, when describing several new species : " They frequent deep and dark forests and groves exclusively, feed chiefly on the ground, eat insects, berries, and caterpillars, and are incapable of a sustained flight. They are frequently met with on the roads and pathways in the forests, attracted by the dung of cattle, for the grain, larvæ, and insects it affords them. On the whole they are more insectivorous than frugivorous or graminivorous, yet they are more capable of a graminivorous diet than the true Thrushes.* They scrape the earth with their bill, and sometimes with their feet ; many of them are caged and tamed with facility, and in Nepal are often kept in walled gardens, when they are very useful, destroying larvæ and insects."

To these remarks I can only add that they are almost exclusively monticolous, one (or two perhaps) frequenting forests in the plains. All are very social, and have loud voices, some harsh, others mellow and pleasing ; a few lay white eggs, the majority blue.

Gen. GARRULAX.

Syn. Crateropus, Swainson, apud Jerdon—*Ianthocincla* (partly) Gould.—*Cinclosoma*, Vigors and Hodgson.

Char.—Bill rather long, moderately stout, nearly straight ; the culmen gently curved towards the tip, which is slightly hooked and notched ; nostrils advanced, more or less impended by nareal tufts ; rictal bristles rather long ; wings moderate, 5th and 6th quills longest ; tail long, much rounded ; legs and feet very strong ; lateral toes nearly equal ; claws long.

The birds composing this genus are of rather large size, with longer bills than the next ; the plumage plain, in masses, and with fewer marks and variegations. In their habits they are the most gregarious and noisy of their tribe.

There are several sections, distinguished chiefly by the mode of coloration.

---

* I presume that Mr. Hodgson had here partly in view the Malacocirci, or Babblers, which are much greater grain-eaters than the Laughing-thrushes.

The first have the head crested, that and the breast white, and a black ear-stripe; and the only species known to the older authors is the first on our list. The bill is furnished with tufts of bristly feathers advancing to the base of the nostrils; the tarsus is very strong; the middle toe elongated, and the outer toe distinctly longer than the inner.

407. Garrulax leucolophus, HARDWICKE.

Corvus, apud HARDWICKE, Lin. Tr. XI.—BLYTH, Cat. 482—HORSF., Cat. 284—GOULD, Cent. II. Birds, pl. 18—*Rawil-kahy,* H. in the N. W. P.—*Karrio-pho,* Lepch.—*Karria goka,* Bhot.—Laughing Crow of Europeans in the N. W. Himalayas.

THE WHITE-CRESTED LAUGHING-THRUSH.

Descr.—The whole head with the crest, nape, sides of neck, throat, and breast, pure white, tinged with cinereous on the nape and back of the neck; a black streak from the nostrils through the eye to the ear-coverts; the rest of the plumage rich olive rufescent brown, tinged with chesnut where it joins the white, and darker on the tail; quills and tail dusky on their inner webs.

Bill black; legs plumbeous; irides red-brown (or brownish yellow in some). Length 12 inches; extent $15\frac{1}{2}$; wing 5; tail 5; bill at front $1\frac{5}{8}$; tarsus $1\frac{7}{8}$.

The White-crested Laughing-thrush is found throughout the whole extent of the Himalayas from the far north-west to Bootan, and thence through the Khasia hills to Arrakan. It assembles in large flocks of twenty or more, every now and then bursting out into a chorus of most discordant laughter, quite startling at first, and screaming and chattering for some time. They feed on the ground a good deal, turning over dead leaves for insects, but also eat various berries. They frequent the hill zone from about 2,000 to 6,000 feet of elevation (rarely higher), but are most numerous between 3,000 and 4,500 feet.

I have had the nest and eggs brought me more than once when at Darjeeling; the former being a large mass of roots, moss, and grass, with a few pure white eggs.

A nearly allied species is found in Burmah, *G. Belangeri*, Lesson.
Another sub-division, very similar in form, is exemplified by *G.
strepitans* of Tickell, and this extends into China, where represented by *G. perspicillatus*, and *G. chinensis* (which last also occurs
in the Tenasserim Provinces); indeed, it is doubtful if it really do
occur in China. *G. bicolor* and *G. mitratus*, Müller, from Sumatra,
perhaps belong to this section. An interesting account of the
habits of *G. chinensis* in confinement is recorded by Blyth,
from Mr. Frith, which, as throwing light on the manners of the
group, I shall here transcribe: "The bird was excessively tame
and familiar, and delighted in being caressed and tickled by the
hand, when it would spread its wing, and assume very singular
attitudes. It was naturally a fine songster, and a most universal
imitator. Whenever chopped meat, or other food, was put into its
cage, it always evinced the propensity to deposit the bits one by
one between the wires; and when a bee or wasp was offered, the
bird would seize it instantly, and invariably turn its tail round
and make the insect sting it several times successively before
eating it. A large beetle it would place on the ground and
pierce it with a violent downward stroke of its bill; a small snake
(about a foot long) it treated in like manner, transfixing the centre
of the head; it afterwards devoured about half the snake, holding
it by one foot, while it picked with the bill, as was its common
mode of feeding." Swinhoe relates that he has more than once
found the remains of small birds in the gizzard of *G. perspicillatus*,
and he states that it also pilfers eggs.

The two next birds, with two others found out of our limits,
form a small group of allied species, of similar habits to those of
the last section, but with a particular coloration; the bill is a trifle
more curved; and the nareal bristles almost conceal the nostrils.

408. Garrulax cærulatus, HODGSON.

Cinclosoma, apud HODGS., As. Res. XIX.—BLYTH, Cat. 487—
HORSF., Cat. 291—*Tarmol-pho*, Lepch.—*Piang-kam*, Bhot.

THE GREY-SIDED LAUGHING-THRUSH.

Descr.—Above rich olive-brown, tinged with chesnut; the head
darker, with some black marks, each feather being narrowly tipped

black; a black frontal zone reaching through the lores to the ears; wings and tibial feathers dull blue or ashy grey.

Bill dusky, livid at the base; legs fleshy white; irides red brown; orbitar skin livid. Length 11 inches; extent 13; wing $4\frac{1}{4}$; tail 5; bill at front $\frac{7}{8}$; tarsus $1\frac{3}{8}$.

This Laughing-thrush is found in the S. E. Himalayas. It is not rare in Sikhim, from about 2,000 to 4.000 feet or so. A nest and eggs, said to be of this bird, were brought to me at Darjeeling, the nest loosely made with roots and grass, and containing two pale-blue eggs.

409. Garrulax Delesserti, JERDON.

Crateropus, apud JERDON, Cat. 88—JERDON, Ill. Ind. Orn., pl. 13—C. griseiceps, DELESSERT.

THE WYNAAD LAUGHING-THRUSH.

Descr.—Head and nape dusky blackish grey; the rest of the plumage above dark brownish rufous, lighter and ferruginous on the rump and tail-coverts, and darker on the wings and tail; chin, throat, neck, and breast, white; the sides of the breast shaded with dull cinereous, belly and vent light reddish brown.

Bill dusky, yellow at the base beneath; legs fleshy; irides dull red. Length 11 inches; wing $4\frac{5}{10}$; tail $4\frac{3}{4}$; tarsus $1\frac{1}{2}$.

This is a somewhat rare bird. I first saw it in possession of M. Delessert, who got it in the slopes of the Neilgherries; and I afterwards procured it in the same locality, at about 3,000 feet of elevation. I also saw it several times in the Wynaad, associating in large flocks, wandering about among the under-wood and bamboos, and occasionally bringing out a chorus of peculiar, but clear, chattering notes.

A nearly allied species is found in Ceylon, *G. cinereifrons*, Blyth; another in Assam, *G. gularis*, McLelland, which last I lately procured in the Khasia hills.

The next bird noticed differs in some points: the bill is shorter and more arched, the frontal plumes are bristly; the tarsus is distinctly scutated, and the coloration is peculiar.

410. Garrulax ruficollis, JARD. and SELBY.

Ianthocincla, apud JARDINE and SELBY, Ill. Orn., 2nd Series,
pl. 21—BLYTH, Cat. 496—HORSF. Cat. 293—Ianthoc. lunaris,
McLELLAND—*Pobduya*, Beng.—*Rapchen-pho*, Lepch.

THE RUFOUS-NECKED LAUGHING-THRUSH.

Descr.—General plumage olive-brown, darker on the tail, which
is almost black at the tip, and passing into deep ashy on the crown
and occiput ; forehead, orbitar region, ear-coverts, throat, and fore-
neck, deep black ; a crescent-like patch of deep rufous on the sides
of the neck; middle of the lower abdomen, vent, and under tail-
coverts, rufous.

Bill black; legs livid brown; irides dull red.   Length $9\frac{1}{2}$
inches ; extent $12\frac{1}{2}$; wing 4 ; tail $5\frac{1}{2}$; bill at front $\frac{3}{4}$; tarsus $1\frac{1}{2}$.

This Garrulax is found at the foot of the Himalayas, extending
up the slopes of the hills, to perhaps 2,000 feet ; and is also common in the forests of Assam, Sylhet, and Cachar, and the eastern
frontier of Bengal. I first observed it in the Sikhim Terai, where I
was absolutely startled by a large troop of them, twenty or thirty
at least, suddenly breaking out into a most extraordinary cackling, chattering, crowing chorus, some of the notes being clear,
others harsh.   The birds were in some bamboo jungle on the road
side, some feeding on the ground, others perched on the bamboos
and trees around ; and they did not leave the spot, nor cease their
calling, till I had shot two or three of them.   I found that they had
been feeding chiefly on insects, also on seeds.   Buchanan Hamilton
says that this bird is easily tamed, sings with a fine full mellow
note, like a Blackbird, and lives on insects and plantains, &c.

The next group is distinguished by their dull plumage, by the tail
feathers tipped with white, and by a tendency of the outer web of the
primaries to be lighter colored, as in the next genus. The bill is stronger than in the last, the nostrils more apert, the rictal bristles feeble,
the tarsus strongly scutated, and the middle toe less lengthened.

411. Garrulax albogularis, GOULD.

Ianthocincla, apud GOULD, P. Z. S., 1835—BLYTH, Cat. 484—
HORSF., Cat. 286—Cinclos. albigula, HODGSON—*Karreum-pho*,
Lepch.

THE WHITE-THROATED LAUGHING-THRUSH.

Descr.—Above dull olive-brown, with some fulvous on the forehead and near the eyes; lores, and under the eyes, black; terminal third of the lateral tail feathers white; beneath, the chin and throat white; breast the same colour as the back; abdomen, vent, and under tail-coverts, rusty, darker on the flanks and under tail-coverts.

Bill dusky; legs plumbeous grey; irides glaucous; orbitar skin greenish. Length 12 inches; extent 15; wing $5\frac{1}{4}$; tail $5\frac{3}{4}$; bill at front nearly 1; tarsus $1\frac{1}{2}$.

The White-throated Laughing-thrush is found throughout the Himalayas, from Bootan to Simla, more common in the North-west, than in the eastern portion of the range. It prefers rather high elevations, from 6,000 to 9,000 feet and upwards; lives in large flocks, feeding mostly on the ground, among bamboos and brush-wood, and every now and then screaming and chattering, but not so loudly or discordantly as some of the others. Hutton, who says that it is very common at Mussooree, found the nest "about seven or eight feet from the ground, of woody tendrils, twigs, fibres, or at times of grass and leaves, and with three beautiful shining green eggs." It is not very common at Darjeeling, and is not found below 6,000 or 7,000 feet.

412. Garrulax pectoralis, GOULD.

Ianthocincla, apud GOULD, P. Z. S., 1835—BLYTH, Cat. 485—HORSF., Cat. 288—Cinclos. grisaure, HODGSON—G. melanotis, BLYTH—G. uropygialis, CABANIS—*Ol-pho*, Lepch.

THE BLACK-GORGETED LAUGHING-THRUSH.

Descr.—Plumage above light olivaceous brown, with a rusty tinge on the back and rump, and the nape and hind neck bright rusty; quills edged whitish, or pale cinereous, and the terminal third of all the lateral tail-feathers with a double band of black and white; a narrow white supercilium; cheeks, lores, and ear-coverts silvery grey or white (in some, however, pure black), enclosed by two narrow black lines, which originate at the base of the bill, and circling round the eyes and ears, unite into a broad band, which descends on the sides of the neck, and thence form a gorget on the top of the breast; beneath, the chin is white; the neck, throat, breast, and sides of the abdomen, very pale fulvous, in some bright rusty throughout, except on the middle of the lower abdomen, sometimes white on the throat and breast; the rest of the body beneath, white.

Bill bluish horny, dusky above; legs greenish plumbeous; irides brown; orbitar skin dusky leaden. Length 13 inches; extent $16\frac{1}{2}$; wing $5\frac{3}{4}$; tail $5\frac{1}{2}$; bill at front $1\frac{1}{8}$; tarsus $1\frac{1}{2}$.

This species varies a good deal (according to the locality) in the markings on the ear-coverts, which in some are black, in others white mixed with black; and in some the pectoral band is obsolete. Specimens from the Himalayas have usually the ears silver-grey, whilst those from Arrakan have them black and grey in every gradation. It is found in the Himalayas, extending through Assam into Burmah.

Bonaparte, in his Conspectus, gives *G. uropygialis*, Cabanis, from Assam, as distinct from this, 'the wings of a duller shade, and the rump rufescent, not concolorous with the body.' It does not appear to me to differ.

413. Garrulax moniliger, Hodgson.

Cinclosoma, apud Hodgson, As. Res. XIX.—Blyth, Cat. 486—Horsf., Cat. 289—Ianthoc. pectoralis, apud McLelland—Garr. McLellandi, Blyth—*Ol-pho*, Lepch.—*Piang-kam*, Bhot.

The Neck-laced Laughing-thrush.

Descr.—Very like the last; above pale olive-brown; the whole neck and throat rusty; the lateral tail feathers with a double band of black and white, but the white much less broad than in the last; the rest of the body beneath white, more or less tinged with rusty on the breast, flanks, and middle of the abdomen; a white supercilium from the bill to the occiput; below it a black line proceeding from the bill, through the eyes and ear-coverts (which are black, more or less mixed with white or grey), and sweeping round the bottom of the breast like a necklace.

Bill dusky horny; legs fleshy grey; irides yellow, or pale brownish, or orange; orbitar skin evanescent. Length $11\frac{1}{2}$ inches; wing $5\frac{1}{2}$; tail 5; bill at front 1; tarsus $1\frac{1}{2}$.

This species differs from the last in its smaller size, shorter wing, the less development of the pectoral band, less white on the tail feathers, and in the ear-coverts seldom having any white, or, it is only seen in the lower part; the legs and irides, too, differ in color. It is found in the S. E. Himalayas, also extending into Assam, Arrakan, and the Tenass erim Provinces.

I procured both this and the last at Darjeeling, and have also seen one, or both, in Sylhet, Cachar, and Upper Burmah. They both associate in large flocks, and frequent more open forests than most of the previous species. The eggs are greenish blue.

Other species of *Garrulax*, which, without being very closely allied, may yet be classed near this section, are *G. merulinus*, Blyth, from the Khasia hills, remarkable for its Thrush-like appearance, and perhaps *G. rufifrons*, Swains. and Lesson, from Java. The former I found to be rare near Cherra Poonjee, at least during the rainy season.

The next species differs somewhat from those previously noticed by its shorter wing, lengthened tail, and coloration. In its habits it is intermediate between the species of *Garrulax* and *Trochalopteron*, having the loud call and numerous flocks of the former, whilst the members keep individually more apart, as in the succeeding birds. Gray separates it generically, retaining for it Gould's name, *Ianthocincla*, but, with Horsfield, I shall still keep it as *Garrulax*.

414. **Garrulax ocellatus**, Vigors.

Cinclosoma, apud Vigors, P. Z. S., 1831—Gould, Cent. II. B., pl. 15—Blyth, Cat. 488—Horsf., Cat. 292—*Lho-karreumpho*, Lepch.

The White-spotted Laughing-Thrush.

Descr.—Forehead, sides of the head, and body above, reddish brown; top of the head, and neck in front, blackish brown; the nape, back, wings, and upper tail-coverts, marked with white ocelli, black anteriorly; quills, and lateral tail-feathers, greenish dusky, with white tips; outer webs of the middle quills grey, showing a grey alar band ; the lower wing-coverts variegated with red, black, and white ; beneath, the breast whitish rufous with black bands ; abdomen pale rufous.

Bill yellowish, dusky on the ridge and tip ; legs dull yellow ; irides yellow-brown.   Length 14 inches ; wing 5 ; tail 7 ; bill at front 1 ; tarsus $1\frac{7}{10}$.

I have seen no record of this handsome bird having been procured elsewhere than in Nepal and Sikhim.   About Darjeeling it is not found below 8,000 feet, and is most abundant between that elevation and 10,000 feet.   I saw it between Darjeeling and Tongloo in large flocks, with a fine loud clear call, which, when begun by one, was immediately answered on all sides.   It was feeding on various fruit and seeds.

Crocias guttatus, Temm., P. C. 592, from Java, judging from the figure, appears to me allied to this species ; and Bonaparte places near these birds *Timalia palliata* and *T. lugubris*, Müller, both from Sumatra.

The following birds differ considerably from *Garrulax*, as restricted, in their smaller size, more variegated plumage, more rounded wings, and also in habits ; for, though still associating in flocks, they do not keep so close together, but scatter through the brushwood.   They have all peculiar calls, which, however, in general, they do not utter in such full chorus as *Garrulax*.   They have of late been divided into two genera, which, however, differ but very slightly from each other, and chiefly in the more complete rounding of the wings.   I shall not separate them, but class them both under Hodgson's genus *Trochalopteron ; Pterocyclos*, in which Gray places them, being pre-occupied in Malacology.

Gen. Trochalopteron, Hodgson.

Syn. *Garrulax* (in part) Auct.—*Pterocyclos*, Gray.

Char.—Bill moderate or short, nearly straight, very slightly hooked at the tip, distinctly notched ; nostrils impended at their base by the frontal plumes ; wings short, much rounded, the tertiaries being as long as the primaries ; tail moderately long, broad ; tarsus and feet moderately strong ; hind claw large.

The birds of this genus are pleasingly varied in their plumage, and the outer webs of the first primaries of many are colored yellow, or bluish, or red.

415 Trochalopteron erythrocephalum, Vigors.

Cinclosoma, apud Vigors, P. Z. S., 1831—Gould, Cent. H. B., pl. 17—Blyth, Cat. 495—Horsf., Cat. 294.

The Red-headed Laughing-thrush.

Descr.—Head and nape deep rich chesnut; lores, chin, and throat black; ear-coverts mixed rufous and dark brown; neck posteriorly olivaceous, with black marks; the rest of the upper plumage ashy olive; shoulders of the wings and lesser coverts deep ferruginous or chesnut; primaries olivaceous, tinged, more or less, with ferruginous, and with black spots on the breast, especially on the sides; these vary in number and size, probably accordingto age; the flanks, lower abdomen, vent, and under tail-coverts, olivaceous.

Bill horny brown; legs dull yellow. Length $11\frac{1}{2}$ inches; wing $4\frac{1}{4}$; tail $5\frac{1}{2}$; bill at front $\frac{7}{8}$; tarsus $1\frac{1}{2}$.

The Red-headed Laughing-thrush appears to be confined to the N. W. Himalayas and the western districts of Nepal. It is unknown in Sikhim, where it is represented by a very closely allied species. Shore, as quoted by Gould in his " Century," says that " it is by no means uncommon in Kumaon, where it frequents shady ravines, building in hollows and their precipitous sides, and making its nest of small sticks and grasses, the eggs being five in number, of a sky-blue colour."

416. Trochalopteron chrysopterum, Gould.

Ianthocincla, apud Gould, P. Z. S., 1835—Blyth, Cat. 494—Horsf., Cat. 294—*Turphom-pho*, Lepch.—*Paniong*, Bhot.

The Yellow-winged Laughing-thrush.

Descr.—Forehead dark rufous; sinciput dusky grey, continuing behind the eyes as a darky band; occiput dark chesnut; back of neck reddish, with large black spots; back, rump, and upper tail-coverts, olivaceous, tinged rufescent on the interscapulars; shoulder of wings and lesser coverts deep chesnut; primaries olivaceous,

edged with bright yellow; tertiaries dull cinereous, black tipped;
beneath, the chin and throat are black, ear-coverts black, edged
with white; the rest rufous, with black crescentic spots on the
neck and breast; olivaceous on the flanks, vent, and under-tail-
coverts.

Bill dusky brown; legs horny yellow brown; irides red.
Length 10 inches; wing 4; tail 4½; bill at front ¾; tarsus 1⅜.

This is perhaps 'the most common and abundant species about
Darjeeling. It is often seen on the road, picking up insects or
grain among the dung of cattle, but rapidly hopping off, and
diving into the nearest thicket on being approached. If one
utter its call, it is answered in all directions, though not very noisily.

The eggs are greenish blue, in a nest neatly made with roots and
moss. It extends from Sikhim and Bootan to Nepal, and is very
closely allied to the last, which it replaces in the S. E. Himalayas.
T. ruficapillum, Bl., from the Khasia hills, and *T. melanostigma*, Bl.,
from Tenasserim, are also representative species in their respective localities.

417. **Trochalopteron subunicolor,** Hodgson.

J. A. S., XII., 952—Blyth, Cat. 491—Horsf., Cat. 306—
Tarmal-pho, Lepch.—*Nabom,* Bhot.

The Plain-colored Laughing-thrush.

Descr.—Above olive-brown, with black marks; the crown dashed
with dusky cinereous, and the feathers slightly edged dark; lores
blackish; ear-coverts, and the feathers beneath them, margined
with silvery ash; the outer primaries, and the emarginate portion
of the others, edged with bright yellow; the central tail-feathers
golden olive-green; lateral tail feathers blackish, olivaceous at
their base, with narrow white tips; the under parts, like those above,
viz., olive-brown with dark marks, but paler, and with the dark
markings less defined.

Bill dusky; legs reddish brown; irides red-brown. Length
10 inches; wing 3½; tail 4½; bill at front ⅝; tarsus 1⅜.

This bird is classed as a *Trochalopteron* in Horsfield's Catalogue,
whilst the two former are placed in *Pterocyclos,* but there is no

essential distinction. The bill is a little shorter in this species, and the wing a trifle more rounded.

It is nearly as abundant as the last in the vicinity of Darjeeling, and its habits do not differ.

418. Trochalopteron variegatum, VIGORS.

Cinclosoma, apud VIGORS, P. Z. S., 1831—GOULD, Cent. II. B., pl. 16—BLYTH, Cat. 493—HORSF, Cat. 296—*Ganza*, Nepal.

THE VARIEGATED LAUGHING-THRUSH.

Descr.—Plumage above brownish grey, rusty on the forehead, and cinereous on the head and neck; a stripe from the nape through the eyes black, surmounted by a narrow white line behind the eye; ear-coverts dark brown; wings with a black spot on the primary coverts, and another on the middle of the wings; the greater coverts rufous; outer webs of the primaries pale ashy-white, tinged yellowish (probably bright yellow in the fresh bird); the last of the primaries and all the secondaries tipped white; tail, with the tips of four middle feathers, ashy grey, the four outer feathers on each side edged with olive-yellow, and white tipped, and all, except the outer ones, black at the base; beneath, the chin, throat, and middle of the neck, are black; the sides of the neck pale rusty whitish, olivaceous on the breast and flanks; and the abdomen and vent rufous.

Bill black; legs reddish; irides brown. Length 10 inches; wing 4; tail 4½; bill at front $\frac{11}{16}$; tarsus 1¼.

This species has been sent from Nepal, Kumaon, and Simla, but it does not appear to extend into Sikhim.

419. Trochalopteron affine, HODGSON.

Garrulax, apud HODGSON, J. A. S., XII., 950—BLYTH, Cat. 492—HORSF., Cat. 297.

THE BLACK-FACED LAUGHING-THRUSH.

Descr.—Above rufescent olive-brown, more or less mottled with paler on the back; rump dingy greenish, and the upper tail-coverts rufous; sides of head, lores, cheeks, and ear-coverts, black, occasionally this hue even suffusing the crown; shoulder of wings and wing-coverts like the back; a jet black spot on the primary coverts; winglet, and the outer margin of the quills, pearl grey; those of the secondaries and some of the tertiaries greenish yellow; the rest of the tertiaries and tips of the secondaries slaty grey; a broad white moustachial spot, and one behind the ears also white; beneath, the chin is black; the breast rufous brown, the feathers edged laterally with grey; the belly uniform faint rufous brown; lower tail-coverts the same, but darker.

Bill black; feet reddish brown; irides brown. Length $10\frac{1}{4}$ inches; wing 4; tail $4\frac{1}{2}$; bill at front nearly $\frac{7}{8}$; tarsus $1\frac{1}{2}$.

This rare species of Laughing-thrush may be said in some measure to take the place, in the S. E. Himalayas, of the last. It has been sent from Bootan, Sikhim, and Nepal. I saw it in thick bamboo jungle between 8,000 and 9,000 feet of elevation, on the road from Darjeeling to Tongloo, and I imagine that it only frequents the higher mountains.

420. **Trochalopteron squamatum,** Gould.

Ianthocincla, apud Gould, P. Z. S., 1835—Blyth, Cat. 492 —Horsf., Cat. 305—Jard. and Selby, Ill. Orn. 2, pl. 4— Cinclos. melanura, Hodgson—*Tarmal-pho,* Lepch.—*Nabom,* Bhot.

The Blue-winged Laughing-thrush.

Descr.—Head, neck, and body above, olive-brown, with black lunules; rump unspotted dark chesnut; brows black; wings black internally, visible as such on the tertiaries, but the edges of the first primaries blue; margins of the other quills, and the coverts, dark castaneous; tail black, overlaid with glossy green, and obsoletely barred with a terminal band of rusty; beneath, the chin is black, and the rest of the lower plumage olivaceous in some, in others inclined to rufous or chesnut; vent and under tail-coverts rufescent or chesnut.

Bill black; legs shining fleshy brown; irides red-brown (glaucous according to Hodgson). Length $10\frac{1}{2}$ inches; extent 12; wing $3\frac{3}{4}$; tail $4\frac{1}{2}$; bill at front $\frac{3}{4}$; tarsus $1\frac{4}{10}$.

This is a common bird in the neighbourhood of Darjeeling, and has similar habits with the others. It has very short and highly rounded wings, and was placed by Horsfield as a restricted *Trocha-lopteron*. It has hitherto only been found in Nepal and Sikhim, but I quite recently obtained it in the Khasia hills, where not un-common.

421. Trochalopteron rufogulare, GOULD.

Ianthocincla, apud GOULD, P. Z. S., 1831—BLYTH, Cat. 482 —HORSF., Cat. 303—Cinclos. rufimenta, HODGSON —*Narbigivanpho*, Lepch.

THE RUFOUS-CHINNED LAUGHING-THRUSH.

Descr.—Above olive-brown, broadly lunated with black; the entire cap black; tail dark rufescent olivaceous, unspotted, but with a double band of black and rusty at the tip; winglet, and outer edges of the primaries, bluish, the last white tipped; the long coverts of the wings tipped with black, barwise; a pale white roundish spot before the eyes, and a broad longitudinal black patch behind the gape, extending under and behind the ear-coverts, which are olive rufescent; beneath, the chin is rusty; the throat white (rusty in some individuals, the females?); breast and belly pale smoky grey, with black drops; vent and under tail-coverts rusty; the lower part of the flanks and thighs olive-brown.

Bill horny yellow; legs fleshy brown; orbitar skin blue. Length 10 inches; extent 10¾; wing 3½; tail 4½; bill at front not ⅝; tarsus 1¾. The bill is somewhat straighter than in the others, and very indistinctly notched.

This bird is found throughout the whole extent of the Hima-layas, from Bootan to Cashmere, and also in the Khasia hills. It is not common at Darjeeling, and I found it at from 5,000 to 8,000 feet. Hutton obtained the nest and eggs at Mussooree in May. The eggs are white; a color rare, but not unknown, in this group, *vide* p. 35. Adams states that it is common in the dense jungles of the lower Himalayan ranges in the N. W., and around the vale of Cashmere. It is generally seen in flocks, and its call is loud and harsh.

The next bird stands alone in its coloration, and is perhaps the richest colored in the family.

422. Trochalopteron phœniceum, Gould.

Ianthocincla, apud Gould, Icon. Av., pl. 3—Blyth, Cat.
497—Horsf., Cat 302—Crateropus puniceus, Blyth—*Tilji-pho*, Lepch.—*Repcha*, Bhot.

The Crimson-winged Laughing-thrush.

Descr.—Above, plumage rich olive-brown, rufous on the wings;
tail dusky black above, each feather tipped with bright orange, the
lateral ones most broadly so; the feathers on the sides of the
crown, and over the eye, margined laterally with black, forming a superciliary streak; eye-streak, ear-coverts, sides of the
neck, outer edge of primaries, of the terminal portions of the
secondaries, and of the longest tertiaries, crimson; the secondaries
black internally, and partially margined with light grey; beneath,
as the upper plumage, but paler, and tinged with ruddy; tail
beneath almost entirely dull-orange.

Bill black; legs livid brown; irides red-brown. Length $8\frac{1}{2}$
inches; extent $10\frac{1}{2}$; wing $3\frac{1}{2}$; tail $4\frac{1}{8}$; bill at front $\frac{5}{8}$; tarsus $1\frac{2}{10}$.

This richly-plumaged Laughing-thrush is found in the S. E.
Himalayas, and also in the Khasia hills. It is tolerably abundant
in Sikhim, and frequents the zone from 4,000 to 6,000 feet or so.
A nest and eggs, said to be of this bird, were brought to me at
Darjeeling, the nest made of roots and grass, and the eggs, three
in number, pale blue, with a few narrow and wavy dusky streaks.

The two next birds belong to a peculiar type, and are the only
representatives of the genus found in Southern India, where they,
as was to be expected, are confined to the summits of the highest
mountain ranges.

423. Trochalopteron cachinnans, Jerdon.

Crateropus, apud Jerdon, Cat. 87, with figure—Blyth, Cat.
598—Horsf., Cat. 298—Crat. Lafresnayii, Delessert—C. Dele-
serti, Lafresnaye.

The Neilgherry Laughing-thrush.

Descr.—Above olive-brown; the head dusky black; eye-brows,
lores, and eyelids, white; ear-coverts rufous; beneath, the chin

white ; the rest of the body bright rufous, olivaceous on the flanks and lower tail-coverts.

Bill black ; legs dusky greenish ; irides fine red. Length 9¼ inches ; wing $3\frac{6}{10}$; tail 4 ; bill at front $\frac{7}{10}$; tarsus 1⅜.

This noisy bird is abundant in all the woods on the summit of the Neilgherries, and its loud laughing call is often heard when the bird itself remains unseen. I have found it nowhere else than on the Neilgherries, but it very probably will be found on the top of the Pulneys, Animalies, and other high ranges of Southern India.

Like others of the genus, it lives in small scattered flocks, foraging about the thick brushwood. It often wanders apparently alone, though at no great distance from the flock, with whom it keeps up a communication as a signal of the direction it is going, or, perhaps, of the abundance of food obtained. On being watched they hop and climb up the stems and thick branches of the nearest tree, never however ascending to the tops of trees. They feed partly on the ground, and partly on bushes ; and their chief food appears to be fruit, especially that of the *Physalis peruviana*, so perfectly acclimatized on the Neilgherries ; but they occasionally eat caterpillars and other insects. The nest is made of roots and moss, and the eggs are blue, with a few brownish spots.

I was in error in stating in my Illustrations of Indian Ornithology that the eggs were white, for, on the occasion alluded to, I mistook the bird (of which I had only a hurried glance) ; it was the *Pomatorhinus Horsfieldii* whose nest I then obtained, as I had afterwards several opportunities of confirming.

424. Trochalopteron Jerdoni, BLYTH.

Garrulax, apud BLYTH, J. A S., XX. 522.

THE BANASORE LAUGHING-THRUSH.

Descr.—Above olivaceous ; the head bluish, passing to dull ashy on the nape ; white supercilia ; lores black, less developed than in *cachinnans* ; fore-neck and breast pale ashy, passing to whitish on the ear-coverts ; middle of the abdomen rufous ; flanks and under tail-coverts olivaceous.

Bill black ; legs horny ; irides red. Length 8¾ inches ; wing $3\frac{7}{10}$; tail 3¾ ; tarsus $1\frac{3}{10}$.

G

This Laughing-thrush is very closely allied to the last, differing chiefly by the ashy breast, and some few other particulars. I procured it near the top of the Banasore peak, a high hill at the edge of the Ghats separating Malabar from the Wynaad, at an elevation of from 5,000 to 6,000 feet. Its voice is very like that of its Neilgherry congener, but more subdued. I did not hear it in Coorg, nor in any other part of the Wynaad, but I have no doubt that it will be found on some of the higher elevations along the range of Western Ghats.

The two next species also differ from all in their mode of coloration, and, to a small extent, structurally, and they exhibit some affinity for *Actinodura*, and also, though more distantly, to the *Malacocircus* group.

425. Trochalopteron lineatum, VIGORS.

Cinclosoma, apud VIGORS, P. Z. S., 1831—BLYTH, Cat. 599— HORSF., Cat. 300.

THE STREAKED LAUGHING-THRUSH.

Descr.—Head and back olivaceous ashy, the feathers of the head and neck centred with reddish brown; wings chesnut; tail the same, more or less olivaceous, and with a broad ashy-white tip, preceded by a narrow dark band, and obsoletely barred (most distinctly seen beneath); ear-coverts rufescent; lores, and over the eyes, whitish; beneath the plumage is mixed ashy and rufescent, lighter and more ashy on the chin and throat; lower abdomen, vent, and under tail-coverts, olivaceous; the feathers of the back and of the neck and breast white-shafted; and the feathers of the breast and lower parts are all edged with olive ashy.

Length 8½ inches; wing 3¼; tail 3¾; bill at front $\frac{9}{10}$; tarsus 1¼.

This species has not been found in the Sikhim Himalayas, but extend from Nepal to Cashmere, where Adams says that it is not rare. He found it living in flocks, very tame, and with a low chattering note. Hutton says that it is seen in pairs, or four or five together. He found the nest, either in a low bush, or the sides of a bank, loosely constructed of grass, stalks, and roots, and with usually three eggs, whose color he does not mention.

426. **Trochalopteron setafer**, Hodgson.

Cinclosoma, apud Hodgson, As. Res. XIX.—Garr. imbricatus, Blyth, J. A. S., XII., 951*—Blyth, Cat. 500—Horsf., Cat. 299.

THE BRISTLY LAUGHING-THRUSH.

Descr.—Above rufescent brown, darker on the head, and more rufous on the wings and tail; rump and flanks olive-green; tail rufescent, its feathers broadly subterminated with dull black, and the extreme tip whitish; feathers of the crown, nape, and neck, slightly margined with dull olive-green, and with shining black shafts, and these feathers and those of the back slightly rigid to the feel; lores albescent; beneath, rufescent olive-brown, more inclining to rufous than the upper parts, and the ear-coverts, sides of neck, and all the under parts are more or less white-shafted, chiefly towards the tips of the feathers; the primaries are inconspicuously margined with grey, and the secondaries with yellowish olive.

Bill and feet brown. Length $8\frac{3}{4}$ inches; wing 3; tail 4; bill at front $\frac{3}{4}$; tarsus $1\frac{1}{8}$.

This curious species shows some affinities for *Acanthoptila,* placed by Hodgson in the *Malacocircus* series, both by its more lengthened bill and the spinous character of the plumage. It has only as yet been sent from Nepal and Bootan, but it will probably be found in Sikhim. Hodgson states that the stomach of this bird is very thick, almost like a gizzard.

No other species of this genus appear to be recorded, except one from China, said by Blyth to be very *Malacocircus*-like. *Psophodes* of Australia appears to belong to this family, near the present series, and indeed has been placed in it by Bonaparte; and this Ornithologist also classes next to it the peculiar Malayan genus *Lophocitta, Vanga cristata* of Griffith's Cuvier, which appears to have some affinity for *Thamnocataphus.* The European *Dysornithia infansta,* usually placed among the Jays, perhaps belongs to this family and section, but most of the African *Crateropi* come nearer the *Malacocircus* group.

---

* Blyth's *imbricatus* agrees with the description of *setafer,* but Hodgson appears to have mixed up specimens of both species, for he sent specimens of the last bird as *setafer,* as I am informed by Mr. Blyth.

We have next in order two genera which differ somewhat, both in structure and habits, from the others of this family, but which, nevertheless, appear to belong to it. They are more arboreal in their habits, less social and noisy, and they appear to have some affinities for the *Leiotrichinæ*, and analogies for the Jays.

Gen. ACTINODURA, Gould,

Syn. *Ixops*, Hodgs.—*Leiocincla*, Bl.

Char.—Bill moderately long and compressed, rather slender, slightly curved; nostrils linear, basal; rictal bristles few and weak; wings short, rounded, 5th, 6th, and 7th quills about equal; tail long, graduated; tarsus moderate, stout; lateral toes unequal; anterior claws long, moderately curved; hind toe with the claw strong and well curved. Plumage copious, dense, and silky; wings barred; tail obscurely banded; head crested.

This genus was considered by Hodgson to be a link between *Sibia* and *Cinclosoma*. Bonaparte in his Conspectus placed it next to *Malacocircus*, but afterwards removed it to the *Garrulax* series. Blyth, Horsfield, and Gray all recognise its affinity to this family, and I think it may be considered to lead from *Trochalopteron* to *Malacocircus*. There are only two species known.

427. **Actinodura Egertoni,** GOULD.

P. Z. S., 1836—BLYTH, Cat. 501—HORSF., Cat. 307—Ixops rufifrons, HODGSON—Leiocincla plumosa, BLYTH—GOULD, Birds of Asia, pl.—*Ramnio-pho*, Lepch.

THE RUFOUS BAR-WING.

Descr.—Crown and nape soft brown, passing into ashy pink on the crest; forehead deep red-brown; ear-coverts silky ashy brown; back, rump, shoulder of wing, and coverts, red-brown; primaries, except the first three, barred with black on a reddish ash ground; the secondaries and tertiaries with narrow dark bars on a more rufous ground; tail dark ruddy brown, faintly barred with dusky (except the two central tail-feathers), and white tipped; beneath pale rufescent, tinged with ashy on the neck and breast, and with red-brown on the throat.

Bill light horny; legs pale brown; irides brown. Length 9 inches; wing $3\frac{3}{8}$; tail 5; bill at front $\frac{3}{4}$; tarsus 1.

The rufous Bar-wing is found from Nepal, to the hill ranges of Assam and Sylhet. It is very common near Darjeeling, from 3,000 to 6,000 feet or so, associates in small flocks, wandering from tree to tree, and carefully examining the foliage and branches, never descending to the ground, and feeding both on fruit and (especially) on insects.

Horsfield gives Afghanistan as a locality, but I have no doubt that Griffith's specimens were from the Khasia hills, where I found it far from rare.

428. Actinodura nipalensis, Hodgson.

Cinclosoma, apud Hodgson, As. Res. XIX., subsequently Ixops,—Blyth, Cat. 502—Horsf., Cat. 308—*Ramnio-pho*, Lepch.

The Hoary Bar-wing.

Descr.—Plumage above rufescent brown, with an olivaceous tinge; head and nape, with the full soft crest, pure brown, the centre of each feather, hoary; ear-coverts and cheeks dark grey; a black moustache from the lower mandible, bounding the ear-coverts beneath; the greater coverts black; the wings castaneous, with numerous cross bars of black, and the quills externally and at tip black; tail also castaneous, with numerous black bands, except the two middle tail-feathers; the inner web quite black, and the tip white, broadly ended with pure black; beneath, rufescent ashy with a yellow tint; the flanks, thighs, vent, and under tail-coverts, of the same color as the back.

Bill dusky horny; legs pale fleshy brown; irides brown. Length 8 inches; extent 10; wing $3\frac{3}{4}$; tail $3\frac{1}{2}$; bill at front $\frac{5}{8}$; tarsus $1\frac{2}{10}$.

The Hoary Bar-wing replaces the last species at higher elevations, being found from about 7,000 to 10,000 feet and upwards. It has only been procured in the S. E. Himalayas, in Nepal, Sikhim, and Bootan. It may be said to be still more arboreal than the last, for it is frequently seen perched on the very tops of moderate-sized trees. It feeds chiefly on insects, and I found it, on Mt. Tongloo, feeding on the various insects that infest the flowers of the

Rhododendrons. As I did not obtain the nest, either of this or of the last species, I presume that they build on high trees.

Gen. SIBIA, Hodgson.

Syn. *Alcopus*, Hodgson—*Heterophosia*, Blyth, partly.

Char.—Bill rather long, slender, gently curved, barely hooked at the tip, and almost entire; nares lateral, lengthened; wings moderate, rounded; tarsi stout, moderately long; toes moderate, lateral toes unequal, hind toe broad and large; nails acute, moderately curved.

The form of the birds of this genus is slender, and the bill is more lengthened and attenuated than in most of the members of this family. The tongue, moreover, is forked and slightly brushed, somewhat as in *Phyllornis*. Gray includes it in the *Pycnonotinæ*, or Bulbuls, as Bonaparte formerly did, near to *Hypsipetes* (the most slender billed of the Bulbuls); and McLelland, indeed, described one species as a *Hypsipetes*. Blyth, however, described this very species as an *Actinodura*; and, taking their strong legs and feet as the most important character, I quite agree with Hodgson, Blyth, and Horsfield, in placing *Sibia* next to *Actinodura* in this family, of which it may be considered a tenuirostral or Melliphagous type, as Hodgson asserts.

There are two forms in this genus, to one of which Cabanis, and Gray, following him, have given the generic name *Malacias*, but I shall not adopt it here; and, moreover, if the genus is to be divided, I would retain *Sibia* for the species classed by Cabanis as *Malacias*, and apply Blyth's prior name of *Heterophasia* for the long-tailed species.

429. **Sibia capistrata**, VIGORS.

Cinclosoma, apud VIGORS, P. Z. S., 1831—BLYTH, Cat. 514—HORSF., Cat. 314—S. nigriceps, HODGSON—Cinclos. melanocephalum, ROYLE, List of Birds—*Sambriak-pho*, Lepch.—*Sesigona*, Bhot.—*Sibya*, Nepal.

THE BLACK-HEADED SIBIA.

Descr.—Head above, cheeks, and ear-coverts, black; nape pale rufous; back brownish grey in the middle, deep rufous posteriorly and on the upper tail-coverts; tail rufous, black at the base (except the central feathers, which are rufous grey), with a subterminal broad band of black, tipped grey; the inner webs rufous; neck in front, breast, and upper part of the abdomen, pale rufous; the rest deep rufous.

Bill black; legs yellowish brown; irides brown. Length 9 to 10 inches; extent 11; wing 4; tail 5; bill at front $\frac{11}{16}$; tarsus $1\frac{1}{8}$.

The black-headed *Sibia* is found throughout the whole Himalayas, from Simla to Bootan, and is one of the most abundant birds about Darjeeling. It is found from 4,000 feet to 8,000 feet, but most common about 7,000 feet. It frequents the highest trees, climbing up the larger branches, and clinging round and below the smaller branches, almost like a Wood-pecker, or Nuthatch.

It is often seen alone, or in pairs, but occasionally in small parties; and is constantly uttering its twittering call, which Hutton syllabizes as *titteeree, titteree, tweeyo*, often answered by one at some little distance. It is very fond of concealing itself in the thick masses of Epiphytic plants found on all lofty trees in Sikhim, and its favorite food is the fruit of the Epiphytic Andromedæ so abundant about Darjeeling; it occasionally, however, picks insects from moss, or crevices of the bark.

I on one occasion saw it at Kursion, 4,500 feet high, in winter, climbing up and down the thatched roof of a bungalow. Hutton procured the nest at Mussooree, made of coarse grass, moss, wool, and roots; and the one egg he got was pale bluish-white, with rufous freckles.

430. Sibia picaoides, HODGSON.

J. A. S., VIII., 38—BLYTH, Cat. 508—HORSF., Cat. 312—Heterophasia cuculopsis, BLYTH—*Malcheo-pho*, Lepch.

THE LONG-TAILED SIBIA.

Descr.—Above greenish fuscous, slightly darker on the forehead; lores black; wings dusky, with a large white wing-spot formed by the middle third of the outer webs of four of the secondaries; tail dusky, with broad white tip; beneath dark ashy, paler on the belly.

Bill and legs blackish; irides red-brown. Length 14 inches; extent 14; wing $4\frac{3}{4}$; tail $8\frac{3}{4}$; bill at front $\frac{7}{8}$; tarsus $1\frac{1}{10}$.

This curious looking bird is the type of Blyth's *Heterophasia*, which, as he says, has a very cuculideous appearance altogether. It differs from the more common species in its longer bill, longer wings, and gently lengthened tail, as well as in its mode of coloration; and, if other species are discovered resembling it, will deserve separation. It bears towards *S. capistrata* much the same relation as *Volvocivora silens* does towards *V. Sykesii*.

It has only been found in Nepal, Sikhim, and Bootan. I found it not uncommon near Darjeeling at about 4,000 feet of elevation, associating in flocks of six or seven, and flying from tree to tree, feeding both on fruit and insects, and keeping up a continual whistling sort of call.

Two other species of *Sibia* are on record; one from Assam, *S. gracilis*, McLell., which I found rather common on the Khasia hills at about 5,000 feet high; and *S. melanoleuca*, Tickell, from Tenasserim. They both belong to the type of *Capistrata*.

The bird described and figured by Nicholson in the Proc. Zool. Soc. for 1851, page 195, as *Artamus cucullatus*, has much the aspect of *Sibia gracilis*. Its habits, as described, are certainly not those of *Artamus*, or any similar bird; but, unless it be a *Sibia* or allied form, I know not where else to class it. I shall here transcribe the account of the bird from the work above quoted. It is said to be from India, but the locality is not mentioned. The Tailor-bird described in the previous page was from Western India, Rajcote and Surat.

" Head large; bill strong, narrow, and sharp, gently arched on the culmen; a distinct notch near the tip of upper mandible; gape wide; tongue horny and divided at the point; nostrils basal, small; eye rather small; iris of a silvery colour, tinged with yellow; wings rounded; first quill very short, third longest, second, third, and fourth quills emarginate on outer web; tail short, and nearly even at the end, of twelve feathers, $2\frac{3}{4}$ inches long; tarsus strong; hallux and claw stronger than the other toes, and as long as the inner toe, and has a large pad at its base; the outer toe is shorter; the claws are much hooked; plumage is soft and loose.

" *Colours*.—The whole top of the head is covered with a cap of black. Bill lead-colour at base and black at the point. The chin, the breast, and all underneath white; the body all above of a leaden colour. Quills and tail of a light black, edged with light on both webs; the outer web of the outer tail-feather is white, as well as the tips of the first five on each side. Feet and legs black. Male: weight $6\frac{1}{2}$ oz. Length from bill to tip of tail $7\frac{2}{9}$ inches. Alar extent 10 inches.

" Contents of stomach were a few grains of *Holcus spicatus* and the exuviæ of insects.

" These birds are only found in very thick jungles among the brushwood, where they are always moving about, and are shot with great difficulty, and even then, if not killed outright, they are so tenacious of life, that they creep into the first hole or crevice they come to. The only note I ever heard was like ' chick, chick.' I think they are residents, but the few I have seen just appear and are lost again in a moment, so that I know little of their habits; the one figured here had one leg and both wings broken, and still crept into the hole of a jerboa-rat, from which I dug it out dead."

The next bird is a very interesting form which appears to unite the *Garrulax* group with the Babblers; and also resembles *Sibia* in the form of its bill. It resembles *Trochalopteron setafer* in the general character of its plumage, and specially in the black and spiny shafts of many of the body feathers, whilst it is more like *Malacocircus* in its bill and general structure, and Hodgson classed it with the members of that genus.

Gen. ACANTHOPTILA, Blyth.

Char.—Bill moderately long, compressed, very gently curved, pointed, entire; rictal bristles few and small; wings feeble, much rounded; tail long, broad; tarsus moderately long, stout; lateral toes nearly equal; claws moderately curved; plumage with black and shining shafts.

431. **Acanthoptila nipalensis,** Hodgson.

Timalia, apud Hodgson, As. Res. XIX.—Blyth, Cat. 789—Horsf., Cat. 320—T. pellotis and T. leucotis, Hodgson.

The Spiny Babbler.

Descr.—Above brown ; chin, throat, neck, and upper breast, rufescent ; the lower part of the breast, belly, and vent, albescent, shaded with brown, and passing into brown on the flanks, thighs, and under tail-coverts ; cheeks pure white ; outer webs of the primaries pale ; the plumage generally with black and somewhat spiny shafts to the feathers.

Bill and legs dark plumbeous ; irides hoary blue. Length 10 inches ; extent 10 ; wing 4 ; tail 5 ; bill at front $\frac{7}{8}$; tarsus $1\frac{7}{10}$.

This highly interesting bird appears to be rare, having only been sent from Nepal, and I did not procure it in Sikhim or in the Terai. Nothing is recorded of its habits.

The next group is that peculiarly Indian one the Babblers. It includes several more or less marked types of form, the most typical of which appears to be only found in the continent of India and Ceylon, and is one of the few generic types quite peculiar to the plains of India. The birds composing this group are all gregarious, somewhat garrulous, chiefly ground feeders, and mostly familiar birds. They construct a loose nest of twigs, and all lay blue eggs.

Gen. MALACOCIRCUS, Swainson.

Syn. *Timalia*, Auct.

Char.—Bill short or moderate, much compressed, rather deep, curving from the base, barely hooked at the tip, entire ; commissure slightly curved ; gonys ascending ; nostrils apert ; a few short pale rictal setæ ; wings short, much rounded, 4th, 5th, and 6th quills nearly equal and longest ; tail moderately long, broad ; tarsus stout, scutellate ; feet rather large ; claws moderately curved.

The birds composing this genus resemble one another so closely that they are with difficulty recognised as distinct. The frontal plumes are broad and round, but slightly rigid. They are clad in sombre earthy grey, more or less mixed with rufescent, and striated, and were formerly, by some authors, referred to the Mynas. One or more species are to be found in every part of the plains of India, and it is the type alluded to above as being perhaps the most characteristic form in this geographical district.

432. Malacocircus terricolor, Hodgson.

Pastor, apud Hodgson, J. A. S., V., 771—M. Bengalensis, Blyth, Cat. 790—M. canorus, L., apud Horsf., Cat. 318— *Sat bhai*, H. *i. e.*, the seven brothers—*Chatarhia*, Beng.—*Pengya maina*, H., in the Upper Provinces.

The Bengal Babbler.

Descr.—Above brownish ashy, paler and somewhat cinereous on the head and neck; browner on the back, where the feathers are faintly pale shafted; quills brown, with outer webs paler, and narrowly bordered with ashy; tail reddish brown, faintly barred, and the outer feathers tipped with pale whitey brown; beneath pale ashy brown on the throat and breast, the feathers very faintly edged and shafted lighter; abdomen, vent, and under-tail-coverts, pale fulvescent.

Bill horny brown; irides pale yellow; legs dingy or fleshy yellow. Length 9 to 10 inches; extent 13; wing 4⅛; tail 4½; bill at front ¾; tarsus 1½.

This species very closely resembles *M. striatus* of Ceylon, excepting that all its colors are less brought out, the cross rays on the tail being faint and inconspicuous, barely discernible on the tertiaries, and not at all on the secondaries; it has a very weak tinge of fulvous on the abdominal region, whilst the Ceylon bird is deeper ferruginous. The closed wing of *striatus* shows more ashy, the bill too is a trifle longer, and more gradually curved.

The Bengal Babbler is found throughout all Bengal proper, extending south to Goomsoor, and perhaps further westward, through the Terai of Nepal to the Dehra Doon; and as far as the Nerbudda at all events in Central India. "It is," says Pearson, "a most abundant and conspicuous species in Bengal and Nepal. It is the *Sat bhai*, or seven brothers, of the natives, so called from being always found in a company of about that number. It is one of the chattering, noisiest birds in India, squeaking and hopping about, now on the ground then upon a tree, the flock being constantly on the move; when one starts, all the rest follow it, one after the other, making generally but a short flight of not more than forty or fifty yards at a time, and when alighted they hold a sort of consultation, hopping and chattering about all the time, till, after a few minutes, they move up to another tree, and so on for the greater part of the day, rarely staying for more than half an hour in the same place : they feed on insects." '

I may add to this that this bird becomes more rare to the eastwards, and I did not observe it at Cachar.

433. Malacocircus griseus, GMELIN.

Turdus, apud GMELIN—BLYTH, Cat. 792—HORSF., Cat. 319— Timalia, apud JERDON, Cat. 92—JERDON, Ill. Ind. Orn., pl. 19— M. affinis, JERD.—*Khyr*, H.—*Chinda* or *Sida*, Tel.—*Kalli-kuravi*, Tam., *i. e.*, Hedge-bird—*Fouille-merde* of the French in India (Vieillot)—*Dirt-bird* popularly in the South of India.

THE WHITE-HEADED BABBLER.

Descr.—Head, lores, and nape, fulvescent or dirty whitish ; plumage above darker brown than in the last, the feathers with pale shafts ; quills not barred ; tail brown, very faintly barred, and the outer feathers tipped pale ; beneath, the chin and throat are mixed brown and ashy, conspicuously darker than the neighbouring parts, each feather being ashy at the base, and with a dark band, tipped paler ; as the pale tip gets worn away, the dark tinge becomes more apparent ; from the breast the rest of the lower parts are pale fulvescent, inclining to rufescent.

Bill yellowish ; irides yellowish white ; legs fleshy yellow. Length 9 inches ; wing 4 ; tail 4 ; bill at front $\frac{11}{16}$; tarsus $1\frac{1}{4}$.

The chief distinguishing marks of this species are the whitish head, and the dark throat, both of which contrast strongly with the neighbouring parts. It is found throughout the whole Carnatic, extending northwards into the Northern Circars, and westwards into the neighbouring portion of the table land, to a greater or less distance. Either this, or a very closely allied race (*M. affinis* of my Illustrations of Indian Ornithology, text to plate 19) is found in the south of Malabar.

It is extremely common and abundant in the Carnatic, and is to be found in every hedge, avenue, and garden. Like the others of its genus it always associates in families of six, seven, eight, or more; even in the breeding season the parent birds feeding in company with their former companions. One may be seen suddenly dropping to the ground from some tree, and is followed in succession, though perhaps not immediately, by each of the flock. They hop about, turning over fallen leaves, and examining all the herbage around the base of trees, a very favorite spot, or on a hedge side, never venturing to any distance from cover, being aware of their tardy powers of flight. They are occasionally seen seeking insects or grain, from heaps of dung, whence they have received their common denomination, as well from the French (Fouille merde) as from the English (Dirt-bird), who are on this account prejudiced against them. They generally feed at some little distance apart from each other, but now and then, if a richer prize than usual is spied out, two or more will meet and struggle for it; and now and then one of them will make a clumsy flight after a grasshopper seeking safety by its wings, and not unfrequently eluding its awkward pursuer. On being driven from the ground, or leaving it from choice, their hunger being satisfied, they fly up to the nearest tree, hopping and climbing up the larger branches, and if you happen to be watching them they do not stop till they have reached the top, or the opposite side, whence they fly off in single and extended file as before. They often appear to pick insects off the branches of trees. They are familiar, if undisturbed,.feeding often close to houses, but if watched or followed, they become circumspect, disperse, and hide themselves. Their cry is a loud sibilous or whispering sort of chatter, which they repeat all at once, sometimes when feeding, or when any unusual sight attracts their attention, and often without any apparent object at all. They have no song. Their flight is slow and laborious, performed by a few rapid strokes of the wings alternating with a sailing with outspread pinions. I have often found the nest of this bird, which is composed of small twigs and roots, carelessly and loosely put together, in general at no great height from the ground; it lays three or four blue eggs. I have found them breeding at all times from January to July, and even later, but do not know if they ever have two broods in the year. The black and white crested Cuckoo, (*Coccystes melanoleucos*) appears to select this bird

to act as foster parent to her own progeny, and she lays a greenish
blue egg. They are readily caught by a spring trap baited with grain,
with one of their kind put in the centre as a lure. The Shikra or
Chipka (*Micronisus badius*) is sometimes flown at them, and causes
a general consternation. After the first burst of alarm and gabbling,
they cease their chattering, separate, and disperse, and do not, like
the bolder Mahratta Babbler (*M. Malcolmi*), come to the rescue
of their unfortunate companion.

The variety or race I named *M. affinis* is so very similar that
I shall not separate it. It appeared to me to differ slightly in the
white of the head being less pure, and the band on the throat
less dark. The hind toe and claw also appeared larger, and the
bill shorter. My specimens were procured in Travancore.

434. Malacocircus Malabaricus, Jerdon.

Ill. Ind. Orn., text to M. griseus, pl. 19—Blyth, Cat. 791—
M. Somervillei, apud Jerdon, Cat. 91—and Horsf., Cat. 317 (in
part)—M. orientalis, Jerdon—*Jangli-khyr* H.—*Pedda sida*, Tel.

The Jungle Babbler.

Descr.—Very like *M. terricolor*, but somewhat darker in color,
with broader and more distinct pale mesial streaks on the feathers
of the back, and especially of the breast; the tertiaries are but
very obscurely striated, but the tail is distinctly so.

Bill and gape dark yellow; orbits yellow; irides pale yellow;
legs dirty yellow, with a fleshy tinge. Length 9 inches; wing $4\frac{1}{10}$;
tail $4\frac{1}{2}$; tarsus $1\frac{2}{10}$; bill at front $\frac{3}{4}$.

The Jungle Babbler is found in forests and jungles throughout
the greater part of the Peninsula of India, in the Carnatic, the
N. Circars, the Malabar Coast, the slopes of the Neilgherries, and
the table land, in suitable places, as far as Nagpore, and to the
latitude of Bombay on the Western Ghats. It is replaced in the
North by *M. terricolor* and *M. Malcolmi* respectively in the east and
west. Royle, in his List of Birds procured in the N. W. P., gives
M. Somervillei as found in the Dhoon, but this appears doubtful.
Horsfield gives my *Malabaricus* as synonymous with Sykes'
Somervillei, but I procured another species in Bombay and vicinity

which corresponds with Sykes' description. Col. Sykes doubtless obtained both species, and probably mixed them up under one name, for Horsfield declares that one of Sykes' own specimens is identical with one of the present species, transmitted from myself through the Asiatic Society of Bengal.

I have always found this species of Babbler either in dense and hilly forest, or in highly-wooded districts, such as Malabar. There I found it not uncommon even in my own compound at Tellicherry, but, in general, it avoids dwellings. In other respects it is similar in habits to *M. griseus*, but its voice is very different, much more like that of *M. terricolor*. In my ' Illustrations,' I separated those from the Eastern ghats under the name of *M. orientalis*. This race, however, has not been considered distinct from *Malabaricus*, and I have accordingly for the present merged it in that species. Malabar specimens appeared to me to have more rufous; those from the Eastern ghats more grey.

435. Malacocircus Somervillei, SYKES.

Cat. 68.

THE RUFOUS-TAILED BABBLER.

Descr.—Above ashy brown, the feathers of the back barely lighter shafted, passing into rufescent on the rump and upper tail-coverts; quills dark brown on both webs; tail rufous brown, obsoletely banded; beneath. the chin, and throat are mixed dark brown and ashy as in *griseus*; the upper part of the breast pale whitey-brown, the feathers dark at their base; the lower breast, belly, vent, and under tail-coverts, rufescent.

Bill horny yellow; legs dirty yellow; irides pale yellow. Length 9½ inches; wing 4¼; tail 4; bill at front ¾; tarsus 1⅛.

This is a very distinct species, and, if it be not Sykes' *M. Somervillei*, is new, and may have the name of *M. Sykesii;* but I feel certain that Sykes had this species in view when he de-scribed *M. Somervillei*, and I append a translation of his description for reference :—" Reddish brown ; abdomen, vent, lower back, and tail, pale rufous; the tail obsoletely banded with darker; quills brown; feathers of the throat and breast bluish in the middle. Bill and feet yellow. Length 9½ inches; tail 4½."

I found this to be the common species of Babbler in Bombay, entering compounds and gardens; and I also saw it above the ghats, though less common there. A specimen obtained at Bombay by myself is now in the Museum of the Asiatic Society of Calcutta.

It is possible that some of the races alluded to by me in the " Illustrations" may turn out to be distinct; but I have not had an opportunity of verifying them since those remarks were penned.

The next bird is of a slightly different type, and has been separated by Mr. Blyth as distinct, under the name of *Malcolmia*, but the distinctive marks are not prominent, and I shall not adopt it here. It differs from restricted *Malacocircus* by its larger size, more uniform color, the tail longer and more narrow; the frontal feathers are stiff and pointed, the bill is a trifle shorter, and the wings are somewhat longer and more pointed. It associates usually in still larger flocks.

436. Malacocircus Malcolmi, Sykes.

Timalia, apud Sykes, Cat. 67—Blyth, Cat. 794—Horsf., Cat. 316—Jerdon, Cat. 90—Garrulus albifrons, Gray, Hardwicke, Ill. Ind. Zool. 2, pl. 36, f. 1—*Ghogoi*, H.—*Gangai*, H. in the N. W. Provinces—*Gongya*, Can.—*Kokatti*, Mahr.—*Verrichinda*, i. e. Mad-babbler, Tel.—also *Gowa sida*, Tel.

The Large Grey Babbler.

Descr.—Above of a pale brownish grey, lighter and more cinereous on the rump; quills and middle rectrices darker, the latter with some faint cross bands, and the lateral feathers whitish; forehead pale bluish, the feathers with white shafts; the first three quills with the outer webs pale yellowish; beneath uniform whitish grey, with a tinge of fulvescent or rufescent, most distinct on the breast and upper part of the abdomen.

Bill horny; legs dirty yellow; irides light yellow. Length 11 inches; wing $4\frac{6}{10}$; tail $5\frac{3}{4}$; bill at front $\frac{9}{10}$; tarsus $1\frac{5}{10}$.

This large Babbler has a peculiar distribution. In the south of India it is found, though not very common, only in jungly and hilly ground, apart from cultivation. I have seen it near Nellore, on the slopes of the Shervaroy and Neilgherry Hills, in Mysore, always in jungly places; but as we go north on the table land, it leaves the jungles and wilds, and becomes the familiar and unscared representative of the *Khyr* or *Sat bhai*. It is particularly abundant at Jaulna in the Deccan, and the country round about. From this it extends north and north-west to the valley of the Ganges, as at Cawnpore, barely extending eastwards, for it is rare at Mhow, and unknown at Saugor in Central India. About Jaulna it frequents fields, hedges, orchards, and the vicinity of villages, generally associating in large flocks, more numerous than those of *Malacocircus griseus*, or *Malabaricus*. It feeds chiefly on the ground, and especially round the trunks of large trees, and near hedge-rows, turning over the fallen leaves with their bills and sometimes with their claws, and picking up various insects, beetles, cockroaches, grasshoppers, &c., and also seeds and grain. I once saw one in vain attempt to capture a grass-hopper on the wing. The flock keep up a continued chattering, occasionally changed to a more sonorous call, resembling "*quey, quey, quey, quo, quo*," pronounced gutturally. Their flight is feeble and straggling. If the *Shikra* sparrow-hawk be thrown at them, they defend each other with great courage, mobbing the hawk, and endeavouring to release the one she has seized. I think that Mr. Philipps must have had this species in view, and not *M. terricolor*, when he writes of the latter attacking a hawk and severely handling it. I have no doubt that this bird extends through most of the N. W. Provinces, whilst *M. terricolor*, so far as we know, is not found there; and the name he gives is nearly that applied to the former bird in other districts.

I have frequently found the nest and eggs, the former a loose structure of roots, twigs, and grass, with usually four verditer blue eggs. Burgess says that he found the nest of this bird in a tuft of grass in some boggy ground. This is a very unusual spot for them to select, and, from the small size of the eggs, I suspect that he must have got the nest and eggs of *Chatarrhœa caudata*, or, it may be, of *Megalurus palustris*.

Mr. Blyth considers that some African birds may perhaps be found to range in *Malcolmia*, especially *Malurus squamiceps* and *M. acaciæ* of Rüppell, the former from Eastern Africa, and the latter from Arabia Petræa, which belongs to the African Fauna.

If this is found to be the case, I would then accord the generic rank proposed by Blyth.

The following bird has also been lately separated from *Malacocircus* by Blyth, and as its distinguishing features are more prominent, I shall adopt it.

Gen. LAYARDIA, Blyth.

Similar to *Malacocircus*, but of more decided colors, the bill shorter and deeper, the wings shorter and more rounded; the frontal plumes hispid, but of open texture, and monticolous in its habits. In its coloration, as in its habitat, it makes an approach to the *Garrulax* series. But two species are known, one from Southern India, the other, a somewhat aberrant species, from Ceylon; but Blyth thinks it probable that *Crateropus rubiginosus*, Rüppell, of E. Africa, may belong to it.

437. Layardia subrufa, JERDON.

Timalia, apud JERDON, Cat. 93—BLYTH, Cat. 795—HORSF., Cat. 315—Tim. pœcilorhyncha, LAFRESNAYE—*Jungli khyr*, H.

THE RUFOUS BABBLER.

Descr.—Above darkish brown olive; forehead pale bluish ash, the frontal feathers somewhat rigid; beneath deep rufous, paler on the chin.

Bill dusky above, yellow beneath; legs dull yellow; irides light yellow. Length $9\frac{1}{2}$ inches; wing $3\frac{7}{10}$; tail $4\frac{1}{4}$; bill at front $\frac{7}{10}$; tarsus $1\frac{3}{10}$.

The Rufous Babbler is found in the higher wooded regions of Malabar, the Wynaad, Coorg, and all along the crest of the Western Ghats, as far as the Southern Mahratta country. I have seen it, though rarely, below the Ghats in Malabar.

It always frequents thick jungles, more especially bamboos; has similar habits to the *Malacocirci*, feeding chiefly on the ground in parties of eight or ten; and, on being disturbed, retreating through the thick clumps of Bamboos, and concealing themselves from view, chattering all the time. Their note, though similar in character to that of the *Malacocirci*, is quite distinct, clearer, and less harsh.

An allied species, *L. rufescens*, Blyth, is found in Ceylon, somewhat darker, the head tinged with ashy, and the whole bill yellow.

We now come to a group which differs in the more slender body, lengthened and narrow tail, and striated plumage.

Gen. CHATARRHŒA, Blyth.

Syn. *Timalia* and *Malacocircus* (in part). Auct.

Char.—Bill longer than in *Malacocircus*, more slender, and very gently curved, both on the commissure and culmen; tail long, narrow; lateral toes about equal; hind toe very long; claws slightly curved.

438. Chatarrhœa caudata, DUMÉRIL.

Copyphus, apud DUMÉRIL—BLYTH, Cat. 797—HORSF., Cat. 322—Tim. chatarrhœa, FRANKLIN—SYKES, Cat. 69—JERDON, Cat. 94—M. Huttoni, BLYTH—Megalurus isabellinus, SWAINSON—*Dumri*, H. in the South—*Huni*, Tam.—*Hedo* and *Lailo*, Sindh—*Chilchil* H. in the N. W. P. (ROYLE)—*Peng* or *Chota-phenga*, Hindi—*Sor* in the N. W. (THEOBALD)—*Chinna sida*, Tel.

THE STRIATED BUSH-BABBLER.

Descr.—Above pale ashy brown, with numerous dusky striæ, each feather being centred brown; tail pale olive-brown, obsoletely barred with dusky; beneath, the chin white, the rest of the plumage rufescent ashy, darkest on the flanks.

Bill pale brownish horny; legs dull yellow; irides red brown. Length 9 inches; wing 3; tail 4½; bill at front ⅝; tarsus 1.

This Babbler is the most extensively spread of all the Indian members of this group, being found throughout the whole country from Assam to Sindh, and from the N. W. Provinces and Afghanistan to Cape Comorin. The only district in which I have not seen it, is Malabar. In the south of India it is usually found away from houses and villages, in the open plains, that are clad with a few low and scattered bushes, and indeed it is to be met with in low jungle throughout India; but, towards the north, in Central India, and in some of the Gangetic provinces, it frequents cultivated

grounds, entering gardens and compounds, and sheltering itself
in hedge-rows. In the south it is a shy bird, flying before you
from bush to bush with a sibilant sort of whistle, or, as Mr. Philipps
says " a low under-toned warbling whistle," which it often repeats.
It runs or rather hops along the ground at a great rate, and with
its long tail held straight out and drooping on the ground, it looks
more like a rat than a bird. This likeness is so striking, that it has
occurred to more than one observer. It flies low, from bush to
bush, with a few rapid beats of the wing alternating with a sailing
motion, and outstretched wings; and though, from the nature of
the ground it frequents, it is obliged to take longer flights than the
Malacocerci, yet its powers of wing are very feeble, and a person
on horseback can easily overtake the flock. In such case they
take refuge in the nearest bush, and are with great difficulty dislodged. I have frequently seen the nest and eggs, the former
almost always in a thorny bush, at no height, made of roots and
grasses loosely put together, and with three or four verditer blue
eggs.

Mr. Philipps says that " they bear confinement well, feeding on
grain, and that all day long they are jumping from side to side of
the aviary, responding to each other."

439.   Chatarrhœa Earlei, BLYTH.

Malacocircus, apud BLYTH, J. A. S., XIII., 369—BLYTH. Cat.
796—HORSF. Cat. 321—*Burra-phenga*, Hindi.

THE STRIATED REED-BABBLER.

Descr.—Above pale ashy brown, with dark brown streaks on
the head and back, fading on the upper tail-coverts; tail concolorous with the back, still paler perhaps, and with no trace of
striæ; chin, throat, and upper part of the breast dull reddish
fulvous, edged paler, and with faint dark central lines; the rest
of the under-parts dingy fulvous or albescent brown.

Bill pale greenish yellow, dusky above and at the tip; legs
dirty greenish horn; irides bright yellow. Length not quite 10
inches; extent 11; wing $3\frac{1}{2}$; tail $5\frac{1}{2}$; bill at front $\frac{3}{4}$; tarsus $1\frac{3}{8}$;
extent of foot $1\frac{1}{2}$.

This species is very similar to the last, but differs in being a little larger, in the frontal feathers being less rufescent, and more distinctly streaked, in the tail being barely striated, and the chin not being white, &c. &c.

It is found throughout Lower Bengal and the Nepal Terai, extending along the valley of Assam and southwards to Burmah, where it is very abundant; but has not yet been noticed in Southern or Central India, nor in the N. W. Provinces. It frequents heavy grass and reed jungle, exclusively, especially near water, and is a most common bird along all the rivers of Eastern Bengal, and its note, which is something like that of its congener, but clearer and louder, is often the only sound heard whilst tracking along the river banks. It associates in large flocks, and a sentinel is generally posted on some high perch to warn the rest of any danger. They feed more exclusively on insects perhaps than the last species.

C. gularis, Blyth, from Burmah, is the familiar Garden-babbler of Thyetmyo, and is still more abundant and familiar higher up the river Irrawaddy, as Mr. W. Blanford informs me. Other species belonging to the group of Babblers are found in Africa, such as *Crateropus Jardinii*, A. Smith, and perhaps some ranked under *Ixos*, viz., *I. plebeius*, *I. leucocephalos*, and *I. leucopygius* of Rüppell. The former of these, indeed, is very like a true *Malacocircus*. Some of the other African *Crateropi* appear immediate between this group and *Garrulax*; but their habits, as described by Tristram, are very similar to those of *Malacocircus* or *Chatarrhœa*. *Chætops*, Swainson, perhaps should also be placed in this group.

Next the Babblers I place a small series of Reed and Grass birds, some of them striated, others of plain plumage; they are somewhat aberrant members of this family, and their location here is not adopted by all. Gray and Horsfield place them among the Warblers, and Bonaparte makes of them a section, *Sphenureæ*, of his *Calamoherpinæ*, including most of our birds, and others greatly affined to them from other regions; but he places them next the *Timalidæ*. Blyth, too, classes them near *Chatarrhœa*, to which the larger species are certainly nearly related, whilst the smaller members approach the *Locustellæ* and *Drymoicæ* of our *Sylviadæ*. Hodgson, too, had, I suspect, similar views of their affinities, for he ranges *Acrocephalus* (which, though allied to our birds, I yet consider more strictly a Sylviadean type) as *Malacocircus abnormis*; and Swainson placed *Chatarrhœa caudata* as a *Megalurus*. Those whose nidification is known lay blue eggs, and although they are less social in their habits than the Babblers, they are perhaps nearer to this group than to any other. They may be said to bear the same relation to the restricted Babblers that *Sibia* and *Actinodura* do to the *Garrulax* group, or *Alcippe* to the *Timaliæ*.

Gen. MEGALURUS, Horsfield.

Char.—Bill slender, compressed, of moderate length, gently hooked at the tip and notched; nostrils apert; rictal bristles few, strong; wing somewhat lengthened, third quill longest, 4th and 5th nearly equal to it; tail long, graduated; tarsus long, with large scutæ; middle toe very long; lateral toes unequal; hind toe long; all the claws long, slender, acute, moderately curved; hind claw large. Sexes differ in size.

This genus, of which there is one species in India and the Malayan isles, comprises several others from Australia and the oceanic province.

440. **Megalurus palustris,** HORSF.

Lin. Trans., XIII., 159—BLYTH, Cat 781—HORSF., Cat. 512—Malurus marginalis, REINWARDT, pl. col. 65, f. 2—*Takko*, Beng.—*Jal-aggin*, H. *i. e.* Water-lark.

THE STRIATED MARSH-BABBLER.

Descr.—Upper parts bright olive-brown, with a mesial broad black stripe to each feather of the back and the scapulars; the edges of the wing-feathers also brown; tail pale dusky-brown, with light edges to the feathers; crown rufescent, with mesial dark lines, obsolete towards the front, and the feathers small, rigid, and oppressed; a pale whitish streak over the eye; beneath, the chin and throat are white, the rest whitish, tinged with earthy brown; the breast and flanks slightly speckled with brown.

Bill horny brown above, paler beneath; legs dull purplish or greenish-brown; irides pale brown. Length of male $9\frac{1}{2}$ to 10 inches; ext. 12; wing $3\frac{3}{4}$; tail 5; bill at front $\frac{5}{8}$; tarsus $1\frac{3}{8}$. The female is only $8\frac{1}{4}$ inches long.

This bird has an extensive geographical distribution, being found in Bengal and Central India, extending to Assam, Burmah, the Malayan peninsula, and Java. I have seen it on the banks of the Wein-Ganga and Indrawatty, tributaries of the Godavery; also on the Nerbudda, where it frequents the grass and reeds on the banks, or on the islets. But it is most abundant in Lower Bengal, where the country is intersected by rivers, and where long grass and reeds cover miles of country. It does not appear to associate in flocks, but hunts about the reeds and grass for various insects, chiefly grasshoppers and coleoptera, and, as Mr. Blyth remarks, it has a remarkable freedom of the action of its legs enabling it to sprawl widely as it clambers among the reeds and grass stems.

Every now and then one rises to the air with a fine song, which Blyth calls a fine flute-like voice, and after fluttering slowly along for a few seconds, warbling all the time, descends again. The song is not confined to the breeding season, for I have heard it at all times. Its nest and eggs have not been observed yet, abundant though it be in many districts. In the breeding season the bill becomes livid blackish, and the whole inside of the mouth wholly black.

Gen. CILÆTORNIS, Gray.

Char.—Bill very short, strong, high, compressed, curved on the culmen, strongly hooked at the tip, and notched; five remarkably strong bristles between the gape and the eyes, forming an almost vertical range curved stiffly outwards; wings somewhat long, 3rd quill longest, 4th and 5th nearly equal to it; 2nd equal to the 7th; feet and legs strong; tarsus moderately long, the middle toe elongate, laterals unequal, inner toe very versatile, hind toe long, all the claws slightly curved.

This genus chiefly differs from *Megalurus* by the very remarkable bill, which, from its compression, is quite Timaline in character.

441. Chætornis striatus, JERDON.

Megalurus, apud JERDON, Suppl. Cat. 88 bis—BLYTH, Cat. 782
—HORSF., Cat. 513—Dasyornis locustelloides, BLYTH—*Genta-pitta,* Tel, *i. e.,* Grass-bird.

THE GRASS-BABBLER.

Descr.—Above olive or yellowish brown, the feathers all centred
with deep brown; tail brownish, banded with dusky externally,
and dusky along the centre of each feather, which is tipped
fulvous white, and the outer feathers have further a dark brown
subterminal band; beneath, the color is white, tinged with earthy-
brown on the breast, and with a few dark specks.

Bill dusky-brown above, fleshy-brown beneath; legs brownish
fleshy; irides yellow-brown or dull grey in some. Length of male
$8\frac{1}{4}$ inches; extent 11; wing $3\frac{1}{2}$; tail $3\frac{3}{4}$; bill at front not quite $\frac{1}{2}$;
tarsus $1\frac{1}{10}$; extent of the foot $1\frac{3}{4}$. The female is 7 inches long
and the wing 3.

I first obtained this bird on the Neilgherries in swampy ground,
but afterwards found it not rare at Nellore, during the cold season,
in long grass and rice fields; and I again found it in Central India,
during the rains, in grass meadows. It is also abundant all over
Lower Bengal in high grass, though not frequenting such dense
thickets of reeds as *Megalurus,* or *Chatarrhœa Earlei..* It most
probably will be found in all suitable localities through the greater
part of India.

It has similar habits to *Megalurus,* soaring into the air like a
lark, with a fine clear song. I have not procured the nest, but
Mr. Blyth mentions that it nearly accords with that of *Malacocircus,* and that the eggs are blue. It feeds chiefly, if not entirely,
on insects. The great difference of size between the sexes at one
time led Mr. Blyth to believe them to be distinct species.

Mr. Frith suggests that the very remarkable outer orbital
bristles of this bird are admirably adapted to protect its eyes
when it is forcing its way through dense tufts of grass and
reeds.

Near these two birds probably should be placed the African
genera *Sphenœacus* and *Sphenura*; and the Australian *Cincloramphus,*

two of the species of which latter have been considered to belong to *Megalurus*.

From these Reed and Grass-babblers there is an evident transition to the Reed-warblers, such as *Locustella*, *Acrocephalus*, and *Arundinax*, in all of which, however, the characters of this family are lost, or nearly so. But it will, perhaps, be advisable to class here two small Grass or Reed birds, which, by their strongly compressed bill, apparently belong to this group, leading to the Warblers. They belong to two distinct forms, and both are rare, and but little known. Mr. Blyth also places them in this family, between *Chætornis* and *Dumetia*.

Gen. Schænicola, Blyth.

Char.—Bill moderate, rather deep, much compressed, slightly curved on the culmen; a few strong rictal bristles, but less developed than in *Chætornis*; wings moderate, slightly rounded, 4th quill longest, 3rd equal to 5th; tail moderate, very broad, soft; tarsus long; toes grasping; plumage somewhat lax.

442. Schænicola platyura, Jerdon.

Timalia, apud Jerdon, Suppl. Cat. 96 bis.

The Broad-tailed Reed-bird.

Descr.—Above dark olive-brown; the feathers of the tail obsoletely barred; beneath ochrey yellowish.

Bill horny yellow; legs fleshy yellow; irides yellowish brown. Length $5\frac{1}{4}$ inches; wing $2\frac{1}{2}$; tail $2\frac{1}{2}$; bill at front $\frac{4}{10}$, tarsus $\frac{9}{10}$.

I only once observed this curious bird among some reeds in swampy ground close to Goodaloor in the Wynaad, at the foot of the Neilgherries. It took short flights, and endeavoured to conceal itself among the thick herbage. Its food had consisted wholly of small insects. I only procured one specimen, which is now lost, but Mr. Blyth had previously seen it, and recognising its peculiarities, had given it the above generic appellation.

Gen. Eurycercus, Blyth.

Syn. *Laticilla* olim, Blyth—*Sphenæacus*, Strickland.

Char.—Bill of moderate length, compressed, slender, nearly straight; culmen gently curved, barely hooked at the tip; a few distant short rictal setæ; wings short, rounded; 4th and 5th quills longest; tail long, graduated, the feathers very broad and soft; tarsus long; middle toe elongated, lateral toes unequal, hind toe rather short.

This curious bird has so much the aspect of a *Drymoica* that it would by some be placed in that genus, but its more compressed bill, broad tail, and, to a certain extent, its coloration, all evince a tendency to this present family. It differs from the last type by its lengthened tail and streaked plumage.

Blyth notices its affinity for *Chætornis*, of which says he "it has the general form, but a weaker and more compressed bill, feebler vibrissæ, shorter feet, and the tail much broader."

443. Eurycercus Burnesii, Blyth.

J. A. S., XIII., 374—Blyth, Cat. 786—*Hidela*, Sindh.

The Long-tailed Reed-bird.

Descr.—Above brownish grey, with dark central streaks, mostly on the scapulars and back; tail faintly barred; under parts whitish, tinged with fulvescent on the flanks, and a shade of the same on the sides of the neck, where also a few mesial streaks are distinct; under tail-coverts ferruginous.

Bill horny above, yellowish beneath; legs yellow-brown; irides brownish yellow. Length $6\frac{1}{4}$ inches; wing $2\frac{1}{8}$; tail $3\frac{3}{4}$; bill at front $\frac{3}{8}$; tarsus $\frac{8}{10}$.

This bird was originally sent from Sindh by Sir A. Burnes, and a drawing of it is also among his collection in the Asiatic Society's Library. Quite recently I found it at Monghyr on the Ganges in March, frequenting grass mixed with Jhow bushes. When flushed, it flew close to the ground, and endeavoured to escape observation, hiding itself in the grass, and with more of the aspect of a *Chatarrhæa* than of a *Drymoica*. It will probably be found in suitable spots all along the Gangetic valley. In its rufous under tail-coverts, and slightly spotted breast, it recalls the coloring of the African genus *Parisoma*.*

The *Miminæ* or Mocking Thrushes of America are the only group, not Asiatic, included by Bonaparte in this family, *Toxostoma,*

* *Salicaria leucoptera*, Rüppell, appears to me to belong to this division of the *Timalinæ*.

by its long and curved beak representing *Pomatorhinus*. *Turdus rulpinus*, Hartlaub, one of the *Miminæ*, figured in P. Z. S. 1850, could not, by the Indian ornithologist, be mistaken for ought but a Timaline form.

Fam. BRACHYPODIDÆ—Short-legged Thrushes.

Legs and feet very short, only suited for perching; wings moderate or rather long; bill various, long and Thrush-like in some, short and somewhat depressed in others.

In this family I include both the Bulbuls and Orioles, which agree in their short legs and feet, food, and arboreal habits.

As in the last sub-family we found that the strong legs and feet afforded the most certain guide to their classification, to the exclusion of the bill, so, in these, the short feet are the most characteristic feature. It has not been usual to class the Bulbuls and Orioles together, but they are, in most systems, placed near each other; the green Bulbuls are by some arranged with the Orioles, and by others with the Bulbuls; and I see no essential difference between them, more than warranting a sectional separation. I was at one time inclined to place them in the family *Merulidæ*, as Gray and Horsfield do, but, on full consideration, have now considered them distinct.

The Short-legged Thrushes are peculiar to the old world, being most abundant in India and Malayana, not rare in Africa, one or two species extending to the south of Europe, and one or two to Australia. The bill varies from somewhat long and slender, as in *Hypsipetes*, to thick and Finch-like in *Spizixos*. It is generally more or less wide and depressed at the base, and usually slightly notched at the tip. The wings are moderate, rather long in a few, and somewhat pointed. The tail is usually short or moderate, even or slightly rounded. The tongue of several is slightly pencilled or brushed, and, in consequence, some of them have been classified as a division of the *Melliphagidæ*, or Honey-eaters of Australia; but the structure and habits of these last, with their geographic distribution, forbid the association, though there is a good deal of mutual resemblance between some of the species of each group, and they perhaps pass into each other. Mr. Blyth re-

marks that the affinity of the family for that of the *Melliphagidæ*
is, I think, undeniable. With regard to other external relations,
they appear to have affinities with the *Ampelidæ*, and particularly
perhaps for some of the *Leiotrichinæ*, as will be pointed out
hereafter.

They live both on fruit and insects, more particularly on the
former food. Only a few species ever descend to the ground.
Most of them construct neat nests, and the eggs are either pale
reddish, or pinkish white, more or less spotted with red.

The *Brachypodidæ* may be sub-divided into—

1st.—Pycnonotinæ, true Bulbuls.

2nd.—Phyllornithinæ, Green Bulbuls.

3rd.—Ireninæ, Blue-birds.

4th.—Oriolinæ, Orioles.

Sub-fam. PYCNONOTINÆ.

The true Bulbuls are distinguished from the members of the
other sub-families by the bill being generally shorter, straighter,
and more depressed at the base, with the rictal bristles more
developed. The tongue is more simple, though bifid in some,
and slightly pencilled in a few. Their plumage is usually full,
sometimes puffy, and, in very many instances, there are various
hairs or bristles (undeveloped feathers) conspicuous, especially
on the head and nape; so much so, that some have received
generic names (*Trichophorus, Criniger*,) from that character.
The sexes are in most cases exactly alike in colour. They
are birds of rather small size, and, as a general rule, of plain,
though, in many instances, pleasing plumage, green, brown, and
yellow being the predominant tints. They are mostly denizens
of the forests and jungles, a very few only frequenting gardens
or groves. They feed both on fruit and insects. Their wings
enable them to fly with ease, and some have a tolerably swift
flight. They make a rather neat nest, and the eggs of most
are pale reddish or pink, with numerous darker red specks. They
are tolerably numerous in India, Burmah, and Malayana; and
many species are found in Africa; one occurs in Spain. They are
active and sprightly in their movements, and usually have a

chirruping call or warble, which seldom could be called a song;
and the name of Bulbul, by which the most common species are
known in India, being the Persian name for the Nightingale, has
led to many misconceptions about their powers of voice and song.
The few known to the older authors were classed in *Lanius*,
Muscicapa, and *Turdus*.

Gen. HYPSIPETES, Vigors.

Char.—Bill moderately strong, lengthened, nearly straight; culmen very slightly arched; nostrils long, with some short tufts and
a few hairs at their base; wings long, 4th and 5th longest, 3rd
nearly as long; tail rather long, square or emarginate; feet and
legs very short. The head is sub-crested, the feathers being
lanceolate, and the rictal bristles are very few and weak.

This is one of the best marked forms in this division, and
comprises two types, the one with red bills, more or less black
plumage, and the tail distinctly emarginate; the other, with more
normal family colouring, the bill dark, and the tail square.

With red bill.

444. Hypsipetes psaroides, Vigors.

P. Z. S., 1831—GOULD, Cent. II. Birds, pl. 10—BLYTH, Cat.
1246—HORSF., Cat. 388—*Ban bakra*, at Mussooree, *i. e.*, Jungle
Goat—*Phakki-pho*, Lepch.

THE HIMALAYAN BLACK BULBUL.

Descr.—Head subcrested, black; body and wings dark ashy or
iron grey; tips of the quills and the tail black; beneath dull grey,
as above, the lower part of the abdomen and vent paler; under
tail-coverts edged white.

Bill bright red; irides red-brown; legs red. Length 11 inches;
wing 5; tail 4¼; bill at front ⅞; tarsus ⅝.

This bird is found throughout the whole extent of the Himalayas, from Simla to Bootan. It is not common about Darjeeling,
and I have found it usually at from 3,000 to 5,000 feet of elevation.
Like the others, it is gregarious generally, and its flight strong
and rapid. Dr. Adams says that it is very noisy, and imitates
the songs of other birds. Hutton says " that it is exceedingly

common at Mussooree, in large flocks, during winter and spring; in the latter season, when the *Rhododendron arboreum* is covered with its branches of deep crimson flowers, these birds may be seen thrusting their beaks into every flower in search of insects and nectar, and the forehead is, in consequence, then generally covered with the pollen derived from the flowers. It is fond of wild mulberries and cherries. They make a rather neat cup-shaped nest of leaves, grass stalks, and spider-web, lined with grasses, lichens and wood-shavings, and placed on a tall tree. The eggs are usually three, rosy or purplish white, sprinkled over rather numerously with deep claret or rufescent-purple specks and spots, but very variable in colour and distribution." I obtained the nest and eggs once only, agreeing very well with Hutton's description.

445. Hypsipetes Neilgherriensis, JERDON.

JERDON, Cat. 68—BLYTH, Cat. 1247.

THE NEILGHERRY BLACK BULBUL.

Descr.—Head, with crest of lanceolate feathers, glossy black; wings and tail black, rest of the body dark blackish grey; under tail-coverts more or less edged with white.

Bill deep red; legs orange-red; irides brownish red. Length 10 inches; extent 14; wing 5; tail $4\frac{2}{10}$; bill at front nearly $\frac{9}{10}$; tarsus $\frac{7}{10}$.

This species differs from the last in its somewhat smaller size, and the prevalent darkness of the body plumage. It abounds on the summit of the Neilgherries from 6,000 to 8,000 feet. I have seen it also in Coorg. It lives in small flocks, in the dense woods, feeding on various fruits and berries, usually on the tops of trees. It keeps up a lively and agreeable warbling, which it often continues during its occasional flight from one tree, or patch of wood, to another. Its flight is undulating, easy, and rapid. It has also been found in Ceylon.

446. Hypsipetes Ganeesa, SYKES.

SYKES, Cat. 49—HORSF.; Cat. 389.

The Ghat Black Bulbul.

Descr.—Above grey-brown, paler beneath ; wings and tail brown ; head slightly crested, metallic black ; irides deep brown. Length 10 inches ; tail 4.

Such is Col. Sykes' description ; but the figure in Jardine and Selby's Illustration represents the upper plumage as more blackish ashy.

This species has only as yet been procured by Col. Sykes, who says that it inhabits the Western ghats. It is most probably found on the Mahableshwar Hills. Col. Sykes remarks, "stony fruit found in its stomach ; flight rapid." Dr. Horsfield in his Catalogue gives Assam also as a locality. This would be a very remarkable distribution, and more probably he has not thoroughly compared them, and the Assam bird will prove to be Blyth's *H. concolor*, from Assam, the Khasia Hills, &c., which he states to be very closely allied to the two last species. The wing and tail of *Ganeesa*, described as being brown, had probably faded, as indeed the whole colours of the birds of this section appear to do, more or less.

Turdas ourovang, from Madagascar, figured P. E. 557, f. 2, appears to belong to this genus and section ; and *H. olivacea*, Jard. and Selby, Ill. Orn. 1, pl. 148, from Mauritius, is another species.

The next group are coloured more or less green, with dusky bills.

447. Hypsipetes McLellandi, Horsfield.

P. Z. S., 1839—Blyth, Cat. 1249—Horsf., Cat. 390—H. viridis, Hodgs.—*Chinchiok-pho*, Lepch.—*Chichiam*, Bhot.

The Rufous-bellied Bulbul.

Descr.—Head brown, sub-crested, the feathers with pale centres; the rest of the upper plumage olive-green ; ear coverts brownish ; chin and throat white, the feathers edged dusky ; sides of neck, breast, and belly, light reddish brown, with pale centres to the feathers, albescent on the lower part of the abdomen ; under tail-coverts yellowish.

Bill dusky olive, horny fleshy beneath ; legs yellowish brown. Irides light brown. Length 9 inches ; extent 13 ; wing $4\frac{1}{8}$; tail 4 ; bill at front $\frac{7}{8}$; tarsus $\frac{3}{4}$.

This species of *Hypsipetes* is found from Nepal to Bootan ; also in the hill ranges of Assam and Arrakan. In Sikhim it occurs from 2,000 feet or so; frequents high trees, lives chiefly on fruit, and has a loud cheerful note.

Other species of *Hypsipetes*, more or less allied to the above, are *H. virescens*, from the Nicobars ; *H. Malaccensis*, from Malacca; *H. Philippensis*, from the Philippines ; and *H. Tickelli*, Bl., from Tenasserim.

Near *Hypsipetes*, perhaps between it and *Hemixos*, should be placed Blyth's genus *Iole*, with one species from the Khasia Hills and Arrakan, *I. virescens*, and two others from Malacca; and the *Turdus amaurotis*, Temm., from Japan, should either be placed here, or in *Hypsipetes*.

Gen. HEMIXOS, Hodgson.

Bill moderately slender, inclining to arch on the culmen, nareal and rictal bristles distinct and strong; wings with the 5th and 6th quills longest; tail moderately long, even, almost emarginate ; tarsus strong, smooth ; toes short, unequal, depressed; nails acute, much curved ; tongue bifid; feathers of the head lanceolate, lengthened.

448. **Hemixos flavala,** HODGSON.

J. A. S., XIV., 572—BLYTH, Cat. 1254—HORSF., Cat. 378— *Nalli-pindi,* Lepch.

THE BROWN-EARED BULBUL.

Descr.—Crown dusky greyish, the coronal feathers lengthened and pointed; rest of the plumage above ashy; wings and tail dusky; the feathers of the greater coverts and the outer webs of the secondaries margined with bright greenish yellow; lores, and a streak from the lower mandible, black ; ear coverts silky brown ; throat and lower tail-coverts white; breast pale ashy ; belly greyish white.

Bill black ; legs dark plumbeous ; irides dark brown. Length $8\frac{1}{2}$ inches, extent 12 ; wing $3\frac{9}{10}$; tail $3\frac{1}{2}$; bill at front $\frac{5}{8}$; tarsus $1\frac{5}{16}$.

The Brown-eared Bulbul is found in the Eastern Himalayas, from Nepal to Bootan, also in the Khasia hills. It is not very rare near

Darjeeling, at elevations from 3,000 to 6,000 feet. It associates in small parties, feeds both on berries and insects, and has a loud warbling note.

The pointed feathers of its crest, and its long square tail, show its affinity to *Hypsipetes*.

Gen. ALCURUS, Hodgson.

Char.—Bill slightly stronger than in the preceding genera, and somewhat wider at the base; rictal bristles weak; tail almost even; the outermost feathers barely shorter; head sub-crested.

This form appears to be immediate between *Hemixos* and its allies, and *Criniger*, from which last it is distinguished by the much feebler bill. In its habits too it is more allied to *Hypsipetes*. The peculiar striation of the plumage is faintly shadowed forth in *H. McLellandi*, but is more marked in *Pycnonotus Finlaysonii*, Blyth, a very beautiful species from Arracan, which appears to belong to this type; as does, perhaps, *Ixos tigus*, Müll., from Sumatra.

449. Alcurus striatus, BLYTH.

Tricophorus, apud BLYTH, J. A. S., XI., 184—BLYTH, Cat. 1256—HORSF., Cat. 384—Alcurus Nipalensis, HODGSON—*Senimplek-pho*, Lepch.—*Chichiam*, Bhot.

THE STRIATED GREEN-BULBUL.

Descr.—Above olive-green, brightest on the rump and wings; feathers of the occiput lengthened and somewhat pointed; crown of the head and back darker green, with a slight tinge of cinereous on the back, and the feathers of both the head and back narrowly streaked with white; tail dusky, with the outer web greenish, obsoletely barred above, and tinged with yellow beneath; the two outer rectrices, and the third partially, tipped with yellowish white; part of throat, chin, and under tail-coverts pale canary yellow; a yellow streak from the nostril to near the eye; throat, foreneck, and belly, pale yellowish, albescent on the breast, the feathers all edged with dusky greenish, most broadly so on the breast, giving a generally striated aspect to the under parts; ear-coverts black.

Bill horny black; legs greenish brown; irides brown-red. Length 8¾ inches; wing 4⅞; tail 4; bill at front ⅝; tarsus not ¾.

This bird is exceedingly abundant about Darjeeling, and is most common from 7,000 feet and upwards. It in general keeps to the tops of high trees, going in small parties, and having a loud mellow warble, which it is continually repeating, both when feeding and on the wing. It feeds chiefly on fruit, sometimes on insects. This bird, like *Hemixos flavala*, has also affinities for *Hypsipetes*, shewn, as well in the structure, as in its habits of flying high, and the frequent repetition of its call.

Gen. CRINIGER, Temm.

Syn. *Tricophorus*, Temm.—*Alcurus*, pars, Hodgson.

Char.—Bill of moderate length, strong and deep; the culmen well curved; rictal bristles distinct, long; tail nearly even, with the outermost feathers distinctly shorter. Head more or less crested.

The first species noticed has the bill somewhat less strong than the second and more typical one, and has been placed under *Hemixos*, but its colours and general characters are more those of the present genus.

450. Criniger ictericus, STRICLAND.

Ann. Nat. Hist., XIII.—BLYTH, Cat. 1255—HORSF., Cat. 379— Tricophorus Indicus, JERDON, Cat. 75.

THE YELLOW-BROWED BULBUL.

Descr.—Plumage above bright olive-green; superciliary streak extending to the forehead, and the whole plumage beneath, bright yellow; quills dusky on their inner webs; the shafts of the tail feathers beneath yellow.

Bill black; legs dark plumbeous; irides blood-red. Length 8 inches; wing $3\frac{7}{10}$; tail $3\frac{1}{2}$; bill at front $\frac{6}{10}$; tarsus $\frac{8}{10}$.

This species has only been found in the Malabar forests and Ceylon. It prefers mountainous regions, at from 3,000 to 5,000 feet of elevation, being very abundant on the slopes of the Neilgherries at that elevation; but it is also found occasionally down to a few hundred feet above the sea level. It lives in small flocks, flying from tree to tree, and keeping up a continual and pleasing mellow bulbul-like warble. I have chiefly found it to have partaken of fruit; but I dare say at times, insects are captured. I first described this bird, considering that it might be the *Turdus indicus* of the older authors. I am not aware what species is now supposed to have been described under that name, or whether it has been identified at all. This bird has the crest only moderately developed, and the tail more even than the next bird.

The next species has the bill proportionally stronger, the crest more developed, and the tail with the outer feathers distinctly shorter.

451. Criniger flaveolus, GOULD.

Tricophorus, apud GOULD, P. Z. S., 1836—BLYTH, Cat. 1257.—HORSF., Cat. 382—Tr. xanthogaster, HODGS.—*Kussop eechiop-pho*, Lepch.

THE WHITE-THROATED BULBUL.

Descr.—Head crested, the feathers progressively lengthened, and mixed with hairs; plumage above dull yellow olive, with a tinge of reddish brown on the wings and tail; cheeks and throat ashy white; the rest beneath bright yellow.

Bill light plumbeous; legs pale fleshy yellow; irides brown-red. Length $8\frac{1}{2}$ inches; extent 13; wing $4\frac{1}{8}$; tail $3\frac{3}{4}$; bill at front $\frac{2}{8}$; tarsus $\frac{3}{4}$.

This bird in its plumage much resembles the last. It is an inhabitant of the Himalayas from Nepal to Bootan, extending to the hill ranges of Assam, Sylhet, and Arrakan. It is chiefly found at from 2,000 to 5,000 feet. I got several specimens from the vicinity of Darjeeling, but did not myself observe it. The name which the Lepchas give it is taken from its call.

Near here should be placed several species of Bulbul, *viz.* *C. ochrocephalus*, Gmel., (*crispiceps*, Blyth,) the giant of the family; *Pyc. inornatus* and *P. simplex*, Kuhl, from Sumatra; *Pycn. rufocaudatus*, Eyton, (*Tricophorus gularis*, Horsf.) from Java and Malacca; with *Tric. gutturalis*, and *sulphurata*, Müll., · from Borneo; and *flavicaudus*, Bon., from Amboyna; also *Setornis criniger*, Blyth, from Malacca; all which tend to grade into *Iole*, previously mentioned.

Not far from these birds should be placed *Spizixos*, Blyth, with a short thick conical bill. The best known species, *S. canifrons*,

Blyth, from the Khasia hills, lives in small flocks, has a pleasant call, keeps to the top of trees, and lives entirely on fruit. Another has lately been sent from China.

The next division only includes two birds belonging to our province, but several Burmese and Malayan species. The colors are not so vivid as in the last, the form is larger and more plump, and it is somewhat related to *Hemixos*. As I imagine that *Musc. psidii*, of the older authors, belongs to this group, I shall put it as *Ixos*, under which genus that bird is classed by Gray.

Gen. Ixos, Temm. (restricted).

Char.—Bill rather short, slightly arching on the culmen; the tip bent over, distinctly notched; commissure nearly straight; a few rictal bristles, mixed with some smaller tufts; hairs on the nape distinct, and some of the feathers of the throat bristle-ended; lateral toes nearly equal; hind toe shorter than middle toe; 4th, 5th, and 6th quills sub-equal and longest, 7th barely shorter; tail slightly rounded in some, almost even in others, with the outer feathers slightly shorter.

452. **Ixos luteolus**, LESS.

Hœmatornis, apud LESSON, Rev. Zool., 1840—HORSF., Cat. 362 —Pycnonotus flavirictus, STRICKLAND—BLYTH, Cat. 1270—Ixos virescens, apud TICKELL, and JERDON, Cat. 74—Criniger Tickelli, BLYTH—*Poda-pigli*, Tel.

THE WHITE-BROWED BUSH BULBUL.

Descr.—Above dull brownish olive-green, palest on the head, where it is slightly ashy, and yellowish on the rump; quills and coverts edged with brighter green; over the eye to the ear-coverts, and from the base of the upper mandible extending below the eye, obscure white; chin, and base of lower mandible, pale clear yellow; lower parts whitish ashy, tinged with pale yellow; the breast dashed with brownish grey, and the vent and under tail-coverts pale yellow.

Bill blackish; legs dark plumbeous; irides blood-red. Length $7\frac{1}{2}$ inches; wing $3\frac{1}{2}$; tail $3\frac{1}{2}$; bill at front $\frac{6}{10}$; tarsus $\frac{8}{10}$.

This is a tolerably common bird in many parts of the South of India; rare in others. It is not found in the forests of Malabar, but in low jungle in that province it is common, and on the skirts of forests occasionally. In the Carnatic it is tolerably common in bushy jungle, and even in gardens, in wooded districts; also throughout the Northern Circars to Goomsoor; and Tickell found it in Central India. It is not however known at Jubbulpore, Saugor, Nagpore, nor Mhow, nor in the bare table land of the Deccan.

It associates less in flocks than most of this family, being usually seen alone, but it avoids observation, and keeps to the thickets. It flies about from bush to bush with a fine loud, clear, thrush-like warble, and feeds entirely on fruit of various kinds. I found the nest in my garden at Nellore. It was rather loosely made with roots, grass, and hair, placed in a hedge; and the eggs, four in number, were reddish-white, with darker lake-red spots, exceedingly like those of the common Bulbul.

I see that the *Ixos virescens* of Temminck, which in my Catalogue I considered the same as this bird, now ranks as an *Hypsipetes*.

453. Ixos xantholæmus, Jerdon.

Brachypus xantholæmus, Jerdon, 2nd Suppl., Cat. 69 bis—Ill. Ind. Orn., pl. 35—Blyth, Cat. 1269—Horsf., Cat. 369—*Konda-poda-pigli*, Tel.

The Yellow-throated Bush Bulbul.

Descr.—Head and face yellowish green; upper plumage grey, tinged with green, especially on the upper tail-coverts; wings dusky, edged with yellow green; tail dusky, the feathers edged with yellow green, and, except the central ones, all the feathers tipped with yellowish white, most broadly on the outermost ones; chin, throat, and forehead pure canary yellow; breast grey, paling to whitish on the abdomen; under tail-coverts pure yellow.

Bill and legs black, irides red. Length nearly 8 inches; wing $3\frac{6}{10}$; tail $3\frac{4}{10}$; bill at front $\frac{6}{10}$; tarsus $\frac{8}{10}$.

This bird is one of exceedingly limited geographical distribution. I have only met with it from the Eastern Ghâts, west of Nellore, whence it was brought me by some Shikarees. It probably may extend along this range South to Royacottah, and Northwards [along the hills towards Goomsoor, but, as yet, I believe, specimens have not been obtained from any other locality. Bonaparte in his Conspectus states that it very closely resembles *I. leucogrammicus*, Müller, from Sumatra, but is larger, and has the throat yellow, which the other has not.

Other species apparently belonging to the present group are *I flavescens*, Blyth, from the Khasia hills and Arrakan, very close to *flaveolus*; *I. tristis*, Blyth, from Arracan; *I. Blanfordi*, Jerdon, (*familiaris*, Blyth) very abundant at Thayetmyo; *I plumosus*, Brand; *I. brunneus*, Bl., from Malacca; *I tigus*, Müll., from Sumatra, and other species from the Islands of Malayana.

Gen. KELAARTIA, Blyth.

Char.—Bill short, wide, tolerably curved, strongly notched; rictal bristles feeble; tarsus somewhat long.

This form is distinguished by having a longer tarsus than any member of the family. It at present consists of but a single species; but *Pyc. Sinensis* is very closely allied to, if indeed it does not belong to it, chiefly differing in its shorter tarsus.

454. **Kelaartia penicillata**, BLYTH.

JERDON, Suppl. Cat. 70 bis.

THE YELLOW-EARED BULBUL.

Descr.—Head above brown; the feathers scale-like; a white spot at the base of the upper mandible, not extending over the eyes; lores, under the eye, and the ear-coverts dusky blackish, paling posteriorly; behind the eye a tuft of lengthened, lanceolate, bright yellow feathers; upper plumage olive-green, with the inner webs of the quills and tail feathers dusky brown; beneath, the chin white, the rest of the lower parts olivaceous yellow, clearer on the abdomen and under tail-coverts, and olivaceous on the sides of the breast and flanks.

Length 7 inches; wing $3\frac{1}{4}$; tail 3; bill at front $\frac{9}{16}$; tarsus $\frac{7}{8}$.

I believe that this Ceylon bird is identical with one procured by me from the Mysore country, below the Neilgherries, which was accidentally destroyed before I had taken a description; but

I had a coloured sketch drawn, from which I briefly described it in my Supplement Cat. Birds.

The succeeding group of Bulbuls differ somewhat from the preceding ones in their generally smaller size, more slender bills, somewhat more rounded tails, and also in a more marked form of coloration. They are mostly Malayan forms, Southern India possessing two, representing different types; and Northern India, including Assam and Burmah, three.

The first genus comprises two species from India, one from Northern India, the other from the South. Blyth named one of these *Rubigula*; Cabanis subsequently *Sphagias*; and Hodgson classed the northern one under his genus *Alcurus*; but it does not correspond with the type of that genus, and both forms I think may safely be classed together.

Genus. RUBIGULA, Blyth.

Syn. *Sphagias*, Cab.

Char.—Bill rather short, moderately stout; rictal bristles small or moderate; tail slightly rounded, or almost even; head black, more or less crested; the feather of the back loose and decomposed; irides yellow.

455. Rubigula gularis, GOULD.

Brachypus, apud GOULD, P. Z. S., 1835—BLYTH, Cat. 1277—HORSF., Cat. 368—Brachypus rubineus, JERDON, Cat. 69, and Ill. Ind. Orn. pl. 37.

THE RUBY-THROATED BULBUL.

Descr.—Head and cheeks pure glossy black; plumage above yellowish olive-green; a small chin spot black; throat beautiful shining ruby-red, the feathers much divided and somewhat bristly; the rest of the plumage beneath bright yellow; quills with a tinge of dusky on the inner webs.

Bill black; legs greenish dusky; irides light yellow. Length $6\frac{1}{2}$ inches; wing 3; tail $2\frac{3}{4}$; tarsus rather more than $\frac{1}{2}$ inch; bill at front $\frac{3}{8}$.

This pretty species is found only in the forests of Malabar, extending from Travancore to North Canara. It is found from the level of the sea nearly to about 2,000 feet of elevation. It is not common, frequents the more open spots and glades in thick jungle, and is usually found in the neighbourhood of water. It lives in small families, is sprightly and active, hopping about the smaller branches of trees, and uttering now and then its pleasant twitter, much in the manner of the crested Bulbuls. Its food consists chiefly of fruits and berries.

A very closely allied species is the *Ixos dispar* of Horsfield, Temm., Pl. col. 137 ; and another has lately been procured in Ceylon, *R. aberrans*, Blyth.

The next species has the head conspicuously crested, and the bill is shorter than in the foregoing; but it has a general similarity of character and plumage, and the irides of both (which is unusual in this family) are pale yellow.

456. Rubigula flaviventris, Tickell.

Vanga, apud Tickell, J. A. S., 2—Blyth, Cat. 1275—Horsf., Cat. 371—Brachypus melanocephalus, Gray, Hardw., Ill. Ind. Zool. 2, pl. 35, f. 1.—Br. plumifera, Gould—*Zurd bulbul, H.*— *Pahariya kangdhara*, at Goruckpore—*Mancliph-kur*, Lepch.

The Black-crested Yellow-bulbul.

Descr.—Above olive-green, beneath yellow, with a greenish tinge, strongest on the breast; head (with a long slender erectile crest), cheeks, and throat, glossy black; primaries within dusky black; the tail brown, the feathers edged with green on the outer webs.

Bill black; legs dark horn; irides pale yellow. Length nearly 8 inches; wing $3\frac{3}{4}$; tail $3\frac{1}{2}$; bill at front $\frac{1}{2}$; tarsus $\frac{9}{16}$.

This Bulbul is found in the Himalayas from Nepal to Bootan, extending into Assam, Arrakan, and Burmah; also in the forests of Central India, where it was procured by Tickell. I found it in Sikhim in the warm valleys from 1,200 feet to 3,000, most abundant in the lower elevations, as on the banks of the Rungeet. It associates in small flocks, is lively and active, and has the usual twittering notes of this family. It feeds chiefly on fruits.

An allied species is *I. bimaculatus*, Lesson, from Java, with the cheeks orange-red.

It is in this group that we find an approach to the color of the common Bulbuls of India, *Hæmatornis* and *Pycnonotus*, as in no other genus is there any red tint.

Gen. BRACHYPODIUS, Blyth.

Char.—Bill somewhat as in *Rubigula*, short, rather deep at the base, but the rictal bristles more feeble; tail more or less rounded.

This form is chiefly developed in Malayana, only one species from Southern India, and one from Tipperah, occurring elsewhere.

457. Brachypodius poiocephalus, JERDON.

Brachypus, apud JERDON, Cat. 70—Ill. Ind. Orn., pl. 31—BLYTH, Cat. 1282.

THE GRAY-HEADED BULBUL.

Descr.—Crown of head, occiput and throat, bluish gray; forehead siskin green; back, wings, and plumage beneath, oil-green, lighter towards the vent; feathers of the rump light yellowish green, broadly streaked with black; tail with the centre feathers greenish, broadly edged with gray, lateral feathers black, also gray-edged; under tail-coverts light gray.

Bill greenish horn; legs reddish yellow; irides bluish white. Length about 7 inches; extent 9; wing 3; tail $2\frac{8}{10}$; tarsus $\frac{1}{2}$ inch; bill at front $\frac{7}{10}$.

The Gray-headed Bulbul is confined to the forests of the Malabar Coast, extending from Travancore to Honore. It is found from near the sea level to about 2,000 feet or so of elevation, living in small families, and feeding chiefly on stony fruit. The plumage of the back and rump is very copious and puffy, recalling the structure of *Iora*, and, like that bird, the present has whitish irides, which are rare in this, or indeed in any group.

A species with very similar markings, *Brachypus eutilotus*, from Malacca, is figured by Jardine and Selby; and of this Gray makes his sub-genus, *Euptilotus*, to which perhaps the present species would appertain.

M

Other species of *Brachypodius* are found in the Malay countries and Burmah, *viz.*, *B. melanocephalus*, Gmelin, from Burmah, and another allied species from Malacca, probably *Ixos metallicus* of Eyton (which two have much the coloration of the Orioles); *Ixos squamatus* Temm., and *I. chalcocephalus*, Temm., from Java and Malacca; *B. cinereoventris*, Blyth, from the Tipperah hills; *Ixidia cyaniventer*, Blyth, from Malacca, and *I. poliopsis*, of Bonaparte's Conspectus. Near here branches off *Microtarsus*, with black plumage, a long and slender bill, and well rounded tail, comprising two species from Malacca.

We have next two forms, the most common of all the Bulbuls, and also with extensive distribution, one or more being found in every part of India Proper, Assam, and Burmah. Both forms have the under tail-coverts bright red in most, yellow in a few, and one group has in addition a crimson cheek stripe.

The first group has been named *Otocompsa* by Cabanis. It was founded apparently on *P. jocosus*, and includes the two yellow-vented crested Bulbuls, whose markings are similar to the first named species.

Gen. OTOCOMPSA, Cabanis.

Char.—Bill short or moderate, slightly curved; rictus bristled; the head black, with an erectile pointed crest; the upper plumage brown and the under tail-coverts yellow or red.

1st. with the lower tail-coverts yellow.

458. Otocompsa leucogenys, GRAY.

Brachypus, apud GRAY, HARDW. Ill. Ind. Zool. 2, pl. 35, f. 3—BLYTH, Cat. 1266—HORSF., Cat. 360—Ix. plumigerus, LAFRESN.—*Manglio-kur or Mancliph-kur*, Lepch.—*Kungdhara*, Beng.

THE WHITE-CHEEKED CRESTED-BULBUL.

Descr.—Top of head and nape hair brown, the feathers long and forming an erectile occipital crest; a faint white supercilium, only reaching the middle of the eye; lores, and round the eyes, black; ear-coverts white; plumage above pale earthy-brown, the quills somewhat darker brown ; tail brown at the base, black for the terminal half, with a white tip ; chin and throat blackish brown, this colour extending round to the back of the ears ; breast and lower parts pale whity-brown, more albescent on the middle of the abdomen ; under tail-coverts bright yellow.

Bill black ; legs plumbeous ; irides brown. Length nearly 8 inches ; extent 11 ; wing $3\frac{5}{8}$; tail $3\frac{1}{2}$; bill at front $\frac{5}{8}$; tarsus $\frac{9}{16}$.

The White-cheeked Bulbul is found throughout the whole extent of the Himalayas, from Cashmere to Bootan. It is most abundant, in Sikhim, from about 2,500 to 5,000 feet of elevation. It feeds both on seeds, fruits, and insects. Hutton found the nest neatly made with stalks and grass, and containing three or four eggs, rosy or purplish white, with specks and spots of dark purple or claret.

459. Otocompsa leucotis, GOULD.

Ixos, apud GOULD, P. Z. S., 1836—BLYTH, Cat. 1265—HORSF., Cat. 359—*Kangdhara*, Beng.—*Kushandra,* or *Kushanbra* of the Punjab—*Bhooroo* of Sindh.

THE WHITE-EARED CRESTED-BULBUL.

Descr.—Whole head and neck black, passing into rich brown on the neck; ear-coverts, and a patch below them, white, edged black ; upper plumage earthy brown; tail brown at the base, the terminal half blackish brown, with the edges white, most broadly so on the outer feathers; beneath, from the breast, whity-brown ; the under tail-coverts rich saffron-yellow.

Length 7 inches ; wing $3\frac{1}{2}$; tail $3\frac{1}{4}$; bill at front $\frac{7}{16}$; tarsus $\frac{3}{4}$. This species has the tail slightly rounded, the bill is rather short, deep, and strong, and in these points it makes approach to *Pyc. sinensis*, V., p. 86.

This Bulbul is found in the Punjab, extending down the Indus and Sutlej, through Ferozepore and Bhawulpore, into Sindh and Guzrat. Nothing is recorded of its habits.

Ixos tympanistrigus, Müll., of Bonaparte's Conspect., may perhaps belong to the present group ; as does certainly *chrysorhæus*, Latham, from Java, figured in Brown's Ill. Zool.

460. **Otocompsa jocosa,** Lin.

Lanius, apud Linnæus—L. Emeria, Shaw—Blyth, Cat. 1260
—Horsf., Cat. 354—Jerdon, Cat. 77—Sykes, Cat. 70—Ix.
monticolus, McLell., P. Z. S., 1839—I. pyrrhotis, Hodgs.—*Kanera
bulbul,* H. in the north—*Phari-bulbul,* H. in the south—*Kara
bulbul,* and *Sipahi bulbul,* Beng.—*Turaka pigli-pitta,* Tel.

The Red-Whiskered Bulbul.

Descr.—Head, with crest, black; ear-coverts white, with a tuft
of glossy hair-like crimson feathers over the ears, and reaching
beyond them; a narrow line of black borders the ear-coverts
beneath; plumage above light hair-brown, darker on the quills and
on the tail, especially towards the tip, which is white on all, except
the central feathers, but only on the inner web, except on the
outermost pair; beneath, from the chin, white, the sides of the
breast dark-brown, forming an interrupted gorget.

Length 8 inches; extent 11; wing $3\frac{1}{2}$; tail $3\frac{9}{10}$; tarsus $\frac{9}{10}$;
bill at front $\frac{1}{2}$.

The Red-whiskered or Hill-bulbul is found throughout India, but
often affects particular localities. As a general rule it is most
common in jungly and well-wooded districts. In the Carnatic it is
rare, found now and then in low jungle, and periodically visiting
Madras and other wooded towns in large flocks. On the western
coast it is more generally spread, but even there you may pass
over considerable tracts of ground without seeing it. On the
Neilgherries it is very abundant. It is rare in the central table
land, tolerably common on the Northern Circars, in Lower Bengal,
and here and there throughout the Upper Provinces, extending to
the Sub-Himalayan range; but not apparently ascending the hills
to any height, as it does in the South. Out of our province it is
found in Assam and Arrakan. It is a most lively and active bird,
always on the move, and warbling its pleasant chirruping notes,
which are more agreeable than those of the next species. Its flight
is steady, but not very rapid, and its crest is always raised the
moment it alights. I have frequently had its nest and eggs brought
me on the Neilgherries. The nest was very neatly made, deep, cup-

shaped, of moss, lichens, and small roots, lined with hair and down. The eggs are barely distinguishable from those of the next bird, being reddish white with spots of purplish or lake-red all over, larger at the thick end. It lives chiefly on fruit and seeds, on the Neilgherries, robbing the gardens of peas, strawberries, &c.; now and then it takes insects; and I have seen it come to the ground to secure them.

An affined race or species is found in Burmah and Malayana, which differs in having the red whiskers shorter, truncated, and of a much deeper crimson colour. It only reaches the basal third of the white ear-coverts, whilst, in the Indian bird, it measures ⅝ of an inch or more, and passes beyond the ear-coverts.

Bonaparte, in his Conspectus, applies the name of Linnæus to the race of Burmah and China; and to the Indian species Hodgson's name *pyrrhotis*; he has also a third species, *erythrotis*, Bonap., from Java. McLelland's *P. monticolus*, which I procured from the Khasia hills, does not appear to me to differ from the Indian race.

Gen. PYCNONOTUS, Kuhl.

Syn. *Hæmatornis* partly, Swainson.

Char.—Bill moderately long, strong, tolerably curved, with strongish rictal bristles; legs and feet stout; tail barely rounded, almost square; under tail-coverts red.

With Gray, I have kept the genus *Pycnonotus* for the common Bulbuls of India. These differ from the last in their darker plumage, and in the want of the pointed crest.

One of the following species is to be seen in every part of India, and a nearly allied race in Burmah, and the Malayan provinces.

461. Pycnonotus pygæus, HODGSON.

HORSF., Cat. 239—P. Bengalensis, BLYTH, Cat. 1261—P. cafer of India, auctorum—*Bulbul*, Hind.—*Kala bulbul*, Beng.—*Mancliph-pho*, Lepch.—*Paklom*, Bhot.

THE COMMON BENGAL BULBUL.

Descr.—Head, nape, hind neck, chin, throat, and breast, glossy black; ear-coverts glossy hair brown; from the hind neck dark smoky brown, edged with ashy, which is the colour of the rump ; the upper tail-coverts white ; tail brownish-black, tipped with white, except the central pair ; wings as the back ; the shoulders and wing-coverts, edged with whitish ; below, from the breast, dark brown, edged with ashy, passing to ashy on the lower abdomen ; vent, and under tail-coverts rich crimson.

Length $8\frac{3}{4}$ inches ; extent $12\frac{1}{4}$; wing $3\frac{7}{8}$; tail $3\frac{1}{4}$; bill at front $\frac{5}{8}$; tarsus $\frac{7}{8}$. Bill black ; legs dark brown ; irides deep brown.

The Bengal Bulbul is found throughout Lower Bengal, and the Upper Provinces, extending to the Himalayas on the north, and south to Midnapore, and the jungles stretching thence to Central India, north of the Nerbudda river. It is doubtful if it is found in Rajpootana and the Punjab. It is also found in Assam ; but in Southern Burmah it is replaced by a nearly affined race, *P. nigropileus*, Blyth.

This bird, whose habits and manners precisely resemble those of the next, ascends the Himalayas, at Darjeeling, to 7,000 feet, at least, being common in the station ; whilst our Southern species is not found beyond Kotagherry and Coonoor, 6,000 feet high, on the Neilgherries.

462. Pycnonotus hæmorhous, GMELIN.

Muscicapa, apud GMELIN—BLYTH, Cat. 1262—HORSF., Cat. 356—Ixos Cafer, apud SYKES, Cat. 71—Hamatornis cafer, JERD., Cat. 76—H. pusillus, and psendo-cafer, BLYTH (olim)— BROWN, Ill. Zool., pl. 31, f. 1—*Bulbul*, Hind—*Tonki bulbul*, Beng.—*Pigli-pitta*, Tel.—*Kunda-lati*, Tam.

THE COMMON MADRAS BULBUL.

Descr.—Head, chin and throat, black ; nape and back smoky brown, more or less edged paler, and the pale edging often extends to the darker feathers of the hind head and nape, giving it a speckled appearance ; rump somewhat cinerascent ; upper tail-coverts white ; beneath, from the top of the breast, brown, edged with ash, paling posteriorly, and becoming albescent on the lower abdomen and vent ; under tail-coverts crimson ; wings and tail as in the last.

Bill black; legs greenish slaty; irides deep brown. Length about 8 inches; extent 11; wing $3\frac{6}{10}$; tail $3\frac{5}{10}$; tarsus $\frac{8}{10}$; bill at front $\frac{9}{16}$.

It differs from the Bengal Bulbul in only having the head black, the nape being of the same colour as the back; also in the black of the lower parts only reaching the upper part of the breast, whilst in the Bengal one the whole breast is black. It is also decidedly a smaller bird.

This is one the of most common and generally spread birds in the South of India. It extends throughout the southern part of the Peninsula to the Nerbudda river, and beyond it, apparently, in the North-west. A specimen from Wuzeerabad, in the Punjab, resembles this species in having only a black cap, but the wing is longer; it is altogether a larger bird, and the ear-coverts are shining dark brown, not so conspicuous as in the Bengal bird, more so than in the Madras species. The plumage, too, is generally lighter, and more deeply edged pale. This may be a hybrid between the two races, but it is probably a distinct race, and will perhaps be found to be the common species throughout the Punjab and other parts of the North-Western Provinces, but I do not like to give it a distinct specific rank at present on the faith of one speci- man. I see, however, that Lord A. Hay considered it distinct, and suggested for it the name of *P. intermedius.* Mr. Blyth moreover states that our present bird is also found in Arrakan, and one specimen from thence, in the Asiatic Society's Museum, certainly very closely resembles the species from Southern India; but two others, one from Arrakan and another from Tonghoo, have the decidedly brown ears of the Bengal species, and are more probably a peculiar race, replaced in the South of Burmah by *P. nigropileus.*

It frequents gardens and cultivated ground, and low bushy jungle, but is never found in forests, and it ascends the Neilgherries to about 6,000 feet only. It is usually seen in pairs, or in small families, flying briskly about, restless and inquisitive, feeding chiefly on fruits, but occasionally descending to the ground, and even hopping a step or two and picking up insects. It destroys various buds and blossoms also, and is very destructive to peas, strawberries, brazil cherries (*Physalis peruviana*), and other soft fruit. Its note, which it is frequently uttering, is an unmusical rather harsh chirrup. It has at times, however, a sweeter note, and it is said to be able to imitate the notes of other birds when caged. Its flight is direct, performed by a continued quick flapping of the wings. It breeds from June to September according to the locality. The nest is rather neat cup-shaped, made of roots and grass, lined with hair, fibres, and spiders' webs, placed at no great height in a shrub or hedge. The eggs are pale-pinkish, with spots of darker lake-red, most crowded at the thick end. Burgess describes them as rich madder colour, spotted and blotched with gray and madder-brown; Layard, as pale cream, with darker markings.

The Bulbul is very commonly caged in various parts of the country, and in the Carnatic it is kept for fighting, being held on the finger with a cord attached. They fight sometimes with great spirit, often, I am assured, seizing their antagonist by the red feathers, and endeavouring to pull them out. When excited they often spread out these feathers laterally, so as to be seen even from above.

Besides *P. nigropileus*, and the races already alluded to, there is one, *P. atricapillus* from China. Two species of Bulbul placed by Pr. Bonaparte under *Tricophorus*, viz., *T. pulverulentus*, and *T. striolatus*, S. Müller, both from Sumatra, appear, by their dingy coloration, either to belong to the present genus, or to be links uniting it to some of the other forms.

Of non-Asiatic *Brachypodinæ*, we have *Andropadus* with three or four species, and *Tricophorus* and *Ixos*, with many species from Africa. Of the last genus there are several from Northern Africa, one of which, *I. obscurus*, has been killed in Spain; and *I. arsinoe* and *I. vallumbrosæ* have been procured, respectively, in Arabia and Palestine.

Sub-Fam. PHYLLORNITHINÆ.

Bill slightly lengthened, more or less curved, of variable strength; wings moderate; tail short; tarsus and feet short, stout. Of a beautiful grass green colour, more or less adorned with various glistening blue patches on the throat and shoulder of the wings.

This is a small group of very pretty birds found in India, Burmah, and Malayana, the species being, as usual, rather locally distributed. Bonaparte places this sub-family among the *Melliphagidæ*. Gray also places *Phyllornis* at the end of the *Melliphagidæ*, and Blyth considers that it is allied to that family (though not so nearly as are the Orioles); but, in his Catalogue, places it and *Iora* in his sub-family *Phyllorninæ* of the *Pycnonotidæ*, with which views I entirely agree. Their general structure and habits are quite like those of the short-footed Thrushes in general, and their geographic distribution coincides with that of the present family. The birds, however, as a rule, are more insectivorous than the true Bulbuls.

Gen. PHYLLORNIS, Boie.

Syn. *Chloropsis*, Jard. and Selby.

Char.—Bill moderate or rather long; culmen keeled, and more or less curved; tip bent down and notched; nostrils basal, lengthened; wings moderately long, with the 4th and 5th quills subequal, but the 4th longest; tail moderate or rather short, even; tarsus short, smooth.

The bill in this genus is of very variable strength and curvature. The plumage of all is bright grass-green, varied with blue and yellow markings about the head and neck. In one or more species the wings are fine blue, showing an approximation towards *Irena*. There are four species found in our province, two in Southern, and two in Northern India.

463. **Phyllornis Jerdoni**, BLYTH.

J. A. S., XII., 392—BLYTH, Cat. 1287—HORSF., Cat. 396—JERDON, Ill. Ind. Orn., pl. 43—Chloropsis cœsmarhynchos, apud TICKELL—Chl. cochinsinensis, apud JERDON, Cat. 72—*Harrewa*, H.—*Wanna bojanum*, Tel. *i. e.*, Ornament of the forest.

THE COMMON GREEN BULBUL.

Descr.—Male, pale grass-green, shoulder patch pale shining blue, quills dusky internally; chin, throat and gorge, deep black, surrounded by a greenish yellow band, which extends through the eyes to the forehead; maxillary streak hyacinth blue, short. The female

N

has the parts that are black in the male light bluish green, surrounded by the yellowish band, and the maxillary streak light azure.

Bill dusky; legs plumbeous; irides light brown. Length $7\frac{1}{4}$
inches; wing $3\frac{1}{2}$; tail $2\frac{3}{4}$; bill at front barely $\frac{7}{10}$; tarsus not
quite $\frac{8}{10}$.

P. cochinchinensis, with which this species was for long confounded, differs in being a smaller bird; in having more yellow
on the forehead and breast; in the maxillary streak being still
shorter, &c., &c.

This Green Bulbul, is spread over great part of the continent
of India, not extending however to Lower Bengal, or to the sub-
Himalayan forests. It is extremely common in all the Western
provinces, and in the jungles of the Eastern Ghâts; but is more
rare in the open country of the Carnatic, Mysore, and Hydrabad.
It is found in Central India at Mhow, Saugor, &c., and through
the vast jungles of Chota Nagpore up to Midnapore. It is usually
met with in pairs, sometimes in small parties, flitting about the
extreme branches of trees, examining the leaves for various insects,
in pursuit of which it occasionally takes a short flight of a foot or
two, or searching for some suitable fruit. It has various notes;
its usual call being, as Mr. Blyth remarks, not unlike that of the
King-crow (*Dicrurus macrocercus*), though softened down and
mellowed; and, at times, it has a very pretty song. Tickell says
" it is an excellent mocker, and imitates the notes of almost
every small bird of the country." I have seen the nest only once.
It was neatly but slightly made, cup-shaped, composed chiefly
of fine grass, with some hairs, and was placed near the extremity
of a branch, one or two of the nearest leaves being brought down,
and loosely fixed to it. It contained two eggs, white, with a few
claret-coloured blotches. Layard also found the nest in Ceylon
" with four eggs, white, thickly mottled at the obtuse end with
purplish spots."

464. Phyllornis Malabaricus, Latham.

Turdus, apud Latham—Blyth, Cat. 1286—Chl. aurifrons,
apud Sykes, Cat. 131—Jerdon, Cat. 71—Chlor. Malabaricus,
Jerdon, 2nd Suppl. Cat., page 124.

THE MALABAR GREEN BULBUL.

Descr.—Male bright grass-green; forehead golden-yellow; chin and throat black, with a small blue moustachial streak; flexure of the wing verdigris blue.

The female wants the golden forehead of the male, and has the black gorget and blue maxillary streak somewhat smaller.

Bill dusky blackish; legs plumbeous; irides light yellowish-brown. Length nearly 8 inches; extent 11; wing $3\frac{1}{2}$; tail 3; bill at front $\frac{3}{4}$; tarsus $\frac{7}{10}$. Female a little smaller.

This species is found most abundantly in the forests of Malabar, in Wynaad, Coorg, and on the sides of the Neilgherries, up to about 4,000 feet of elevation. It is also found, though rarely, on the Eastern Ghâts, and in some of the forests of Central India. Like the last it is seen in pairs, or small parties, hopping and flying actively about the branches of trees, and lives both on fruits and insects, chiefly the latter.

465. **Phyllornis aurifrons,** TEMM.

Pl. col. 484, f. 1—BLYTH, Cat. 1285—HORSF., Cat. 395—Chl. Malabaricus, apud JARD. and SELBY, Ill. Orn., pl. 5—*Subzharewa*, Nepal—*Hurriba*, Beng.—*Skalem-pho*, Lepch.

THE GOLD-FRONTED GREEN BULBUL.

Descr.—Male, green, paler beneath, with the flexure of the wings verdigris blue; forehead and front of crown, brilliant golden orange, the feathers rigid and glistening; the throat wholly shining smalt-blue; fore-neck black, surrounded by a yellow zone; wings and tail beneath dusky-gray.

The female has the black of the neck of smaller extent, and wants the golden forehead.

Bill black; legs greenish plumbeous; feet dusky blue; irides brown. Length 8 inches; extent 12; wing $3\frac{3}{8}$; tail $2\frac{3}{4}$; bill at front $\frac{3}{4}$; tarsus $\frac{5}{8}$.

This species is found in all the sub-Himalayan region, from Dehra Doon into Sikhim; also in Lower Bengal and Midnapore, and it extends into Assam, Arrakan, and Burmah. It is often caged in Calcutta, many being brought to Monghyr from the Nepal

Terai. I procured it in Sikhim up to 4,000 feet or so. It has a sweet song, and, like the others, when caged, is quite a mocking bird.

466. Phyllornis Hardwickii, JARD. and SELBY.

Chloropsis, apud JARD. and SELBY—BLYTH, Cat. 1284—HORSF., Cat. 394—C. curvirostris, SWAINS.—C. chrysogaster, McLELL., P. Z. S., 1839—C. auriventris, GUERIN, Mag. Zool. 1840, pl. 17— C. cyanopterus, HODGS.—*Sahlem-pho*, Lepch.

THE BLUE-WINGED GREEN BULBUL.

Descr.—Male above green; the head and neck tinged with yellowish, and a brilliant smalt-blue moustachial streak; shoulder of the wings verdigris blue; wings and tail fine violet or purple; throat and fore-neck black, passing into glossy dark-purple on the breast; abdomen rich orange saffron.

Females want the black neck and throat; the moustachial streak is less vivid, and the lower parts are more mixed with green.

Bill black; legs plumbeous; irides light brown. Length 8 inches; extent 12; wing 3¾; tail 3; bill at front $\frac{11}{16}$; tarsus ¾.

This beautiful bird is found in the South-East Himalayas, from Nepal to Bootan, spreading south to the hill ranges of Assam, Sylhet, and Arrakan. In Sikhim I found it from 2,000 feet upwards, most common about 4,000 feet. It has a fine song, and the usual habits of its genus.

Several other species of *Phyllornis* are found in Malayana and the eastern island, *viz*, *P. Cochinsinensis*, already alluded to; *icterocephalus*, Temm., P. C. 512, 2, very closely allied to the last, and both having, like *Hardwickii*, blue wings and tail; *cyanopogon* of Malacca; and *Sonneratii*, J. and S., also from Malacca and the islands, the largest of the group, and with the bill proportionally strong and curved. Bonaparte, in his Conspectus, gives two additional species, *media*, Müll., like *Sonneratii*, but with the bill smaller; and *venusta*, Temm., both from Sumatra.

The next genus, *Iora*, has been considered rather an isolated form, although its relationship to the Bulbuls had been allowed by many; but the discovery of a fine and large species of this genus, with undoubted affinities for *Phyllornis*, has settled conclusively its place along with that genus as a group of the Brachypodine Thrushes. *Iora* is one of those forms that has certain affinities both of structure and habits for some of the Parine and Leiotrichine groups. Bonaparte classes it along with *Phyllornis*, but associates with them *Yuhina* and *Zosterops*, which I prefer placing with the *Leiotrichinæ*, albeit there is a considerable resemblance to those genera, and more especially to *Erpornis*, another member of the same family. But the still closer affinities for *Phyllornis*, shewn in *Iora Lafresnayii*, the nest and the color of the eggs, which are those of the Bulbuls, have determined me to place it here.

Gen. IORA, Horsf.

Syn. *Ægithina* Vieill.

Char.—Bill moderate or rather long, somewhat compressed, very slightly curving; culmen rounded, slightly hooked at the tip, and notched; rictal bristles almost wanting; nostrils apert; wings rather short, with 4th, 5th, and 6th quills sub-equal and longest; secondaries long, nearly equal to the primaries; tail even, short; tarsus rather short with scales divided; toes short; middle toe very little longer than the outer, which is slightly syndactyle; claws slightly curved; hind toe shorter than the middle toe.

467. **Iora Zeylonica,** GMELIN.

Motacilla, apud GMEL.—BLYTH, Cat. 1291—HORSF., Cat. 409—BROWN, Ill. Zool., pl. 15 f. 2—I. melaceps, SWAINS.—I. typhia, apud JERDON, Cat. 73—*Shoubiga* or *Shoubhigi*, Hind.—*Patsu-jitta*, Tel. and *Pacha-pora*, Tam.; both names meaning *green-bird*.

THE BLACK-HEADED GREEN BULBUL.

Descr.—Male in full plumage, with the head, back, wings, and tail, deep black; the former with two white bars, caused by the tips of the greater coverts; scapulars also partly white; the tail tipped with yellowish white; beneath bright yellow; abdomen and lower tail-coverts pale yellow; the flanks have a tuft of white silky feathers, and the base of the clothing feathers is mostly white.

In non-breeding plumage, and in males not fully adult, the
black of the upper plumage is less in extent, and more mixed
with green; the white of the quills are faintly edged with pale
yellow externally, and the innermost ones are white internally,
near the tip; and the pale tips to the tail feathers are more distinct.
I believe that the black plumage is mostly seasonal, and that
the change takes place either by a partial moult, or by a change
in the feathers.   One specimen in the Museum, Asiatic Society,
from Southern India, has the central tail feathers partly green and
partly black.   In the cold weather we generally find the males
having more or less green mixed with the black.

The female is entirely grass-green above, pale yellow beneath;
the wings blackish, with whitish bars and yellow edges; and the
tail green, pale tipped.

Bill light plumbeous, darker on the ridge; irides greyish white;
legs dusky plumbeous.   Length $5\frac{1}{4}$ inches; extent 8; wing
$2\frac{1}{2}$; tail 2; bill at front $\frac{1}{2}$; tarsus $\frac{5}{8}$.

This is one of the most common birds in Southern India.   It
extends up to 16° or 17° N. L. if not further, and it is possible
that it may be met with in the N. W. Provinces, for Blyth gives
one, though with a query, from Dehra Doon.   In Bengal and in
the north of India generally, it is replaced by the next species.

It may be seen in almost every garden in the south of India.   Its
habits are more active and restless than those of any other member
of this family, being much like those of the Tits.   It may be seen
diligently and carefully searching the smaller branches and twigs
of trees, climbing actively among them, poring under the leaves,
and occasionally clinging like a titmouse from a slender twig; all
the while keeping up a loud warbling strain, or a low querulous
sort of note, very different from each other.   It is not confined to
cultivated ground, but is also a denizen of the open spaces of
jungles.   Its flight is performed by a succession of quick vibrations
of the wing, and causes a loud whirring sound.   Its food consists
of various insects and larvæ, spiders, &c.

The male, at the breeding season, now and then takes a short
flight from one tree to another, slowly, and in a fluttering manner,
with his black tail spread, and the white feathers of the flanks

puffed outwards and upwards, so as to give the appearance of a pure white rump. I have seen the nest and eggs on several occasions. The nest is deep, cup-shaped, very neatly made with grass, various fibres, hairs, and spiders' web; and the eggs, two or three in number, are reddish white with numerous darker red spots, chiefly at the thicker end. It breeds in the South of India in August and September; perhaps however twice a year. Burgess, speaking of its notes, says " truly, it has a wonderful power of voice; at one moment uttering a low plaintive cry, at the next a shrill whistle." Layard, too, who observed it in Ceylon, states that "the note is a clear bell-like whistle, which may be imitated on an octave flute." One of its notes, the low plaintive one, is not unlike the word 'Chee-too,' the last syllable much lengthened out, which Horsfield gives as the note of its Malayan congener. It is said by the natives of the south of India to repeat the word " Shoubhiga, Shoubhiga," before rain.

468. Iora typhia, LIN.

Motacilla, apud LINNÆUS—BLYTH, Cat. 1293—HORSF., Cat. 408—SYKES, Cat. 74—Mot. sub-viridis, TICKELL—Chah-tuk, Beng.—Taphika, or Fatickja tonjik, also, Beng.

THE WHITE-WINGED GREEN BULBUL.

Descr.—Male, above olive-green, beneath yellow; wings black, faintly edged with yellow; greater coverts broadly tipped with white; scapulars also partly white; tail black. The female has the tail concolorous with the body, but slightly infuscated, and the wings paler than in the male.

Bill and legs pale bluish brown; eyes light hazel. Length 5½ inches; wing 2⅝; tail 2; bill at front $\frac{9}{16}$.

This species of Iora is found in Nepal, Bengal, Central India, Assam, Arrakan, and the Malayan Peninsula. Horsfield, in his Catalogue, asserts that it is Col. Sykes' species from the Deccan, and I believe that it was the species common at Jaulnah, as it certainly was at Nagpore and Saugor. It differs in the want of black on the head and back, in the bill being slightly longer, in being altogether a larger bird; also in the color of the irides. Blyth however says that a dusky tinge is often observable on the

crown and back ; and occasionally specimens are met with which
have assumed more or less of the black. These perhaps may be
hybrids, for males, colored exactly as birds from Southern India
and Ceylon, are not met with in the North. The females are
barely distinguishable.

Another very closely allined species, *Iora scapularis,* is found in
Java and the other islands ; and a large species, of plain plumage,
has lately been discovered in Arrakan, *I. Lafresnayii,* Hartlaub,
(*innotata,* Blyth), which, as before remarked, by its size, shape
of bill, and other points, distinctly shows the relationship of this
genus for *Phyllornis.*

There are two other species recorded in Bonaparte's Conspectus,
I. viridis, and *I. viridissima,* Temm., the first from Borneo, the
other from Sumatra.

Sub-fam. IRENINÆ, Blue-birds.

Bill stout, of moderate length, somewhat widened at the base ;
culmen elevated, and slightly arching from the base; the tip not
much hooked, but distinctly toothed ; nostrils partially concealed
by short plumes; rictus with short but distinct bristles ; wings
moderate or rather long; 4th quill longest, 3rd nearly as long ;
tail moderate, even ; feet with the tarsus very short ; lateral toes
very slightly unequal ; claws short, well curved.

The fairy Blue-birds have been bandied about by various
authors, and it is by no means agreed on even yet where their final
resting place is to be. Gray, most unfortunately as I consider it,
places them near the Drongo Shrikes, from some similarity in the
bill. Others would place them in the *Campephaginæ,* but their
strictly fruit-eating habits, though not entirely unknown in that
family, are still the exception to the usual habits. Swainson
placed them, with more regard to both structure and habits, among
the Orioles, and, in his Catalogue, Blyth placed it between
Phyllornis and the Orioles ; and I think that this is pretty nearly
its true situation. The rich blue, glistering color of *Irena* is
present, in more or less extent, in *Phyllornis,* and in few other
Indian birds ; the feet and wings are quite those of the Brachypodine Thrushes, and its full rich notes are those of the Orioles.

I was at one time inclined to class it as an aberrant form of *Ampelidæ*, not far from *Cochoa ;* and Bonaparte, in his Conspectus, places *Irena* together with *Cochoa* in the *Dicrurinæ*, but next to the Orioles. Its much shorter legs and feet, and the less depressed bill, are, however, more those of the present family.

Gen. IRENA, Horsf.

Char.—Those of the sub-family of which it is the sole genus.

469. Irena puella, LATHAM.

Coracias, apud LATHAM—JERDON, Cat. 100—BLYTH, Cat. 1295—HORSF., Cat. 420—I. Indica, A. HAY.

THE FAIRY BLUE-BIRD.

Descr.—Male, the whole upper parts with the lower tail-coverts, brilliant glistening cobalt-blue ; wings, tail, and lower plumage, deep velvet black.

The female is of a dull, slightly mottled, Antwerp-blue throughout.

Bill and legs black ; irides ruby-red. Length 10 inches ; wing $5\frac{1}{4}$; tail 4 ; tarsus $\frac{7}{10}$; bill at front .

This most lovely plumaged bird is only found in our province in the dense and lofty forests of Malabar, from Travancore upwards to about N. L. 15°. It is also found in Assam, Arrakan, and Burmah ; but has not been procured in any of the sub-Himalayan forests. It ascends mountain ranges up to 4,000 feet and upwards, and lives in small parties of five, six, or more, frequenting the loftiest trees near their summit, and wandering from tree to tree. It has a fine loud mellow warble, which it is constantly repeating, both when feeding and as it flies from one tree to another. It feeds chiefly on fruits of various kinds, but I dare say may take caterpillars occasionally. Mr. Ward obtained what he was informed was the nest and eggs ; the nest was large, made of roots and fibres and lined with moss ; and the eggs, two in number, were pale greenish, much spotted with dusky.

A race from Malayana differs in having the under tail-coverts reaching to the end of the tail, whilst, in the Indian bird, they are never less than 1¼ inch short of the tail-tip. Lord A. Hay, thinking that the name *puella* of Latham applied to the Javanese bird, called our species *I. indica;* but in Horsfield's Catalogue it is mentioned by Moore that Latham's bird came from India; consequently the Malayan race is without a name, and Moore accordingly named it *I. malayensis.* It is figured in Horsfield's Zool. Res. in Java.

A third species exists in *I. cyanogastra,* Vigors, from the Phillipines, figured in Gray's Genera of Birds.

Sub-fam. ORIOLINÆ.

Bill Thrush-like, rather long, strong, moderately broad at the base, slightly curving, tolerably hooked, and the tip distinctly notched; wings long, 3rd or 4th quill longest; tail rather short, nearly even; tarsus short; feet small; lateral toes unequal, and the outer one syndactyle; claws well curved.

The Orioles comprise a small number of genera, chiefly natives of the Old World and Australia. They may be said to be true Thrushes by their bills, with the legs of the short-footed Thrushes. The tongue is slightly cleft or pencilled at the tip. Their food is fruit, and soft insects, such as caterpillars. They frequent woods and forests, and rarely or never descend to the ground. Van Hoeven places them with the Birds of Paradise; Blyth in the *Melliphagidæ;* Cuvier, Gray, and Horsfield among the Thrushes.

Gen. ORIOLUS, Linnæus.

Char.—Bill long, slightly broad at the base, somewhat curved on the culmen, which is keeled, slightly hooked at tip, distinctly notched; nostrils basal and lateral, longitudinal, pierced in membrane, nearly apert; wings lengthened, 1st quill very short, 2nd a little shorter than the 3rd, which is longest; tail sub-even, with long coverts; tarsus short; feet moderately strong; anterior scales of tarsus divided; claws moderate, well curved.

The true Orioles are confined to Asia, Africa, and Australia, one species extending to the South of Europe, and rarely straggling to England. They are almost uniformly of a yellow color, with

more or less black. Several species are found in India, and others
in Malayana. They may be divided into four groups: 1st, Golden
Orioles; 2nd, Black-naped Orioles; 3rd, Black-headed Orioles;
4th, Maroon Orioles.

1st, Golden Orioles, (*Galbulus* of Bonaparte).

470. Oriolus kundoo, SYKES.

SYKES, Cat. 60 (the young or female)—O. galbula, apud SYKES,
Cat. 58—BLYTH, Cat. 1304—HORSF., Cat. 418—O. aureus, apud
JERDON, Cat. 97—O. galbuloides, GOULD—*Piluk*, Hind. *i. e.*,
the yellow bird—*Vanga-pandu*, Tel.—*Pawseh*, Mahr.—*Mango-bird*
of Europeans in India.

THE INDIAN ORIOLE.

Descr.—Male, bright yellow; a black stripe from the base of
the bill through the eyes for a short distance beyond; wings black,
with a yellow bar formed by the primary coverts and the tips
and outer edges of the quills; tail with the central feathers black;
the next pair black with a broad yellow tip; and the others black
at the base, and yellow for the greater part of their terminal
length.

Bill deep lake-red; legs plumbeous; irides rich blood-red.
Length 9½ inches, wing 5½; tail 3½; bill at front 1; tarsus 1.

The young bird is yellowish-green above; the rump, vent, the
inner webs of the tail feathers at their tips, and the sides of
abdomen, bright yellow; wings olive-brown; body beneath
whitish, with brown stripes; bill black.

The adult female differs from the male in a slightly
greenish tint above. This Oriole differs from the European
O. galbula, only in the black eye streak extending to the ear-
coverts, in the wing being shorter, and the bill proportionally
longer. It extends over the whole peninsula of India (except
Lower Bengal) up to the base of the Himalayas. On the Malabar
Coast it is perhaps not so common as *O. melanocephalus*. It does
not occur in the countries to the east of the Bay of Bengal. In
the South of India it is most abundant in the cold weather; in the
Deccan, according to Sykes, in the hot weather just before the
rains; and in Central India, during the rains, when it breeds; but

it is to be found, at all seasons, in every part of the country in small numbers. It prefers a well-wooded country, but not deep forests ; and lives in large groves of trees, gardens, and avenues. It chiefly feeds on fruit, especially on the figs of the *Banian* and *Pakur*, on Mulberries, &c., also occasionally on caterpillars, and other soft-bodied insects. Its flight is strong, but undulating, with interrupted flappings. Its call is a loud mellow whistle, something resembling *pee-ho* ; and the voice of the European Oriole must be very similar, as it is given as *puh-lo* and *bülow* ; and the French name *Loriot* is said to be also given from its call.

I have seen the nest several times, and I described one in my Illustration of Indian Ornithology, under *O. indicus*, as follows :— "It was a cup-shaped nest, slightly made with fine grass and roots, and suspended from a rather high branch by a few long fibres of grass ; these did not surround the nest but only supported it on two sides. It contained three eggs, white, spotted, chiefly at the large end, with a very few large dark purple blotches." I procured a nest at Saugor, from a high branch of a banian tree in cantonment. It was situated between the forks of a branch, made of fine roots and grass, with some hair and a feather or two internally, and suspended by a long roll of cloth about ¾ inch wide, which it must have pilferred from the neighbouring verandah, where the tailor worked. This strip was wound round each fork, then passed round the nest beneath, fixed to the other fork and again brought round the nest, to the opposite side ; there were four or five of these supports on each side. It was, indeed, a most curious nest, and so securely fixed that it could not have been removed till the supporting bands had been cut or rotted away. The eggs were, as before described, white, with a few dark claret-colored spots. Burgess describes a nest made of grass, spiders' web, hemp, and pieces of paper, placed in the fork of a tree, and two of the branches were bound together with the hemp. Theobald also found the nest, a neat cup of woven grass, attached by its side to the bough of a tree, and he describes the eggs as white, with black spots. The only other species of Oriole of this section in Bonaparte's Conspectus, is *O. auratus*, of Africa ; but others are recorded elsewhere.

2nd, Black-naped Orioles (*Broderipus,* of Bonaparte), peculiar
to the Indian region.

471. Oriolus indicus, Brisson.

Jerdon, Ill. Ind. Orn., pl. 15—Blyth, Cat. 1302—Horsf.,
Cat. 415—O. chinensis, Jerdon, Cat. 99—and of other authors.

The Black-naped Indian Oriole.

Descr.—Bright yellow, greenish on the back and coverts; a
black horse-shoe mark extending from the base of the bill through
the eyes to the nape; tail black, the central feathers barely tipped
yellow, the others tipped broadly, the outermost feathers for $1\frac{1}{2}$
inches or so; wings black, the secondaries, broadly margined with
pale yellow; the tertiaries with the whole outer web, and part of the
inner web, greenish yellow; primaries also tipped with the same;
a bright yellow wing-spot formed by the tips of the coverts of the
primaries. Females only differ in being slightly greenish above,
and in the yellow generally being not quite so vivid.

The young are yellowish green above, with little or no trace
of the occipital crescent, whitish beneath, with dark central lines;
bill infuscated. In a further stage the under-parts are weaker
yellow, with black shafts to the breast feathers more or less
developed.

Bill of adult pinky-red; feet plumbeous; irides rich blood-red.
Length 10 inches; wing 6; tail $3\frac{1}{2}$; bill at front $1\frac{1}{8}$; tarsus $\frac{3}{4}$.

This species, which I first characterized in my Illustrations as
distinct from *O. chinensis (acrorhynchus,* Vigors), differs from that
species and from another nearly allied one from the Nicobars (*O.
macrourus,* Blyth), by its much smaller bill, the smaller black
crescent on the nape, and in the much greater extent of the
yellow upon the wings, whilst the tail has less yellow. The present
species however appears also to be found in China, and, it is possible, may have been the original *chinensis,* instead of *acrorhynchus.*

This Black-naped Oriole is spread more or less through India,
but rare everywhere, and it has not been observed in the Himalayas.   I have procured it from the Malabar jungles; Mr. Elliot
obtained it at Dharwar, and it is found near Calcutta. It appears
however to be much more common in the countries to the east of

the Bay of Bengal, Arrakan, Pegu, and Tenasserim, extending to
Malacca, and it is more confined to the forest regions than the
other Indian Orioles.

Besides the two allied species mentioned above, a fourth has
been found in the Burmese countries, and named *O. tenuirostris*,
by Blyth; and another exists in Java, *O. hippocrepis*, Wagler,
probably *coronatus* of Swainson.   Bonaparte also gives *O. Horsfieldii* from Java (*galbula* of Horsfield); and *O. Broderipi*, from
Sumbava, figured in the Ill. P. Z. S. for 1850.

3rd, Black-headed Orioles (*Oriolus* of Bonaparte for the Indian
species, and *Baruffius*, Bon., for the African ones).

There are two races of Black-headed Orioles in India; and, as
they are well marked apart, and, constantly, as it would appear, I
shall follow Prince Bonaparte in separating them.

472. Oriolus melanocephalus, Linnæus.

Blyth, Cat. 1297 (in part)—Horsf., Cat. 411 (in part)—O.
maderaspatanus, Franklin (the young)—O. McCoshii, Tickell,
(the young)—*Pilk*, and *Zardak*, H— *Pirola*, at Goruckpore.

THE BENGAL BLACK-HEADED ORIOLE.

Descr.—Whole head, neck and breast in front, deep black;
rest of the plumage rich dark yellow above, slightly paler beneath,
on the lower abdomen and under tail-coverts; wings black, with a
small yellow band formed by the primary coverts; tertiaries
with the tips and outer webs pale yellow; the secondaries also
broadly tipped with yellow, gradually diminishing in extent to
the last primaries, some of which are tipped and edged with
yellow; tail pale yellow, the two central feathers with a broad
black band about half inch, tipped with yellow, the next pair with
barely one inch of black, and the yellow tip nearly $\frac{1}{2}$ inch; the
next pair with a narrow and sometimes interrupted black band about
the terminal third, and the three outer pair on each side nearly
wholly yellow; the outer pair with an occasional smear of black on
the outer margin; all the tail feathers with black shafts diminishing
in intensity towards the outermost feathers.

Bill pale lake-red; legs plumbeous; irides rich red. Length
$9\frac{1}{2}$ inches; extent 16; wing $5\frac{1}{2}$; tail $3\frac{1}{2}$; bill at front 1; tarsus $\frac{3}{4}$.

The young bird has the forehead yellow, the head more or less blackish, the neck white with blackish streaks, the belly yellow with longitudinally dark streaks, and the yellow duller in tint.

This black-headed Oriole is found throughout Bengal and Northern India generally, extending into Central India, and spreading to all the countries to the eastward, Assam, Burmah, and the Malay peninsula. In the south of India and Ceylon it is replaced by the next bird. It frequents both forests, and gardens and groves; is a lively and noisy bird, constantly flying from tree to tree, and uttering its loud mellow whistle, which Sundevall has put into musical form.

It feeds chiefly on fruit, especially on the figs of the Banian, Peepal, and other *Fici*, and it is said also to eat blossoms and buds. Buchanan Hamilton states that he found the nest, made of bamboo leaves and the fibres that invest the top of the Cocoanut and other palms, in March, with the young unfledged.

473. Oriolus ceylonensis, BONAPARTE

O. melanocephalus, BLYTH, Cat. 1297 (in part) JERDON, Cat. 98—SYKES, Cat. 59—*Konda-vanga pandu*, Tel.

THE SOUTHERN BLACK-HEADED ORIOLE.

Descr.—Head and neck deep black ; rest of the plumage rich yellow ; wings black ; the wing-spot formed by the tips of the primary coverts smaller than in the last ; the tertiaries only tipped with yellow ; and the black on the tail of greater extent especially on the central feathers.

Bill, legs, and irides as in the last.

This species is found in Southern India and Ceylon, but how far it extends towards Central India, I am not aware. Its note, as might have been expected, is very similar to that of its Northern congener. It is very common in the Malabar Coast, more so indeed than *O. Kundoo*, but is comparatively rare in the Carnatic, and almost unknown in the bare Deccan.

Other black-headed Orioles from the East are *O. xanthonotus*, Horsfield, from Malacca and Java, the smallest of the genus, placed as a separate division by Bonaparte, under the sub-generic

name of *Xanthonotus;* and *O. Philippensis,* Gray : and there are
several similarly colored Orioles in Africa.

4th, Marroon Orioles, *Psarolophus,* J. and S.

The only bird of this division is a remarkably plumaged species,
and has been considered to belong to a different type, but it is
essentially an Oriole. The glistening maronne color recals that of
some of the American *Ampelidæ* (*Cotinga pompadoura*); and this
remarkable variation of color, from the usual yellow tints of most of
the group, serves, in some manner, to show us that the glistening
blue of the *Irena* is not an unique anomaly in the coloration of this
family.

474. Oriolus Traillii, VIGORS.

Pastor, apud VIGORS, P. Z. S., 1831—GOULD, Cent. Him.
Birds, pl. 35—BLYTH., Cat. 1296—HORSF., Cat. 419—Psarolophus
Traillii, JARD. and SELBY, Ill. Orn. 2nd Ser., pl. 26—*Melambok,*
Lepch.— *Tania-pia,* Bhot.

THE MARONNE ORIOLE.

Descr.—Whole head, neck, and wings, glossy black; the rest
of the plumage, both above and below, glistening maroon red; tail
dull Indian red.

The young bird is brown above, darker on the head, and the tail
red; beneath sullied white, with numerous longitudinal brown streaks.

Bill bluish; legs dark plumbeous; irides pale yellow. Length
$11\frac{1}{2}$ inches; wing 6; tail $4\frac{1}{2}$; bill at front 1; tarsus $1\frac{1}{10}$.

This curiously plumaged Oriole is found in the eastern part of
the Himalayas, Nepal, and Sikhim, extending into Assam, Arrakan,
and Tenasserim. It is found from 2,000 feet, or so, to at least
7,000 feet, generally in small flocks, keeping to high trees, and has
a fine loud mellow call. I found those I examined to have partaken
of caterpillars only. In the young bird the iris is yellow-brown.

Other genera placed in this sub-family are *Mimeta* and *Sphe-
cotheres,* from Australia, and the Oceanic region. Some species,
formerly ranked under the former genus, are now considered to be
true Orioles. *Sericulus* is classed by some among the Orioles, but
is more generally considered to belong to the Birds of Paradise.

Oriolia, from Madagascar, probably belongs also to this family, and shows some affinity in its coloring to *O. Traillii*.

Fam. SYLVIADÆ.

Of small size mostly; bill slender; wing usually somewhat lengthened, and tail moderate or short; tarsus long; feet moderate.

The family of Warblers comprise several distinct groups which I have classed together, partly in accordance with Gray and Hors-field, and partly because I consider that the birds thus arranged form a parallel series of equal value with the Thrushes, Shrikes, and the other dentirostral families, in all of which there are certain marked differences of type. They agree in being mostly of small size, some very minute, and none equalling a Thrush; the wings of most are moderate or somewhat long, short and rounded in one sub-family; the tail is usually moderate or rather short, lengthened in a few; the tarsus of all is moderately long and stout, and the feet moderate, suited in some for perching, in others for terrestrial habits. The majority feed solely on insects, a very few on flower-buds, and even on fruit. They may be divided into the following sub-families :—

1.—*Saxicolinæ*, Stone-chats and Wheat-ears.

2.—*Ruticillinæ*, Redstarts and Bush-chats.

3.—*Calamoherpinæ*, Grass Warblers.

4.—*Drymoicinæ*, Wren Warblers.

5.—*Phylloscopinæ*, Tree Warblers.

6.—*Sylviinæ*, Grey Warblers.

7.—*Motacillinæ*, Wagtails and Pipits.

Prince Bonaparte divides them into *Saxicolinæ*, including our two first sub-families; *Calamoherpinæ*, comprising our two next; *Sylviinæ*, with our 5th and 6th; and *Motacillinæ*.

Although the chain of affinities is not uninterrupted in this grouping, yet it appears, upon the whole, that this is not far from the natural order of succession. The Stone-chats and Wagtails perhaps ought to be placed next each other, as they have various affinities of color and habits. Some of the larger species appear to grade into the Rock-thrushes; a few have affinities for the Timaline Thrushes; several approach the Saxicoline Fly-catchers; others

P

perhaps join the Titmice in the next family; and lastly the Pipits are barely separable from the Larks, a conirostral group.

Sub-fam. SAXICOLINÆ.

Bill stouter, more depressed at the base than in the other sub-families; wings moderate or somewhat long; tail moderate in most, short in some, long in a very few; tarsus moderately long, stout; feet moderate, fitted for terrestrial habits; claws slightly curved.

The *Saxicolinæ* are a group of ground birds, of solitary habits, frequenting in general open and rocky ground, and affecting the neighbourhood of man; a few however being more sylvan, and courting concealment. The song of most is pleasing, very fine in a few, and they are exceedingly pugnacious. They nestle on banks, or rocks, or holes in buildings, occasionally in a hole of a tree; and the eggs of most are bluish white, with a few dark spots. The plumage of many is pied, and the sexes usually differ more or less in colour. The young are usually spotted like the young of Thrushes. They comprise some of the largest birds of the present family, and Bonaparte unites with them some of the Rock-thrushes of the Old World. They are chiefly inhabitants of the Old World, many of them being migratory; but there is a peculiar group in Australia, and another in America. They approach the Wagtails on one side, and certainly grade into the next sub-family, *Ruticillinæ.*

Gen. COPSYCHUS, Wagler.

Syn. *Gryllivora,* Sw.—*Dahila,* Hodgs.

Char.—Bill moderately long and strong, straight, tip slightly bent, distinctly notched; rictal bristles almost absent; nostrils large, exposed, basal; wings moderate, 4th and 5th quills longest, 3rd nearly equal to them; tail rather long, graduated, or with the six central feathers equal, the outer ones graduated; tarsus moderately long, stout, nearly entire; feet moderate, middle toe long, hind toe and claw moderate; claws slightly curved.

475. **Copsychus saularis,** LINN.

Gracula, apud LINNÆUS—BLYTH, Cat. 970—HORSF., Cat. 422 —SYKES, Cat. 62—Gryllivora intermedia, SWAINSON, and JERDON

Cat. 101—Dahila docilis, Hodgs.—*Dayar*, or *Dayal*, H. and Beng.
—*Peddu nalanchi*, Tel., also *Sarela-gadu*, *i. e.*, the Pict—*Zannid-pho*, Lepch.

THE MAGPIE-ROBIN.

Descr.—Head, neck, breast, body above, and wings, black, glossed blue on all parts except the wings; abdomen, vent, and under tail-coverts white, the four outer tail-feathers on each side, white.

The female is duller black than the male, and somwhat ashy on the breast. The young birds have the breast dusky with ruddy spots, the upper surface olive-brown turning to slaty.

Bill and legs black; irides brown. Length $8\frac{1}{2}$ inches; wing 4; tail $3\frac{5}{10}$; extent $11\frac{1}{2}$; bill at front $\frac{11}{10}$; tarsus $1\frac{1}{8}$.

The Magpie-robin is found throughout all India, from the Himalayas to Cape Comorin and Ceylon; and eastwards to Arrakan and Tenasserim. Hutton says that at Mussooree it occurs up to 5,000 feet. It is rare near Darjeeling, and I never saw it above 3,000 feet. It affects chiefly wooded districts, but does not inhabit the deep jungles. Towards the South of India it is less familiar than it is in the North, for in Central India, Bengal &c., it is often seen feeding close to houses. It is generally seen alone or in pairs, usually seeks its prey on the ground from a low perch, often hopping a few steps to pick up an insect. When it returns to its perch, it generally elevates its tail and often utters a pleasing warble. Though it frequently raises and depresses its tail, both when perched and on the ground, I cannot say that I have observed the Wagtail-like flirtation of its tail noted by Hodgson, or that it throws its tail back till it nearly touches its head, as Layard has seen. Towards the evening it may often be seen near the top of some tolerably large tree, or other elevated perch, pouring forth its song. I have always found its food to consist of insects of various kinds, small grasshoppers, beetles, worms, &c. Hodgson asserts that in winter they like unripe vetches, and such like; but this is quite opposed to the usual habits of this group. It breeds generally in thick bushes, or hedges; some-times in a hole in a bank or tree, and occasionally in a hole in a wall, or on the rafter of a house. The nest is made of roots and grass; and the eggs, four in number, are bluish white, or pale bluish, with pale brown spots and blotches. Layard says that the eggs are bright blue, and Hutton that they are carneous cream color, but these observers must, I think, have been mistaken in the identity of the owner of the nest.

The Dayal is often caged, as well for its song, as for its pugnacious qualities, which, according to Hodgson, are made use of to capture others. " Fighting these tame birds," says Hodgson, " is a favorite amusement with the rich (in Nepal), nor can any race of game-cocks combat with more energy and resolution than do these birds. Latham called it the *Dial* bird from its native name, and Linnæus, apparently thinking that it had some connection with a sundial, called it *solaris*, by *lapsus pennæ, saularis*. I may here state that in my Catalogue published in 1839, I called it the Magpie-robin, by which name Mr. Layard says it is now known in Ceylon.

A nearly allied race is found in Ceylon, *C. ceylonensis*, Sclater, P. Z. S., 1861, p. 186 (*brevirostris*, apud Blyth); *C. mindanensis*, in Malacca, Siam and China; and *C. amœnus*, Horsf. (*brevirostris*, Swains.) in Java; and these are all representatives of our Indian species; besides which there are *C. luzoniensis*, Kittlitz, in the Philippines, and *C. pluto*, Temm., in Borneo.

Gen. KITTACINCLA, Gould.

Char.—Bill more slender than in the last; tail very long, graduated; wings slightly more rounded; tarsus slender, pale; lateral toes very short.

This form is considered by some not to be distinct from the last, but the few structural points noted above, its more slender form, retired habits, and the fact of there being several species, exhibiting all these characters, from various parts of the Indian region, lead me to keep it distinct.

476. **Kittacincla macroura**, GMEL.

Turdus, apud GMELIN—BLYTH, Cat. 968—HORSF., Cat. 425—SYKES, Cat. 61—Gryllivora longicauda, SWAINSON—JERDON, Cat. 102—*Shama*, H.—*Poda nalanchi*, Tel., also *Tonka nalanchi*.

THE SHAMA.

Descr.—Head, neck, back, wing-coverts, breast, and tail, glossy black; rump white; wings dull black; outer tail feathers broadly tipped with white; breast, belly, and under tail-coverts deep chesnut.

Bill black; legs pale fleshy; irides deep brown. Length 12 inches; wing 3¾; tail nearly 8; bill at front ¾; tarsus 1.

The female has the colors less pure and duller than the male.

This most charming songster is found over all India where there are sufficiently dense or lofty jungles, and it never affects cultivated country, however well wooded.* It is common in all Malabar, especially in the upland districts, as in the Wynaad; more rare in the Eastern Gháts; and not unfrequent in all the jungles of Central India to Midnapore and Cuttack. It also frequents all the sub-Himalayan forests, and extends to the hill tracts of Assam, Sylhet, Burmah, and Malacca, as also to Ceylon.

The Shama frequents the densest thickets, and is very partial to thick bamboo jungles. It is almost always solitary, perches on low branches, and hops to the ground to secure a small grasshopper or other insect. When alarmed, it flies before you from tree to tree at no great height. Its song is chiefly heard in the evening, just before and after sunset. It is a most gushing melody, of great power, surpassed by no Indian bird. In confinement it imitates the notes of other birds, and of various animals, with ease and accuracy. It is caught in great number and caged for its song. Many are brought from the Nepal Terai to Monghyr, chiefly young birds. It is the practice throughout India to cover the cages of singing birds with cloth, and in some places a fresh piece of cloth is added every year. The birds certainly sing away readily when thus caged, but not more so perhaps, than others freely exposed. The Shama is usually fed on a paste made of parched chenna mixed with the yolk of hard-boiled eggs, and it appears to thrive well on this diet, if a few maggots or insects are given occasionally. It will also eat pieces of raw meat in lieu of insects.

A new species has lately been discovered in the Andaman Islands, *K. albiventris*, Blyth; there is another from Labuan, *K. Stricklandi*, Mottl. and Dillwyn; and a fourth species has quite

---

* I can scarcely believe that this is Mr. Philipps' Shama, which, says he, in the N. W. P., may be seen perched on walls, and building in houses.

recently been described by Sclater, P. Z. S., 1861, p. 187, *Copsychus suavis* from Borneo, which has the tail of a *Copsychus*, and the colours and form of *Kittacincla*.

Gen. MYIOMELA, Hodgson.

Syn. *Muscisylvia*, Hodgs.—*Notodela*, Lesson, apud Blyth.

Char.—Bill short, tolerably slender, compressed, slightly bending at the tip and notched; rictus very feebly bristled; wings rather long, ample, reaching half way down the tail; 5th quill longest; tail moderate, broad, very slightly rounded; tarsi rather long, smooth; toes moderate, slender; claws gracile, longish.

This genus has the general structure of *Copsychus*, but less robust in form, with a more even tail, a smaller bill, and larger feet. Blyth considers this form barely distinct from *Ruticilla*, to which it certainly has affinities; but its general structure, coloration, and sylvan habits, induce me to consider it as more nearly allied to the present group.

477. Myiomela leucura, HODGSON.

Muscisylvia, apud HODGSON, Ann. Nat. Hist., 1845—J. A. S., XIII.,138—BLYTH, Cat. 971—HORSF.,Cat.426—*Mangshia*, Lepch.

THE WHITE-TAILED BLUE-CHAT.

Descr.—General color dark blackish indigo-blue; forehead, over the eyes, and shoulder, bright smalt-blue; alars and caudals dull black, with the base of the outer web of the three tail feathers on each side, next the outer ones, white, this white increasing outwardly; a concealed white spot on the sides of the neck, formed by part of the outer webs of some of the feathers. The female is rufescent brown, paler beneath; the quills dusky, edged with deep ferruginous; tail the same; the base of the feathers white, as in the male.

Bill black; feet brown-black; irides dark brown. Length $7\frac{1}{2}$ inches; extent 12; wing $3\frac{3}{4}$; tail $3\frac{1}{4}$; bill at front $\frac{9}{16}$; tarsus $1\frac{1}{8}$. The wingsreach to within $1\frac{1}{4}$ inches or so from the end of the tail.

The White-tailed Blue chat is found throughout the Himalayas, from Mussooree to Sikhim, and also in the Khasia hills. It affects high altitudes, being found from 5,000 to nearly 9,000 feet. It frequents dense underwood, or very thick forest, perching low, and seeking its food chiefly on the ground. I have found only insects of various kinds in its stomach. Hodgson, indeed, says that it feeds equally on pulpy berries. It is very shy, and from the density of the cover it frequents, it is difficult to observe closely.

From its tone of coloring, the white neck spot, and especially the mode of coloration of the female, it appears to me to be somewhat allied to *Niltava*, and the Lepchas brought me a nest and eggs, alleged to belong to this bird, exactly resembling those of *Niltava sundara*, but they may have been mistaken in the identity of the bird, the females being so like each other.

A somewhat allied species is found in Pegu, *Notodela diana*, of Lesson, in Belanger's voyage, and *Eupetes cærulescens*, Temm., P. C. 574, from New Guinea, appears to me also related.

The next bird noticed is a somewhat anomalous form, albeit having some distant affinities for the last species.

Gen. GRANDALA, Hodgson.

Char.—Bill moderate, slender, straight, phœnicuran, but slightly depressed at the base; nostrils oval, free, in the front of a large fossa; gape perfectly smooth; wings long, ample and firm, 1st quill spurious, 2nd longest; the tertials only half the length of the primaries; tail moderate, firm, slightly emarginate; tarsus longish, entire; toes long, slender, suitable for progression on the ground; hind toe rather short.

This is a very peculiar genus. Hodgson says that " it has the general structure of a Thrush with the wings greatly enlarged, and a sylvian bill." Blyth says that it is allied to the Wheat-ears. It differs from all the other members of this family by its excessively long wings. I was at one time inclined to class it not far from *Hartlaubius*, Bonaparte, an African genus of *Sturnidæ*, judging from the brief characters given by the Prince, and the long wings and sturnideous habits of the only species, as noticed by some observers.

478. Grandala cœlicolor, HODGSON.

J. A. S., XII., 447, with fig.—BLYTH, Cat. 972—HORSF., Cat. 427—G. schistacea, HODGSON, the young female.

THE LONG-WINGED BLUE CHAT.

Descr.—Whole head and body glistening externally with brilliant dark smalt-blue, but the feathers black internally; wings and tail black. The female is sordid slaty, or blue-black, with a brown smear; alars and caudals darker, and a white bar through the wing; the feathers of the lower parts striped down the shafts with luteous white.

Bill and feet jet black; irides dark brown. Length of male 9 inches; wing 6; tail $3\frac{3}{4}$; bill at front $\frac{9}{10}$; tarsus $1\frac{1}{8}$. The female is considerably smaller than the male.

This magnificent bird inhabits the Northern region of Nepal, or the Cachar, in under spots near the snows. It is stated by Hodgson to be solitary in its habits, and that insects and gravel were found in its stomach. It has also been found in the North-west Himalayas, near the snowy region, and Mr. Blyth was informed by Lieutenant Speke, that he observed it in flocks, with a rapid flight like that of the Starlings.

The next group, from its slender, and slightly curved beak, was formerly classed under the heterogeneous *Leos* of Temminck; but its place in this family is now universally conceded.

Gen. THAMNOBIA, Swainson.

Char.—Bill slender, very slightly widened at the base, the sides compressed, slightly arched throughout: tip deflected, not notched; gape smooth; wings short, rounded, the 4th and 5th quills longest, the primaries hardly exceeding the tertiaries and secondaries, which are broad; tail moderate, broad, much rounded; tarsus long, the feet moderate, inner toe much shorter than the outer; hind toe short, all the claws slightly curved.

I have no doubt myself of the propriety of placing this genus among the Stone-chats or Robins. Blyth, at one time, from observation of a caged specimen, held that it was a Wren. Swainson was the first naturalist who, from specimens alone, with great acumen fixed its true position; which subsequent observations of its habits have certainly confirmed. The Telingas, it will be observed, call both *Copsychus* and *Thamnobia* by the same name, with a specific prefix. There are two species known in India, one from the south, the other from the north.

479. **Thamnobia fulicata,** Linn.

Motacilla, apud Linnæus—Jerdon, Cat. 103—Blyth, Cat. 967—Horsf., Cat. 428—Ixos, apud Sykes, Cat. 72—Tham. leucoptera, Swains.—*Kalchuri,* **H.**—*Nalanchi,* Tel.—*Wannatikurari,* Tam., *i. e.,* Washerman-bird.

The Indian Black Robin.

Descr.—Male, shining deep black, with a white wing spot; the middle of the abdomen and the under tail-coverts deep chesnut. The female is dull sooty-brown, darkened on the wings and tail, the under tail-coverts chesnut.

Length 6 inches; wing $2\frac{8}{10}$ to 3; tail $2\frac{3}{4}$; tarsus $1\frac{1}{16}$; bill at front barely $\frac{1}{2}$ inch. Bill black; irides dark brown.

This well known bird is found throughout Southern India as far north as the Taptee on the West, but only extending to the Godavery on the East. North of this it is replaced by the next species.

Its familiar habits well entitle it to the name of Indian Robin. It is mostly found about villages, pagodas, old buildings, and mud walls, often perching on the roofs of houses and tops of walls, and feeding in verandahs, or occasionally even entering houses. It is, however, not confined to the vicinity of houses or villages, but is very common on rocky and stony hills, and in groves of palmyra or date palms. It is generally seen single, or in pairs, feeds on the ground, on which it hops with great agility, frequently pursuing and capturing several insects before it re-seats itself on its perch either on a house or on a neighbouring tree or bush. At all times, but especially when feeding, it has the habit of jerking up its tail by successive efforts, so as almost to overshadow its head. The male has a very sweet little song, which it warbles forth from the top of a wall or low tree, and it is occasionally caged. It builds among rocks, on holes in houses or mud walls; also low down on the stem of palm trees, where the broken stalk of the frond juts out from the trunk: Burgess says, ' under tussocks of grass.' On one occasion a pair built their nest, at Jalnah, among a heap of stones raised from a well. It was being deepened, and they made their nest during the time the rock was being

Q

blasted, and continued the incubation till the young ones were hatched, when it was accidentally destroyed. The nest is made with grass, roots, and hairs; and the eggs, four or five in number, are bluish white, spotted with purplish brown.

480. **Thamnobia Cambaiensis**, LATH.

Sylvia, apud LATHAM—BLYTH, Cat. 966—HORSF., Cat. 429.— M. fulicata, apud TICKELL—Th. scapularis, HODGS.—Saxicoloides erythrurus, LESSON (the female), and Cinnyricinclus melasoma, LESSON (male.)

THE BROWN-BACKED INDIAN ROBIN.

Descr.—The male has the back, wings, and upper tail-coverts, dusky olive-brown; the wings and the tail black; the lores, ear-coverts, and lower plumage also black; a white wing spot as in the last; the vent and centre of belly deep chesnut. The female is sooty-brown throughout, except the chesnut beneath.

Dimension of the last nearly, or a trifle smaller. The Brown-backed Robin is found throughout all Central and Northern India, up to the base of the Himalayas, and as far as the Punjab. It is found at Nagpore, Mhow, Saugor, Chota Nagpore, and Midnapore, and thence throughout northwards. It differs in nowise in its habits from the last. Theobald found the nest in holes of trees and banks, made of grass, and almost invariably with cast snake-skins; and the eggs were greenish-white, ringed and spotted with pale reddish.

To this series of the Shama, Dayal, and Robins, belong several African forms, but it does not appear to be developed further in Malayana. *Thamnolœa, Cercotrichas,* and *Dromolœa* of Cabanis are African groups, a few of them coloured like the Shamas, others like the Dayals, and some more like *Thamnobia,* to which last genus several African birds are referred. *Turdus Madagascariensis,* figd. Pl. Enl. 557, 1, appears very like a *Copsychus.*

The next group, that of the Chats, have the bill short and stout, a short tail, and wings of mean length. They frequent bushy places and cultivated land, occasionally seize insects on the wing, and sometimes sing while hovering in the air.

Gen. Pratincola, Koch.

Syn. *Rubetra*, Gray.

Char.—Bill short, straight, somewhat wide at base, strongly curving at tip, which is faintly notched; nostrils concealed by tufts of hairs and plumes; strong rictal bristles; wings moderate, 4th, 5th, and 6th quills nearly equal and longest; tail moderate, nearly even; tarsus moderate, longish; feet moderate; claws slightly curved, slender.

This genus has been instituted for the Whin-chat and some allied birds, which are usually smaller than the true *Saxicolæ*, and differ in some other points, and they more affect wooded and cultivated country. It includes two or three minor divisions. The first and third peculiar to India, the second common to Europe, Africa, and Asia, and containing several representative species.

481. Pratincola caprata, Linn.

Motacilla, apud Linnæus—Mot-sylvatica, Tickell—Sax. fruti-cola, Horsf.—S. bicolor (male), and S. erythropygia (female), Sykes, Cat. 90 and 92—Jerdon, Cat. 105 (in part)—Blyth, Cat. 995—Horsf., Cat. 433—Sax-melaleuca, Hodgson—*Pidha*, and *Kala pidha*, H.—*Kumpa nalanchi*, Tel., *i. e.*, Bush Robin.

The White-winged Black Robin.

Descr.—Male black; a longitudinal band on the wings, the rump and the upper tail-coverts, and the middle of the lower part of the abdomen, vent, and under tail-coverts, white. When newly moulted, the black is fringed with brown edgings, which gradually get worn away. Female dusky brown, the feathers edged paler, with a rufous rump and upper tail-coverts; beneath pale reddish brown, albescent on the throat and vent; abdomen slightly streaked; vent and under tail-coverts tinged with rufous.

Length about 5 inches; wing $2\frac{3}{4}$; tail $2\frac{2}{10}$; bill at front $\frac{3}{8}$; tarsus $\frac{7}{8}$.

Bill black; legs brown-black, irides deep brown.

This Bush-chat is common over all India, frequenting bushy ground, hedges, gardens, and the like, but not found in forests or

jungle. It extends to Burmah and the Malayan countries, and
even to the Philippines. It has the usual habits of the tribe, dart-
ing down to the ground from its perch, usually on the top of a bush
or branch of a tree, and, having secured an insect, returning to
its seat. It has a pleasant song, which Blyth compares to that
of the English Robin, but more uniformly plaintive. It is rather
a favorite cage-bird in Bengal. Tickell got the nest in a bush,
made of grass, with three pale greenish white eggs, sprinkled
equally throughout, with brown spots.

482. **Pratincola atrata**, Blyth.

J. A. S. XX., 177—Jerdon, Cat. 105 (in part).

The Neilgherry Black Robin.

Descr.—Very similar to the last, larger. No gradation of size
has been observed between this and the last species. Length $6\frac{1}{4}$
inches; wing $3\frac{1}{4}$; tail $2\frac{1}{4}$; tarsus $\frac{9}{10}$.

In my Catalogue I did not distinguish this specifically from the
last, but called attention to the difference of size between it and
the low country one, *P. caprata*. This species is very common
on the Neilgherries as well as the upland hilly regions of Ceylon,
frequenting the skirts of woods, bushes, and gardens; and it gets
the name of Hill-robin from its familiar habits. I have seen the
nest of this bird several times, always on banks, on the road side,
neatly made of moss, roots, and hairs, and with usually three or
four eggs, bluish-white, with brown specks and spots.

The next group comprises the Whin-chat of Europe and several
allied species.

483. **Pratincola Indica**, Blyth.

J. A. S. XVI., 129—Blyth, Cat. 997—Horsf., Cat. 434—
Sax. rubicola, Sykes, Cat. 89—Jerdon, Cat. 104—P. saturatior,
Hodgson—*Adavi kampa nalanchi*, Tel., *i. e.*, Jungle Bush-robin
and *Adavi-kampa-jitta*, *i. e.*, Jungle Bramble-bird.

The Indian Bush-chat.

Descr.—The male, in summer plumage, has the whole head and
neck, back, wings, and tail, black; the back and wings edged with

pale rufous; wing spot, rump, and upper tail-coverts. white; breast and lower parts, bright ferruginous. deep on the breast, paler on the flanks and belly, and albescent on the vent and under tail-coverts; a demi-collar of white almost meets on the nape, dividing the black of the head and neck. In winter plumage the black is almost replaced by earthy brown; the rump and upper tail-coverts are ferruginous brown; the lores, ear-coverts, and chin, however, are always more or less black; the white wing spot is less prominent; the whole lower parts are dull ferruginous. albescent on the under tail-coverts; and the demi-collar is deficient or rusty. The female resembles the male in winter dress, being brown above, margined with paler brown, and rufescent towards the tail; but the chin and throat are white, and there is a white supercilium. The wing spot too is a little sullied.

Length 5¼ inches; wing 2¾; tail 1¾; tarsus $\frac{9}{10}$; bill at front ⅜. Bill and legs black; irides deep brown.

This species, which was first discriminated by Mr. Blyth, differs from the English bird chiefly by the paler tint of the lower plumage, the deeper hue being confined to the breast, by the white demi-collar extending further backwards, in the black of the throat not descending so low in the breast, and in the female having the chin and throat white, instead of pale brown. The wing, too, is somewhat longer than in the European bird. Strickland once considered the Indian bird identical with his *P. pastor* from Africa, but Horsfield in his Catalogue places the two as distinct.

The Indian Whin-chat is only a winter visitant to India, coming in about the end of September or beginning of October. It is found throughout all India, extending to Assam, Burmah, and Tenasserim, but has not yet been noticed in Ceylon. Buchanan Hamilton in his MSS. Notes, says that in the Bhagulpore and Gya districts it remains all the year, building in thickets of reeds, but he has doubtless not discriminated it from the next species, which I found a resident in those districts. It is probably Pallas' *Mot. rubicola*, of Central Asia, which breeds, he says, in deserted rat-holes, laying its eggs on the bare ground, or under fallen trees. It frequents bushes in the plains, hedges, and cultivated fields, but avoids the vicinity of villages; hence called the *Jungle Bramble-robin* by the Telingas, in contra-distinction to the familiar *P. caprata*. It feeds on various insects, taking them on the ground from a low perch. Many of the males have assumed their summer plumage before they leave the North of India. I have seen it in every part of the country except the more wooded parts of the Malabar Coast, and it is never seen in thick or lofty jungle.

484. **Pratincola leucura,** Blyth.

J. A. S. XVI., 474—Blyth, Cat. 998—*Khar-pidda,* H., at Monghyr.

The White-tailed Bush-chat.

Descr.—Male, above black with the usual white wing patch; the breast bright rufous in the centre; sides of neck, breast, and lower parts, pure white; the four outer tail-feathers wholly white on their inner webs, except the tip of the two outermost; and the pair next the centrals (which are wholly black) have the greater portion of the inner web also white. The female is brown above, the feathers edged paler, with a smaller white wing-spot, but no white on the tail; beneath earthy white, tinged rufous on the breast. In winter the dorsal feathers are more or less edged with brown.

Length 5 inches; wing $2\frac{1}{2}$; tail 2; bill at front $\frac{7}{16}$; tarsus $1\frac{3}{16}$.

This White-tailed Bush-chat, till lately, had only been procured in Sindh, whence it was sent by Sir A. Burnes to the Museum of the Asiatic Society, and it is figured in his drawings. I found it far from rare at Thyet-myo in Upper Burmah, frequenting grassy churrs on the Irrawaddy, but never the low jungles that lined the banks. Somewhat to my surprise I found it most abundant in the Gangetic valley, from Rajmehal to Monghyr, frequenting fields and long grasses. It is a permanent resident, and breeds here; for I found the young birds just flown in April, but did not succeed in procuring the nest. On referring to Buchanan Hamilton's MSS. Notes I find that he has confounded it with the last, for, writing of *rubicola*, he says that he found them breeding in the Bhagulpore and Gya districts, making their nests among thick tufts of grass, but whether attached to the grass, or on the ground, he does not state. He gives the native name as *Kat-pidda*.

485. **Pratincola insignis,** HODGSON.

J. A. S. XVI., 129.

THE LARGE BUSH-CHAT.

Descr.—Male (in summer dress) above black; throat, sides of the neck, upper tail-coverts, a large patch on the wings, the base of the primaries, and most of the large coverts, white; the breast bright ferruginous; belly white, slightly tinged with ferruginous.

Bill and feet black. Length 6½ inches; wing 3½; tail 2¼; tarsus 1⅛.

It is very similar to *P. rubicola*, but larger, differs in having a white throat, and also in the much larger wing spot. This species of *Pratincola* has only as yet been found in Nepal, and probably comes from the most Northern districts, perhaps, as Mr. Blyth hints, from Tibet. I did not observe it at Darjeeling.

Besides the *Pratincola rubicola*, and *P. rubetra* of Europe, *P. pastor*, of Africa (placed as *sybilla*, Gmelin, in Bonaparte's Conspectus,) *P. Hemprichii*, Ehrenb., and *P. salax*, Verreaux, also from Africa, belong to this genus and section.

The next species differs slightly in its mode of coloration, longer tail, which is slightly rounded, stronger bill, and short tarsi.

486. **Pratincola ferrea,** HODGSON.

J. A. S. XVI., 129—BLYTH, Cat. 1000—HORSF., Cat. 436— *Sarrak-chak-pho*, Lepch.

THE DARK GRAY BUSH-CHAT.

Descr.—Male, above darkish ashy grey; the feathers centred with blackish, lighter and less streaked on the rump; lores and ear-coverts black, and a white supercilium; tail black, with a narrow edging of white externally, and the outer pair of feathers (which are ¼ inch shorter than the centre ones) are partially albescent; wings blackish, with white wing-spot usually concealed;

secondaries slightly edged with whitish; beneath white, tinged with earthy rufescent on the breast and abdomen. The female is wholly brown above, passing to ferruginous on the upper tail-coverts, and partially on the tail-feathers; beneath, paler earthy brown, rufescent on the flanks and lower tail-coverts, and whitish on the throat.

Bill black; feet brown-black; irides brown. Length 5¾ inches; wing 2⅝; tail 2½; bill at front $\frac{7}{10}$; tarsus nearly 1.

The Grey Bush-chat is found throughout the whole extent of the Himalayas, and is tolerably common about Darjeeling. It frequents the skirts of forests and brushwood, perches on shrubs or low trees, and descends to the ground to pick up insects. It also occasionally takes one from a leaf. It has a very pleasing song; breeds in holes in banks, making a nest of moss, leaves, or grass and roots; and lays 3 or 4 eggs, pale blue, with numerous pale brownish spots.

The next bird is somewhat related in form to *Pr. ferrea*, but differs in some points, and especially in its mode of coloration, so that I have thought it necessary to give it separate generic rank.

Gen. RHODOPHILA, Jerdon.

Char.—Much as in *Pratincola*, but the bill longer, deeper, barely depressed at the base; nostrils longitudinal, slightly impended by some nareal tufts; rictus strongly bristled; wing moderate or rather short, rounded; 1st quill short, 2nd, 3rd, and 4th graduated, 4th longest, 5th and 6th nearly equal to it; tail moderate, distinctly rounded; tarsus moderate; feet moderately long, toes slender; hind toe and claw lengthened.

This form approaches that of *Prat. ferrea*, but the bill is still less depressed, and the tail more distinctly rounded. The coloration, too, is peculiar, as are its thicket-loving habits; and the sexes, moreover, are presumed to be alike.

487. Rhodophila melanoleuca, Jerdon.

THE BLACK AND WHITE BUSH-CHAT.

Above, with lores, and cheeks pure glossy black; beneath pure white.

Bill and legs black; irides dark brown. Length 5½ inches; wing 2⅝; tail 2½; bill at front $\frac{7}{16}$; tarsus not quite ⅞.

I first procured this bird in dense swampy rose-thickets in Purneah, near the banks of the Ganges, when beating for game; and subsequently observed it along the reedy edge of some of the rivers in Eastern Bengal and Cachar. Mr. W. Blanford obtained it in Burmah, in long Elephant grass, and I doubt not it will be found in similar situations throughout Lower Bengal and the countries to the Eastward. It is with difficulty dislodged from the thick coverts it frequents; and quickly returns to its shelter. It is probably, from the structure of its feet, a ground feeder, like the rest of this family.

It is possible that some of the Oceanic *Saxicolæ* of Prince Bonaparte, which he named *Oreicola*, may belong to the same type. One of these is *Sax. melanoleuca*, Müll., black above and white beneath, but this has a white wing-spot, and ear-spot. Another is *S. luctuosa*, Müll., black above and white beneath, but the wings varied with white; and *S. pyrrhonota*, Müll., has the back rufous. All three are from Timor. *Lanius silens*, Shaw, of which Bonaparte makes his genus *Sigelus*, perhaps should come near this last form, which appears to have some affinities for *Curruca*.

The next group are rather larger birds than the Chats, with longer and more slender bills, longer wings, and a somewhat square tail. They chiefly belong to the more barren regions of Asia and Africa, frequenting the open plains, and most of them are migratory in India, breeding probably in Central Asia. They breed on the ground in some convenient nook, laying four or five eggs, bluish white, with ferruginous speckles.

Gen. SAXICOLA, Bechstein.

Bill moderate, slender, straight and compressed, very slightly inflected, with a blunt notch; nostrils apert; rictal bristles feeble or wanting; wings moderately long, pointed; the 1st short, 2nd half an inch shorter than the 3rd, 4th, and 5th, which are equal and longest; tail moderate, even, or very slightly rounded; tarsus long, strong; feet moderate.

This genus, as here restricted, comprises two groups; one, with pied plumage, of which *S. leucura* of Southern Europe may be

R

considered the type; and the Wheat-ears. Some of the first group are placed by Bonaparte under *Dromolæa* of Cabanis.

488. Saxicola leucuroides, GUERIN.

Mag. de Zool. 1843—S. opistholeuca, STRICKLAND—S. leucura, apud BLYTH, J. A. S. XVI., 137—BLYTH, Cat. 974—figd., JARDINE, Contrib. to Ornithology.

THE INDIAN WHITE-TAILED STONE-CHAT.

Descr.—Sooty black; the thigh coverts, lower abdomen, vent, and under tail-coverts, white; the upper tail-coverts and the greater part of the tail also white, the lateral feathers tipped with black for not quite half an inch, the middle feathers for about ⅓ inch. The female is said to be of a duller and browner hue.

An immature bird described by Blyth formerly as the supposed female, has the head, neck, breast, wings, and two centre tail-feathers, dusky brownish black; a patch of deep black on each jaw; breast, belly, rump, and tail-coverts white, except for about half an inch at the end.

Bill and legs black; irides dark brown. Length 6¼ inches; wing 3¾; tail 2⅝; bill at front ½; tarsus 1.

This species differs from true *S. leucura* (*S. cachinnans,* Temm.), with which it was at first confounded, in being less robust, and the bill and feet smaller; in the lateral tail-feathers being all black tipped, and in the white being less pure.

This fine Stone-chat is not uncommon about Mhow in Central India, in the cold weather, and I have seen it on the banks of the Nerbudda, near Mundleysur, but nowhere else. It frequents bushes on the plains, but also comes into Cantonments, and may be seen seated on the hedges or on the low trees bordering the roads. It descends to the ground to feed on insects, returning to its perch. I saw a plain brown-plumaged bird in company with it, on more than one occasion, but I did not procure it.

This species probably extends throughout the North-West Provinces, having been killed near Agra, and in Sindh. In summer it doubtless migrates to Tibet and Central Asia.

489. Saxicola picata, BLYTH.

J. A. S. XVI., 131—BLYTH, Cat. 75—HORSF., Cat. 439.

THE PIED STONE-CHAT.

Descr.—Whole head, neck, and upper breast, back, and wings, black ; the rump, upper tail-coverts, and all the lower parts from the breast, white ; tail white, except the terminal two-thirds of the two central feathers, and the tips of the others, which are black. Length $6\frac{1}{4}$ to $6\frac{1}{2}$ inches ; wing $3\frac{3}{8}$; tail $2\frac{3}{4}$; bill at front $\frac{1}{2}$; tarsus 1. Bill and legs black.

This species has the black somewhat deeper, and the white purer than in the last, of which it has much the size and proportion.

The pied Stone-chat has only been found in the Upper Provinces of India, and in Sindh; also in Afghanistan. Adams observed it in Sindh, frequenting gardens, and also in the Punjab. It is probably only a winter visitant.

The next bird is very similar, but differs in having the head white instead of black.

490. Saxicola leucomela, PALLAS.

Motacilla, apud PALLAS—BLYTH, Cat 976—HORSF., Cat. 438.

THE WHITE-HEADED STONE-CHAT.

Descr.—Crown of the head greyish white ; the rump and upper tail-coverts, and all the lower parts, from the top of the breast, white ; rest of the upper part, neck, and breast, black ; tail black, with the base of the central feathers, and all the lateral ones, white ; the outer-most tipped with black, and part of the outer-web also black. Young birds have the white cap more or less tinged with dingy greyish brown.

Bill and legs black ; irides dark brown. Length $6\frac{1}{2}$ inches ; wing $3\frac{3}{4}$; tail $2\frac{3}{4}$; bill at front barely $\frac{1}{2}$; tarsus $1\frac{1}{6}$.

This bird differs somewhat from Temminck's *S. leucomela*, (*S. lugens* of Lichtenstein), found in the South of Europe and North Africa, which is said to have the lower abdomen and under tail-coverts rufous. Our bird has been found in the Upper Provinces of Hindostan, during the cold weather only, and is common in Afghanistan. *S. aurita*, Temm., is another European species.

The next group is that of the Wheat-ears, by some separated as *Œnanthe*.

491. **Saxicola œnanthe,** LINN.

Motacilla, apud LINNÆUS—BLYTH, Cat. 980—GOULD, Birds of Europe, pl. 90.

THE WHEAT-EAR.

Descr.—Male, above ashy, with a brown tinge; the rump and upper tail-coverts white, and a white supercilium; lores and eye streak black; wings dusky, edged with brown; tail with the two central feathers black for the terminal two thirds, the rest white; the outer feathers black tipped; under surface pale rusty brown, albescent on the belly and under tail-coverts; under wing-coverts blackish with white edgings.

The female is ashy-brown above, wings dusky brown, tail black tipped. In winter the feathers are broadly edged with rufous, most conspicuous on the wing-coverts and tertiaries.

Length nearly 7 inches, extent 11; wing 4; tail $2\frac{3}{4}$; bill at front not quite half; tarsus more than 1.

The Wheat-ear is found, according to the season, over Europe, Northern Africa, and part of Asia. I got a specimen near Mhow, in the cold whether, and it is known to be found, though rarely, in the Upper Provinces. It is a larger bird than the black-throated Wheat-ear, which it otherwise somewhat resembles, and has a much stronger bill and legs.*

492. **Saxicola deserti,** RUPPELL.

TEMMINCK, Pl. Col. 359—S. atrogularis, BLYTH, J. A. S. XVI., 130—BLYTH, Cat. 977—HORSF., Cat. 440.

THE BLACK-THROATED WHEAT-EAR.

Descr.—Above pale isabelline, greyish on the crown and nape, and a whitish eyebrow; rump and upper tail-coverts buffy white;

---

* The name of Wheat-ear is supposed to be an imitation of its call *wheet-jur*; but Mr. Blyth considers that the English names of Stone-chat and Wheat-ear have been transposed.

tail white at base, the rest black ; chin, throat, lores, and ears, pure black, extending down the sides of the neck to the shoulder; wing black, with a white patch on the bend of the wing ; beneath, pale isabelline, the lower tail-coverts buffy white.

Bill and legs black ; irides brown. Length nearly 7 inches; wing 4 ; tail $2\frac{3}{4}$; tarsus $1\frac{1}{16}$; bill at front $\frac{1}{2}$.

The Black-throated Wheat-ear is nearly affined to *S. stapazina* of Arabia,|S. Europe, and Africa, from which it differs in having the upper parts less rufous, and in the greater extent of the black of the neck. It is common at Mhow, in the cold weather, frequenting stones and bushes in the open plains. It is also tolerably common in the Upper Provinces of India, in Sindh, the Punjab, and Afghanistan.

A nearly allied species is *S. philothamna*, Tristram, figured in the Ibis for 1859. Various other species of this group are found in Africa, some of them extending to the South of Europe, and Western Asia. One, *S. lugubris*, has the white head and black body of *leucomela*, and the tail rufous, like a *Ruticilla*.

The two last species of this series are remarkable for having no white at the base of the tail.

Gen. Cercomela, Bon.

Char.—Bill moderate, slender, straight, tolerably curving at the tip, and barely notched ; rictal bristles small but distinct ; wings as in *Saxicola*, 2nd quill a trifle longer ; tail somewhat lengthened ; feet stout, middle toe not elongated, hind toe rather long.

This form of Stone-chat differs from *Saxicola* in its more sober and dull tints, and in the tail not being partly white.

493. Cercomela melanura, Rupp.

Saxicola, apud Ruppell—Temm., Pl. col. 257, f. 2—Blyth, J. A. S. XVI., 131.

The Black-tailed Rock-chat.

Descr.—Of an uniform ashy brown tint above, paler on the throat and breast, and passing to whitish below ; under tail-coverts white ; the tail and upper coverts black.

Length 6 inches; wing 3⅛; tail 2⅜; tarsus ⅞. Bill blackish;
legs black.

Among the drawings of Sir A. Burnes is one of a Saxicoline bird,
procured, in Sindh, which Mr. Blyth identifies with Rüppell's bird,
which is a native of N. E. Africa and Arabia.

494. Cercomela fusca, BLYTH.

Saxicola, apud BLYTH, J. A. S. XX., 523, and XXIV., 188—
BLYTH, Cat. 1907.

THE BROWN ROCK-CHAT.

Descr.—Above light fuscous brown or rufous olive, tinged
with fawn color on the back; tail dark sepia brown, obsoletely
banded, as seen in a strong light; beneath rufescent fawn or dull
ferruginous.

Bill and legs black, irides deep brown. Length 6½ inches;
wing 3_{10}^{6}; tail 2_{10}^{8}; tarsus 1_{10}^{1}; bill at front nearly ½ inch.

This plain-colored Stone-chat, colored somewhat similarly to
Mirafra phœnicura, is found at Saugor, Bhopal, and Bundlecund,
extending towards Gwalior and the N. W. Provinces. It is
a permanent resident at Saugor, and I have always found it on the
sandstone hills there, among the rocks, cliffs, and loose stones, never
coming to the cultivated ground below, and rarely found on the
trap-hills that occur in close proximity to the others. It feeds
on the ground, on various coleopterous insects, ants, &c. Mr. Blyth
remarks that it approaches in color *Saxicola infuscata* of S. Africa.
It forms an easy transition to the Redstarts, the next group.

Pr. Bonaparte gives two other species of this genus from
Palestine and Arabia, *S. lypura*, Ehr., and *S. asthenia*, Bonap. *S.
erythrœa*, Ehr., from Palestine, should also, perhaps, be classed here.
S. infuscata and *S. baroica*, Smith, from S. Africa, appear allied,
though the Prince makes of them a separate division, *Agricola*.
If *Bradornis* of A. Smith belongs to the *Saxicolinæ*, it probably
should be placed not far from these last birds.

Two other African genera of Saxicoline birds are recorded by
Bonaparte, viz. *Campicola*, and *Pogonocichla*. *Sialia*, containing
the Blue Robins of America, and the Australian genera, *Petroica*
and *Erythrodryas*, appear to appertain to this sub-family, or at

all events to represent them respectively in N. America and
Australia.

We next pass to birds more sylvan in their habit, viz., the
Redstarts and Robins, most of which perch more freely on trees
than the Stone-chats. Still many are partial to rocks and buildings,
and nidificate in their crevices. Certain among them of still more
retired habits, *Larvicorinæ*, Blyth (in lit.), are peculiar, or nearly
so, to the Himalayas and part of Central Asia; and these have
sometimes been classed apart, but they are placed together by
Gray and Bonaparte, and cannot, I think, be well separated. The
well known Robin and Redstart of Europe are the types of this
sub-family.

Sub-fam. RUTICILLINÆ.

They are distinguished from the true Stone-chats by a
more slender beak, somewhat longer tarsi and feet; and their
coloration is peculiar. Most have more or less rufous on the tail,
(hence the name of *Phœnicura*,) also on the lower parts, and
the prevalent hue of the upper plumage is ashy grey, dull
black-blue in a few. Their tail is somewhat longer than in most
of the Chats, and many have the habit of shaking and flirting it
continually, hence the names given it in several languages, both
Native and European. The sexes ordinarily differ in plumage,
though the female sometimes is said to assume the plumage of
the male. They have a pleasing song, usually delivered from
the top of a building or rock, or tree. They nestle in holes in
trees, or buildings, or on the ground, and the eggs of most known
are blue; of one, at least, pure white. They are found chiefly in
the temperate parts of the Old World; and the Himalayan district,
and adjoining part of Tibet, is peculiarly rich in species.

Gen. RUTICILLA, Brehm.

Syn. *Phœnicura*, Swains.

Char.—Bill rather short, straight, slender, slightly notched;
rictus nearly smooth; wings moderately long, pointed; 1st primary
about one-third the length of the 4th; 5th and 6th equal and
longest; tail moderate, even, or slightly rounded; tarsus long,
slender, nearly smooth; feet moderate; lateral toes nearly equal,
hind toe not much lengthened; claws slender, moderately curved.

The Redstarts form a very natural group of birds, chiefly found in the northern and temperate parts of the Old World, and a few migrating to the tropics in winter. Only one species is found in the plains of India, but a considerable number occur in the Himalayas, chiefly as winter visitants perhaps; and others occur in Western Asia and Africa.

495. Ruticilla phænicura, LINN.

Motacilla, apud LINNÆUS—GOULD, Birds of Europe, pl. 95— R. tithys, apud HUTTON, J. A. S. XV., 780—BLYTH, Cat. 984— HORSF., Cat. 467.

THE EUROPEAN REDSTART.

Descr.—Narrow frontal band black, behind this a broad white patch, continued as a line over the eyes; lores, ear-coverts, throat, and upper part of breast, black; the rest of the body above brownish-ashy; wings dark brown; beneath, the rump, and upper and under tail-coverts, and tail (except the two centre feathers which are dark brown), bright ferruginous, albescent on the middle of the belly.

The female is olive-brown above, paler below, and with a rufous tinge on the abdomen; rump and tail, as in the male, but less bright. She is said, however, sometimes to assume the full male plumage. In the newly-moulted bird the white of the head is more or less concealed by dark terminal edgings to the feathers, and the black of the throat and breast has whitish edgings.

Bill black; legs dark brown; irides brown. Length $5\frac{1}{2}$ inches; wing $3\frac{1}{8}$; tail $2\frac{3}{8}$; bill at front $\frac{1}{2}$; tarsus $1\frac{5}{16}$.

The European Redstart has been found, but rarely, in the N. W. Provinces and Afghanistan. One was sent from Saharunpore to the Museum at the India House by Dr. Jameson. It is a summer visitant to Europe, where it breeds in holes of trees and buildings, and its eggs are beautiful verditer-blue; it retires to Northern Africa in winter.

496. Ruticilla phænicuroides, MOORE.

P. Z. S. 1854, pl. 57—HORSF., Cat. 468—BLYTH, Cat. 984— (in part).

THE ALLIED REDSTART.

Descr.—A narrow band on the forehead, lores, ear-coverts, throat and head, black ; crown, neck, back, and upper wing-coverts, ashy, with a rufous tint, the ash palest on the crown; wings brown, with the edges of the exterior webs paler ; from breast to vent, under wing-coverts, rump, upper and lower tail-coverts, and the tail (except the two middle feathers which are brown) rufous red.

Bill and legs black. Length nearly 6 inches ; wing $3\frac{1}{4}$; tail $2\frac{1}{2}$; bill at front $\frac{7}{16}$; tarsus $\frac{7}{8}$.

This species is exceedingly close to *R. phœnicura*, but differs in wanting the white on the forehead, in the black color of the breast extending lower down, in the 1st primary being longer, and the 2nd shorter than in that species, and the 6th is nearly as long as the 5th, whilst, in *phœnicura*, it is fully $\frac{1}{4}$ inch shorter. It has only been found in the extreme N. W. Provinces of India, Sindh, and Afghanistan.

497. **Ruticilla rufiventris,** VIEILLOT.

(Œnanthe, apud VIEILLOT—R. indica, BLYTH, Cat. 986—R. nipalensis, HODGS., apud MOORE, HORSF., Cat. 470—Phænicura atrata, apud JARD. and SELBY, Ill. Orn., pl. 86, -f. 3—SYKES, Cat. 90—JERDON, Cat. 108—*Thir-thira*, H. *i. e.*, Quaker or trembler—*Thirtir-hampa*, in N. W. Provinces—*Phir-ira* and *Lal-girdi*, Beng. —*Nuni-budi-gadu*, Tel., *i. e.*, Oil-bottle bird.

THE INDIAN REDSTART.

Descr.—Crown dark ashy-grey ; lores, ear-coverts, neck, throat, breast, back and upper wing-coverts, black, with greyish edges to the feathers; wings dusky brown ; the primaries margined with pale rufous, the secondaries with dull grey, forming an inconspicuous patch ; under wing-coverts, flanks, belly, rump, upper and lower tail-coverts, and tail (except half the inner and a little of the outer webs of the two middle tail feathers near the tip, which are brown), bright cinnamon rufous. The female is brown above, with the edges of the wings, the abdomen, and under tail-coverts, pale rufous ; below, dusky on the throat and breast, changing to clear

s

light rufous on the abdomen, and under tail-coverts; rump and tail, as in the male.

Bill black; legs brown black; irides brown.   Length 6 inches; extent $10\frac{1}{2}$; wing $3\frac{1}{2}$; tail $2\frac{7}{10}$; bill at front $\frac{7}{16}$; tarsus nearly 1.

The Indian Redstart is very regular in its appearance in the plains of India, from the end of September to the first week or so of October, according to the locality.   It is generally spread throughout the country, to the extreme south of the peninsula, but has not been observed in Ceylon; frequenting groves of trees, orchards, gardens, and the vicinity of old buildings, walls, and houses, and it is often seen perched on the roof of a house.   It feeds on the ground, on various insects.   It has a most peculiar quivering motion of its tail, especially when seating itself on its perch after feeding; hence some of the native names.   I never heard of its breeding in this country, and I cannot help thinking that Col. Sykes must have been mistaken when he mentions that "a pair built their nest in an out-house constantly frequented by my servants, and within reach of the hand."   It was more probably a *Thamnobia*.

498. Ruticilla Hodgsonii, Moore.

P. Z. S., 1854, pl. 58—Horsf., Cat. 471—Phœn. Reevesii, apud Blyth, J. A. S., XII., 963—R. erythrogastra, apud Blyth, Cat. 983 (in part)—*Thar-capmi*, Nep.

Hodgson's Redstart.

Descr.—A narrow band on the forehead, lores, ear-coverts, throat, and breast, black; the fore-part of the crown clear white, much narrower than in *R. phœnicura;* hind part of crown, neck, back, and upper wing-coverts, fine ash, lightest on the crown; wings dusky brown; the outer half of the basal half of the secondaries white, forming a wing patch; from the breast to vent, under wing-coverts, rump, upper and lower tail-coverts, and tail (except the inner and outer margins of the two middle feathers, which are dusky brown), bright rufous red.

The female has the usual colors of this genus, like the female of the last; but may be distinguished by a general puffy appearance, by the relative length of wing, and by the under parts being more grey and less rufescent.

Bill and legs black. Length 6½ inches; wing 3⅜; tail 2¾; tarsus ⅞; bill at front ₁⁷₀.

This Redstart has been found in Nepal, Bootan, and other parts of the Himalayas, but only, I suspect, in winter. It probably breeds in some parts of Central Asia. I only procured one female of this species when at Darjeeling, and this was during the winter.

499. **Ruticilla erythrogastra,** GULDENSTADT.

Motacilla, apud GULDENSTADT—Mot. ceraunia, PALLAS—GOULD, Birds of Asia, pl. 50—HORSF., Cat. 472—R. grandis, GOULD, P. Z. S., 1849—BLYTH, Cat. 983 (in part)—R. Vigorsii, MOORE (the female).

THE WHITE-WINGED REDSTART.

Descr.—Male with a narrow band on the forehead, the lores, ear-coverts, throat, fore-part of breast, back, wing-coverts, and apical portion of the primaries and secondaries, deep black; crown of head, back of neck, and basal portion of the primaries and secondaries, white, the white on the head being tinged with silvery grey; breast, belly, vent, rump, upper and lower tail-coverts, and tail, rich dark rufous.

Bill and legs black. Length 7 inches; wing 4¼; tail 3; tarsus 1; bill at front ₁⁷₀: the 4th primary is equal to the 5th and a little longer than the 6th.

This large Redstart has been found in Bootan, Nepal, Kumaon, and Cashmere, chiefly in the higher regions of the Himalayas, rarely lower than 10,000 feet. It is found in summer in the Caucasian hills, frequenting the gravelly hollows of torrents, and breeding in bushes. One pair was seen by Dr. Stewart, near Landour, by the side of a stream, and it is said to frequent mountain streams only, like *Chæmorrornis leucocephala*.

500. **Ruticilla aurorea,** PALLAS.

Motacilla, apud PALLAS—HORSF., Cat. 474—BLYTH, Cat. 983 (in part)—SCHLEGEL, Faun. Japon, pl. 21—Phœn. Reevesii, GRAY, and McLELLAND, P. Z. S., 1839—R. leucoptera, BLYTH.

REEVES' REDSTART.

Descr.—A narrow band on the forehead, lores, ear-coverts, throat, fore-part of breast, back, upper wing-coverts, apical and basal portion of the secondaries and tertiaries, and the two middle tail feathers, black; the latter changing to dusky brown; exterior margin of the outer tail feathers, and apical margin of the rest dusky brown black; medial portion of both webs of the secondaries and tertiaries, white; crown of head and back of neck slaty ash, rather whitish above the ear-coverts, and on the nape; breast, abdomen, under wing-coverts, upper and lower tail-coverts, and the tail, deep rufous.

The female is brown above, the wing patch rufescent white; beneath rufescent, upper and lower tail-coverts and the tail (except the medial feathers which are dusky brown), rufous.

Bill and legs black. Length $5\frac{3}{4}$ inches; wing $2\frac{7}{8}$; tail $2\frac{1}{2}$; bill at front $\frac{3}{8}$; tarsus rather more than $\frac{3}{4}$.

This Redstart has only been found in the more eastern portion of the Himalayas, in Bootan, coming south into the hill ranges of Assam, during the cold season. In the summer it is found in Siberia, Japan, and probably through great part of China.

501. Ruticilla schisticeps, HODGSON.

GRAY, Cat., Birds of Nepal, App. p. 153—HORSF., Cat., note to p. 307.

THE SLATY-HEADED REDSTART.

Descr.—Side of head and neck, black; wings and tail, black; top of head pale slaty blue; throat, and a large patch on each wing, white; lower part of breast and abdomen rufous chesnut. Length 6 inches; wing $3\frac{4}{12}$; tarsus $\frac{10\frac{1}{2}}{12}$; bill at front $\frac{4}{12}$.

From Nepal. Rare.

502. Ruticilla nigrogularis, HODGSON.

MOORE, P. Z. S., 1854—HORSF., Cat. 477.

THE BLACK-THROATED REDSTART.

Descr.—Crown of head slaty blue, lightest on the forehead; lores, ear-coverts, throat, back of neck, back, upper wing-coverts, two middle tail feathers entirely, and the rest (except the basal portion) black; wings blackish brown; the scapulars, outer edges of the secondaries, and under wing-coverts, white; breast, belly, flanks, rump, upper and lower tail-coverts, and base of tail (except the two middle feathers) bright chesnut; vent and under tail-coverts mixed with white.

Bill and legs black. Length 6 inches; wing 3⅜; tail 2¾.

From Nepal. This species is nearly allied to the last, but differs in having the throat black instead of white.

503. Ruticilla frontalis, VIGORS.

Phœnicura, apud VIGORS—GOULD, Cent. Him. Birds, pl. 26, f. 1—BLYTH, Cat. 982—HORSF., Cat. 478—Ph. tricolor, HODGSON.—R. melanura, LESSON—*Tak-tirriri-pho*, Lepch.

THE BLUE-FRONTED REDSTART.

Descr.—Top of head, back, throat and breast, dusky cyaneous, with terminal brown edgings; forehead, and above the eyes, lazuline blue; wings dusky blackish; rump, upper tail-coverts, and under parts, bright rufous; tail feathers rufous, with black tips, except the two middle ones, which are wholly black. The female is brown above, paler below, and rufescent on the lower belly and flanks; the rest as in the male.

Bill black; legs brown; irides brown. Length 6½ inches; extent 11; wing 3½; tail 3; bill at front ⅔; tarsus 1.

This species, as well in its coloration, as in its habits and haunts, approximates somewhat to the next group, that of the Blue Robins of India.

This pretty Redstart is found throughout the Himalayas, and also in the Khasia hills. It is very common at Darjeeling, in the winter only, extending from 4,000 feet to 8,000 feet. It is found on roads in the more open parts of the forest, and in cleared ground. When alarmed it flies into the thick under-wood. It feeds on the ground on various insects.

504. Ruticilla cœruleocephala, VIGORS.

Phœnicura, apud VIGORS, P. Z. S., 1830—GOULD, Cent. Il. Birds, pl. 25, f. 2—BLYTH, Cat. 988—HORSF., Cat. 476.

THE BLUE-HEADED REDSTART.

Descr.—Top of the head pale whitish blue; lores, ear-coverts, throat, breast, back, rump, upper tail-coverts and tail, black; wings dark brown, the scapulars, and outer edges of the secondaries, white; the under wing-coverts, belly, and vent, whitish.

Bill and legs black. Length 6 to 6¼ inches; wing 2¼; tail 2¾; bill at front $\frac{7}{16}$; tarsus about 1; 4th, 5th, and 6th quills about equal. The female is probably similarly colored to the male.

In this species the typical rufous tail is entirely absent, some of the feathers of the rump, in winter only, having a rufous tinge. Bonaparte makes of it the genus *Adelura,* but strangely joins with it certain Fly-catchers.

This prettily-colored Redstart is found throughout the whole extent of the Himalayas, from the N. W. Provinces to Bootan, but appears more common in the N. W. Himalayas, and I did not procure it at Darjeeling, nor has it been yet observed there; but it will probably be found in the interior of Sikhim, at higher elevations.

505. **Ruticilla fuliginosa,** VIGORS.

P. Z. S., 1831—BLYTH, Cat. 989—HORSF., Cat. 479—Ph. plumbea, GOULD—Rut. simplex, LESSON—Ph. rubricauda and P. lineoventris (the female), HODGSON—*Suradum parbo-pho,* Lepch. —*Chubia nakki,* Bhot.

THE PLUMBEOUS WATER-ROBIN.

Descr.—Male uniform dusky cyaneous; wings dusky blackish, margined with cyaneous; vent, upper and lower tail-coverts, and tail, dark ferruginous. The female is much paler ashy above, and still paler below; from the throat to the vent, each feather spotted with white, and margined with dusky, and then pale ash; wings brown, spotted with white on the coverts; tail white at its base, extending to near the tip on the outermost tail feathers; the rest brown; upper and lower tail-coverts also white.

Bill black; legs vinaceous brown; irides dark brown. Length 5¼ inches; extent 9; wing nearly 3; tail 2; bill at front $\frac{5}{16}$; tarsus $\frac{7}{8}$.

The coloration of this bird, especially that of the female, is very peculiar, and indeed unique in this group, and the sexes would hardly be recognised as belonging to the same species. It probably ought to form a distinct type. Hodgson classed it with *Chæmorrornis*, with which it agrees in the shorter and somewhat rounded tail, as also in its habits; but the wings are proportionally longer, and the bill shorter.

This plumbeous Redstart is found throughout the Himalayas, the Khasia hills, and, according to Griffiths, all the hill ranges between Assam and Burmah. In Sikhim it is common from 1,300 feet to 5,000 feet or so, and is a permanent resident there. It lives entirely along rivers and mountain torrents, and may often be seen on a wet and slippery rock, just above a boiling rapid; it climbs up the wet rocks with great facility, and every now then alighting on a rock, it spreads its tail, but does not vibrate it like some of the Redstarts. It is a pugnacious little fellow, and often gives battle to the little *Enicurus Scouleri*, which delights in similar spots, and it generally drives its antagonist away. Its flight is rapid and direct. It feeds on various aquatic insects and larvæ, some kinds of which are always found just at the edge of the water, and which a wave often leaves behind it on the rock.

Griffiths in his private journal states that he observed and shot it in Kaffiristan, while it was "examining a wall for insects, and fluttering about the holes in it."

Gen. CHÆMORRORNIS, Hodgson.

Differs from true *Ruticilla* by its more rounded wings and tail, and by the intense ruddy hue. Sexes alike.

506. **Chæmorrornis leucocephala**, Vigors.

Phœnicura, apud VIGORS, P. Z. S., 1830—GOULD, Cent. Him. Birds, pl. 26, f. 2—BLYTH, Cat. 99.—HORSF., Cat. 480—*Gir-chaondia*, Hind.—*Kali-pholia* at Mohun Ghat—*Mati-tap-pho*, Lepch.—*Chubia-mati*, Bhot.

THE WHITE-CAPPED REDSTART.

Descr.—Frontal band, lores, ear-coverts, throat, neck, breast, back, wings, and tips of the tail feathers, black; abdomen, rump, upper and lower tail-coverts, and more than two-thirds of the tail, deep rich chesnut; crown of head and nape, pure white.

Bill black; legs vinaceous brown; irides dark brown. Length 7½ inches; extent 12; wing 4; tail 3; bill at front ½; tarsus 1¼.

This very handsome Redstart is found throughout the Himalayas, from the extreme N. W., Affghanistan and Kaffiristan, to the Khasia Hills in the south east; and, according to Griffiths, still further towards Burmah. In Sikhim it occurs from a level of 1,000 feet, to 5,000 feet, but it is only a winter resident, going northwards to breed. It is found on the banks of rivers and streams, but does not affect the rapids of torrents so much as the last bird, preferring the more level and shingly rivers, and picking up insects at the brink of the water. I did not observe it flirting or spreading its tail so much as Hutton represents it to do. Its flight is moderately strong, but more wavy than that of the last.

Among other recorded species of Redstart are *R. tithys*, of Europe; *R. erythroprocta*, Gould, from Western Asia, and *R. rufogularis*, Moore, figd. in P. Z. S., 1854, pl. 59, found in Affghanistan, and which, perhaps, may occur in our North-western limits.

The following birds differ somewhat from the Redstarts both in coloration and structure, but are too intimately connected with them to be separable, some of the group, *viz*, the Blue-breasts, (*Cyanecula*) having the tail of *Ruticilla*. The group comprises several distinct forms, some of them peculiar, or nearly so, to the Himalayas and adjoining parts of Asia; others spread over Europe, Asia, and Northern Africa. The Robin belongs to this group, and is the best known European form. They agree among themselves in having a rather slender, straight bill, of mean length, more or less compressed, very feebly notched at the tip, and slightly deflected, with the ridge of the upper mandible very slightly elevated between the nostrils, and the gape very feebly bristled. The legs and feet are lengthened, and rather slender, and the claws are elongated and very slightly curved. The wings vary somewhat in structure, some having these organs more rounded than others, and the tail is either square or very slightly rounded.

They are mostly ground birds, feeding on insects, but fond of shelter; some frequenting thickets, others, long grass; a few being more arboreal. They usually nidificate on the ground.

Gen. LARVIVORA, Hodgson.

Bill as noticed above; wings moderate, strong, 1st quill short, 3rd, 4th, and 5th quills about equal and longest; tail rather short, and the feathers slightly mucronate at the tip, even, or nearly so; tarsus long, slender, nearly smooth; toes long slender; claws long, moderately curved, much compressed.

507. **Larvivora cyana,** HODGSON.

J. A. S., VI., 102—BLYTH, Cat. 993—HORSF., Cat. 481—Phœnicura superciliaris, JERDON, Cat. Suppl. 190—L. brunnea, HODGS. (the female)—*Manzhil-pho,* Lepch.

THE BLUE WOOD-CHAT.

Descr.—Above dusky indigo-blue, with a white superciliary streak; lores and ears black; beneath bright rufous (the feathers all dusky blue at their base), albescent towards the vent and under tail-coverts; thigh coverts cross-barred with blue and white.

The female, according to Hodgson, is brown above; white beneath; cheeks, breast, and flanks rusty.

Bill dusky; legs pale fleshy; irides brown. Length 6 inches; extent 10; wing 3; tail 2; tarsus $1\frac{1}{6}$; bill at front $\frac{1}{2}$.

This bird is nearly related both to *Ianthia* and *Calliope*, with which genus Mr. Blyth formerly classed it, and I described it as a *Phœnicura.* Its shorter tail, lengthened legs, as well as partly the coloring, tend towards *Brachypteryx* in the *Myiotherine* group.

The blue Wood-chat is found in the Himalayas, from Cashmere to Sikhim, and in the cold weather extending, but in very small numbers, to the plains, for it has been procured near Calcutta. It is also an inhabitant of the Neilgherries and Ceylon; and I once killed it among some brush-wood in a large mangoe-grove at Nellore. Whether this bird had come from the Himalayas, or the Neilgherries, it is impossible to say, but from the season at which I procured it, *viz.,* the end of March, it was probably migrating northwards.

I do not know if it is a permanent resident on the Neilgherries, but rather think that it is.

It frequents open forests in the hills, perching low, and descending to the ground to pick up insects. Hodgson says, that "from the number of insects' nests and larvæ he found in its stomach, he has given the generic name." Dr. Adams found it in the forests of Cashmere, and remarked that it had the habits of a Redstart. Some specimens have the white superciliary mark very short, stopping at the eye; in others it extends far beyond it. Hodgson at first stated that the sexes were alike, but he afterwards described the female as differing in her plumage. A second species of *Larvivora* has been noticed by Mr. Swinhoe from China.

Gen. IANTHIA, Blyth.

Syn. *Nemura*, Hodgson.

Char.—Bill short, slender, straight, rictal bristles rather long; wings rather long; 4th and 5th quills equal and longest; 3rd and 6th nearly equal; tail almost even, moderate, slightly mucronate; tarsus long, slender; toes and claws long and slender.

This genus comprises a few birds, the males of which are blue above, and more or less rufous beneath; the plumage soft, silky and lax, but copious. They are very nearly allied to the true Robins, *Erythaca*, but differ in their more delicate make, longer wings, longer toes and claws; and the sexes differ in coloring. They are all foresters and shy, and, as far as I have observed, insectivorous; but Mr. Hodgson states that they sometimes eat pulpy berries.

508. Ianthia cyanura, PALLAS.

Motacilla, apud PALLAS—Nemura rufilata, and N. cyanura, HODGSON—JARDINE, Contrib. Ornith. Pl.—BLYTH, Cat. 1002— HORSF., Cat. 464—Erythaca Tytleri, JAMESON—*Mangzhil-pho*, Lepch.

THE WHITE-BREASTED BLUE WOOD-CHAT.

Descr.—Male above prussian-blue, brightening and inclining to ultramarine on the forehead, over the eyes, on the shoulder and rump; the lower parts are white, confined to a narrow streak on the throat and foreneck; the breast more or less brown, and the flanks bright ferruginous.

The female is pale brown, with a trace of blue on the shoulder, a greyish blue supercilium; margins to the tertiaries, rump, upper tail-coverts, and tail, blue, as in the male, but much lighter; sides of the neck and breast pale olive-brown; the middle of the belly, lower tail-coverts, and the middle line of the throat white; the flanks ferruginous as in the male.

Bill dusky; legs brown; irides dark brown. Length $5\frac{3}{4}$ inches; extent 10; wing $3\frac{1}{4}$; tail $2\frac{5}{8}$; bill at front $\frac{3}{8}$; tarsus 1.

This very prettily plumaged bird is found throughout the Himalayas from the N. W. to Sikhim. It is only a winter resident in Sikhim, however, and I suspect throughout the hills also. It is said to be common in China, Central and Northern Asia, and in Japan. It is very numerous about Darjeeling in the cold weather, from 4,000 feet upwards. It keeps to the forests, perches low on small trees and brushwood, and descends to the ground to feed on insects of various kinds. It is not unfrequently seen feeding on the bridle paths and roads. The name *Manzhil-pho* is properly applied to this species, which is a well known bird, but it is given indiscriminately to other species of this genus, to *Larvivora*, and even to the blue Fly-catchers, *Cyornis* and *Muscicapula*.

509. Ianthia hyperythra, BLYTH.

J. A. S., XVI., 132—BLYTH, Cat. 1001—HORSF., Cat. 465.

THE RUSTY-THROATED BLUE WOOD-CHAT.

Descr.—Male, upper parts deep indigo-blue, brightening to ultramarine above the eyes and on the shoulder; wings and tail black, the feathers outwardly edged blue; beneath dark yellowish ferruginous, confined to a narrow streak on the middle of the throat and foreneck; lower tail-coverts, and centre of the lower parts of the belly, white.

The female is a rich brown olive; the tail blue as in the male; the rump lighter and more greyish; there is also a little blue on the shoulder, and a greyish blue supercilium; the lower parts are tawny brown, or subdued fulvous; the lower tail-coverts white.

Bill dusky; legs brown. Length $5\frac{1}{2}$ inches, wing $3\frac{1}{8}$; tail $2\frac{1}{4}$; bill at front $\frac{3}{8}$; tarsus 1.

This bird, which differs from the last by the deep ferruginous on the lower plumage, as also by the deeper blue of the upper parts, and in the shorter tail, has only been procured from Nepal and Sikhim. It appears to be very rare, and is probably a migratory species also.

510. Ianthia superciliaris, Hodgson.

MOORE, P. Z. S., 1854—HORSF., Cat. 483—I. flavolivacea, HODGSON (the female)—Erythaca, apud BLYTH, Cat. 1003.

THE RUFOUS-BELLIED BUSH-CHAT.

Descr.—Male, above deep indigo or cyaneous; wings dusky black or brown, the outer edges margined with cyaneous, and rufous on the shoulder; the primaries also faintly margined with rufous, and the secondaries with cyaneous; lores and cheeks black; a white superciliary streak extending from the nares to the back of the neck; beneath rufous; middle of the belly white.

The female is olive-brown above; wings and tail brown, the former margined with rusty olive; white superciliary streak not so clear as in male; beneath dull pale rufous, inclining to oil yellow, the middle of the lower belly and vent partially white.

Bill black; legs pale horny-brown; irides brown. Length nearly 6 inches; wing $3\frac{5}{10}$; tail $2\frac{3}{8}$; tarsus $1\frac{1}{8}$; bill at front $\frac{7}{16}$.

This species has been classed as a *Tarsiger*, but its coloration is quite that of the present genus. Blyth at one time made it a true Robin (*Erythaca*), but he has since located it here. It is remarkable for the great length of its hind claw. This bird greatly resembles in its mode of coloration *Larvivora cyana*. It is rare in Nepal and Sikhim. I got two or three specimens at Darjeeling, but did not observe it myself. It has hitherto been only procured in the S. E. Himalayas.

Gen. TARSIGER, Hodgson.

Syn. *Sericornis*, Blyth.

Char.—Bill straight, slender; gape rather wide, distinctly ciliated; wings moderate; 5th quill longest, 4th and 6th sub-equal to it;

tail moderate, barely rounded, conspicuously mucronate ; tarsus long, very slender, smooth ; feet rather large, middle toe elongate, hind toe rather large ; claws long, slender, moderately curved. This genus differs from the two last by its more slender bill and less rounded tail. The coloration, too, is peculiar and unique.

511. Tarsiger chrsyæus, HODGSON.

P. Z. S., 1845, 28—JARDINE, Contrib. Orn. pl.—BLYTH, Cat. 994—HORSF., Cat. 482—*Manshil-pho*, Lepch.

THE GOLDEN BUSH-CHAT.

Descr.—Male, head, nape, sides of neck above, and back, olive-green ; a stripe through the eyes, widening at the ears, black ; superciliary streak, rump, tail, and whole lower surface, deep golden yellow ; tail with a broad black tip and the two centre feathers black ; wings dusky, edged with olivaceous, some of the greater wing-coverts deeper black, edged with yellowish.

The female is olivaceous above, the orbits whitish ; beneath oil yellow ; supercilium dull yellow ; wings dusky, edged with olive, and the tail olive-brown ; the inner webs of all, except the centre pair, dull golden yellow ; two central feathers dusky, and part of the inner web of the next pair also dusky.

Bill dusky above, deep fleshy yellow beneath ; irides dark brown. Length $5\frac{3}{4}$th inches ; extent 9 ; wing $2\frac{3}{4}$; tail $2\frac{1}{4}$; bill at front $\frac{3}{8}$; tarsus $1\frac{1}{4}$ nearly.

This very beautiful bird has only been procured in Nepal and Sikhim. It is not uncommon near Darjeeling, and is a permanent resident, I believe. It is found in the valleys, from 3,000 to 5,000 feet chiefly, keeps to the forest amongst thick underwood, and feeds on the ground on insects. Hodgson says : "It is shy, solitary, and bush-loving. It breeds on the ground, making a compact saucer-like nest of moss, under the roots of a tree or a stone, and the eggs are verditer-blue."

Gen. CALLIOPE, Gould.

Char.—Bill of moderate length and strength ; wings moderate, 1st quill very short, 2nd equal to 7th ; tail very slightly rounded, the outer feathers being a little shorter than the penultimate pair; tarsus moderately long, stout, the feet large, hind toe long ; claws long, not much curved.

This form is closely allied to *Larvivora*, but differs by its longer and more rounded tail.

512. Calliope Kamtschatkensis, GMEL.

Turdus, apud GMELIN—BLYTH, Cat. 992—HORSF., Cat. 485— Mot. calliope, PALLAS and TICKELL.—C. Lathami, GOULD, Birds of Europe, pl. 118—*Gunpiyora*, Beng.—*Gangula*, in Nepal.

THE COMMON RUBY-THROAT.

Descr.—Above olive-brown ; beneath dull whitish ; a band above and below the eyes, whitish ; intermediate space black ; feathers of the throat somewhat scaly and stiff, light scarlet or ruby red, with silvery edges, more or less surrounded with black ; the breast ashy, flanks bright olive-brown, and belly whitish ; axillaries slightly rufescent.

The female has in general no trace of the ruby throat, which is whitish, and the lores brown ; but some old females have a tinge of the ruby colour.

Bill horny brown ; irides dark brown ; legs livid or purplish. Length 6 inches ; wing 3 ; tail $2\frac{1}{2}$; bill at front $\frac{1}{2}$; tarsus $1\frac{1}{4}$.

This pretty bird is found chiefly in Northern and Central India. I never saw it south of the Nerbudda, except once, on boardship, a little south of Bombay, where one took refuge in the month of November. It is most common in Bengal and the Eastern side of India, and is a cold weather visitant only. It extends throughout Central and Northern Asia as far as Kamtschatka, whence it was first brought; and it has been occasionally killed in Europe. In its manners it is shy, solitary, and silent; haunts thickets and underwood, and feeds on the ground on various insects. It is said especially to frequent the covered plantations of the Betel-vine.

513. Calliope pectoralis, GOULD.

Icones Avium, pl.—BLYTH, Cat. 991—HORSF., Cat. 486— Bradybates, apud GRAY, Genera of Birds.

The White-tailed Ruby Throat.

Descr.—General color dark brownish ashy, with a white supercilium; lores black, and a small moustachial spot white; the breast and sides of the throat black, and the chin and the middle of the throat and upper part of the neck bright glistening crimson; the belly, vent, and under tail-coverts, white, ashy on the flanks and mixed with dusky on the under tail-coverts; tail white on the basal half, except the centre pair, and white tipped; also some white on the outer-web of the outermost feathers. In winter the black of the breast is broadly edged with grey, and the red of the throat is less intense; the back too is not so dark. The female is plain olive-brown, paler on the breast, and whitish on the throat and belly; supercilia pale rufescent, there is much less white at the base of the tail, and the terminal spots are light rufescent.

Bill dusky; legs pale reddish brown; irides dark brown. Length 6 inches; wing barely 3; tail $2\frac{3}{4}$; bill at front nearly $\frac{1}{2}$; tarsus $1\frac{1}{8}$.

The tail is more graduated than in the last species, and the wings are more rounded. It is found throughout the Himalayas, from Cashmere to Sikhim. I saw it at Darjeeling, where not common, frequenting thick brush-wood, and coming to the road to feed on insects. Adams found it at high elevations, among rocks and precipices, in the N. W. Himalayas. I quite recently procured one specimen, and saw others, frequenting long grass jungle, not far from the banks of the Ganges at Caragola Ghat. It came to the small foot paths, especially near the edge of water, to feed. It is only a cold weather visitor at Darjeeling, but may probably breed in the interior.

Gen. Cyanecula, Brehm.

Char.—Bill rather short, slightly conic, straight; wings moderate, 3rd and 4th quills equal and longest, 5th a little shorter, 2nd equal to 6th, tail rather short, nearly even; tarsus moderately long; claws very slightly curved.

The Blue-throats differ from the other members of this section by their firmer wings, and plumage generally, the wings being somewhat more pointed, and the tail is sub-even, and somewhat fan-shaped, the feathers scarcely, if at all, mucronate, and bright rufous at its base, thus reverting towards the Redstarts. The throat has more or less bright azure blue in the males.

There appear to be four or five nearly allied races or species inhabiting Europe, Asia, and the North of Africa; and there is some doubt as to which of the races the Indian bird belongs. It is generally allowed that the birds that visit India during the cold weather, most closely resemble those of Northern Europe, as distinguished from the race of Middle and Southern Europe, which visit England occasionally. Bonaparte, however, made it distinct, as indeed Blyth formerly did.

514, Cyaneula suecica, LINN.

Motacilla, apud LINNÆUS—BLYTH, Cat. 981—HORSF., Cat. 484 —SYKES, Cat. 94—JERDON, Cat. 109—C. succicoides, HODGSON—Motac. cœrulecula, PALLAS—C. indica, BONAP.—*Husenipidda*, H.—also *Nil kunthi*, H. in the North.—*Gunpigera* and *Gurpedra*, Beng.—*Dumbak*, Sindh.

THE INDIAN BLUE-THROAT.

Descr.—Above pale olive-brown, the feathers of the crown slightly centred darker, and with a whitish supercilium; lower parts whitish; the under tail-coverts more or less tinged with rufescent; throat and breast bright shining azure-blue, the former generally mingled with whitish along the middle, and having a large ferruginous spot in front of the neck; below, and bordering the azure of the breast, is a narrow blackish band, then a narrow whitish band, and below this again a broad ferruginous band; the upper tail-coverts are brown, mingled with ferruginous; tail rufous, the two centre feathers, and the tips of all the others, dark brown.

Bill dusky horn, the gape yellow; legs brownish; irides dark brown. Length nearly $6\frac{1}{4}$ inches; wing 3; tail $2\frac{1}{4}$; extent $9\frac{1}{4}$ tarsus $1\frac{1}{10}$; bill at front $\frac{7}{10}$. Female a little smaller.

Young males have much less blue on the breast, which is often confined to a moustachial streak on either side, and a comparatively narrow gorget; they have also scarcely any tinge of ferruginous on the throat and breast, the former being chiefly of a dull white, but there is never the pure silky-white pectoral spot of *C. Wolfi* of Southern Europe. The females have commonly the throat and fore-neck dull white, encircled with dusky spots, which are more developed in old females, and these have sometimes a tolerably broad dusky gorget, mingled with a little blue.

The Indian Blue-throat is found over all India in suitable localities. It is migratory, leaving for the North at the end of the cold weather, March and April. This species appears to visit the North of Europe and Northern and Western Asia in summer, and is described as being a pleasing songster, breeding in moss on the ground, and laying four or five eggs of a greenish color. It is found in India, in open country, in hedge-rows, gardens, fields of pulse and *Cucurbitaceæ*, corn fields, and reeds or long grass, especially near water. In gardens it haunts the pea-rows, beans, and any thick cover; and it feeds on the ground, running along and picking up various insects. It makes its way very adroitly through thick reeds, and when observed it tries to conceal itself. When feeding it occasionally displays its rufous tail, and sometimes jerks it up, but does not quiver it like the Redstarts. I have seen it feeding close to houses in various parts of Central India.

The allied species are, besides *C. Wolfi*, already referred to, *C. cyane*, Eversman, of Eastern Siberia, which ought to occur in China; *C. dichrosterna*, Cabanis, from Arabia; and *C. major* from Abyssinia.

Besides the well known European Robin, one or two species from Japan have been classed under *Erythaca*, but it appears doubtful if they really belong to this group of birds. Mr. Blyth would class the Nightingale here, but it appears to me to associate more naturally with the birds of the next sub-family.

Sub-fam. CALAMOHERPINÆ, Grass-warblers.

The following birds comprise a series of plain plumaged species, of mostly small size, frequenting reeds, long grass, and other thick coverts near the ground. They may be said to grade from the last group by *Cyanecula*, which has the habits of the Reed-warblers. They nestle on the ground, or among reeds, and feed entirely on insects. They are most developed in the temperate and warmer

U

parts of Europe, Asia, and Northern Africa, migrating southwards in winter. They are part of the *Calamoherpinæ* of Bonaparte, and of the *Sylviinæ* of Gray. One only is known to breed on the plains, and one on the Hills; but the last species recorded are probably permanent residents on the Himalayas. Their feet are less fitted for terrestrial habits than those of the last sub-families. They approximate the Wren-warblers by *Horeites,* and also *Phyllopneustæ* and *Phylloscopus* through *Horornis,* and the smaller *Acrocephali.*

Gen. ACROCEPHALUS, Naumann.

Syn.   *Calamoherpe,* Boie.

Char.—Bill Thrush-like, moderate or rather long, straight, very slightly deflected and notched; a few short, but stout, rictal bristles; wings moderately long, somewhat pointed, 1st quill minute, 3rd and 4th about equal and longest; tail rounded, of moderate length; tarsus somewhat lengthened, feet moderate, claws long, slightly curved, hind claw much curved.

515. Acrocephalus brunnescens, JERDON.

Agrobates, apud JERDON, Cat. 113—BLYTH, Cat., 1078—HORSF. Cat. 515—Malacocircus abnormis, HODGSON—A. arundinaceus, apud BLYTH, olim—*Bora-jitta,* Tel.

THE LARGE REED-WARBLER.

Descr.—Above light olive-brown, darkest on the wings and tail, and lightest on the rump; beneath, and eyebrow, with a tinge of olive-yellow; the chin pure white; wings and tail beneath cinereous; plumage soft and silky.

Bill dark brown, fleshy at base beneath; legs horny brown; irides dull greenish yellow. Length $8\frac{1}{2}$ inches; wing $3\frac{5}{8}$; tail $3\frac{1}{4}$; bill at front $\frac{7}{10}$; tarsus $1\frac{2}{10}$; extent $10\frac{5}{8}$. Female somewhat smaller.

This species is very similar to the European *A. arundinaceus,* or *Sylvia turdoides,* Temm., but differs in being something smaller, in the first long primary being 3-16th shorter than the next, and the 3rd, if any thing, longer than the 2nd, whereas in the European analogue the 1st long primary is, if any thing, longer than the 2nd. The wing too is longer, 3¾ in the European bird, and it is more intense in its color; in both the first primary is very minute.

The larger Reed-warbler is found in most parts of India in the cold weather, for it is only a winter visitant. It extends into Assam, Arracan, and China, in some parts of which latter country it most probably breeds. It frequents high reeds and grasses, high grain fields and gardens, where it hunts among the pea-rows, beans, and other vegetables. It clings strongly to the stalks of grain, and makes its way adroitly through thick grass or bushes, concealing itself when observed and being with difficulty driven out. It feeds on small grasshoppers, ants, and other insects. I have heard it occasionally utter a harsh clucking kind of note. The European bird is said to have a charming song, to make a neat nest among reeds, and to lay four or five greenish white eggs with grey and brown speckles.

516. Acrocephalus dumetorum, BLYTH.

J. A. S., XVIII., 815—Horsf., Cat. 517—A. montanus, BLYTH, Cat. 1079—Sylvia montana, SYKES, Cat. 78—and JERDON, Cat. 123—Salic. arundinacea, HODGSON—*Podena*, II.—*Tik-tikki* of Mussulmans—*Tikra*, Beng.—*Kumpa-jitta*. Tel.

THE LESSER REED-WARBLER.

Descr.—Above olive-brown, with a pale supercilium; beneath whitish, tinged with pale earthy brown.

Bill dusky, fleshy at base beneath; legs red brown; irides yellow brown. Length 6 inches; wing $2\frac{4}{10}$; bill at front $\frac{4}{10}$; tarsus $\frac{9}{10}$.

This bird so closely resembles the *A. salicaria* of Europe, that Mr. Strickland, at one time, pronounced it to be the same. It differs, however, besides in some proportions of the quills, in having less brown tint above and on the breast and flanks, and in the bill being less compressed, though vertically deeper. It has the same proportions of the quills as the last species, and thus differs from *A. montana* of Java, the 1st quill being very minute and pointed, and the 2nd equal to or longer than the 6th.

The lesser Reed-warbler is found in bushy and grassy ground on the Neilgherries and West Coast, also more rarely in the Carnatic, in Central India, and in Bengal, to Nepal and Assam. Blyth says that it is not met with in the wilder marshy district about Calcutta, but chiefly in gardens. It is migratory in the plains, but breeds in some parts of the Himalayas. Hutton found the nest, which was a round ball of dry grasses; the eggs three in number, pearl-white, with minute scattered specks of rufous, chiefly at the larger end. Its note, he states, is "a sharp *titick titick*, resembling the sound made by a flint and steel." He further states that many leave the hills in May without breeding, so they probably go still further north.

517. Acrocephalus agricolus, JERDON.

Sylvia, apud JERDON, 2nd Suppl. Cat. 124 bis—BLYTH, Cat. 1081—HORSF., Cat. 518—*Yerra kumpa jitta*, Tel.

THE PADDY FIELD WARBLER.

Descr.—Above pale rufous brown, brightest on the rump; wings brown, edged with rufous; tail dull brown; beneath whitish tinged with fulvous, and brownish on the flanks.

Bill brown, paler beneath; legs brown; irides yellow brown. Length 5¼ inches; wing 2¼ ; tail 2¼ ; bill at front $\frac{4}{10}$; tarsus $\frac{9}{10}$.

This Warbler is a good deal smaller than the last, with a considerably smaller bill, and a more rufous tone of coloring. It is also very like *A. salicaria* of Europe, but differs in having the same proportion of primaries as *A. brunnescens*.

I first found this species in growing paddy fields in Nellore in the cold weather, and in reedy ground near tanks in Central India. It is also found in the vicinity of Calcutta, and in various parts of India to Nepal and Affghanistan. Like the others it feeds entirely on insects. It is migratory in India, going north to breed.

Mr. Blyth remarks that these Indian species of Reed-warblers tend to approximate *Phylloscopus*, in the form of wing, and are less aquatic in their habits than their European congeners.

Gen. ARUNDINAX, Blyth.

Bill wide at the base, not much compressed, of moderate length; tip well deflected, and very slightly notched; wings rather short,

1st quill nearly half the length of the 2nd, which is a little shorter than the 3rd and 4th, which are equal and longest, and the 5th is nearly as long; tail somewhat long, much graduated, the feathers narrow; tarsus moderate, stout; feet strong; claws lengthened, moderately curved.

The peculiar form has quite the general aspect of *Acrocephalus*, but differs in its much wider bill, and the form of the wing. Some class it along with *Megalurus* and *Chætornis*, but its somewhat more lengthened wing, and broad, little compressed, bill, are against this view, whilst its colors are quite those of *Acrocephalus brunnescens*, to which its general resemblance is so strong that I at first passed it over.

518. Arundinax olivaceus, BLYTH.

Phragmaticola olivacea, BLYTH, apud JERDON, 2nd Suppl. Cat. No. 113 bis—BLYTH, Cat. 1075—HORSF., Cat. 514.

THE THICK-BILLED REED-WARBLER.

Descr.—Uniform olive-brown above, a little rufescent towards the tail; throat whitish, and the rest of the under parts tinged with fulvous brown; lores pale.

Bill dark brown above; fleshy yellow at base of lower mandible; legs pale horny red, and toes fleshy grey; irides hazel. Length 8 inches; wing $3\frac{1}{4}$; tail $3\frac{3}{4}$; bill at front $\frac{9}{16}$; tarsus $1\frac{1}{10}$; extent $10\frac{1}{4}$.

I first procured this species in the Carnatic near Nellore, where, however, it is not very common; and Mr. Blyth subsequently obtained it tolerably abundant in the vicinity of Calcutta. It has also been procured in the Nepal Terai, and in Tenasserim, and probably frequents suitable localities over most parts of India. I presume that like the last it is migratory.

Gen. DUMETICOLA, Blyth.

Char.—Bill straight, as in *Cinclus*, but shorter, stout, compressed, strongly notched at the tip; gape smooth; tail rounded, moderate; wings short, the first three somewhat graduate, 4th longest and

5th sub-equal; tarsus moderate, stout; toes and claws long, not much curved; plumage puffy and full.

This genus is not separated from *Acrocephalus* by Bonaparte and Gray, but differs by its spotted breast and more cincline bill.

519. Dumeticola affinis, HODGSON.

Salicaria, apud HODGSON, GRAY, Zool. Misc., and Cat. Nep. Birds--GRAY, Genera of Birds, pl. 49, f. 2.—D. thoracica, BLYTH, J. A. S., XIV. 584—BLYTH, Cat. 1087—HORSF., Cat. 520.

THE SPOTTED REED-WARBLER.

Descr.—Above dark olive-brown, with a faint ruddy tinge on the lower part of the back; throat, and above the lores, white, passing into ashy on the breast, which, with the fore-neck, is marked with largish round dusky spots; lower parts, and sides of breast, plain brownish ashy; the middle portion of the belly white; the flanks fulvescent brown, and the under tail-coverts dark olive brown, with whitish tips.

Bill dusky; legs pale. Length 5 inches; wing $2\frac{1}{2}$; tail 2; bill at front $\frac{3}{8}$; tarsus $\frac{3}{4}$.

This bird has only been procured in Nepal, and no notice of its habits or haunts is on record.

Besides the European species casually alluded to above, there are a few others of this group found in Europe, Asia, and Africa, *Acrocephalus montanus* from Java, several of the same genus from Japan, and others from China, North Africa, and Australia; *Calamodyta* and *Lusciniopsis* comprise several species of Southern Europe and North Africa; *Luscinia*, containing the Nightingale of Europe, and a nearly affined species from Eastern Europe and Persia, *L. Major*, Bonap., is placed among the Robins by many authors; but its coloration and general habits appear to me to entitle it to a place in this group. *Aedon*, comprising *Sylvia galactodes* of Europe, and others, is placed by Gray next the Nightingale, but some of the species appear to me to belong to the *Timalinœ*, or at all events to the short-winged Warblers; and some of the species of *Erythropygia*, A. Smith, of Southern Africa (placed as a synonym of *Aedon* by Bonaparte), even approximate *Eurycercus* in their mode of coloration.

The next group comprises the Grasshopper Warblers, and some allined forms, corresponding to the section *Locustelleæ* of Bonaparte. Their plumage is striped or lark-like above, and they frequent reeds and grass. The European species make their nests among reeds.

Gen. LOCUSTELLA, Gould.

Char.—Bill of moderate length, slender, straight, compressed, barely deflected at the tip, which is slightly notched; wings long, with the 1st quill minute; 2nd nearly equal to the third, which is longest; tail moderate, rounded or graduated; hind claw very long, much curved.

520. **Locustella certhiola**, PALLAS.

Turdus, apud PALLAS—Locustella Raii, GOULD, apud BLYTH.

THE LESSER REED-WARBLER.

Descr.—Above pale olive-brown, all the feathers centred dark brown; tail uniform brown, tipped pale, especially as seen from below; beneath white, tinged with earthy brown on the neck, breast, and flanks; lower tail-coverts fulvescent white, with narrow longitudinal striæ. In the spring moult the lower plumage is at first a somewhat rich yellow.

Bill dusky above, pale beneath; irides hazel; legs fleshy brown. Length $5\frac{1}{2}$ inches; wing $2\frac{1}{4}$; tail $2\frac{1}{8}$; bill at front 11 mill.

I first found this bird in long grass in the neighbourhood of Mhow, in Central India, during the rains, and Mr. Blyth then considered it to be identical with the European *Locustella Raii*. He subsequently procured it from Lower Bengal, not far from Calcutta; and I quite recently obtained it near Monghyr, and also observed it in other places along the Ganges, and it probably will be found in suitable localities throughout India. From the specimens then procured, towards the end of March and beginning of April, Mr. Blyth was led to doubt their identity with the English bird. On comparing it with Temminck's description of *L. certhiola*, it appears to me to correspond sufficiently well, the pale tip to the tail, one of the distinguishing points of the latter from *S. locustella*, being distinctly present, in which however it agrees with the next bird. It is, possibly, a distinct species, and in that case I would propose the name of LOCUSTELLA TEMPORALIS.

This bird frequents long grass and grain, and is with some difficulty procured, as it always tries to conceal itself among the long grass; and, when flushed, takes but a very short flight, again hides itself, and is with difficulty dislodged. It probably breeds in this country. It feeds entirely on insects.

521. Locustella rubescens, BLYTH.

J. A. S. XIV., 582—BLYTH, Cat. 1084

THE RUDDY REED-WARBLER.

Descr.—Back ruddy-brown, with blackish centres to the feathers; crown dusky olive; sides of neck and breast olivaceous; throat and belly white, fulvescent brown on the sides of the neck, flanks, and under tail-coverts; some of the latter brown, tipped white; rump and tail dark ruddy-brown, all the outer feathers tipped with grey and obsoletely barred; wing-coverts edged with olivaceous, and the quills with ruddy-brown; tips of tertiaries slightly albescent; a narrow whitish line from bill to occiput.

Bill dusky horn, pale beneath; legs light brown; irides hazel. Length 6½ inches; wing 2½; extent 7¾; tail 2; tarsus ⅞; bill at front 12 mill.

This interesting bird has been found frequenting reeds and long grass in the neighbourhood of Calcutta, in the cold weather only. It probably extends into other parts of Lower Bengal, Assam, and the Burmese countries. I got one specimen in a reedy tank near Jounpore, in March 1848. Mr. Blyth suggested that this species may be the *Sylvia certhiola* of Pallas, from Northern Asia; but Temminck's description, I think, applies better to the previous species.

Some Australian forms appear to belong to this section, which is not very distinct from the last.

The three following genera differ from the previous ones by their shorter and more rounded wings, and thus lead to the next sub-family, *Drymoicinæ.* They are mountain forms, peculiar to the Himalayas, and some of them are classed by Gray and Bonaparte with the latter group. In their habits they resemble *Acrocephalus* and *Locustella.*

Gen. Tribura, Hodgson.

Syn. *Pseudoluscinia,* apud Blyth.

Char.—Bill straight, moderately compressed, culmen distinctly raised, acute at the base and notched; gape smooth; wing short, rounded and feeble, 3rd, 4th and 5th quills about equal; tail lengthened, graduated; tarsus stout and smooth; hind toe short.

Blyth considers that this form is nearly allied to *Locustella. Salicaria cinnamomea,* Rüppell, is considered to belong to it.

522. **Tribura luteoventris,** Hodgson.

P. Z. S., 1845, p. 30, and J. A. S., XIV., 588—Blyth, Cat. 1086—Horsf., Cat. 521.

The plain brown Reed-Warbler.

Descr.—Above uniform olive-brown; beneath paler, except the flanks, which are slightly rufescent; throat, and middle of the breast and belly, yellowish, inclining to whitish.

Bill dark horny above, pale below; legs light brown. Length 5½ inches; wing 2; tail 2½; bill at front 11 mill; tarsus ¾ inch.

Gray in his Genera places this bird as a *Calamodyta.* From the Cachar of Nepal.

Gen. Horornis, Hodgs.

Char.—Bill feeble, slender, compressed, with rictal hairs scarcely perceptible, distinct in some; wings moderately short, the 4th and 5th quills equal and longest; tail short, broad, much graduated, tarsus long and strong; feet moderate.

This genus was considered, by its founder, to have the general form of *Tribura,* (with some of the characters of *Horeites*) and indeed was placed as a sub-genus of the former. Gray, in his Genera, placed the species under *Regulus,* and Dr. Gray, in his last list of Genera, and Bonaparte, place it next *Abrornis.* Their habits are not recorded, and, in their mode of coloration they are allied to *Tribura,* but with a tendency towards the Tree-warblers.

523. Horornis fulviventris, Hodgson.

P. Z. S., 1845, p. 32.

THE FULVOUS-BELLIED HILL-WARBLER.

Descr.—Above olive-brown, below sordid luteous, the flanks shaded with olive; chin, and line over the eye, albescent.

Bill dusky brown; legs fleshy grey. Length $4\frac{3}{8}$ inches; wing not 2; tail $1\frac{5}{8}$; tarsus $\frac{13}{16}$ths.

From the Cachar of Nepal.

524. Horornis flaviventris, Hodgson.

P. Z. S., 1845, p.

THE YELLOW-BELLIED HILL-WARBLER.

Above olive-green, beneath pale yellow; chin, and line over the eye albescent.

Bill dusky-brown; legs fleshy. Length $4\frac{3}{8}$; wing not quite 2; tail $1\frac{5}{8}$; tarsus $\frac{13}{16}$.

From the Cachar region of the hills of Nepal.

525. Horornis fuliginiventer, Hodgson.

P. Z. S., 1845, p. 31.

THE SMOKY HILL-WARBLER.

Descr.—Above dusky olive-brown, diluted into a dusky greenish cast below.

Bill and legs dark. Length 5 inches; wing $2\frac{1}{4}$; tail 2; tarsus $\frac{7}{8}$.

Hodgson says " perhaps more probably a *Tribura*." From Nepal.

526. Horornis fortipes, Hodgson.

J. A. S., XIV., 584.

THE STRONG-FOOTED HILL-WARBLER.

Descr.—Above olive-brown, below pale ochraceous brown, approaching to albescent. Length $4\frac{3}{8}$ inches; wing $2\frac{1}{16}$; tail $1\frac{1}{4}$; tarsus nearly 1 inch.

From Nepal.

All these species appear to be rare, and only found in the higher regions of the Himalayas. I was not fortunate enough to procure any specimens when at Darjeeling.

Gen. HOREITES, Hodgson.

Syn.—*Nivicola*, Hodgs., J. A. S., XIV., 586.

Char.—Bill slender, short, straight, barely bent down at tip, slightly notched; wings as in *Prinia*; tail moderate, rounded, broad and soft; tarsus long; toes moderate; middle toe longer than in *Prinia*; nails slender, less curved.

This genus appears to be the hill representative of the *Prinia* of the plains, from which they chiefly differ in their more ambulant toes, and broader and shorter tail, but, at the same time, are more nearly allied in colours and habits to the grass warblers. Blyth at one time considered that they had some of the characters of *Tesia*, which Bonaparte also latterly classed with the *Drymoicinæ*.

527. Horeites brunneifrons, Hodgson.

J. A. S., XIV., 585—BLYTH, Cat. 819—HORSF., Cat. 499— Nivicola schistilata, HODGS.?—*Liklik-pho*, Lepch.

THE RUFOUS-CAPPED HILL-WARBLER.

Descr.—Above olive-brown, slightly redder on the wings and tail; cap red-brown; below, pale ashy, with a white central streak.

Bill dusky above, pale fleshy beneath; legs light-brown; irides brown.   Length $4\frac{3}{8}$ inches; wing $1\frac{3}{4}$; extent $6\frac{1}{4}$; tail $7\frac{3}{8}$; bill at front $\frac{3}{8}$; tarsus $\frac{3}{4}$.

Hodgson says these birds are only found, in Nepal, in the Northern region, near the snows, living among brushwood, and feeding on the ground.   I observed it only on the top of Tonglo, 10,000 feet high, among brushwood.

528. Horeites pollicaris, HODGSON.

J. A. S., XIV., 585.

THE STRONG-CLAWED HILL-WARBLER.

Descr.—Above dark olive, beneath and eye-brow yellowish; legs and bill fleshy grey. Length $3\frac{1}{2}$ inches; wing $1\frac{5}{8}$; tail $1\frac{3}{8}$; bill $\frac{7}{8}$; tarsus $\frac{13}{16}$.

This species is said to have a large hind claw, and a slender *Regulus*-like bill. Blyth suggests that it may be the young of *H. brunneifrons*.

From the same locality as the last.

529. **Horeites major**, Hodgson.

MOORE, P. Z. S., 1854.

The Large Hill-Warbler.

Descr.— Above olive-brown reddish, on the wings; tail rounded, and of a dusky brown, the outer webs fringed with olive-brown; cap red-brown; a yellowish ferruginous superciliary streak extending over the ear-coverts, which are ruddy brown above, ashy beneath; throat, sides of neck, centre of breast, and abdomen, ashy white; sides of the breast and flanks olive-brown.

Bill dark horny, fleshy at the base beneath; feet yellowish. Length 5 inches; wing $2\frac{1}{2}$; tail $2\frac{2}{10}$; bill at front $\frac{3}{8}$; tarsus $\frac{9}{10}$.

This species has a comparatively larger bill, and longer wing than the others of the genus, and also stronger feet. From Nepal.

I obtained two species, apparently of this genus, on the Khasia hills, from 5,000 to 6,000 feet of elevation. They frequent the grassy hills, hiding themselves with celerity, and in their habits closely resemble *Locustella*.

Sub-fam. Drymoicinæ, Wren-Warblers.

Bill moderately long and compressed; wings short, rounded; tail long, more or less graduated; legs and feet moderately strong.

This group comprises a considerable series of birds, highly characteristic of the Indian region, but found throughout the warmer portions of the old world, and very abundant in Africa, a few species only extending to the South of Europe, and several to Australia. They are mostly of diminutive size; and, except in a remarkable Australian group, of dull plumage. They chiefly frequent bushy ground, hedge-rows and the like, a few only being found in tree jungle, and a few in long grass. They are active and sprightly in their habits, and are somewhat garrulous, but few of them capable of what could be called a song. They feed exclusively on insects, which they pick off leaves or branches occasionally from the ground. The nests of some are remarkable for the ingenuity with which they are made; and the eggs are red in some, white with red spots in others, and in many blue, pure, or with blotches.

The *Drymoicinæ* form part of the *Malurinæ* of Gray, and the section *Drymoicinæ* of Bonaparte's *Calamoherpinæ*. Blyth, at one time, classed them as portion of the great Timaline series; but their less social habits, and other points, tend, in our opinion, to keep them distinct, but with strong analogies for that group. They appear to grade into the Grass-warblers by *Horeites*, and into the Tree-warblers by *Neornis*.

Gen. ORTHOTOMUS, Horsfield.

Char.—Bill long, slender, rather wide at the base, nearly entire, straight, very slightly deflexed at the tip; a few weak rictal bristles; wing short, feeble, much rounded, 5th and 6th quills equal and longest; tail narrow, feeble, typically short and rounded, or graduated, the two centre feathers elongated in some; tarsus moderately long, stout; feet short; hind toe short; claws moderately curved, compressed.

This genus comprises the Tailor-birds, which sew leaves together to form their nest. They are natives of India, and the Malayan peninsula is especially rich in species. They form a group of small species, generally green above, with more or less ferruginous on the head, and with somewhat the manners of the Wrens. They have a remarkably loud chirp.

530. **Orthotomus longicauda,** GMELIN.

Motacilla, apud GMELIN—BLYTH, Cat. 815—HORSF., Cat. 492 —Orth. Bennettii, SYKES, Cat. 80—and JERDON, Cat. 114—O. lingoo, SYKES, (the young)—O. sphenurus, SWAINSON—Sylvia ruficapilla, HUTTON—S. guzurata, LATHAM—O. sutoria and O. patia, HODGSON—*Phutki, H.—Tuntuni,* Beng.--*Patia,* Nepal. —*Likku-jitta,* Tel.

THE INDIAN TAILOR-BIRD.

Descr.—Crown rufous; nape somewhat cinereous, with a tinge of rufous; back, scapulars, rump, and upper tail-coverts, yellowish

olive-green; wings brown, edged with green; tail narrow, light
brown with a green tinge, and the outer feathers on each side with
a narrow white tip; beneath white, with a concealed black spot on
each side of the throat, formed by the bases of some of the
feathers, and only seen at times.

Bill dark horny above, pale fleshy beneath; legs fleshy; irides
reddish-yellow.   Length, male 6½ inches; wing nearly 2; tail
3½; bill at front ½; tarsus nearly ₁⁹₀.

There are four dark brown hairs arising from the nape, two on
each side.   In the male the two centre tail feathers are much
elongated, 1½ inches or so longer than the next pair, and the rest
are rounded and slightly graduated.   The female is barely 5 inches
long; tail 2.   In some specimens (especially in those from Ceylon)
the ashy nape is inconspicuous, being nearly overlaid with rufous,
and passing into the green of the back; and Ceylon birds appear to
have the bill also somewhat longer than those of continental India.

The well known Tailor-bird is found throughout all India,
from the Himalayas to Cape Comorin and Ceylon, and extending
into the Burmese countries.   It is most common in well-wooded districts, frequenting gardens, hedge-rows, orchards, low jungle, and
even now and then the more open parts of high tree jungles.   It is
usually in pairs, at times in small flocks, incessantly hopping about
the branches of trees, shrubs, pea-rows and the like, with a loud
reiterated call; and picking various insects, chiefly ants, cicadellæ,
and various small larvæ, off the bark and leaves, and not unfrequently seeking them on the ground.   It has the habit of raising its tail
whilst feeding and hopping about, and at times, especially when
calling, it raises the feathers and displays the concealed black stripe
on its neck.   The ordinary note of the Tailor is *to-wee-to-wee-to-
wee;* or as syllabized by Layard *pretty-pretty-pretty;* when alarmed
or angry, it has a different call.   It is a familiar bird, venturing
close to houses, but when aware that it is being watched, it
becomes wary and shy.

The Tailor-bird makes its nest with cotton, wool, and various
other soft materials, sometimes also lined with hair, and draws together one leaf or more, generally two leaves, on each side of the
nest, and stitches them together with cotton, either woven by itself,

or cotton thread picked up; and after passing the thread through
the leaf, it makes a knot at the end to fix it. I have seen a Tailor-
bird at Saugor watch till the Dirzee (native tailor) had left the
verandah where he had been working, fly in, seize some pieces of
thread that were laying about, and go off in triumph with them;
this was repeated in my presence several days running. I have
known many different trees selected to build in; in gardens very
often a Guava tree. The nest is generally built at from two to
four feet above the ground. The eggs are two, three, or four in
number, and in every case which I have seen, were white, spotted
with reddish brown, and chiefly at the large end. Col. Sykes says
that the eggs are crimson, but he has probably mistaken the nest
and eggs of *Prinia socialis*, which last are sometimes brick-red
throughout.

Hodgson suspects that there are two species confounded under
one name, as he has on several occasions got unspotted blue eggs
from a Tailor-bird's nest. These were probably those of *Prinia
gracilis*, the eggs of which are blue. Layard describes one nest
made of cocoanut fibre entirely, with a dozen leaves of Oleander
drawn and stretched together. I cannot call to recollection ever
having seen a nest made with more than two leaves. The bird
and its nest are very well figured in Guerin, Magasin de Zoologie,
for 1839.

Pennant, in his Indian Zoology, gives the earliest, though somewhat erroneous, account of the nest of the Tailor-bird. He says.
" The bird picks up a dead leaf, and, surprising to relate, sews it to
the side of a living one." Hutton gave the first authentic account
of the bird and nest in the J. A. S., II., 504. The Tailor-bird
described and figured by Forbes, in his Oriental Memoirs, appears
to be a species of *Nectarinia*. Nicholson's supposed new species
(P. Z. S., 1851), *O. agilis*, which, he says, often selects the
Brinjal (*Solanum esculeutum*) to build in, is of course the same
as our bird.

A very closely allied species exists in the *O. phyllorapheus* of
Swinhoe from China. This species is said to drop its lengthened
central tail feathers at the antumnal moult, when they are suc-
ceeded by others of the usual length.

531. Orthotomus coronatus, JERDON and BLYTH.

P. Z. S., 1861, p. 200—*Sing-kaneel*, Lepch.

THE GOLD-HEADED TAILOR-BIRD.

Descr.—Forehead and top of head golden fulvous; lores, ear-coverts, occiput and nape ashy; a narrow pale yellow stripe over the eye; back and wings pale olive-green; chin, throat, breast, and narrow stripe down the middle of the abdomen, milky white; flanks, lower part of abdomen, under tail-coverts, and lining of the wings, pale canary yellow; quills internally, and tail dusky, edged with greenish; the two outer tail-feathers with the inner web white.

Bill horny brown, darker above; legs pale fleshy yellow; irides light yellow brown. Length $4\frac{1}{2}$ inches; extent $5\frac{3}{4}$; wing $1\frac{5}{8}$; tail $1\frac{3}{4}$; bill at front $\frac{1}{2}$; tarsus $\frac{3}{4}$.

The bill in this species is somewhat depressed throughout, and flat on the culmen.

I procured specimens of this new species of Tailor-bird from the vicinity of Darjeeling, where it occurs in the warmer valleys. A nest and eggs were brought to me, said to be those of this bird, similar to that of the last, but not so carefully made; the leaves were loosely attached and with fewer stitches. The eggs were two in number, white with rusty spots. It exceedingly resembles the description of *O. cucullatus*, Temminck, from Sumatra, but there are points of difference, *viz.* the presence of a yellowish superciliary streak, and the white on the tail, in our bird; and the locality alone would warrant the probability of the two being distinct.

Moore has published a monograph of this genus in the Proceedings Zoological Society for 1854. Other species on record are as follows: *O. edela*, Temm., P. C. 599, 2, (*sepium*, Raffles) from Malacca and Sumatra; *O. ruficeps* Lesson, and *O. atrogularis* Temm., from Malacca and Borneo; *O. flavo-viridis*, Moore (*edela*, apud Blyth), very common at Malacca; *O. cineraceus*, Blyth, (*sepium*, Lafresnaye), also from Malacca; *O. longirostris*, Swainson; *O. Derbianus*, Moore, the giant of the group; and others.

Gen. PRINIA, Horsfield.

Char.—Bill moderately long, very slender, straight, entire; rictal bristles distinct ; tail much graduated, rather long, of ten or twelve feathers ; feet much as in *Orthotomus.*

This genus differs from *Orthotomus* by its shorter and more slender bill, more lengthened and graduated tail, and coloration. In habits it differs but little, and some of them are quite Tailor-birds as regards the nest.

With ten tail-feathers.

The first species differs from the others in its longer toes and claws, especially the posterior one ; also in its mode of coloration.

532. **Prinia flaviventris,** DELESSERT.

Orthotomus, apud DELESSERT—BLYTH, Cat. 813—HORSF., Cat. 494.

THE YELLOW-BELLIED WREN-WARBLER.

Descr.—Head, with lores and ear-coverts, dark ashy; back, wings, and tail, dull olive-green; the quills dusky brown ; chin, throat, and breast, white; the abdomen, vent, and under tail-coverts, bright canary yellow.

Bill black, fleshy at the base beneath ; legs deep yellow ; irides reddish yellow. Length $5\frac{1}{4}$ inches; wing $1\frac{7}{8}$; tail nearly 3 ; tarsus $\frac{13}{16}$; bill at front $\frac{1}{2}$.

This pretty little bird is found, within our province, in the Nepal Terai, and thence through Bengal to the Sunderbuns, extending into Assam, Sylhet, all the Burmese countries, and the Malayan Peninsula. It is abundant in the high grass jungles throughout Lower Bengal, especially near the Ganges, where I have frequently seen it, when beating for game. It is not found, that I am aware of, in forest or tree jungle. It makes its way through the thick grass and reeds, with great facility, and is generally seen in small parties. It is certainly not found in the Neilgherries, as stated by Delessert, nor, I believe, in Southern India; but an allied species has been lately noticed in Western India. Tickell describes the nest to be " pensile," but quite open, being a hemisphere with one side prolonged, by which it is suspended from a twig. The eggs are bright brick-red, without spot.

Y

533. Prinia Adamsi, Jerdon.

Prinia, No. 127—Adams, List of Birds, P. Z. S., 1858.

The white-bellied Wren-Warbler.

Descr.—" Above greenish, the tail tipped with white; cheeks, throat and breast, whitish yellow; belly and vent white, tinged with yellow; tail long, graduated.

" Bill black; legs long, yellow.

" Found at Poonah in cornfields." This is evidently a nearly allied species to the last, but apparently distinct, wanting the ashy head and the pure white breast of the last bird; its haunts also appear to be similar. As Dr. Adams appears to be a faithful observer, I have ventured to include this bird on his authority alone.

A nearly allied species to the two last, *Pr. sonitans*, Swinhoe, occurs in China, and of this the eggs are described as 'strangely red.'

534. Prinia socialis, Sykes.

Sykes, Cat. 78—Jerdon, Cat. 116—Blyth, Cat. 811— Horsf., Cat. 493—*Phutki*, H.—*Relu-jitta* Tel.—*Pit-pitta*, H. in the South.

The dark-ashy Wren-Warbler.

Descr.—Head and back dark-ashy; quills and tail reddish brown, the latter with a dusky band near the tip, and the outer feathers with a small white tip; beneath, rufescent whitish, the flanks rufous.

Bill black; legs deep yellow; irides orange buff. Length $5\frac{1}{4}$ inches; wing $2\frac{1}{10}$; tail $2\frac{3}{10}$; bill at front not quite $\frac{1}{2}$; tarsus nearly $\frac{9}{10}$.

This bird is found throughout Southern India only, and Ceylon, and I have not seen it to the north of the Godavery. It frequents long grass and reeds, sugar-cane fields, and occasionally low jungle mixed with grass. It is found on the Neilgherries, to about 6,000 feet or so, very abundant in bushy ground mixed with grass. It is active and restless, making its way adroitly through the reeds or bushes, with a loud reiterated note, something like that of the Tailor-bird, but louder. Col. Sykes remarks " has the same ingenious nest, the same habits and note, and feeds in the same •

manner as *Orthotomus longicauda.*" I have found the nest on several occasions, and verified Col. Sykes' observations, but it is not so neatly sewn together as the nest of the true Tailor-bird, and there is generally more grass and other vegetable fibres used in the construction. The eggs are usually reddish white, with numerous darker red dots at the large end, often coalescing, and sometimes the eggs are uniform brick-red throughout.

535. **Prinia Stewarti,** BLYTH.

J. A. S., XIV., 455—BLYTH, Cat. 812—*Kala-phutki,* H.

STEWART'S WREN-WARBLER.

Descr.—Above dark ashy, brown on the wings, and rufescent on the tail, with a faint subterminal dark band (as seen from above); throat white; the rest of the body beneath pale rufescent, darker on the flanks, and rusty on the vent and under tail-coverts.

Bill black; legs deep yellow; irides buff. Length $5\frac{2}{10}$ inches; wing $1\frac{8}{10}$; tail $2\frac{3}{4}$; bill at front not $\frac{7}{10}$; tarsus $\frac{3}{4}$.

Mr. Blyth got some specimens of this bird from Agra, and at first considered them distinct from *P. socialis,* to which it is certainly very closely allied. He has since been inclined to consider them the same, but having observed this bird, and obtained specimens at Mhow, in Central India, I am fully convinced of its specific difference. It has a considerably smaller and lighter body, when seen fresh, than *socialis,* and probably would not weigh much more than half of the latter bird; the tail is proportionally longer, the dark tip more diffused and less defined, and the vent and under tail-coverts are decidedly darker than in the other, as indeed are the whole colors of the bird; the bill is smaller and feebler, and the feet are smaller. Its geographical distribution too is against the identity.

This species ranges from the Nerbudda northwards through Central India to Agra and the N. W. Provinces; but does not extend far eastwards, I think, as I did not see it at Saugor. At Mhow I found it frequenting gardens and hedges, hunting among peas and other vegetables; and, like the rest of the tribe, occasionally descending to the ground for its food, which consisted of ants and other small insects.

Prinia familiaris, Horsfield, the type of the genus, belongs to this section.

With twelve tail-feathers.

536.   **Prinia gracilis,** Franklin.

P. Z. S., 1831—Blyth, Cat. 809—Orthot. lingoo, Sykes, according to Blyth.

Franklin's Wren-Warbler.

Descr.—Slightly rufescent olive above, tinged greyer on the head and neck; the wing feathers dusky, edged externally with rufous brown; under parts silky white, tinged with yellowish fulvous on the flanks, and faintly on the sides of the neck; tail brown, albescent greyish beneath, with a subterminal dark band, and whitish tips, most conspicuous on the under surface.

Bill black; legs fleshy yellow; irides deep amber; orbits fleshy red.   Length $4\frac{1}{2}$ inches; extent $5\frac{3}{4}$; wing $1\frac{7}{8}$; tail 2; bill at front $\frac{4}{10}$; tarsus $\frac{13}{16}$.

This little Warbler is found in Central and Northern India.   It was first procured and described by Franklin; and I found it abundant on the Vindhian Mountains near Mhow, and in jungles close to Saugor. It frequents tree forest, and has the usual habits of the genus.   It often has its forehead colored yellow by the pollen of flowers which it has been searching for minute insects.   I found its nest, at Saugor, very like that of the Tailor-bird, but smaller, made of cotton, wool, and various soft vegetable fibres, and occasionally bits of cloth, and I invariably found it sewn to one leaf of the *Kydia*, so common in the jungles there.   The eggs were pale blue with some brown or reddish spots, often barely visible. This is perhaps the Tailor-bird described by Lieut. Gifford, J. A. S., II., 648 "light brown above, dirty white below, 4 inches long, called *Phutki*." Hodgson's blue Tailor-bird's eggs may have been of this species, or the next one.

537.   **Prinia cinereo-capilla,** Hodgson.

Moore, P. Z. S., 1854.

Hodgson's Wren-Warbler.

Descr.—Crown of head grey, the shaft and margins of the feathers being darker, nareal and frontal plumes, a streak over and beyond the eye, and the whole under parts rufescent, brightest on the flanks and thighs; lores and upper part of the ears, greyish; nape, back, rump and wings bright rufous brown, the tips of the latter dusky; tail the same as the back, paler beneath, with a terminal dusky band, and rufescent-white tips.

Bill black; legs pale horny; irides buff. Length $4\frac{1}{2}$ inches; wing $1\frac{8}{12}$; tail 2; bill at front $\frac{5}{8}$; tarsus $\frac{3}{4}$.

This species is closely related to *P. gracilis*, but appears to differ by the deeper rufous brown of the upper plumage, by the more rufescent lower plumage, and by the presence of a superciliary stripe. It is an inhabitant of the Nepal Terai and lower hills, and is probably Hodgson's Tailor-bird, with blue eggs; it may be also Lieut. Gifford's, alluded to under the last species.

538. Prinia Hodgsoni, BLYTH.

J. A. S., XIII., 376—BLYTH, Cat .808—HORSF., Cat. 496— P. gracilis, apud JERDON, Cat. 117.

THE MALABAR WREN-WARBLER.

Descr.—Above dark ashy grey, brownish on the wings and tail, the latter with a subterminal dark band, tipped white on the outer feathers; beneath white, slightly tinged with fulvescent, greyish on the edge of the neck and breast.

Bill black; legs yellow; irides buff. Length 4 inches; wing $1\frac{8}{10}$; tail $1\frac{7}{8}$; bill at front $\frac{3}{8}$; tarsus $\frac{11}{16}$.

This is the smallest species of the group. It is found in Southern India, and also, it is said, in Nepal and Bootan, but perhaps, at that time, not discriminated from the last species. It frequents tree jungle. I have seen it all through the Malabar Coast, the Wynaad, the slopes of the Neilgherries, and more rare on the Eastern Ghats, and in wooded valleys at the Northern termination of the Table Land.

Pr. rufescens, Blyth, from Burmah, is a nearly allied species. Several other *Priniæ* are recorded from Malayana, but whether belonging to this genus as now restricted, I know not. Among these are *P. olivacea*, Raffles, *P. icteria*, Strickland, and *P. Stricklandi*, Bonap., from Java and Sumatra.

Gen. CISTICOLA, Lesson.

Char.—Bill rather short, slender, gently curving from the middle, entire at tip; wings short, ample; 1st quill small, 3rd, 4th, and 5th equal and longest, 2nd equal to 7th, shorter than the 6th; tail of twelve feathers, somewhat rounded, short; tarsus long; feet rather large with the lateral toes nearly equal and the hind toe long, the claws lengthened, especially the hind one, only slightly curved.

This genus differs from *Prinia* by its shorter, deeper bill, shorter tail, and less curved claws. It is a small group, of very nearly allied species, from the south of Europe, Asia, and Africa, extending to Australia. They are tiny birds, with a streaked plumage, and frequent chiefly grass and reeds.

539.   Cisticola schœnicola, BONAPARTE.

GOULD, Birds of Europe, pl. 113—Prinia cursitans, FRANKLIN, P. Z. S, 1831—BLYTH, Cat. 821—HORSF., Cat. 503—JERDON, Cat. 122—and JERDON, Ill. Ind. Orn., pl. 6—C. sub-himalayana, HODGSON—*Ghas ka-phutki*, or *Ghas ka-pit-pitti*, Hind., *i. e.*, Grass Prinia—*Yedru-jitta*, Tel.—*Kher-ghusa* H. at Bhagulpore—*Tuntunia* at Monghyr.

THE RUFOUS GRASS-WARBLER.

Descr.—Above rufous brown, all the feathers broadly centred dark brown; rump plain rufous; quills dusky, narrowly edged with brown; tail with the two central feathers pale brown, darker in the middle, and pale tipped; the others all dark brown, deeper towards the end, and with a broad whitish tip; plumage beneath rufescent white, nearly pure white on the chin and throat, and more rufescent on the flanks; tail beneath cinereous at the base, then pale rufous with a black bar, and a broad white tip, in some uniform dusky cinereous.

Bill dusky brown above, fleshy beneath; irides pale olive-brown; legs fleshy. Length 4½ inches; wing 2¼; tail 1⅝ to nearly 2; bill at front not quite 9 mill.; tarsus ¾.

This bird is now considered identical with the European one, and is also spread over the greater part of Africa. It is found in every part of India, frequenting long grass, corn, and rice fields. It makes its way adroitly through the grass or corn, and often descends to the ground to pick up insects; but I do not think that it habitually runs along, as the name given by Franklin would imply, but it rather makes its way through the grass, or reeds, partly hopping and partly flying.. When put up, it takes a short jerking flight for a few yards and then drops down into the grass again. It feeds on ants, larvæ of grasshoppers, and various other small insects. As Blyth remarks, "it may commonly be observed to rise a little way into the air, as is the habit of so many birds that inhabit similar situations, repeating at intervals a single note, *jik, jik*. During the breeding season the male bird may be seen seated on a tall blade of grass pouring forth a feeble little song. The nest is made of delicate vegetable down, woven into the stems of a thick clump of grass, and forming a compact and very beautiful fabric, with a small entrance near the top; and the eggs are four or five in number, translucent white, with reddish spots. It has been noticed that whilst the hen is laying, the male bird builds the nest higher.

540. Cisticola erythrocephala, JERDON.

BLYTH, J. A. S., XX., 523—BLYTH, Cat. 1935.

THE RED-HEADED GRASS-WARBLER.

Descr.—General hue rufous or ferruginous, deepest on the crown, darker on the rump, and brightest on all the lower parts; back olive-brown with black medial streaks to the feathers and wings and tail dusky brown, the former margined with olive-brown, and the latter very slightly tipped or margined round the extremity of the feathers with pale brown.

Bill dusky, fleshy beneath; legs fleshy yellow; irides pale brown. Length 4 inches; wing 2; tail $1\frac{5}{8}$; tarsus $\frac{8}{10}$; bill at front 9 mill.

This species differs from the last in its shorter and less graduated tail.

I have only procured this interesting species of *Cisticola* in one locality, *viz.*, in some open grassy ground, interspersed with bushes, close to the head of the Carcoor Pass, leading from Wynaad into lower Malabar; but I have no doubt that it will be found in suitable localities all through the Wynaad, Coorg, and the Western Ghats. It has a most peculiar loud chuckling, ventrilo-quising note, sometimes uttered on the wing, or from a bush, and it frequently completely deceives you as to its whereabouts. It is so loud as to draw your attention at once.

The next species appears to have somewhat similar habits.

541. **Cisticola Tytleri,** Blyth.
J. A. S.

The Cream-colored Grass-Warbler.

Descr.—The whole head, face and lower parts fulvous white; superciliary line, nape, and back, rusty; wings earthy brown, the feathers edged pale; rump uniform pale brown; tail dark brown, both above and below, very narrowly tipped with white.

Such is the coloration of specimens presented to the Asiatic Society by Colonel Tytler. One I procured at Dacca, differs a good deal; it has the head and upper parts pale rufous throughout, but not nearly so pale as the specimen described; the face and lower parts whitish, tinged with brown yellow.

Bill fleshy brown; legs fleshy yellow; irides buff. Length $4\frac{1}{4}$ inches; extent $5\frac{1}{2}$; wing $1\frac{3}{4}$; tail $1\frac{1}{2}$; bill at front $\frac{5}{10}$; tarsus $\frac{3}{4}$.

Tytler first obtained this species at Dacca, and noticed its dis-tinctness from the common one. He states that he found it in long grass jungle, excessively wild in its habits, and difficult to approach. I observed it in the same locality, but in bushy ground, and I did not hear its note. I think that Blyth is right in con-sidering Tytler's specimens as young; but from the observations I made, and the only good specimen I secured, I am inclined with Tytler to consider it distinct from *C. erythrocephala* of the Wynaad, though allied, both in coloration and habits.

A nearly allied species appears to exist in China, *Cist. tinnin-abulans*, Swinhoe, which is described as 'jerking about high in the air, whilst uttering its strange tinkling notes.'

The next bird is one whose generic location is somewhat doubt-ful. It exactly resembles *Cisticola* in its coloration and habits, but is a much larger bird, and I propose to give it distinct generic rank. Many of the so-called African *Drymœicœ*, figured by Rüppell, appear to approximate it very closely, and are probably co-generic with it. Such are *D. robusta, D. lugubris, and D. ery-throgenys*, Rüppell; also A. Smith's *D. natalensis*, and perhaps others from the same country, and also from Australia.

Gen. GRAMINICOLA, Jerdon.

Char.—Bill moderate, rather stout, compressed; culmen curved; some rather stout rictal bristles curving outwards; wings very short and much rounded: tail of twelve feathers, much graduated and broad; tarsi stout, of moderate length; hind toe not length-ened; claws long, slender, very slightly curved.

This form differs from *Cisticola* in the less elongated hind toe, and the more strongly curved beak, with prominent rictal bristles.

542. **Graminicola Bengalensis**, JERDON.

THE LARGE GRASS-WARBLER.

Descr.—Above, the head and back deep brown, the feathers edged with tawny fulvous; rump dark fulvous; wings with bright fulvous edgings to the feathers of the wing-coverts; the quills edged with yellowish brown; tail deep brown, with indis-tinct brown edging, obsoletely barred and broadly white-tipped, this being continued a short distance along the outer edge of the outermost feathers; beneath white, tinged with fulvous on the neck, breast, and flanks; under-tail-coverts slightly olivaceous.

Bill reddish horny; irides yellow brown; legs fleshy yellow. Length 6¼ inches; wing 2¼; tail 3; bill at front ½; tarsus 1.

Some specimens have the upper parts almost black, mixed with white over the eye and on the nape, but whether this is seasonal, or the effects of age, I am not aware. I first observed this bird in high grass on the banks of the Ganges, but did not procure specimens. I shot several, however, in Cachar, where it appeared to be tolerably abundant. It frequents high grass, in pairs, occa-sionally three or four together; now and then taking a short flight, and rapidly concealing itself when it alights.

Gen. DRYMOIPUS, Bonap.

Char.—Bill short or of moderate length, nearly entire, rather deep at the base; culmen moderately curving; rictus bristled; wings very short and rounded, the first three quills nearly equally graduated, 4th and 5th longest; tail graduated, long, of ten feathers, the feathers obtuse; tarsus long; feet moderate; claws moderately curved.

The genus *Drymoipus* was instituted by Bonaparte for the Asiatic *Drymoicæ*. It differs from *Prinia* in its shorter, deeper, less slender bill, more developed rictal bristles; and they usually frequent low bush cover rather than tree jungle. The species have usually been classed under *Drymoica*, but Bonaparte has separated the Indian species from the African ones, and though unaware in what points they differ, I shall follow Mr. Blyth's example, and keep them distinct.

543. **Drymoipus inornatus,** SYKES.

SYKES, Cat. 79—JERDON, Cat. 118—BLYTH, Cat. 804.—HORSF., Cat. 510—P. macroura, FRANKLIN—P. Franklinii, BLYTH, Cat. 805 (in part)—Prinia fusca, HODGSON—*Lota-kun-jitta,* Tel.—*Niong-pho.* Lepch.

THE COMMON WREN-WARBLER.

Descr.—Head and back greyish brown, with an olivaceous tinge on the head and hind neck; wings brown, edged pale rufous; tail rufous or brownish, with a terminal dark spot, and the centre tail feathers obsoletely banded; a whitish supercilium, and whitish lores and chin; beneath whitish with a faint fulvescent tinge; thighs pale ferruginous brown.

Bill dusky brown above, yellowish or fleshy at the base beneath; legs fleshy yellow; irides brownish yellow. Length 5 to $5\frac{1}{4}$ inches; wing $1\frac{3}{4}$ to $1\frac{8}{10}$; tail $2\frac{3}{4}$; bill at front $\frac{3}{8}$, tarsus $\frac{9}{10}$.

Horsfield, in his Catalogue, has joined Sykes and Franklin's species, which last Mr. Blyth had already united to Hodgson's *fusca.* Under his number 510 he has placed specimens from Col. Sykes, from Mr. Hodgson and from Bengal; and I have no doubt, has carefully compared them together. On examining my notes,

I find specimens described from Southern India, from the Himalayas, and Ghazeepore, which, on the whole, agree very well with
each other; and the few slight differences apparent may depend on
age, or on the more or less abrasion the feathers have under-
gone. Blyth, who at one time considered them distinct. in the J.
A. S., XVIII., 12, note, declared his belief that the two were
identical, and that *inornata* was the worn and abnaded plumage of
macroura. On a previous occasion, when contrasting the supposed
two species, (J. A. S. XVI.) I imagine that he had the next species in view; and Hodgson, in his original description of *fusca*,
had at that time probably not distinguished the next species.
When freshly moulted, the sub-terminal dark band of the tail has
more the character of a large spot, and the whitish tips are then
more conspicuous, but, by abrasion, become lost and the spot appears as a band. In no case does the wing ever come up to 2 inches,
more generally 1¾. The tail of course accidentally varies much
length.

The common Wren-Warbler is found throughout India in low
jungles, bushy ground, hedgerows, in cultivated ground, and even
in gardens. It is generally in pairs, occasionally in small
flocks, flying incessantly from bush to bush, hunting for insects,
and every now and then descending to the ground. It has a
rather loud monotonous note, *twee-twee-twee*; and occasionally
one perches himself on the top of a bush, and gives a sort of feeble,
but sprightly, twittering song. Its flight is feeble, struggling as
it were, by jerks, and. when pursued, they conceal themselves
in the thick bushes. I have found the nest and eggs repeatedly,
usually in a thorny shrub, at about three or four feet from the
ground. The nest is very neatly woven with grass, nearly
globular, with a hole at the side, and lined with some soft down,
generally that of the *Calotropis gigantea*, and sometimes with
feathers. It is firmly fixed to some of the thorny twigs of the
bush, and it is impossible to remove it without cutting the supporting branches. The eggs are from two to four, bright pale
blue, with large blotches of purplish brown, one of the most
beautiful eggs I know. I imagine that the nest described by me,
under 118 of my Cat., probably refers to the next species.

This species probably extends to Ceylon, but Mr. Layard describes the nest as built among reeds, the tops of which it draws together into a dome over the nest. As stated above, I have always found the nest in a thorny shrub.

Mr. Blyth, J. A. S., XI., 883 and XVI., 459, described a Drymoica as *D. Jerdoni*, Cat. 803, from specimens sent by myself from Southern India, which he has since absorbed into *D. longicaudatus*, stating that this supposed species was founded on a rather large specimen with abraded plumage. This specimen is still in existence, though rather in a dilapidated state; and on examination of it, I am by no means certain of its identity, but shall not separate it till other specimens are obtained. It appears to me very similar to some Ceylon birds, which Mr. Blyth doubtfully considered identical with *D. inornatus*. It appears intermediate in form between that species and *D. sylvaticus*.

544. Drymoipus longicaudatus, TICKELL.

J. A. S., II.—P. macroura, apud JERDON, Cat. 119—D. nipalensis, HODGSON, apud MOORE, P. Z. S., 1854, p.—D. fusca, HODGSON (in part), and D. Franklinii, apud BLYTH, J. A. S., XVI.,—and Cat. 805 (in part)—D. Jerdoni, BLYTH?

THE LONG-TAILED WREN-WARBLER.

Descr.—Above pale rufous brown; wings dusky, margined with bright rufous brown; tail rufous brown, paler beneath and distinctly rayed, with a terminal dusky band, seen most conspicuously above; the tips pale, not white; the whole under parts pale rufescent or lutescent, deeper on the flanks, and inclining to olivaceous.

Bill brown, pale fleshy at base of the lower mandible; legs fleshy brown; irides brownish orange. Length 5 to 6 inches according to length of tail; wing $1\frac{1}{12}$; tail $2\frac{1}{2}$ to 3 and more; tarsus $\frac{8}{10}$; bill at front 11 mill.

A specimen from Cashmere, in the Museum, As. Soc., is very pale throughout, the chin and throat more conspicuously white, and the bill darker and slightly shorter. Moore's description and measurements accord pretty exactly with those of mine; and I have little doubt that Blyth's bird is the same. Compared with *D. inornata*, it has always a more rufous tint above, more fulvescent tint beneath, the tail feathers are browner, the wings and tail are more distinctly marked with rufous, and the tail is considerably longer.

The long-tailed Wren-Warbler, like the last, is spread through India, but is only found in the more wooded and jungly districts. I have killed it on the Malabar Coast, on the Vindhian Mountains, and in Lower Bengal; and it has been procured in Central India, and Nepal. I have very little doubt that the nest and eggs described in my Catalogue under *P. inornata*, belonged to this species. I found it in a low bush on the edge of a water-course among some paddy fields in Malabar, near Trichoor. The nest was deep, cup-shaped, one side slightly raised where it was fixed to the bush, made of grass, well woven without any lining, and contained four pale blue eggs without any marks. Some nests, however, in the Museum, Asiatic Society, marked as of this species, correspond well with the nest and eggs of *D. inornatus*, as described above.

545. Drymoipus sylvaticus, JERDON.

Prinia, apud JERDON, Cat. 120—BLYTH, Cat. 799—HORSF., Cat. 508—*Konda lot dkun jitta*, Tel.

THE JUNGLE WREN-WARBLER.

Descr.—Above olive-brown; superciliary streak and beneath white, tinged throughout with yellowish; tail obsoletely barred, with a narrow subterminal dark band, tipped with white, except on the central tail-feathers.

Bill black; legs dark fleshy yellow; irides orange buff. Length 6 inches; wing $2\frac{1}{10}$; tail $2\frac{7}{10}$ to 3; bill at front 12 mill.; tarsus 1. The bill is strong, as are the feet and legs.

This species is only found in Southern India, in low jungle in the Carnatic, in thin tree jungle on the Eastern Ghauts, and in the more open parts of the forest on the Malabar Coast, ranging up the slopes of the Neilgherries to 4,000 feet. It is generally in small flocks, has a loud reiterated note, and one is usually perched on the very top of a bush or low tree, apparently as a sentinel.

I found the nest in low jungle near Nellore, made chiefly of grass, with a few roots and fibres, globular, large, with a hole at one side near the top, and the eggs white, spotted very thickly with rusty red, especially at the thick end. Nearly allied species are *D. validus*, Blyth, from Ceylon, and *D. polychrous*, Temm., from Java (*Suya Blythii*, Bonap.)

546. Drymoipus neglectus, JERDON.

Prinia, apud JERDON, 2nd Suppl. Cat., 121 bis—BLYTH, Cat. 801—HORSF., Cat. 509—D. sylvatica, apud BLYTH, J. A. S., XVI., 458—*Tot-rungi*, H. in Central India.

THE ALLIED WREN-WARBLER.

Descr.—Plumage greenish ashy brown, but with a decided tinge of rufous throughout; beneath whitish, strongly tinged with olive fulvous; tail very faintly barred.

Bill dusky above, fleshy beneath; legs dingy fleshy; irides amber colour. Length nearly 6 inches; wing $2\frac{3}{8}$; tail $2\frac{1}{2}$ to 3; bill at front $\frac{4}{10}$; tarsus $\frac{9}{10}$.

This species chiefly differs from *D. sylvaticus* in its more rufescent tinge throughout. I obtained my specimens from the jungles skirting the base of the Eastern Ghauts and from the Vindhian range near Mhow; and Mr. Blyth observed it in open bushy ground near tree jungle, N. W. of Midnapore, in straggling flocks of a dozen or more. It has also been procured in the N. W. Provinces, and it is Tickell's species, from Central India, J. A. S., 1848, p. 301, where he describes the nest and eggs, which are very similar to that of *sylvatica*, the eggs being described as fleshy white, with patches and scratches as of dried blood, darker spots showing through the shell. "Its note," says Mr. Blyth, "was a long continued and rapid repetition of the sound *twit, twit*."

Gen. SUYA, Hodgs.

Syn. *Decurus*, Hodgs.—*Drymoica*, pars. Auct.

Char.—Bill stout and compressed; gape with strong rictal bristles; tail of ten feathers, very long and much graduated; otherwise as in *Drymoipus*.

This is a mountain group of birds of rather larger size, and stouter form than the *Drymoipi* of the plains, with the tail very much lengthened. The plumage is obscurely striated, or rather with lateral pale edges to the feathers more or less developed, and the frontal feathers are inclined to be stiff.

547. **Suya criniger**, Hodgson.

As. Res. XIX., 183—Blyth, Cat. 798—Horsf., Cat. 504—Trochalopteron? Adams, P. Z. S., 1858, p. 486, No. 125—*Suya*, Nepal—*Dang prim-pho*, Lepch.—*Shik-shillik*, Bhot.

The Brown Mountain Wren-Warbler.

Descr.—Above dusky olive-brown (with pale lateral margins to the feathers, often, however, entirely abraded), somewhat darker on the cap, paler on the tail, which is faintly banded throughout, and with subterminal dusky spots and whitish tips; below rufescent yellow, shaded on the breast and flanks with brownish; lining of the wings buff.

Bill dusky black; legs fleshy grey; irides pale brown. Length nearly 8 inches; extent 7; wing $2\frac{3}{8}$; tail $4\frac{1}{2}$; bill at front $\frac{7}{10}$; tarsus $1\frac{4}{16}$. The female is a little smaller.

This bird is entirely confined to the Himalayas, from Cashmere to Sikhim. It is found among low bushes and brushwood, chiefly, from a moderately low elevation up to 7,000 feet, and upwards. It seeks its food on the ground, and lives on various small insects and larvæ. It makes a large, loosely constructed nest of fine grass, the opening near the top a little at one side, and lays three or four eggs of a fleshy white, with numerous rusty red small spots, tending to form a ring at the large end. It is not common about Darjeeling, but appears more so in the N. W. Himalayas. Hutton says "It delights to sit on the summit of tall grass, or even of an oak tree, from whence it pours forth a loud and long continued grating note, like the filing of a saw."

548. **Suya fuliginosa**, Hodgson.

Decurus fuliginosus, Hodgs., Gray, Zool. Misc., and Cat. of Birds of Nepal—Horsf., Cat. 505.

THE DUSKY HILL-WARBLER.

This species differs from *S. criniger*, in having a more robust bill which is entirely black, the feathers of the breast being dusky black, with rufescent-white shafts and tips. The legs are also shorter.

This species has only been sent from Nepal; it is intermediate to the last and the following species: and, as the next species, which is common about Darjeeling, is not included in Hodgson's list of Nepal birds, it is possible that an imperfect specimen of *atrogularis* was so named by Hodgson.

549. Suya atrogularis, MOORE.

P. Z. S., 1854—HORSF., Cat. 506—*Prim-pho*. Lepch.—*Shik-shillik*, Bhot.

Descr.—Above dusky olive-brown, or dusky brown, distinctly darker and cinereous on the head and neck; edge of wing at the shoulder, and under-wing coverts buff; primaries margined with buffish, and secondaries with rufescent brown; a whitish streak extending from the base of the lower mandible to the end of, and under, the ear-coverts; chin, throat, sides of neck and breast, black; the feather of the latter centred with white; the flanks and sides of abdomen mixed grey-brown and rufescent; vent olivaceous buff; thighs buffy rufous; tail paler than the back, without perceptible terminal band; the feathers narrow.

Bill horny brown; legs pale fleshy brown; irides yellow brown. Length $6\frac{1}{2}$ inches; wing $1\frac{7}{8}$ to 2; tail 4; bill at front $\frac{5}{12}$; tarsus 1.

This black-breasted Wren-Warbler is not uncommon about Darjeeling, frequenting brushwood, among which it generally conceals itself, now and then coming out, and, seated on the top of some shrub, uttering a harsh grating note. It makes its nest of fine grass and withered stalks, large, very loosely put together, globular, with a hole near the top, and lays three or four eggs, entirely dull Indian red color. It has been sent from Nepal as well as from Sikhim, and I lately procured on the Khasia hills.

The next bird has been separated by Mr. Blyth as the type of another genus.

Gen. BURNESIA, Blyth.

Bill very slender, rictal setæ minute and fine ; tail graduate ; legs long ; plumage distinctly streaked ; of small size and delicate form ; otherwise as in *Drymoipus.*

One species is found in India, and others apparently in Africa.

550. **Burnesia lepida,** BLYTH.

Drymoica, apud BLYTH, J. A. S., XIII., 376 ; and XVI., 460 —BLYTH, Cat. 807—HOUSF., Cat. 507—*Khur-phootki,* H. at Monghyr—*Door*, Sindh.

THE STREAKED WREN-WARBLER.

Descr.—General color light olive-grey above, each feather having a medial dusky streak, broader on those of the crown and back ; wings light dusky-brown ; the feathers margined with olive-grey, and the tail throughout distinctly, but obsoletely, banded above with narrow transverse duskyish lines, below pale, with whitish tips and a sub-terminal dusky band, or rather spot, on the inner web of each feather ; the under parts throughout are greyish white ; the lores, and a slight supercilium, of the same hue.

Bill plumbeous above, carneous below ; legs pale carneous-yellow ; irides light yellowish brown   Length 5¼ inches ; wing 1¾ ; extent 5½ ; tail 2⅜ ; tarsus ⅝ ; bill at front ⅜.

This streaked Warbler has hitherto been only found along the banks of the Hooghly and the Indus. Mr. Blyth found it in the former locality, where says he, " It inhabits low scrub intermixed with tufts of coarse sedgy grass, growing in sandy places by the river side, and it frequently flies out to feed among the thin herbage growing along the margin of the sand-dunes." I found it not rare in Tamarisk scrub, on some large churrs on the Ganges, at Monghyr.

Dr. Gould, who observed it near Kurrachee, says, " It frequents marshy bushes at the sea-side, in Scinde ; it is difficult to find and shoot, for it runs among the roots, and now and then it perches on a twig, and gives forth a wheezy feeble song, and then drops again into the thickets." It is also figured among the drawings of Sir A. Burnes, who found it in the same locality as Dr. Gould.

It appears very similar to *Malurus gracilis*, of Rüppell; and
M. clamans, Rüppell, may be another species of the same group.
Mr. Blyth pointed out to me that it was very possibly this species
noticed on the Indus by Lieut. Wood* in the month of July,
'nestling on the half-drowned islands, hanging its neatly constructed little nest to the top of a flexile grass stalk, and
rearing its young in security, where all is flooded beneath and
around it.'

The next species belongs to a different type, and has been named
Franklinia by Mr. Blyth.

Gen FRANKLINIA, Blyth.

Char.—Bill stout, compressed, deep; culmen moderately curved
towards the tip; wings short; tail broad, moderately lengthened,
and graduated, of twelve feathers, white-tipped; tarsi and feet stout.

This small group, composed of one Indian, and perhaps one African species, has much the habits and make of a small *Malacocercus*,
or *Chatarrhœa*.

551. Franklinia Buchanani, BLYTH.

Prinia, apud BLYTH, J. A. S., XIII., 376—P. rufifrons,
JERDON, Cat. 121—BLYTH, Cat. 806—Pr. brunnifrons, HODGSON.

THE RUFOUS-FRONTED WREN-WARBLER.

Descr.—Forehead and head pale rufous; plumage above greenish ashy; beneath white; tail brown, all the feathers except the
two central ones, broadly terminated by white, more broadly
so on the outermost feathers.

Bill brown above, yellowish beneath; legs fleshy; irides pale
orange buff. Length $5\frac{1}{4}$ inches; wing $2\frac{2}{10}$; tail $2\frac{2}{10}$; bill at front
10 mill.; tarsus $\frac{9}{10}$.

This little Wren-Warbler, of all the group, has most of the
manners of the *Malacoceci*. It is always in flocks of six, eight,
or more, is wary, and flies before you from bush to bush with a
low chirping whistle. I have found it in low thorny jungle in the

Carnatic, and all through the Table-land of Southern India. It also extends through Central India to the Upper Provinces, as far as Peshawur, and the Nepal Terai, but not eastwards apparently, for it is unknown in Bengal. A specimen I got near Mhow, in Central India, was so much darker in color, that I at first considered it distinct, but Mr. Blyth, on comparison, pronounced it identical with the bird of Southern India.

Africa possesses a large number of *Drymoicæ*, and affined birds, some of which, as before stated, appear to belong to our new type *Graminicola*. The Australian *Maluri* are conspicuous in this family for the beautiful seasonal plumage of the male, which is richly adorned with shining blue or red. Their habits do not appear to differ much from those of our Indian birds, but the eggs are described as being fleshy white, with red-brown spots. *Amytis* and *Stipiturus*, the latter with only six tail feathers, appear to belong to the same group.

Sub. fam. PHYLLOSCOPINÆ, Tree-Warblers.

Mostly of very small size; plumage more or less green above; bill in some slightly widened and depressed; wings moderate, or rather long; tail moderate or short; tarsus moderate; feet arboreal.

This group comprises a series of birds tolerably abundant throughout India during the cold season, only one, and that not a typical member of the group having been recorded to breed in the plains. Many of them do not appear to leave the Himalayas, where they are probably permanent residents, though wandering to different levels according to the season. They are exclusively insectivorous, feeding on minute insects, flies, cicadellæ, &c., &c., which they pick off the leaves, or occasionally capture on the wing. They are mostly social in the cold season, going about in small, somewhat scattered flocks, and they have a pleasant chirping note. Compared with the other Warblers, they are more strictly arboreal, most of them frequenting high trees; the bill is wider and more flattened on the culmen, and the rictal bristles more developed. A considerable number of species are found as summer residents in Europe and Western Asia, migrating to the North of Africa

in winter; others are found in South Africa. Gray, in his List of
Genera, places these birds, along with our *Calamoherpinæ* and *Sylviinæ*, in his sub-fam. *Sylviinæ*.

I shall commence the series with two birds, each leading to a
former group, and the first of which is, by some, classed apart
from this sub-family; but as it has, in my opinion, stronger affinities for the birds of the present group, I have preferred keeping
it here.

Gen. NEORNIS, Hodgson.

Bill much as in *Phylloscopus, i. e.* straight, moderately slender,
not compressed, with some long hair-like rictal setæ; wings short,
much rounded; tail rather short or moderate, rounded; tarsus
long; feet moderate, arboreal. Coloring as in *Phylloscopus*.

This name, at first applied by Hodgson to Blyth's *Culicipeta*, was
afterwards bestowed by him on the present genus as an aberrant
representative of the same form, which clearly showed that he
considered it to belong to the present sub-family; and Blyth
also places it here, although he at one time classed it under
Drymoica.

552. Neornis flavolivacea, HODGSON.

Cat. Birds Nepal, App. p. 152—BLYTH, J. A. S., XIV., 590—
N. cacharensis, HODGS. (the young)—Drymoica brevicaudata,
BLYTH—BLYTH, Cat. 814—HORSF., Cat. 502.

THE ABERRANT TREE-WARBLER.

Descr.—Above olive-green; beneath, and eyebrow, dull greenish
yellow; quills and tail dusky internally. The young bird is duller
green above, beneath buffy yellow.

Bill dusky; legs pale brown; irides light brown. Length about
5 inches; wing $2\frac{3}{16}$; tail $2\frac{3}{8}$; bill at front nearly $\frac{1}{2}$; tarsus $\frac{14}{16}$.

This Tree-Warbler has been found in Nepal and Sikhim.
The few specimens I procured were shot at a considerable
elevation.

The next bird, though clearly related to some of the *Phyl-
loscopi*, is also connected with the *Acrocephali* of the previous
group.

Gen. PHYLLOPNEUSTE, Meyer.

Char.—Bill straight, moderately slender, slightly widened at the base, entire; a few small rictal bristles; wings moderate, pointed, the 1st quill small, 2nd very little shorter than the third and 4th, which are longest, 5th nearly equal to it; tail moderate, even, or slightly rounded; feet moderate; claws long; hind toe short.

This genus, as restricted, barely differs from *Phylloscopus* by its somewhat thicker bill, stouter form, and shorter 1st primary.

553. **Phyllopneuste rama**, SYKES.

Sylvia, apud SYKES, Cat. 77—JERDON, Cat. 124—BLYTH, Cat. 1088—HORSF., Cat. 524—ADAMS, P. Z. S., 1858, p. 487, No. 126—*Chinna-kampa-jitta*, Tel.

SYKES' WARBLER.

Descr.—Above uniform light greyish brown; below pale or albescent, passing into white on the chin, middle of the belly and vent; lores, continued as a slight streak passing over the eye, and the orbital feathers, pale.

Bill dusky above, fleshy below at base; legs light brown; irides dark. Length 5 inches; extent $7\frac{1}{2}$; wing $2\frac{1}{2}$; tail 2; bill at front $\frac{4}{10}$; tarsus $\frac{3}{4}$; 1st primary about $\frac{1}{2}$ inch; 2nd equal to 7th; 3rd, 4th and 5th nearly equal and longest.

The coloring of this bird, as Mr. Blyth says, approximates it to the *Acrocephalus* group, but the form of the wings and tail differ. I follow Mr. Blyth in referring the present bird to *Phyllopneuste* of Meyer, the type of which is given by Gray as the *Sylvia hippolais* of Europe; but it appears to me to differ somewhat. The former Naturalist remarks that "there appear to be two races of this bird, differing a little in shade of color, but in no other particulars that we can discern." Those from Southern India are more rufous, those from the North more grey in their tints.

Sykes' Warbler is found all through India, frequenting low jungles, groves, hedges, gardens and trees near villages, and also among fields. It is lively and active, hopping about the branches, and capturing various insects, occasionally on the wing. but generally on the leaves or branches. It has a rather harsh chuckling

note, which it incessantly utters on being approached, and it
usually endeavours to hide itself, creeping to the further side of
the tree. I have obtained the nest and eggs of this species on one
occasion only, at Jaulnah in the Deccan ; the nest was cup-shaped,
made of roots, and grass, and contained four pure white eggs.

Gen. PHYLLOSCOPUS, Boie.

Char.—Bill very slender, small, straight, shallow, barely deflected
at the 'tip, entire ; a few small but distinct rictal bristles ; wings
as in the last, but the first primary more developed, and the
wing somewhat shorter ; tail moderate, even or slightly emarginate
in some ; tarsus and feet moderate ; claws slender.

This genus, formed for the *Motacilla trochilus* of Europe, and
allied species, comprises a considerable number of birds found in
various parts of India during the cold season only.   The plumage
is generally green above, inclining to brown in a few, whitish green
or yellow beneath, and, in general, without any paler markings on
the occiput, or bars on the wings.

554.   Phylloscopus tristis, BLYTH.

J. A. S., XII., 966—BLYTH, Cat. 1104—HORSF., Cat. 525—
Sylvia trochilus apud JERDON, Cat. 125.

THE BROWN TREE-WARBLER.

Descr.—Above uniform dull brown, below albescent, with a
faint tinge of ruddy on the pale supercilia, sides of neck, breast
and flanks ; axillaries, and fore part of the wing underneath, pure
light-yellow.

Bill blackish, yellow beneath and at gape ; legs brownish black ;
irides brown. Length 5 inches ; extent 7 ; wing $2\frac{1}{2}$; tail 2 ; tarsus
$\frac{3}{4}$; bill at front nearly 9 mill.

This species appears generally spread through India, during the
cold weather.   Blyth says that it is abundant in Lower Bengal in
swampy places with bushes, or occasionally in groves of trees.
I have seen it perched among some reeds on the banks of a stream,
now and then alighting on a stone in the water, and making short
sallies after insects in the air, or seizing one in the sand of the
rivulet.

555. Phylloscopus fuscatus, Blyth.

J. A. S., XI., 113—Blyth, Cat. 1111—P. brunneus, Blyth, Cat. 1110 (the young).

The Dusky Tree-Warbler.

Descr.—Uniform dusky greenish brown above, somewhat darker on the crown; primaries slightly margined with rufescent; beneath albescent, whitish on the throat and middle of the belly, and tinged with ferruginous or earthy brown on the sides of the neck, flanks, lower tail-coverts and breast; shoulders of the wings beneath fulvous; a pale streak over the eye from the nostril, and the ear-coverts also fulvous.

Bill dusky above, yellowish beneath; legs greenish brown; irides dark hazel. Length $5\frac{3}{4}$ inches; extent $7\frac{3}{8}$; wing $2\frac{1}{4}$ to $2\frac{3}{8}$; tail $2\frac{1}{8}$; bill at front $\frac{7}{16}$; tarsus not quite $\frac{7}{8}$; the 1st primary is about 1 inch long; the 2nd $\frac{3}{16}$ shorter than the 3rd, which is a trifle shorter than the 4th and 5th. The outer tail-feathers are about $\frac{5}{16}$ shorter than the medial ones.

This Warbler is not rare near Calcutta in the cold season, but appears to be more common in the countries to the eastward, especially in Arrakan. I did not procure it in Southern India.

556. Phylloscopus magnirostris, Blyth.

J. A. S., XII., 966—Phyllopneuste indica, Blyth, Cat. 1089 —Horsf., Cat. 526—Phyll., javanicus, Horsf., apud Blyth, Cat 1109—P. trochilus, apud Hodgson.

The Large Billed Tree-Warbler.

Descr.—Above dusky olive-green, with a faint tinge of tawny on the wings and tail; medial wing-coverts tipped with greenish white; a pale yellow supercilium, and the lower ear-coverts partly yellow; beneath, pale, the breast tinged with ashy, mingled with faint yellowish, and the rest of the lower parts more or less pure yellowish white.

Bill dusky plumbeous above, fleshy at base beneath; legs pale plumbeous; irides dusky. Length 5 to $5\frac{1}{4}$ inches; extent $8\frac{1}{4}$; wing $2\frac{5}{8}$ to $2\frac{3}{4}$; tail $2\frac{1}{8}$; tarsus $\frac{3}{4}$; bill at front $\frac{1}{2}$.

This bird, says Mr. Blyth, is something like *P. trochilus* of Europe. but is larger, and has a proportionally larger bill. The tawny hue of the wings and tail resembles that of *P. rufus* of Europe. It appears to be spread, but rare, over all India. I obtained it at Nellore, in the cold weather, and it has been procured near Calcutta, in Nepal, in Arrakan, and in China.

557. Phylloscopus trochilus, Linn.

Motacilla, apud Linnæus.—Gould, Birds of Europe, pl. 131, f. 1—Blyth, Cat. 1102.

The Willow-Warbler.

Descr.—Very similar to the last, but somewhat smaller, and with the lower parts distinctly olive-yellow on the neck, breast, and flanks; abdomen albescent; under wing-coverts yellow, tinging the edge of the wing. Length about 5 inches; wing 2½.

This species is said to have been obtained by Mr. Gould from Western India, though quite possibly not discriminated from some of the allied species. Adams also records it from Western India, P. Z. S., 1858, p. 693. The nest of this European species is said to be built on the ground, and the eggs are white with small red spots, in some cases pure unsullied white.

558. Phylloscopus lugubris, Blyth.

J. A. S., XII., 968—Blyth, Cat. 1108—Horsf., Cat. 527— Sylvia hippolais, Jerdon, Cat. 126 (in part)—Phyllopneuste flaveolus. Gray, Append. Cat. Nepal Birds.—Abrornis xanthogaster, Hodgson, Cat. Birds Nepal.

The Dull-green Tree-Warbler.

Descr.—Above dusky olive-green, with a pale yellowish supercilium, and yellowish tips to the medial wing-coverts; beneath albescent, faintly tinged with yellow medially, and the flanks greenish yellow.

Bill dusky above, amber colored beneath; legs greenish dusky; irides dusky brown. Length 4¾ inches; extent 7½; wing 2½; tail 1⅞; tarsus ¾; bill at front 10 mill. The 1st primary is $\frac{15}{16}$ long, the 2nd $\frac{5}{16}$ shorter than the 3rd, which is very little shorter than the 4th and 5th, which are longest; tail nearly even.

This species is also spread throughout India. I procured it in the Neilgherries, in the Wynaad, and also at Nellore; and it is common near Calcutta, and in Nepal and Sikhim.

559. Phylloscopus nitidus, LATHAM.

Muscicapa, apud LATHAM, and FRANKLIN—BLYTH, J. A. S., XII., 965—BLYTH, Cat. 1100—Sylvia hippolais, JERDON, Cat. 126 (in part)—Hippolais Swainsoni, HODGSON—probably S. sibilatrix of ROYLE.

THE BRIGHT-GREEN TREE-WARBLER.

Descr.—Above lively green, below unsullied pale yellowish, brightest about the breast; a pale wing-band formed by the tips of the larger coverts of the secondaries.

Bill dusky above, fleshy beneath and at the base; legs light brown; irides dark. Length $4\frac{3}{4}$ inches: extent $7\frac{1}{4}$; wing $2\frac{3}{8}$; bill at front 10 mill.: tail $1\frac{7}{8}$ to 2: tarsus $\frac{3}{4}$; the 3rd primary equals the 4th and slightly exceeds the 5th.

This pretty species is generally distributed over India during the cold weather, and is by no means rare. I have got it frequently in Southern India, especially in the hill regions; but it is somewhat rare about Calcutta.

560. Phylloscopus viridanus, BLYTH.

J. A. S., XII., 967—BLYTH, Cat. 1106—HORSF., Cat. 528 —Phyllopneuste affinis, and P. rufa, BLYTH, olim—Abrornis tenuiceps, HODGSON.

THE GREENISH TREE-WARBLER.

Descr.—Above light dull olive-green; beneath greenish albescent, darker on the flanks; a pale yellow supercilium, and an indication of a slight whitish bar on the wings, the coverts being tipped pale. Length $4\frac{3}{4}$ to 5 inches; extent $7\frac{1}{2}$; wing $2\frac{1}{4}$ to $2\frac{1}{2}$; bill at front 10 mill.; tail $1\frac{3}{4}$ to 2; tarsus $\frac{11}{16}$ to $\frac{3}{4}$. The 1st primary is $\frac{3}{4}$ inch; the 2nd $\frac{1}{4}$ shorter than the 3rd, which is nearly equal to the 4th and 5th.

" This species," says Mr. Blyth, " is very common in Lower Bengal in the cold weather, and likewise in Nepal. The note of the bird is weak, and is expressible by the sound *tiss-yip*, *tiss-yip*, frequently uttered." I procured it in various parts of Southern India, and also at Darjeeling. It is possibly the *P. trochilus*, apud Gould and Adams. (*Vide* page 192.)

561. Phylloscopus affinis, TICKELL.

Motacilla, apud TICKELL—BLYTH, Cat. 1107—and J. A. S., XVI., 442.

TICKELL'S TREE-WARBLER.

Descr.—Above fuscous olive-green, with an extremely faint tawny tinge ; no pale tips to the medial wing-coverts ; supercilia, cheeks, and under parts, pale sullied greenish or oil yellow, brightest on the middle of the belly, with a slight tawny tinge in some, and the breast and flanks a little infuscated.

Bill dusky above, amber colored beneath ; legs pale brownish dusky, tinged with yellow. Length $4\frac{1}{2}$ inches; extent 7 ; wing $2\frac{3}{8}$; tail $1\frac{7}{8}$; bill at front 9 mill. ; tarsus nearly $\frac{3}{4}$. The 3rd primary is equal to the 4th and 5th. The outer tail-feathers are slightly graduated.

This species appears to be spread over all India, and is said by Blyth to be very common about Calcutta. It very closely resembles the next bird in coloration, but is a good deal smaller, and the yellow beneath is somewhat brighter. Mr. Atkinson lately procured a specimen in Sikhim, not far from the snows.

562. Phylloscopus indicus, JERDON.

Sylvia, apud JERDON, Cat. 127—Ph. griseolus, BLYTH, J. A. S., XVI., 443.

THE OLIVACEOUS TREE-WARBLER.

Descr.—Above uniform olive-grey, beneath olivaceous yellow, purest on the middle of the belly ; a clear pale yellow supercilium.

Bill dusky above, yellowish beneath; legs greenish brown, yellow internally and on the soles; irides dark brown. Length $5\frac{1}{4}$ inches; extent $7\frac{1}{4}$; wing $2\frac{5}{8}$ to $2\frac{1}{4}$; tail 2; bill at front 10 mill.; tarsus $\frac{3}{4}$.

This Warbler is not common, but I have seen it in many parts of the country. I got it in Central India near Jaulnah, on the Northern Ghâts, at Saugor, and at Mhow. It sometimes frequents trees, but is more common in bushes and shrubs near rocks, and especially on rocky cliffs, which it appears to affect much. It is by no means rare on the cliffs of the Vindhian Mountains near Mhow; and at Saugor, I saw and watched it for some time among some low brush-wood at the foot of a high wall adjoining my house. It appears to be very rare at Calcutta, and I did not obtain it at Darjeeling.

Chloropeta, A. Smith, of S. Africa, appears nearly related to *Phylloscopus*.

The next group differs very slightly from *Phylloscopus*, but can, in general, be readily recognised by a peculiar mode of coloration.

Gen. REGULOIDES, Blyth.

Syn. *Phyllobasileus*, Caban.

Bill much as in *Phylloscopus*, or a trifle shorter comparatively; wings moderately long and more pointed, the 2nd primary being very little shorter than the 4th; tarsus and feet rather small.

The birds placed under this genus, which was founded on the *Regulus modestus* of Gould, are very similar in appearance and structure to the *Phylloscopus* group, from which they may, in general, be distinguished by a smaller size, and the head and wing-coverts being usually variegated with some light markings. They are mostly hill birds, migrating to the plains in the cold weather.

The first on the list is much the largest of the group, and, but for the light marking on the head, might have been classed under *Phylloscopus*; and, indeed, Mr. Blyth at one time observed that the remarkable firmness of its wings and tail is peculiar, and prohibitory of its association with either *Reguloides* or *Abrornis*, but he now, I believe, places it under *Reguloides*.

563. Reguloides occipitalis, JERDON.

Phyllopneuste, JERDON, apud BLYTH, J. A. S., XIV., 593.

THE LARGE CROWNED WARBLER.

Descr.—Above mingled green and ashy, the latter prevailing on the back, the former on the rump, wings, and tail; crown dusky, with whitish supercilia, and a conspicuous pale mesial line, broader and tinged with yellow at the occiput; a very pale yellowish wing band; the fore part of the wing brightish green, and its margin, and the axillaries pure light yellow; lower parts albescent, mingled with yellowish, and very faintly tinged with ruddy; inner webs of the three outer tail-feathers, on each side, narrowly bordered with white.

Bill dusky above, yellow beneath; legs pale brownish; irides hazel. Length $4\frac{3}{4}$ inches; wing $2\frac{5}{8}$; tail 2; bill at front 10 mill.; tarsus $\frac{11}{16}$. The 3rd primary is nearly as long as the 4th and 5th, and $\frac{5}{16}$ longer than the 2nd.

This, the largest species of the group, has been found rarely in different parts of the country. I got it at Nellore; and Mr. Blyth has seen it from Dehra Dhoon.

564. Reguloides trochiloides, SUNDEVALL.

Acanthiza, apud SUNDEVALL—HORSF., Cat. 539—BLYTH, Cat. 1096—Phyllopneuste reguloides, BLYTH, olim.

THE MEDIAN CROWNED WARBLER.

Descr.—Above dull green, yellowish on the rump and upper tail-coverts, with two conspicuous yellowish-white bars on the wings; below albescent greenish, a little tinged with yellow; a broad pale yellow supercilium, and above this a broad dusky band, leaving the middle line of the crown dull green, paling at the occiput; axillaries, and front of the wing beneath, yellow; outer and penultimate tail-feathers with a narrow whitish margin to their inner webs.

Bill dusky above, yellow beneath; legs yellow brown; irides dark. Length $4\frac{3}{8}$ to $4\frac{1}{2}$ inches; extent $7\frac{1}{4}$; wing $2\frac{1}{2}$; bill at front 9 mill.; tail $1\frac{7}{8}$; tarsus $\frac{11}{16}$.

This bird inhabits the Himalayas, migrating to the plains in the cold weather. It does not appear to extend to the south of India, at least I never procured it myself, but it is said to be very common about Calcutta.

565. Reguloides proregulus, PALLAS.

Motacilla, apud PALLAS—HORSF., Cat. 538—Regulus modestus, GOULD, Birds of Europe, pl. 149—R. inornatus, BLYTH—Phyllopneuste reguloides, and P. nitidus, HODGSON.

THE CROWNED TREE-WARBLER.

Descr.—Above olive-green, brightest on the rump, wings, and tail; crown dusky, with a pale mesial line, not always very distinct; two conspicuous yellowish-white bars on the wings, the hind one the broader of the two; and behind this is a dark patch; tertiaries conspicuously margined with whitish; secondaries and some of the primaries slightly tipped with the same; axillaries, with the fore-part of the wing underneath, pale yellow; supercilia and plumage beneath greenish albescent.

Bill dusky above, yellow beneath; legs pale brown; irides dark. Length 4¼ inches; extent 6½; wing 2⅛ to 2¼; tail 1½ to 1¾; bill at front 8 mill.; tarsus $\frac{11}{16}$.

This little Warbler, so rare in Europe, is tolerably common in most parts of India during the cold weather, and at all times on the Himalayas. I have got it at Nellore, on the Malabar Coast, in Central India, and at Darjeeling, and it also appears to be common about Calcutta. Mr. Blyth observes :—"This bird is solitary, and its song note is nearly similar to that of *Phylloscopus sibilatrix* of Europe, but considerably weaker." He also describes a nest which was brought to him as that of this bird, but I cannot help thinking that the person who brought the nest was mistaken, or wished to deceive. It is very like the nest of a *Nectarinia*, and it is certainly unusual for this bird, or any of the tribe, to remain in the plains to breed.

566. Reguloides chloronotus, HODGSON.

Abrornis, apud HODGSON, Cat. Birds Nepal, Appendix 152— BLTYH, Cat. 1098—HORSF., Cat. 540.

The Yellow-rumped Warbler.

Descr.—Above dull olive-green, rump canary yellow ; a con-spicuous mesial coronal pale yellowish line; superciliary streak, extending back to nape and cheeks, also pale yellowish ; beneath, pale yellow-greenish ; the coverts distinctly tipped, and the tertiaries margined with whitish-yellow ; tail dusky, olive externally.

Bill blackish above, pale at the base beneath ; legs pale brown. Length 3½ inches; wing 1⅞ ; bill at front 7 to 8 mill. ; tail 1⅝ ; tarsus ⅝.

This species of Warbler appears to have been found in the Himalayas from Mussooree to Bootan; also in Burmah, China, and the Dehra Dhoon. I got specimens at Darjeeling.

567. Reguloides viridipennis, Blyth.

J. A. S., XXIV., 278.

The Green-winged Warbler.

Descr.—Upper parts vivid olive-green, brightest on the margins of the wings and tail-feathers ; lower parts albescent, tinged with yellow ; crown dusky, mixed with green, with bright yellowish-white supercilia, and coronal streak continued over the occiput, the supercilia more yellowish anteriorly ; a broad pale yellow wing band, formed by the tips of the great-coverts of the secondaries ; and the smaller range of wing-coverts slightly tipped with yellowish; tibial plumes bright yellowish ; the margin of the wing pure canary yellow.

Bill dusky olive, yellow beneath ; irides brown ; legs dark brown. Length 4 inches ; wing 2 ; tail 1⅝ ; tarsus ⅝ ; bill at front 8 mill.

This species most nearly resembles *R. chloronotus*, but is readily distinguished by the rump being concolorous with the back. From *R. proregulus*, it differs by being smaller, and brighter coloured.

It was originally described from the Tenasserim Hills, but I obtained it at Darjeeling, so it probably inhabits all the intervening Hill ranges.

568. Reguloides erochroa, Hodgson.

Abrornis, apud Hodgson, Gray, Cat. Birds of Nepal, Append. p. 152—A. pulchra, Hodgson, (young bird)—Blyth, Cat. 1091—Horsf., Cat. 533.

THE BAR-WINGED WARBLER.

Descr.—Above dull olive-green, with a trace of a light streak on the centre of the crown, and a darker greyish streak on each side of the head; supercilia pale yellowish; orbitar feathers yellow; the checks mixed yellowish and dusky green; the lower parts of the back yellowish white, brightest on the rump and vent; tips of the greater wing-coverts with a broad bar of yellow rufous; quills brownish black, narrowly margined with greenish yellow; tail slaty brown, margined with yellow-green, the three outer tail feathers wholly white, except the terminal half of the outer webs, together with the tip of the inner web of the antepenultimate, and slightly of the penultimate feathers; entire under parts pale greenish yellow, or albescent yellow, greenish on the flanks.

Length 4 inches; wing $2\frac{1}{8}$; tail $1\frac{1}{2}$; bill at front 9 mill., tarsus $\frac{11}{16}$.

This well-marked species has been found in Nipal and Sikhim. I procured specimens from the neighbourhood of Darjeeling.

The next group contains two Indian species, which differ from *Reguloides* by having the markings on the head more pronounced, and darker, and the colours more vivid. The bill too is considerably wider and more Fly-catcher like.

Gen. CULICIPETA, Blyth.

Char.—Bill depressed, rather wide, but evenly attenuating, moderately slender, ridge of the culmen well marked; rictal bristles well developed; claws longer and less curved; otherwise as in *Phylloscopus*, or *Reguloides*.

569. Culicipeta Burkii, Burton.

Sylvia, apud Burton—Blyth, Cat. 1095—Horsf., Cat. 537—Cryptolopha auri-capilla, Swainson—Muscicapa bilineata, Lesson

—Neornis strigiceps, HODGSON—Acanthiza arrogans, SUNDEVALL
—Rhipidura, apud GRAY, Genera of Birds, Appendix.

THE BLACK-BROWED WARBLER.

Descr.—Above bright yellowish olive-green; below full siskin
yellow throughout; cheeks and sides of neck yellow-green; over
each eye a broad black streak, reaching to the occiput, leaving the
middle of the head greenish; tail dusky, its middle feathers margined green, and the inner web of the outermost feather nearly
all white, also the terminal half of the next; some have a slight
yellowish wing band, others not a trace of it.

Bill dusky above, beneath amber; legs brownish yellow; irides
dark.   Length $4\frac{3}{8}$ inches; extent $6\frac{1}{2}$; wing $2\frac{1}{4}$; tail $1\frac{3}{4}$; bill at
front 10 mill.; tarsus $\frac{11}{16}$.

"This pretty little bird is not uncommon in the neighbourhood
of Calcutta, during the cold season, and. like the rest of its tribe,"
says Blyth, "retires to the sub-Himalayan region to breed."   Its
bill, as seen above, is more decidedly of the Fly-catcher form than
in any of the tribe, and Gray even classed it as a Fly-catcher.   I
have only procured this species near Darjeeling.

570. **Culicipeta cantator,** TICKELL.

Motacilla, apud TICKELL—Horsf., Cat. 530—BLYTH, Cat. 1092.

THE LESSER BLACK-BROWED WARBLER.

Descr.—Bright olive-green above, yellower on the wings and
tail; throat, cheeks, supercilia, lower tail-coverts, and margin of
the wing, bright yellow; belly and flanks greyish white; a very
narrow yellow bar on the wing; on each side of the crown a broad
black band, and an intermediate and narrower greenish one,
becoming yellower on the occiput; upper tertiaries slightly margined at the tips with yellowish white, and the tail feathers have
a very narrow yellowish white internal border.

Bill light dusky above, amber beneath; legs fleshy yellow; irides
hazel.   Length $4\frac{1}{4}$ inches; extent $6\frac{1}{4}$; wing $2\frac{1}{4}$; tail $1\frac{3}{4}$; tarsus
$\frac{5}{8}$; bill at front 8 or 9 mill.

This very pretty Warbler is found in Nepal, Central India,
Bengal, and Assam.   It is rare near Calcutta.

Tickell says that it frequents trees in the thickest parts of the jungle, and has a loud and incessant note, '*pio-pio.*' I did not procure either of the last two species in Southern India.

A nearly affined species exist in *Phylloscopus trivirgatus,* Strickland, from Java, figured in Jardine's Contribution to Ornithology for 1849.

Gen. ABRORNIS, HODGSON.

Bill wider than in *Phylloscopus* or *Reguloides*, depressed, moderately deflected, and distinctly notched; nostrils concealed; a few fine rictal setæ; otherwise as in *Phylloscopus*.

The birds of this group only differ structurally from the two last forms by their wider and more depressed bill; but they have a peculiar mode of coloration, and, in this respect, divide into two lesser groups, the one with the head more or less grey, the other with the head chesnut. It is chiefly a Himalayan genus, but extends through Burmah to Malayana.

571. **Abrornis schisticeps**, HODGSON.

GRAY, Zool. Misc.—Culicipeta, Cat. Nep. Birds, App. p. 153— BLYTH, Cat. 1093—HORSF., Cat. 231—A. melanotis, JERDON and BLYTH, P. Z. S., 1861, p. 200.

THE BLACK-EARED WARBLER.

Descr.—Crown, occiput and ear-coverts, greyish slate, tinged greenish on the head, and passing to olive-green on the shoulders and back; yellowish on the rump and upper tail-coverts; wings and tail dusky, margined with olive-green; the inner webs of the outer tail feathers white; abdomen white; a broad streak from the front above each eye, the throat, breast, and vent, bright yellow; lores, base of lower mandible, under and over the eye, and a streak below the ear-coverts, black.

Bill and feet horny. Length $3\frac{1}{2}$ inches; wing $1\frac{9}{16}$; tail $1\frac{3}{4}$; bill at front 7 mill.; tarsus $\frac{5}{8}$.

This species has been found in Nepal, at Mussooric, and I procured it in Sikhim, but there rare. Hutton says that it is common at Mussoorie, and breeds at about 5,000 feet. It makes a round ball-like nest, with a lateral entrance, of grass, moss, wool, cotton, feathers, thread, and hair, and the eggs, three in number, are pure white.

572.　Abrornis xanthoschistos, HODGSON.

Phyllopneuste, apud HODGSON, Cat. Nep. Birds, App. p. 151—A. schisticeps apud BLYTH, J. A. S., XIV., 592—BLYTH, Cat. 1093—HORSF., Cat. 532.

THE GREY-HEADED WARBLER.

Descr.—Head, nape and upper back uniform ash-grey; the rest of the upper plumage bright yellow green; the entire under parts deep yellow; the two outer tail-feathers white on their inner web; a whitish grey supercilium; an ill-defined central pale streak on the middle of the head; and two ill-defined lateral broad streaks, more dusky than the head.

Length $3\frac{3}{4}$; wing 2; tail $1\frac{1}{2}$; tarsus $\frac{11}{16}$. Hodgson's measurements are rather larger. Length 4; wing $2\frac{1}{12}$; tarsus $\frac{3}{4}$.

This species has been found in Nepal, Sikhim, and Bootan, and I obtained it at Darjeeling.

573.　Abrornis albo-superciliaris, BLYTH.

Adams' List of Birds of Cashmere, No. 113—P. Z. S., 1859, p. 182.

THE WHITE-BROWED WARBLER.

Descr.—'Head, neck, and back, leaden ash, a white line over the eye; rump and sides tinged with yellow: tail olive; lower parts lively yellow; wings brownish black, with the edges of the quills tinged with yellow.

Bill dusky; legs light brown. Size of *P. trochilus*. Approximates *A. xanthoschistos*. Common in the woods and thickets of the lesser ranges.'

Adams' description corresponds nearly with a specimen I procured at Darjeeling, and which I had confounded with *xanthoschistos*, but the ashy hue of the head and upper back is much overlaid with green. It differs from what I take to be *xanthoschistos* by its larger size. Length $4\frac{1}{2}$; wing $2\frac{1}{4}$; tail $1\frac{7}{8}$; tarsus $\frac{3}{4}$.

I may remark that Gray's description of *xanthoschistos* does not quite agree with either, as the lower part of the back is said to be rich yellow.

An allied species is *A. superciliaris*, Tickell, from Burmah.

574. Abrornis flaviventris, JERDON.

A albigularis, JERDON and BLYTH, P. Z. S., 1861, p. 200.

THE YELLOW-BELLIED WARBLER.

Descr.—Above yellowish green, with a rufescent tinge on the tail feathers; head greyish, with a white supercilium from the base of the upper mandible; lores black; ear-coverts mingled whitish and greenish; throat and fore-neck white; rest of lower parts bright yellow; no trace of a band on the wings.

Bill dusky; legs pale. Length nearly 4 inches; wing $1\frac{7}{8}$; tail $1\frac{1}{2}$; bill at front 7 mill.; tarsus nearly $\frac{3}{4}$.

I found this species at Darjeeling, not very rare. The name given in the P. Z. S. having been forestalled, I am compelled to change it.

575. Abrornis poliogenys, BLYTH.

Culicipeta, apud BLYTH, J. A. S., XVI., 441—BLYTH, Cat. 1094—HORSF., Cat., 535.

THE GREY-CHEEKED WARBLER.

Descr.—Head, nape, base of lower mandible, and ear-coverts, ash grey; the loral feathers tipped with greyish white; round the eye a clear white ring; back, rump and shoulders, bright olive-green; wings dusky black, margined with olive-green, the greater coverts tipped with whitish yellow; throat greyish white, the rest of the under parts clear yellow; tail dusky on the six central feathers, which are margined with olive-green; the three outer being greenish dusky on the terminal half of the outer web, the basal half, with the whole of the inner web, being white.

Bill blackish horny above, yellowish beneath; feet yellowish horny. Length $4\frac{1}{4}$ inches; wing 2; tail $1\frac{3}{4}$; bill at front $\frac{3}{10}$; tarsus $\frac{1}{2}$.

This Warbler has been found in Nepál and Sikhim. I observed it near Darjeeling, less common than either of the last two, frequenting high trees; and also in the Khasia Hills in the summer, so it probably breeds there.

576. Abrornis affinis, Hodgson.

MOORE, P. Z. S., 1854—HORSF., Cat. 536.

THE ALLIED WARBLER.

Descr.—'Very close to *A. poliogenys*; differs in having the lores, base of lower mandible, lower portion of the ear-coverts, chin, and throat, the same bright yellow as the rest of the under parts; the feathers of the crown are pale-shafted, which does not appear in the last; the tail is pale dusky, the two outer feathers only being white on portion of the inner web, the basal part of which is dusky; the outer web in both is pale dusky green; the other ten are fringed with greenish on the outer web. The wing is $\frac{1}{4}$ inch longer than in *poliogenys*, but similarly marked; the tarsus also is $\frac{1}{10}$ inch longer. The bill in this species and in *poliogenys* is broader than in *A. xanthoschistos*.'

This nearly allied species has hitherto been only found in Nepal, or perhaps in Sikhim, whence, as before noticed, many of Hodgson's last specimens were sent.

The next two birds have chesnut heads.

577. Abrornis albogularis, Hodgson.

MOORE, P. Z. S., 1854—HORSF., Cat. 534—A. albiventris, JERDON and BLYTH, P. Z. S., 1861, p. 200.

THE WHITE-THROATED WARBLER.

Descr.—Forehead, lores, over and under the eyes to the nape and ear coverts, pale rusty ferruginous, the crown being dusky ferruginous, or mixed ferruginous and black, passing to yellowish olive-green on the back and shoulders, the rump being tinged yellowish; wings dusky black, margined with yellow-green; tail pale dusky greenish, edged exteriorly throughout with yellowish green; chin and throat white, the feathers of the latter black at the base; breast bright yellow; abdomen white; vent yellowish.

Length 3½ inches; wing 1¾; tail 1½; bill at front $\frac{3}{12}$ or 7 mill.; tarsus not quite $\frac{6}{10}$.

Rictal bristles black, strong, nearly half as long as the bill; and the hind toe and claw long and strong.

This pretty bird has been found in Nepal and Sikhim, where I procured one or two specimens only.

578. Abrornis castaneoceps, HODGSON.

GRAY, Cat. Nep. Birds, App. p. 152—BLYTH, J. A.S., **XIV.**, 593—HORSF., Cat. 511.

THE CHESNUT-HEADED WARBLER.

Descr.—Top of the head chesnut, edged by black at the sides posteriorly; checks and nape cinereous; above vernal green; wings and coverts edged pale yellow; greater coverts and quills dusky, edged green; outer tail-feathers white; chin to belly bluish white; belly, vent, and sides of the rump, pale canary-yellow.

Bill and legs pale. Length 4 inches; wing nearly 2; tail ⅝; bill at front 7 mill.; tarsus ¾.

This species has only as yet been procured in Nepal, and Sikhim, in which district I procured one or two specimens, near Darjeeling.

A nearly allied species is figured in Jardine's Contributions to Ornithology, as *Pycnosphrys grammiceps*, Strickland, from Java.

Gen. TICKELLIA, Jerdon and Blyth.

Char.—Bill flat, depressed, broad throughout, ending in a blunt point, laterally very slender and shallow; culmen very slightly curved, faintly notched; nostrils apert, at the anterior end of a large hollow; rictal bristles long, slender; wing short, rounded, the first quill graduated, 4th and 5th about equal; tail moderate, even, or slightly rounded; tarsus lengthened; feet rather large; middle and hind claws long.

The sole member of this genus, whilst clearly related to the last-named species of *Abrornis*, has, at the same time, considerable affinity for *Orthotomus*, and more especially for *O. coronatus*, which it very closely resembles in coloration.

579. **Tickellia Hodgsoni**, Moore.

Abrornis, apud Moore, Horsf., Cat. 679.

THE BROAD-BILLED WARBLER.

Descr.—Above olive-green, yellowish on the rump, and upper tail-coverts; forehead and crown deep ferruginous; the infraorbital plumes blackish, tipped white; above and below the eyes, ear-coverts, and sides of neck, grey; throat and breast greyish white; abdomen yellow; wings dusky, margined with ferruginous olive-green; tail dusky, the two outer feathers, with the whole of the inner web, white, the rest margined with olive-green.

Bill horny, yellowish at base beneath; legs yellowish. Length $3\frac{3}{4}$ to 4 inches; wing $1\frac{7}{8}$ to 2; tail $1\frac{3}{4}$; bill at front $\frac{7}{16}$, or 10 mill.; tarsus $\frac{11}{12}$.

I procured one specimen only of this rare bird from the neighbourhood of Darjeeling, and I think that Hodgson's specimens were also probably from Sikhim, and not from Nepal, as given by Moore.

Gen. REGULUS.

Char.—Bill short, straight, somewhat conic; nares protected by one or two rigid plumes; tail of ten feathers; otherwise as in *Reguloides*.

This genus, comprising two species from Europe, the well-known golden-crested Wrens, and other from North America, Japan, and Madeira, approximates *Reguloides* in the coloration of the head, which, however, is much more highly developed. The bill moreover is more conic. It is clearly related to *Ægithalus*, which is usually located among the Tits; and these two forms may be said to join the Warblers and the *Parinæ*, to which sub-family the Gold-crests perhaps more strictly belong.

580. **Regulus Himalayensis**, Blyth.

Reg. cristatus, apud Blyth, Cat. 1113.—Gould, B. Asia, pl.

THE HIMALAYAN FIRE-CREST.

Descr.—Plumage dingy green, yellowish on the rump; head with a central patch of flame color, edged with pale yellow, and tinged with a dark streak from the base of the upper mandible; lores, supercilia, and ear-coverts, greenish grey; wing-coverts dingy, with a few pale spots, and tipped pale ; quills dusky, yellowish externally, and with a dark spot near the middle of the wings, formed by the outer webs of the last primaries and secondaries ; tail dusky, edged with yellow green ; plumage beneath dingy or greenish white.

Length 4 inches ; wing 2¼ to 2⅜ ; tail 1⅝ ; bill at front 8 mill. ; tarsus ⅚.

Very like *Regulus cristatus* of Europe, but larger, and the flame-colored interior of the crest is more developed.

The Himalayan Fire-crested Wren has only been found in the N. W. Himalayas, and, even there, apparently not very common.

Sub-fam. SYLVIINÆ, Grey-Warblers.

These are a small series of birds, with mostly grey plumage, and frequently marked with black on the head or throat ; their bill is moderately slender ; the wings rather lengthened ; the tarsus and the feet short, but strong, and with moderately curved claws. They are less insectivorous than most of the previous groups of Warblers, most of them eating freely both buds of flowers, and fruit, and hence some of them are named Beccaficos or Fig-eaters in Italy (*Ficedula*, Brisson). They are mostly inhabitants of Northern Africa, the South of Europe, and Western (and perhaps Central) Asia, a few only, from the latter region, migrating, in winter, to the tropical regions of India. They are very arboreal in their habits, and in some degree, approximate the Tits (*Parinæ*) in their habits, as in their colours. Many of them sing very sweetly. It appears undecided among Ornithologists under what generic name to rank these birds. Some call them *Curruca* after Brisson ; Horsfield, whom I shall follow here, in his Catalogue places them under *Sylvia*. Gray, in his List of Genera, ignores both *Sylvia* and *Curruca*, and places them under six distinct sub-genera.

Gen. SYLVIA, Latham.

Syn. *Curruca*, Brisson.

Char.—Bill moderate or slightly lengthened and slender, with the rictal bristles almost obsolete ; wings lengthened and somewhat pointed ; 1st quill minute, 2nd a little shorter than the 3rd

and 4th, which are about equal; secondaries broad; tail slightly
rounded ; tarsus moderate or short, stout and scutate; feet strong,
short; lateral toes unequal, hind toe moderate ; claws moderately
curved.

These birds are in some parts of the country called *Phularia*,
i. e., quasi ' Flower-peckers.' The first noticed is placed by Gray
under *Adophoneus*, Kaup., and is distinguished by its somewhat
large size, and stronger bill, but Bonaparte ranks it under *Adophoneus*, and gives *S. nisoria* as the type.

581. Sylvia orphea, Temminck.

Philomela, apud JERDON, Cat. 110—BLYTH, Cat. 1121 and
1122—Curruca Jerdoni, BLYTH, J. A. S., XVI., 439—GOULD,
Birds of Europe, pl. 119—*Pedda nulla kampa-jitta*, Tel.

The Large Black-capped Warbler.

Descr.—Above brownish ashy, tolerably pure ashy on the nape
and rump; cap, lores, and ear-coverts, black in the male, dusky or
blackish grey in the female ; beneath whitish, pure white on the
throat and middle of the belly, tinged albescent on the breast ; tail
blackish, the outer feathers externally white, for the basal two-
thirds, and the next four successively less broadly tipped white ;
quills dusky brown, with pale edgings.

Bill blackish horny ; legs reddish brown ; irides dull greenish
yellow. Length 7 inches ; wing $3\frac{2}{10}$; tail $2\frac{3}{4}$; bill at front $\frac{6}{10}$;
tarsus $\frac{9}{10}$.

This bird was at first thought by Blyth to be distinct from
S. orphea of Southern Europe, with which I had identified it, but
he has lately united them. It is not rare in Southern India
during the cold weather. I have seen it at Trichinopoly, Madras,
and Nellore ; also at Jaulnah, and Mhow in Central India, whence
it appears to extend through the Upper Provinces, for Blyth has
received it from Delhi ; but it does not extend far to the Eastwards,
for I did not see it at Saugor, and it is unknown in Bengal. It
frequents groves, gardens, hedges, single trees, and even low
bushes on the plains; is very active and restless, incessantly
moving about from branch to branch, clinging to the twigs and

feeding on various insects, grubs, and caterpillars, and also on flower-buds. It is sometimes seen alone, at other times two or three together.

The next bird is, I presume, classed by Gray under *Epilais* Kaup.; but Bonaparte places it in his genus *Pyrophthalma*, along with *S. melanocephala* and *S. sarda* of Southern Europe.

582. Sylvia affinis, BLYTH.

J. A. S., XIV., 564, Note—Curruca cinerea, apud JERDON, Cat. 111—BLYTH, Cat. 1124—*Nelia kumpa-jitta,* Tel.

THE ALLIED GREY-WARBLER.

Descr.—Head and neck cinereous; ears dusky; the rest of the plumage above reddish cinereous; wings and tail brownish; outer tail feathers nearly all white, the others only tipped with white; throat white, rest of the plumage beneath white with a tinge of reddish.

Bill and legs brown; irides brownish yellow. Length 6 inches; wing $2\frac{3}{8}$; tail $2\frac{1}{4}$; bill at front 11 mill.; tarsus $\frac{3}{4}$.

This species, which in my Catalogue I considered to be the White-throat of England, has been separated by Mr. Blyth. It is however nearly allied to the European bird. Like the last it is migratory, being only a cold weather visitant. It frequents similar situations and has similar habits and food, and it feeds much on flower buds. On one occasion I found it very numerous in a hedgerow in the Carnatic, and observed it feeding on the pupæ of some ants which were swarming about, to seize which it descended to the ground. I have found it in the Carnatic, at Jaulnah, and other parts of the Deccan, and also at Mhow, but no further east; it does not appear to extend into Bengal, but probably will be found in the N. W. Provinces. It has also been obtained in Ceylon.

The following species would, I imagine, be classed by Gray under *Sterparola*, of which *Mot. sylvia* of Linnæus is given as the type.

583. Sylvia curruca, GMELIN.

Motacilla curruca and M. sylviella, GMEL.—Curruca garrula, BRISSON—JERDON, Cat. 112—BLYTH, Cat. 1125—HORSF., Cat.

543—Sykes, Cat. 76—Gould, Birds of Europe, pl. 125, f. 2—
Cheea in Sindh—*Chinna nalla kumpa jitta*, Tel.

THE LESSER WHITE-THROAT.

Descr.—Plumage above pale reddish cinercous, chiefly ashy on
the head and nape; lores and ears dusky ash; a faint white line
from the base of the bill to the eye; beneath white, tinged with
rufescent on the neck and breast; tail as in the last.

Bill blackish, pale beneath; legs dark slaty; irides brownish yellow.
Length 5¼ inches; wing 2⅜; tail 2; bill at front 9 mill.; tarsus ¾.

The Lesser White-throat is found over the greater part of
India during the cold weather, and it is much more common than
either of the two last species. It frequents similar localities, and has
the same habits and food, feeding both on insects and flower buds,
and incessantly moving about the upper and extreme branches of
trees. Mr. Blyth, who observed it in Bengal, noticed that it frequented Mimosa trees in small parties, and that it kept chiefly to trees.

Other species of this sub-family are *S. cinerea*, *S. leucopogon*, and
S. conspicillata, Europe. *S. atricapilla*, that well known Warbler,
the Blackcap, is placed under *Curruca* by Bonaparte, along with
S. hortensis, and *S. Ruppellii* of N. E. Africa and the Greek Archi-
pelago; and there are two or three more belonging to the
African Fauna.

Other Sylviadean forms not alluded to previously are *Cettia* and
Melizophilus, of Southern Europe, which appear to belong to the
short-winged Warblers, at all events, the latter.

The Warblers may be said to be represented in the New World
by the *Mniotiltinæ*, but, from their colours and structure, these
birds appear more allied to the Titmice than to the true
Warblers. In Australia and Oceanica, *Gerygone* appears to
take their place, but it is located by Bonaparte among his
Acanthizeæ.

Sub-fam. Motacillinæ, Wagtails and Pipits.

Bill generally of moderate length, slender, straight, barely deflected at the tip, and indistinctly notched; rictal vibrissæ minute or
wanting; wings typically long and pointed, and the tertiaries
lengthened; tail long; tarsus moderately long and slender; toes moderate; claws slightly curved; the hind claw often long and straight.

The *Motacillinæ* comprise three groups of birds, the species of each group greatly resembling one another; and, in most, there is more or less white on the outer tail-feathers. Some live by the sides of rivers or lakes, others in damp ground, or even marshes and irrigated fields; others in grass meadows, and many on bare and stony plains; a few only affect woodland situations, and perch on trees. They live almost entirely on the ground, on which they run with tolerable speed, always moving by alternate steps, and not hopping; and they feed chiefly on insects (which they are very dexterous in catching, even on the wing); a few only, at times, partaking of seeds or grain. Their flight is graceful, strong, undulating, and tolerably rapid; and many are highly gregarious in winter. They breed mostly on the ground, rarely on the ledge of a rock or building, and lay whitish or pale clayey-coloured eggs with brown speckles. Some of them have a sweet song and are occasionally caged; and many have the habit of jerking their tails up and down, which has procured for some the familiar name of Wagtails. A considerable number of the known species are migratory, visiting India and other hot countries in winter. They are found in all countries, but most abundant in the Old World, a few only being found in America, and still fewer in Australia and Oceanica. They may be said to approach the *Saxicolinæ*, and perhaps *Accentorinæ*, in this family: and their external affinities appear to lie with the Thrushes on one side through the Fork-tails; and, on the other side, with the Larks through the Pipits.

The *Motacillinæ* may be divided into—

1st.—Hill Wagtails, or Forktails, with rounded wings, and the tertials not lengthened.

2nd.—Wagtails, with lengthened tertials and unstreaked plumage.

3rd.—Titlarks, with streaked plumage.

1st.—Hill Wagtails.

Gen. ENICURUS, Temminck.

Char.—Bill moderate, or long, straight, stout; the culmen strongly keeled; gonys well marked, and inclining upwards; nostrils lateral, apert; two or three rigid bristles at the gape; wings moderate, rounded, with the 1st quill small, the 4th and 5th sub-equal and longest; tail (typically) long and forked; tarsus long and entire; feet moderate, ambulatory, the middle toe lengthened, the hind toe short; claws moderately curved.

This genus is a very aberrant one, tending towards the *Myiotherinæ*, and especially towards *Hydrobata*, and *Grallina*; but also, perhaps, with affinities for *Turdulus*. It differs from the typical Wagtails by the stronger and more cincline bill, shorter and more rounded wings, with the tertials of the usual length, and by the stronger tarsus and feet. Blyth and others class them with *Hydrobata* and *Eupetes;* but whilst allowing their affinities with those genera, on a comparison of all their characters, their more slender body, long tail, more lengthend wings, colours, mode of flight, and progression on the ground, I agree with Gray and Horsfield that they should be brought, within the limits of this sub-family, as the most aberrant group.

Their plumage is uniformly black and white, and they all have very pale fleshy-white legs. They frequent mountain streams in the forests only, and are found, within our limits, in the Himalayas only, extending through the hill ranges of Assam and Burmah to the Malayan Archipelago.

584. Enicurus maculatus, Vigors.

GOULD, Cent. Him. Birds, pl. 27—BLYTH, Cat. 921—HORSF., Cat. 548—E. fuliginosus, HODGS. (the young)—*Khanjan* in the N. W. Himalayas— *Oong-sam ching-pho,* Lepch.—*Chubia leka,* Bhot.

THE SPOTTED FORK-TAIL.

Descr.—Broad frontal band white, the rest of the upper plumage black with white spots; secondaries and tail black, without spots; rump white; the greater wing-coverts white, forming a large oblique white band, and the secondaries and tertials also white at the base, and tipped white; primaries dusky brown, lateral tail-feathers, and the tip of the central ones. white; neck and breast black; abdomen and under tail-coverts white.

Bill black; feet and legs fleshy white; irides dark brown. Length 10 inches; extent 12½; wing 4; tail 5½ to 6; bill at front nearly $\frac{3}{4}$; tarsus $\frac{13}{16}$; the tail is very deeply forked. The young bird has the black dull and sooty, and without spots.

The spotted-backed Fork-tail is found throughout the whole extent of the Himalayas, as far as Simla in the North-west, at all events, and extends into the hilly regions of Assam, Arracan, and Burmah. This beautiful Wagtail may be said to be one of the characteristic adjuncts of Himalayan scenery; if you come suddenly on a mountain stream crossing the road or path, and still more certainly if there be a waterfall, you are sure to see one of these birds, either on the road, or on a rock in the stream. If on the road, it will at times fly before you to the next stream that crosses the path, and so on for a dozen times in succession; but, more generally, it flies rapidly into the jungle, as you approach, and disappears up the stream, but not going far owing to the density of the jungle. I cannot say that I have seen them perch, but on one or two occasions, thought they did. In the larger streams they may be seen running on the shingle, at the edge of the river, but still more frequently on rocks, especially on those in the rapids that are washed over by the spray. There they pick up various small insects and larvæ, which constitute their chief food.

In general it is a solitary bird; occasionally two or three may be seen near each other, and, in that case, one will usually drive away the other. The nest and eggs of this bird have been brought to me, more than once, made of roots, fibres, and a little moss, with three or four eggs, greenish white, with a few rusty brown spots. The Hindustani name, *Khanjan*, is that usually given to the common black and white Wagtail of the plains.

585. Enicurus immaculatus, Hodgson.

As. Res. XIX., 190—BLYTH, Cat. 823—HORSF., Cat., 547.

THE BLACK-BACKED FORK-TAIL.

Form as in *maculatus*; colors similar, but the breast is white instead of being black, and the mantle is not spotted.

Length about 8 inches, of which the tail is $4\frac{3}{4}$; wing $3\frac{3}{4}$; bill at front $\frac{11}{16}$; tarsus $1\frac{1}{16}$.

Mr. Hodgson found this species very rarely in Nepal; and
it appears to be more common in the hill ranges to the South-
east, Colonel Phayre having sent specimens to the Calcutta
Museum from Arracan. Horsfield gives Affghanistan as a locality, but this is probably a mistake, many of Griffith's specimens,
undoubtedly from Assam and the Khasia Hills, being mixed up
with his collections from Affghanistan. I did not procure it at
Darjeeling.

586. Enicurus schistaceus, Hodgson.

As. Res. XIX., 189—Blyth, Cat. 922—Horsf., Cat., 546.

The Slaty-backed Fork-tail.

Descr.—Head, neck, back, and flanks, dark slaty blue; cheeks,
throat, and a very narrow band round the bill, jet black; a white
frontal band above the last, from eye to eye, partially surrounding
the eyes behind; beneath, the whole body from the neck, with the
rump and upper tail-coverts, white; wings and tail as in *maculatus*,
but the white at the base of the quills is more extended, and
shows itself as a speculum on the primaries.

Bill black; legs fleshy-white; irides brown. Length about
10 inches by 12 in extent; wing $3\frac{3}{4}$; tail $5\frac{1}{2}$; tarsus $1\frac{1}{8}$; bill at
front. $\frac{11}{16}$.

The Slaty Enicurus is chiefly found on the larger streams, not
ascending so high as *E. maculatus*. I procured it both from the
little and great Rungeet, but it is much rarer than the spotted-
backed and the short-tailed species. It extends from Nepal to
Bootan, and is also found in the Khasia hills and Burmah; but
has not been sent from the N. W. Himalayas.

587. Enicurus Scouleri, Vigors.

Gould, Cent. Him. Birds, pl. 28—E. heterurus, Hodgs.—
Blyth, Cat. 925—Horsf., Cat. 550—*Oong-sumbrek-pho*, Lepch.

The Short-tailed Fork-tail.

Descr.—Frontal band white, the rest of the head, back, and
wings, black; rump and upper tail-coverts white; tail, with the

central feathers black, except at the base; the outermost white with a black tip, and the intermediate ones with the black gradually increasing to the central feathers; a large white wing band; chin, throat, and upper part of breast, black, the rest below white.

Bill and legs black; irides brown. Length $5\frac{1}{2}$ inches; extent $9\frac{1}{2}$; wing $2\frac{3}{4}$; tail $2\frac{1}{2}$; bill at front $\frac{7}{16}$; tarsus 1.

This little Enicurus, aberrant as regards the shortness of its tail, appears to be found throughout the whole extent of the Himalayas, though more common in their eastern portion, for Jameson says that it is rare in the N. W.; and Adams, who observed it in Cashmere, states that it is not nearly so common as *maculatus*. About Darjeeling it is far from rare, but it does not ascend the streams so high as the spotted Fork-tail, being most abundant between 2,000 and 5,000 feet of elevation. It does not affect the smaller brooks, but chiefly good sized rapid streams, and it may often be seen seated on a rock in the midst of a boiling torrent, which is now and then almost submerged by a wave; and it feeds, almost exclusively, on rocks that are so washed over, following the retreating wave, or climbing up a slippery rock with great ease. It often contends with the plumbeous water Redstart, as already mentioned (page 143) for a choice piece of rock, and is generally vanquished by its more spirited antagonist. It feeds on various water insects, chiefly on the larvæ of various Neuroptera that frequent the wet rocks and the edges of rapids.

A nest was brought to me, said to be that of this bird, found on a ledge of rock near a stream, with three eggs, very similar to those of *E. maculatus*, but smaller.

588. Enicurus nigrifrons, Hodgson.

Gould, P. Z. S. 1859, p. 102.

The Black-fronted Fork-tail.

Descr.—Above black, with the upper tail-coverts, wing-band, base of the central, and the two outer tail-feathers, entirely white; beneath white; the throat and breast mottled with black and white.

Length 6 inches; wing $2\frac{11}{12}$; tarsus 1.

This species has been lately described from specimens transmitted from Sikhim by Mr. Hodgson, but we are ignorant of its particular haunts. It differs from the last species, which it otherwise greatly resembles in size and coloration, by the forehead being black, and the throat and breast being mottled instead of pure black. This latter character however is rather a mark of nonage.

Other recorded species of this genus are *E. Leschenaultii*, T., *E. velatus*, T., and *E. frontalis*, Bl., from Malacca and Java. *E. ruficapillus*, T., by its coloration and stronger bill, appears to belong to a distinct type, leading to the Thrushes.

2nd.—Wagtails.

We next come to the true Wagtails, which differ from the Pipits by their more lengthened tail which they flirt or wag up and down. They never rise singing into the air, as the last-mentioned birds do sometimes. They have a double moult. The Wagtails comprise four groups, distinguished by their mode of coloration, and the length and curvature of the hind claw.

1st.—Water Wagtails.

Gen. MOTACILLA, Lin. (as restricted).

Char.—Bill moderate, straight, slender, compressed at the tip which is very slightly notched; nostrils apert; rictus almost smooth; wings long, pointed, with nine primary quills, the first two subequal and longest; tertiaries lengthened, equal to the primaries; tail long, slender, nearly even; tarsus moderately long, slender, obscurely scutulate; feet moderate; hind toe short; claws slightly curved; hind claw small, more curved.

The Water Wagtails are usually colored black and white, more or less mixed with grey, and their tails are much lengthened. Their summer plumage is usually very distinct from that of the winter, showing much more black. They are in the habit of frequenting the neighbourhood of water, but they also affect towns and villages. They are pretty and lively birds, and some have a sweet song. They are found throughout the Old World, and most of them are migratory, one only being a permanent resident in India.

589. Motacilla Maderaspatana, Brisson.

Blyth, Cat. 766—Horsf., Cat. 551—Jerdon, Cat. 138—
Gould, Birds of Asia, pl.—M. picata, Franklin—M. variegata,
Sykes, Cat. 85—*Mamula,* II., sometimes *Bhuin mamula,* or
Khanjan— Sakala sarela-gadu, Tel.

The Pied Wagtail.

Descr.—Upper plumage, with the chin, throat, and breast, black,
with a broad white supercilium, and a large white wing spot,
formed by the median and greater coverts, and the edges of some
of the primaries; the greater part of the two outermost tail
feathers white, also the edges of the upper tail-coverts ; beneath,
from the breast, white. The female has the black less pure.
In winter the chin, upper part of the throat, and some feathers
just below the eye, are white.

Bill and legs black; irides dark brown. Length 8½ to 9 inches ;
wing nearly 4 ; tail 4; bill at front ⅜; tarsus fully 1.

This is the largest of the group in India, and it changes its
plumage in summer only in a trifling degree. In its mode of
coloration it comes nearest to the *Enicuri,* and it is not unlike
M. lugubris of Europe and Northern Asia. The Pied Wagtail is
found throughout the whole of India (except in lower Bengal),
and in Ceylon ; but it does not appear to extend to the east of the
Bay of Bengal It also occurs within the Himalayas, for I found
it in Sikhim. It is most truly a Water-Wagtail, being rarely
found except on the banks of rivers. It is usually solitary or in
pairs, and it is a permanent resident in India, breeding in a hole
in a pebbly bank, or under a shelf of rock, or even under a large
stone in the dry bed of a river. I have seen it on the top of
Government House, Madras, and had reason to believe that a pair
built their nest there, as others of this group are known to do sometimes in similar situations. The eggs are three or four in number,
pale greenish-white, with numerous light brown spots. The male
has a very sweet song, and is occasionally caged at Madras and
elsewhere.

590. Motacilla luzoniensis, Scopoli.

BLYTH, Cat. 770—HORSF., Cat. 553—M. alboides, HODGS.—
M. leucopsis, GOULD— *Dhobin*, H., *i. e.* washer-woman.— *Tangzhen-fleu*, Lepch.

THE WHITE-FACED WAGTAIL.

Descr.—In summer plumage, the occiput, nape, and upper parts
generally, deep black, also a large patch on the breast; a broad
frontal band, sides of head (including the eye), and neck, large
wing-patch, the two outermost tail-feathers on each side, and the
lower parts, white.

In winter plumage, the back, shoulder, and rump are ashy
grey, the occiput, nape, and breast-band alone being black. The
female is a trifle smaller than the male, and the black perhaps not
quite so deep.

Bill and legs black; irides brown. Length nearly 8 inches;
extent $11\frac{1}{2}$; wing $3\frac{5}{8}$, tail $3\frac{3}{4}$; bill at front $\frac{5}{8}$; tarsus $\frac{6}{8}$.

This and the next Wagtail may be considered the representatives of *M. alba*, and *M. Yarrelli* of Europe. The present species is
found in Northern India chiefly, and most abundant to the Eastward,
extending to Assam, Burmah, China, and the Philippines. It is very
common in Bengal, and extends north and west to Nepal, and
part of Central India, but is replaced in the south and west by the
next species. Adams, indeed, gives it from Cashmere and Ladakh,
but he may not have correctly distinguished it from the next
bird.

It affects the vicinity of houses, huts, and gardens, and runs
about picking up various small insects. Its arrival in India, which
takes place about the end of September, is looked on as the first
intimation of the ensuing cold weather. Most of the birds, in the
north of India, have assumed their summer plumage before quitting
the country. Swinhoe states that a few pairs breed in China, but
that most of them go still further north.

591. Motacilla dukhunensis, Sykes.

Cat. 86—M. alba, JERDON, Cat. 140—BLYTH, Cat. 769—HORSF.,
Cat. 554—*Dhobin*, H.

The Black-faced Wagtail.

Descr.—In summer plumage, the back and scapulars pale grey ; occiput, nape, wings, and tail, black ; a supercilium, wing-patch, and outermost tail-feathers, white ; beneath, the throat, neck, and breast, black, the rest white ; primaries are dusky, edged with white, and the upper tail-coverts ashy, edged with black.

In winter dress, the chin, throat, and beneath the eye, are white, leaving only a small patch of black on the breast ; the occiput and nape also are grey, the white wing-patch smaller ; the coverts and secondaries also grey, edged paler.

Bill and legs black ; irides brown. Length $7\frac{1}{2}$ to 8 inches ; wing $8\frac{4}{9}$; tail $4\frac{3}{4}$; bill at front rather more than $\frac{5}{8}$; tarsus nearly 1.

This species is the representative in Southern and Western India, of the white-faced Wagtail, from which, in its winter dress, it is barely distinguishable ; but a black feather or two on the chin, usually to be found, is a sure indication of the present species. It differs from *luzoniensis* by the permanently grey back. It very closely resembles *M albu* of Europe, but differs by its great wing-patch, and by the neck all round, and the ear-feathers, being black.

This Wagtail is found throughout Southern and Central India, extending into the N. W. Provinces, Sindh, the Punjab, and Affghanistan. Adams, however, says that he did not see it at Peshawur, and that the former species is the common Wagtail of Cashmere. It also is found in Ceylon. It is not very abundant in the extreme south of the peninsula, but is very common in the Deccan, and in Central India, coming in about the beginning of October, and leaving in March or April. It is a very familiar bird, feeding close to houses, stables, and in gardens ; often, indeed, entering verandahs, and coming into an open room if not disturbed. It runs about briskly after small insects, and is very active in catching the flies that infest the vicinity of stables and out-houses. Like the last, a small party of them may be seen towards evening on the bank of a river or tank, though, when feeding, it is usually solitary. Out of India the geographical distribution of these two last Wagtails is not recorded, but they probably breed respectively in the Eastern and Western sides of Central and

Northern Asia. Mr. Blyth remarks that these three species of true Wagtail differ from the European species, in all having more white on the wing-coverts and tertiaries, and in the neck being black all round when in summer dress.

Besides *M. lugubris* of Europe and Northern Asia already alluded to, the only other true Wagtails recorded, are four from Africa; one (*M. longicauda*, figured by Rüppell,) being remarkable for its particularly long tail.

2nd.—Wood Wagtails.

Gen. CALOBATES, Kaup.

Syn —*Pallenura*, Bonap.

Char.—Bill more slender than in *Motacilla;* wing slightly shorter, and tertials less elongated; tarsus shorter, and pale colored; hind toe short, with the claw a little longer and moderately curved; otherwise as in *Motacilla.*

This form chiefly differs in the more slender form, pale feet and legs, and in its mode of coloration, by which it forms a link to the next group.

592. Calobates sulphurea, BECHSTEIN.

Motacilla, apud BECHST.—BLYTH, Cat. 771—HORSF., Cat. 555 —M. boarula, TEMM.—JERDON, Cat. 137—GOULD, Birds of Europe pl. 147—M. bistrigata, RAFFLES—*Mudi-tippudu-jitta*, Tel.

THE GREY AND YELLOW WAGTAIL.

Descr.—Plumage above pale grey, with a wash of olivaceous; upper tail-coverts pale yellow, also the edges of the tertiaries; supercilium, chin, and throat, white; rest of the lower parts pale yellow, greenish on the middle, and laterally pure yellow; under tail-coverts darker yellow; a white wing-band; wings and tail brownish black, the three outer tail-feathers on each side, white on the inner web, the outermost wholly so.

In summer the chin and throat become black with a whitish border, and the yellow of the lower parts is darker.

Bill black; legs pale brown; irides brown. Length $7\frac{1}{2}$ inches; wing $2\frac{1}{4}$; tail $3\frac{1}{2}$; bill at front $\frac{7}{10}$; tarsus $\frac{8}{10}$.

This pretty and delicate Wagtail is widely diffused, inhabiting all Europe, Asia as far as Australia, and Africa. It is migratory in India, appearing about the end of September, and remaining till the first week of May or so. It is spread throughout all India, and Ceylon, but is most general in the hilly and wooded parts, and rare in the open country, especially towards the south of India, in the Carnatic and the bare table land ; being apparently more abundant in Bengal and the North of India.

It occasionally is to be seen on the banks of rivers, but is more generally found in gardens, near houses, in towns and villages, and on walks in the forests, or where there is sufficient shelter. Mr. Blyth states that he has seen it " tripping over the filthiest narrow black drains, between hut and hut, in the native town of Calcutta." It occasionally, though rarely, perches on trees ; and it has the jerking motion of its tail more remarkably than any other of the group, for it appears unable to keep it motionless for a moment.

This is the only recognised species of the genus ; but Bonaparte has separated the bird from Java under the name of *Pallenura javensis;* Blyth. however, states that those which he has examined from all parts of Asia, Africa, and Australia, were perfectly identical.

3rd.—Field Wagtails.

Gen. BUDYTES, Cuvier.

Char.—As in *Motacilla,* but the tertials barely so long. the tail shorter ; tarsus longer and stouter ; hind toe and claw lengthened, the latter very much so, and but slightly curved.

The Field Wagtails have the form of the Pipits, a long tarsus, and a long, nearly straight, hind claw ; and they all have more or less yellow on their under surface. They are found in fields and pasture lands. often in large flocks attending cattle whilst grazing. They are migratory, breeding in Northern countries, on the ground like the Pipits ; and they are said to lay similarly coloured eggs. Several species are known in the Old World, each apparently inhabiting a particular zone of longitude, and migrating South-wards in winter. They have no song like *Motacilla,* only a double chirrup.

There are. it is believed, only two species that visit India, although the changes of plumage of one of them are so great, that several have been recorded; and even now there appears to be some uncertainty about the changes of these and of others that visit South-eastern Europe.

593. **Budytes viridis,** Gmelin.

Motacilla, apud Gmelin— B. beema, Sykes, Cat. 83—B. neglecta, and B. flava, Jerdon, Cat. 135 and 136 bis—B. melanocephala, Sykes, Cat. 84, and Jerdon, Cat. 136—Brown. Ill. Zool. pl. 33—Blyth. Cat. 775 and 776—Horsf., Cat 556 and 557—B. dubius, fulviventer, and schisticeps, Hodgs.—B. melanocephala, Licht.—Rüpp. F. Ab. pl. 33 f. 6—*Pilkya*, H.

The Indian Field-wagtail.

Descr.—The usual plumage of adult birds, in winter, is olive-green above, with a white, or occasionally yellow, superciliary mark; beneath, the chin and throat whitish, the rest yellow, more or less pure; wings dusky, with two dull whitish yellow cross bands, formed by the tips of the coverts, and the tertials broadly margined with yellowish; tail black, slightly margined with greenish, and the two outermost feathers on each side chiefly white. At the spring moult, the whole cap, lores and ear-coverts change to a bluish ash-grey, with, or without, a white or yellow supercilium, which however is not always present, and disappears eventually by the change of color which takes place in the feathers themselves at a later period. The lower parts, too, become more pure and bright yellow; the chin is white, and the throat yellow, with its lateral border white.

A little later in the season, the lores and ear-coverts become darker by a change in the feathers themselves; and finally change to deep black; and, in full breeding plumage, the whole cap, lores, and ear-coverts, are deep black. It is not certain if the females ever assume the black cap, but it is probable that they do, and the only difference between the sexes is stated to be the slightly duller plumage of the female.

Young birds of the year are light brownish grey, purer on the nape and rump; wings and tail dusky, the former with two whitish cross bands; the tail darker than the wings, with the two outermost feathers on each side nearly white; beneath white, sometimes with a yellowish tinge, and a few brown marks on the breast; a white supercilium always present.

Bill black; legs black; irides dusky brown.   Length about $6\frac{1}{2}$ inches; extent $9\frac{1}{2}$; wing $3\frac{1}{4}$; tail $2\frac{3}{4}$; bill at front $\frac{7}{16}$; tarsus nearly $\frac{7}{8}$.

Some naturalists consider that the Black-headed Wagtails of India are a distinct species from the common one, and Horsfield yet retains Sykes' *melanocephala*, as Mr. Blyth and myself formerly did.   Most late writers on the ornithological Fauna of South-eastern Europe maintain *melanocephala* as distinct from the other European species, not, however, stating its identity with the Indian bird, but recording it to be much more rare than the grey-headed species. The distinctions between the various closely allied races are not very exactly laid down.   The species usually recognised are, *B. Rayi* of Western Europe only ; *B. flava*, L. (*neglecta*, Gould) of Europe generally ; *B. cinereo-capilla*, Savi, from South-eastern Europe ; and the so-called *B. melanocephala*, of Lichtenstein and Rüppell, from Africa and S. Europe.   Bonaparte has also *B. nigricapilla* (*melanocephala*, Savi), from various parts of Europe ; and *M. Feldeggi* is recorded, said to be intermediate between *cinereo-capilla*, and *melanocephala*, probably *viridis* in a state of change.   Of these, *B. Rayi*, at the breeding season, has the head, lores, ear-coverts, pale olive, with a yellow supercilium, chin a so yellow. *B. flava* has, in the breeding plumage, the head, lores, and ear-coverts always grey, with a white supercilium, and a white chin, the throat being yellow, bordered by a white line extending from the gape to below the ear-coverts ; *B. cinereo-capilla* appears by the description merely to differ from *flava* by having no superciliary mark, and the chin and throat being always white ; whilst *B. melanocephala* is stated to have the head black without any supercilium, and the throat yellow. *B. nigricapilla* is not described by Bonaparte. but is stated to occur in Italy, Dalmatia, Scandinavia, and Lapland.   Temminck states that *B. flava*, of Europe, is also found in Japan, in India, and the Moluccas, not, however, distinguishing it specifically from *cinereo-capilla* and *melanocephala*, which he gives as races of *flava*.

From the description of *melanocephala* of Southern Europe, there is very little doubt that it is our Indian bird, which thus appears also

to inhabit N. Africa, South-eastern Europe, and Western Asia.
When, with the grey head, a white supercilium be present, I do
not see how it can be discriminated from *flava*, but the ear-
coverts and lores always appear to be a little darker. Is it possible
that those found in India with the white eyebrow may be hybrids
between it and *flava*? or, have we individuals of *flava* mingling
with the majority of *viridis*? From *cinereo-capilla* it is distinguished
only by the throat being yellow instead of white. In spite of
these very close resemblances, we must consider it a distinct race,
as none of the other recognized species are recorded to assume a
black cap whilst breeding; and it has only been observed in Europe,
in the southern and eastern parts thereof * I think it quite possible that all the individuals of *viridis* may not assume the black head
the first year, at all events, which would account for its being considered so much ra·er than the allied species. Birds in winter plumage of *viridis*, *cinereo-capilla* and *flava* appear to differ but little.

Of the range of *viridis* in Central or Northern Asia, we have
no records. Pallas describes *flava*, apparently, as the common
species of Northern and Central Asia; and Swinhoe gives *flava*
as the common Chinese species. In this case our bird winters in
Africa and India. and breeds in South-Eastern Europe, probably
also in Western and perhaps the more Southern parts of Central
Asia. M. Malherbe asserts that *melanocephala* does not nestle in
Sicily, nor in Tuscany, though *cinereo-capilla* does.

In India this Wagtail comes in towards the end of September,
and does not quit the North of India till the end of April. or
beginning of May. It is an exceedingly abundant bird in every
part of India, usually associating in considerable flocks, and feeding
among cattle, picking up the insects disturbed by their feet whilst
grazing. They also frequent damp meadow ground near rivers or
tanks, grain fields, where they may often be put up along with the
so called Ortolan (*Calandrella brachydactyla*) during the heat of the
day; and, late in the season, they may always be seen taking

---

* But what are we to say of *B. nigracapilla*, Bonap., found in the same localities as
flava? Do old birds of *flava* ever assume a black cap, or are these individuals hybrids
with *viridis*?

advantage of any shade, a tree, stone, small clump, or paling, to shelter them from the fierce mid-day heat. Now and then a few may be seen about houses, in gardens and roads; occasionally even perching on a house top, or a wall, or paling, but very rarely on trees. Many are snared at Calcutta and elsewhere to be served up as Ortolan. Most of the birds on first arrival are in their first plumage, but they soon complete the change to the winter livery of the adult; and about the end of March, the new coronal feathers make their appearance, and it is not, in general, till the end of April that individuals with a black cap are met with. The nidification probably closely resembles that of *B. flava*, which is said to breed in cornfields or meadows, or in deserted mole holes, &c., and to lay several eggs of a greenish colour with fleshy spots.

594. Budytes citreola, PALLAS.

Motacilla, apud PALLAS—B. calcaratus, and B. citreoloides, HODGSON—JERDON, Cat. 134—BLYTH, Cat. 772—HORSF., Cat. 559—GOULD, Birds of Europe, pl. 144—*Pani ka pilkya*, H.

THE YELLOW-HEADED WAGTAIL.

Descr.—In winter plumage, above light ash grey, with more or less of the nape black or dusky ashy, as also, sometimes, the sides of the breast; head, and beneath yellow, with dusky olivaceous on the breast and flanks; wings dusky, the primaries edged greyish, and the tertiaries margined with white; wing-coverts broadly tipped white, forming two broad white wing-bands; lower tail-coverts more or less white; tail black, with the outermost feathers on each side white, except a portion of their inner web, and the extreme base of the outer. In full breeding plumage the upper parts become intense black, the yellow on the head and lower parts much brighter and more brilliant; and the shoulders of the wings grey. Young birds have the whole upper parts brownish grey, beneath dingy white, tinged yellow in some, and with a gorget of dusky spots; there is less white on the wing, and the super-cilium, forehead, ear-coverts, and chin are generally yellow.

Bill and feet black; irides brown. Length 6¾ to 7 inches; extent 10½; wing 3¼ to 3½; tail 3½; bill at front nearly ½; tarsus 1; long hind claw sometimes ⅝ of an inch.

This species is remarkable for the great length of the hind claw. It is found all over India in the cold weather, being migratory, and probably breeding in North-Eastern Europe and Northern Asia. It is not very abundant, and is never found in dry places like the last, but on the banks of rivers and lakes, and more particularly in swampy ground, or in inundated rice fields, apparently affecting concealment more than the others of this group. It has been obtained in breeding plumage at Mussooree, and is then a very beautiful bird.

Besides the species of *Budytes* already alluded to, *B. ophthalmica* from N. Africa, and *B. flavescens,* Shaw, from the Moluccas, are recorded. Does this last differ from *viridis*?

4th.—Garden Wagtails.

Gen. NEMORICOLA, Blyth.

Char.—General form that of *Budytes*, but with the short hind claw of *Motacilla,* and a peculiar mode of coloration.

This form appears intermediate between the Wagtails and the Pipits, both in structure, coloration, and habits, in which Mr. Blyth states that it approximates the latter group, but that it does not rise singing in the air, nor indeed is it known to have a song at all. It does not appear to wag its tail. It was founded on a single species.

595. Nemoricola, indica GMELIN.

Motacilla, apud GMELIN—BLYTH, Cat. 765—HORSF., Cat. 560—M. variegata, VIEILLOT—JERDON, Cat. 139—*Uzhalla-jitta,* Tel.

THE BLACK-BREASTED WAGTAIL.

Descr.—Plumage above greenish olive brown; beneath yellowish white; supercilium white; a double black band on the breast; the lower one not complete in the centre, which unites laterally with the upper one; wings blackish, with two broad white bands, and a third at the base of the primaries, a fourth near the tips of the secondaries, continued along the edge of the longest tertiary; tail with the middle feathers brown, the next dusky; the outermost white, with generally a brown outer margin, and blackish base;

the penultimate with white only on its terminal half. Sexes alike.

Bill dusky above, lower mandible whitish ; legs whitish, tinged with purple-brown. Length $6\frac{1}{4}$ inches ; extent 10 ; wing $3\frac{1}{8}$; tail $2\frac{5}{8}$; tarsus $\frac{7}{8}$; hind claw not $\frac{1}{4}$ inch ; bill $\frac{7}{16}$.

The black-breasted Wagtail is found throughout the whole peninsula of India, and Ceylon, but is common nowhere, and indeed rare in the South of India, in the bare table-land of Central India, and it is not recorded from the N. W. Provinces,* nor the Himalayas. It extends to Arracan, Burmah, Malacca, and some of the Malayan Islands, where it is much more common than in Continental India. I have only procured it myself at Nellore, in my own garden, and on the Malabar Coast. It appears not very uncommon about Calcutta, and, according to Blyth, at all seasons. It is quite a wood-loving species, never being found in the open plains, nor, that I have seen, about rivers ; being chiefly found in shady gardens and orchards, and on roads in the forests. It is usually solitary, and feeds on various insects. Layard relates of its habits in Ceylon, that it scratches among the dung of cattle in search of the larvæ of insects, and hence it gets its Cinghalese name *Gomarita*, or dung-spreader. It has no seasonal change of coloring, and appears to be found here, at all events in the more Northern parts of India, all the year round.

The next group comprises the Pipits or Titlarks, distinguished by their lark-like plumage and habits, but with a more slender form, and much less breadth of wing. The Pipits are closely connected with the Wagtails in their general structure, elongated tertials, &c., but, in color, are nearer to the Larks, among which some of them have been placed by Swainson and others. They may, indeed, be considered as a link uniting the two tribes of *Dentirostres* and *Conirostres*. In habits they are as much like one as the other, frequenting grass meadows, fields, and open sandy plains, but not so familiar in their habits as the Wagtails. A few perch habitually on trees. They rise into the air singing, but do not ascend to any height, or sing nearly so long as the Larks ;

---

* I cannot think that Mr. Philipps has rightly identified this bird, for he states that it frequents open fields in flocks of six or eight.

and their notes are feeble and monotonous. They moult in spring,
but hardly change their coloring at this time, or very slightly so ;
and the young of most are colored like their parents, though, in a
few, the pale edgings to the feathers assimilate them to the larks.
A few are migratory, others stationary. They are mostly inhabitants of the Old World, only one or two true Pipits being found
in Australia, and in America, but there are two or three genera
in the latter country, which perhaps belong to this group. The
bill is thicker than in the Wagtails, elevated at the base. They
live chiefly on insects, but also eat grass seeds and other small
grain.

There are at least three or four distant types now recognised
among the Pipits.

1st.—The Tree-Pipits.

Gen. PIPASTES, Kaup.

Syn. *Dendronanthus,* Blyth.

Char.—Bill short, stout ; tarsus short ; hind claw short and
moderately curved. Plumage much spotted beneath.

The Tree-Pipits frequent groves of trees, under which they feed ;
they perch readily, and when seated, have a peculiar motion of their
tail up and down. Mr. Blyth remarks that in confinement their
gait and manners are very different from those of the other Pipits,
being more deliberate. They are migratory, and social in the
winter.

596. Pipastes agilis, SYKES.

Anthus, apud SYKES, Cat. No. 88—A maculatus, HODGSON—
A. arboreus, JERDON, Cat. 141—BLYTH, Cat. 753—HORSF., Cat.
562—*Musarichi,* Hind.—*Khorasani churi,* of some Falconers—
Liku-jitta, Tel. *i. e.* Blind bird.

THE INDIAN TREE-PIPIT.

Descr.—In winter plumage, above fine greenish olive, with
strongly marked dusky streaks on the crown, and some slight
dark centres to the dorsal feathers ; beneath white, with a faint
fulvous tinge, with large dark spots on the throat, breast, and flanks ;
wing-coverts dark brown ; the median, with yellowish white tips ;

the greater coverts broadly edged with olive; the quills brown, edged with olive; tail with the outermost feathers white terminally, and for the greater part of both webs; the penultimate with a white tip; central feathers olive-brown; the intermediate ones brown, with olive edgings. In summer plumage, the upper parts are more brown, and less olive, more broadly streaked with dusky centres, and the under parts always pale fulvescent, passing to white on the abdomen and lower tail-coverts.

Bill dusky above, dull fleshy beneath; legs pale fleshy brown; irides dark brown. Length $6\frac{1}{2}$ inches; extent 11; wing $3\frac{1}{2}$; tail $2\frac{3}{4}$; tarsus $\frac{9}{10}$; bill at front $\frac{7}{10}$.

The Indian Tree-Pipit is very similar to its European congener, but appears to differ slightly. It is found over all India in the cold season, for it is a winter visitant only, coming early in October, and departing about the end of April. It frequents gardens, groves, thin tree-jungle; also occasionally grain fields, beds of woody streams, &c. It is social in its habits, many being generally found together. They usually feed on the ground on various insects, and also on seeds; but, on being disturbed, fly up at once to the nearest tree. They now and then feed on trees, hopping about the upper branches, and occasionally snapping at an insect on the wing. It is said by the natives to kill many mosquitoes, hence some of the native names. Mr. Blyth says he has seen small parties of them flying over their haunts, in a restless unsettled way, now and then alighting on a tree, and uttering a slight chirp, and continuing this till nearly dark. Its flesh is used by Falconers as a restorative to the Bhyri, and is said to be very delicate. It is taken in numbers for the table at Calcutta, and elsewhere in Bengal, and sold as Ortolan. Colonel Sykes' remark (which must have arisen from a mistake), "Found on open stony lands," is of course, not at all applicable to this bird, and misled many in identifying this species with his description.

597. Pipastes arboreus, BECHSTEIN.

Anthus, apud BECHSTEIN—A. trivialis, L.—GOULD, Birds of Europe, pl. 139—BLYTH, Cat. 752—HORSF., Cat. 561.

The European Tree-Pipit.

Descr.—Very similar to the last, but the tone of color less deep, it is less distinctly striated on the body, and more tinged with fulvescent on the throat, breast, and under parts generally. It is also somewhat smaller, the wing only measuring $3\frac{1}{4}$; the bill is stronger, and the hind claw slightly more curved.

This species has been killed in the N. W. Provinces at Ferozepore, Mussooree, and even in Nepal. Adams (distinguishing it from the last) says, "very common in the Lower Himalayan ranges." It is found in Europe (where it breeds); wintering in Africa; also in all Asia, Japan, &c. It is a fine songster, and lives well in captivity. Gray, List of Birds from Molucca, P. Z. S. 1860, has *A. arboreus*, var., from Batchian. Is this *agilis* or *arboreus ?*

598. Pipastes montanus, Jerdon.

Anthus, apud Jerdon, J. A. S., XVI., 435—Blyth, Cat. 759—
A rufescens, Jerdon, Cat. 191.

The Hill Tree-Pipit.

Descr.—Plumage olive-yellow, the feathers centered with dark brown; beneath, and supercilium, of a light rufous or tawny tinge, darkest on the breast, which, with the flanks and abdomen, are streaked with blackish brown; tail with the outer feathers dull fawn-white for the terminal two-thirds; the penultimate one has the terminal third of the same hue, and both, with the antepenultimate, have their tips white.

Bill blackish; legs pale brown; irides dark brown. Length about $6\frac{1}{2}$ inches; wing $3\frac{1}{4}$; tail $2\frac{5}{8}$; tarsus not quite 1 inch; bill at front $\frac{4}{10}$. Bill strong, short; hind claw well curved, nearly $\frac{4}{10}$ long.

The Hill Pipit has hitherto only been found on the top of the Neilgherries, where it is a permanent resident, and tolerably abundant. It frequents grassy hills there, being very commonly found near the woods, and, on being disturbed, flying up and perching on trees. It feeds chiefly on various insects and grass seeds. I can hardly imagine that it is restricted to the limited hill plateaus of

Southern India, most of this tribe having a wide geographical distribution, and I have little doubt that it will hereafter be found more widely dispersed.

2nd.—Titlarks.

The next group may be specially designated as the Titlarks, in which the plumage of the young birds resembles that of young Larks, the feathers being more on less pale edged.

Gen. CORYDALLA, Vigors.

Char.—Bill stout; rictal vibrissæ occasionally present; tarsi moderately long. In these birds the spring moult scarcely causes any change of colour from the hues of winter.

There are two very distinct types in this genus, the first with streaked plumage and long hind claw; the other, with the plumage but little streaked, and a short hind claw.

The first species is remarkable for its very elongated hind claw, approximating it to *Macronyx* of Africa.

599. Corydalla Richardi, VIEILLOT.

Anthus, apud VIEILLOT—JERDON, Cat. 142—BLYTH, Cat. 755—HORSF., Cat. 563—GOULD, Birds of Europe, pl. 135.

THE LARGE MARSH-PIPIT.

Descr.—Dusky brown above, the feathers edged pale olive-brown; beneath, and supercilium, fulvous white, deeper on the breast and flanks, paler on the belly and throat, and marked on the breast and sides of the throat with a few lengthened dusky spots; tail with the terminal two-thirds of the outermost, and nearly as much of the next, dull white, obliquely separated from the dusky colour of the base. The summer plumage is darker, the edgings more distinct.

Bill dusky above, yellow at base of lower mandible, and more or less to the tip; legs yellowish brown; soles bright yellow; inside of mouth also bright yellow; irides brown. Length $7\frac{1}{2}$ to 8 inches; extent $12\frac{1}{2}$; wing $3\frac{8}{10}$; tail $3\frac{1}{4}$; tarsus $1\frac{1}{4}$; bill at front $\frac{9}{10}$; hind claw $\frac{6}{10}$ to $\frac{3}{4}$.

The young bird has the feathers edged whitish, and is of the same tint beneath, with very faint spots. Mr. Blyth remarks that it closely resembles the only Titlark of Australia, *A. australis*, which however has shorter toes and claws; but the same naturalist has procured specimens from the vicinity of Calcutta, that make an exceedingly near approach to the Australian bird, which therefore perhaps may be found in the Eastern portion of Northern and Central Asia. Bonaparte, however, I see, has *C. sinensis*, 'like *Richardi*, but smaller and more rufous beneath.'

This large Pipit occurs throughout the greater part of India, being only found in the cold weather, up to about the end of April. It is found from Nepal and the Himalayas to the extreme South; more rare in Southern India, especially in the Carnatic; but tolerably common, indeed abundant, in Lower Bengal. It is also found in Ceylon, in Burmah, and other countries to the eastward. It always affects swampy or wet ground, grassy beds of rivers, edges of tanks, and especially wet rice fields, either singly or in small parties. Its flight is strong, elegant, and undulating, and it flies some distance in general before it alights again. Swinhoe says that it is very ochreous on arrival in China, but that this wears off; perhaps he here alludes to the race alluded to above as *Sinensis*, Bonap. Out of India, it occurs in Europe, Africa and Asia generally, rare in Britain. It is brought in large numbers to the Calcutta market, and sold as Ortolan.

600. **Corydalla rufula** Vieillot.

Anthus, apud Vieillot—Blyth, Cat. 757—Horsf., Cat. 566 —A. agilis, apud Jerdon, Cat. 190 —A. malaiensis, Eyton— Cichlops ubiquitarius, Hodgson—*Rugel*, H.,—*Chachari*, H., at Monghyr. *Gurapa-madi jitta*, Tel.

The Indian Titlark.

Descr.—Plumage above pale olive-brown, the feathers centered with dusky brown; beneath earthy or fulvous white, the fulvous most developed on the breast; chin white; breast and sides of throat marked with dusky brown striæ; supercilium fulvous white; outermost tail-feathers almost all white; the penultimate white on the whole outer-web, and also a considerable portion, obliquely, of the inner web.

Bill dusky above, yellowish at base of lower mandible; irides brown; legs fleshy yellow with a tinge of brown. Length 6½ to 6¾ inches; wing 3 to 3¼; tail 2¼ to 2½; tarsus about 1; bill at front $\frac{1}{10}$.

This species varies a good deal in size and proportion. Blyth says that it is almost an exact miniature of *A. Richardi*, except in its proportionally short tail, and rather smaller feet. It was generally considered the same bird as *A. Malaiensis* of Eyton, and to be diffused through the Malayan provinces; but Horsfield, in his Catalogue, puts that species as distinct.

Its breeding plumage does not appear to differ from the winter-dress.

This is one of the most common, abundant, and generally spread birds in India, being found in every part of the country, except on the highest elevations; and throughout most parts of Assam and Burmah. It frequents fields, compounds, and open grass plains, the sandy beds of rivers, edges of tanks, &c. It runs rapidly on the ground, and when raised, does not fly far. It feeds on insects and grass seeds. It makes its nest on the ground in April and May, under a slight prominence, or in a tuft of grass, or at the edge of a bush; and lays three or four eggs of a greenish ground color, with numerous small brown specks, chiefly on the larger end. Its song is a mere repetition of one note, during its descent from a short flight of a few feet from the ground.

601. Corydalla striolata, BLYTH.

Anthus, apud BLYTH, J. A. S., XVI., 435—BLYTH, Cat. 758—JERDON, 2nd Suppl. Cat. 190 bis—A. thermophilus, HODGSON, (name only)—HORSF., Cat. 565.

THE LARGE TITLARK.

Descr.—Very similar to *A. rufulus*, but larger, the markings more distinct, and the breast much more spotted, the general tinge at the same time being more fulvous.

Length about 7½ inches; wing 3½; tail 3; tarsus 1⅛; hind claw ½; bill at front nearly ½.

We are not thoroughly acquainted yet with the geographical distribution of this species, which might be sometimes overlooked as a large specimen of the last. Mr. Hodgson sent it from Nepal. Blyth first procured it from Darjeeling, where I found it tolerably common about the Station, and in stubble fields. I also procured it in the Nellore District, in the South of India, generally near low bushy hills, not approaching houses like the last; it is not rare at Saugor, in Central India, in similar localities; and it probably will be found more or less, throughout India, during the cold weather. It does not breed, that I am aware of, in India, even at Darjeeling, coming in towards the end of September. Swinhoe records that it visits China during the winter. I know nothing further of its habits, but that it has a stronger flight than *A. rufula,* and frequently takes shelter under trees or shrubs.

C. Hasselti, Brehm, from Java, is recorded, perhaps the same as *malayensis,* if that species be really distinct from *rufula;* and *A. euonyx,* Caban., may be another synonym. Blyth has also *Corydalla infuscata,* from the Philippines.

3rd Stone-pipits, or Lark Pipits.

Gen. AGRODROMA, Swainson.

Hind claw comparatively short; bill moderately strong; plumage more uniform and less streaked.

The Lark Pipits habitually frequent more bare, rocky, and stony ground than any of the preceding groups, and some affect chiefly mountainous or hilly regions. Besides the obsolete character of the markings of the plumage noted above, the outer tail feathers have less white, and more sullied in its tint. None of the three species inhabiting India are peculiar to it.

602. Agrodroma campestris, LIN.

Alauda, apud LINNÆUS—BLYTH, Cat. 760—A rufulus, apud JERDON, Cat. 192—A rufescens, TEMM.—GOULD, Birds of Europe, pl. 137—*Chillu,* H.

THE STONE-PIPIT.

Descr.—General tone of plumage pale rufous grey, some of the feathers, especially of the head, centred with dusky, those on the back scarcely so at all; beneath, and superciliary stripe, pale fawn color, whitening on the throat and vent; breast very faintly marked with brown streaks; a brown stripe from the gape below the ears, and another from the lower edge of the under mandible, down the throat of each side; wing-coverts brown, broadly edged with pale fawn color; the two centre feathers of the tail brown, edged with fawn, the outermost nearly all of that color; the penultimate tipped and edged only, and the remainder deep brown.

Bill horny above, pale fleshy-yellow beneath; legs fleshy yellow, irides brown. Length nearly 7 inches; extent $10\frac{3}{4}$; wing $3\frac{6}{10}$; tail $2\frac{3}{4}$ to nearly 3; tarsus $\frac{15}{16}$; bill at front $\frac{5}{10}$; hind toe and claw $\frac{7}{10}$; the latter much more curved, and shorter than in *C. rufula.*

The Stone-pipit is found in suitable places throughout India. I have found it most abundant in the Deccan, at Mhow in Central India, and on the Eastern ghauts; it is rare in the Carnatic; Blyth has it from Midnapore, and the N. W. Provinces. It frequents barren, open, stony land; and is never found in rich pastures or meadows, like *C. rufula,* from which it otherwise differs but little in its manners. Out of India, it occurs in parts of Eastern Europe, Asia, and North Africa. It breeds in this country. In Palestine it is recorded as frequenting the higher plains and hills.

The next two birds belong to a slightly different type. They are of large size, with plainer and less spotted plumage; the bill is somewhat more curved towards the tip, and the hind claw is well curved. Moreover they possess a minute 1st primary, as was ascertained by Blyth, which is not present in any other of this sub-family, except in the aberrant *Enicuri.*

I was the first to notice these birds in India, though I did not at the time consider them distinct; but Mr. Blyth identified them with the African birds described by Rüppell.

603. **Agrodroma cinnamomea,** Rüppell.

Anthus, apud Rüppell—A. similis, Jerdon, Cat. 193 (in part)—Blyth, Cat. 754 (in part)—Jerdon, Ill. Ind. Orn., pl. 45.

THE RUFOUS ROCK-PIPIT.

Descr.—Upper parts dusky olive-brown, the feathers more or less edged with pale ferruginous, deepest on the margins of the wing-feathers; beneath, and superciliary stripe, ferruginous, with narrow brown streaks on the foreneck and breast; chin and throat dull white; tail, with its outermost feathers dark, obliquely tipped for its terminal third with ruddy whitish, which extends up the narrow outer web to near its base; and the penultimate feather is tipped, for about $\frac{1}{4}$ of an inch only, with the same.

Bill dusky, pale at the base of lower mandible; legs fleshy; irides brown. Length $8\frac{1}{4}$ inches; wing $3\frac{8}{10}$; tail $3\frac{6}{10}$; tarsus $1\frac{1}{10}$; hind toe $\frac{4}{10}$; hind claw $\frac{4}{10}$, considerably curved.

I procured this fine Pipit on the Segoor Pass of the Neilgherries, seated on rocks by the road side, and occasionally descending to the road to feed on various insects. I believe that it breeds on the hills, for I procured one specimen in nestling plumage. It has hitherto I believe not been noticed by any other observer in this country. Out of India it is only hitherto recorded from Abyssinia, but it will probably be found in various parts of Western Asia.

604.   **Agrodroma sordida**, Rüppell.

Anthus, apud Rüppell, N. W. pl. 39, f. 9—A. similis, apud JERDON, Cat. 193 (in part); and BLYTH, Cat. 754 (in part).

THE BROWN ROCK-PIPIT.

Descr.—Very similar to the last; colors duller, and not so rufous, being of a dull earthy brown, darker on the wings and tail, the feathers edged paler; a fawn coloured superciliary stripe, and a faint brown mandibular stripe; beneath, the chin and throat whitish, and the rest of the body rufescent-vinous or fawn color, with a few indistinct brown blotches; central tail-feathers dark brown; outer ditto rufescent.

Length $7\frac{1}{2}$ to 8 inches; wing nearly 4; tail $3\frac{1}{2}$; bill at front $\frac{3}{8}$; tarsus $1\frac{1}{4}$; hind toe and claw $\frac{2}{10}$.

I procured specimens of this large Pipit at Jalna in the Deccan, on rocky ground, and at the edge of stony ravines; also on stony plains. I noticed at the time that, in their flight, they appeared to flap their wings more frequently than Pipits usually do. Blyth has obtained it from the N. W. Himalayas, and Horsfield's specimens are from Shikarpore, and Kumaon. It appears to be common in the Alpine Punjab, whence specimens were sent by Mr. Theobald; and it also inhabits Africa.

Several other Tit-larks are recorded by authors from Africa, most of which appear to belong to this genus. Bonaparte has *A. australis*, Swainson, from Oceanica, and two other species from the same region.

4th.—True-Pipits.

Gen. ANTHUS (as restricted).

Bill and tarsus slender, and the latter short; form lighter and more like *Budytes*, to which it is nearly allied; hind claw moderately long, slightly curved.

The True-Pipits have a greater change of plumage at the vernal moult than any of the Tit-larks, and the young resemble their parents.

There are two slightly differing forms in this genus; one typified by *A. pratensis* of Europe, to which the generic name *Spipola*, Leach, is applied by Gray; the other, with *aquaticus* for its type, restricted *Anthus* of Gray; but they are barely separable, the winter plumage of both being very similar. The only Indian member of this group belongs to the last.

605. **Anthus cervinus,** PALLAS.

Motacilla, apud PALLAS—BLYTH, Cat. 764—A. rosaceus, HODGSON—HORSF., Cat. 568—A. aquaticus, apud BLYTH, olim—A. rufo-superciliaris, BLYTH, J. A. S., XXIX., 105—A. pratensis, apud GOULD? and BLYTH—A. japonicus, TEMM. and SCHLEGEL?

THE VINOUS-THROATED PIPIT.

Descr.—In winter plumage, tawny brown above, with dark centres to the feathers, and two indistinct pale wing bands; lores, face, and superciliary streak, dull ferruginous; beneath, the chin and throat, white, bordered by a dark line; the rest of the plumage white tinged more or less with fulvous, especially on the flanks, and with large oblong dark spots or blotches on the breast, upper abdomen, and flanks, disappearing on the lower belly, vent and under tail-coverts; the outermost tail-feather nearly half of a sullied white color, the next with only a white spot near the tip.

In summer, the chin, neck, throat, and breast become of a faint vinous or dull roseate tint, and the spots on the breast disappear, or become very faint; the lores, supercilium, and round the eyes, partake of the same vinous tinge; the upper plumage becomes a richer olive-brown, with dusky blotches, and the wing-bands are more conspicuous, broader, and paler; the bend of the wing and margins of the secondaries are somewhat yellowish green, not always observable; the axillaries, and inner margins of the wings beneath, incline to sulphur yellow.

Bill dusky above, yellowish beneath; legs brown; irides brown. Length about 6 inches; wing $3\frac{1}{4}$; tail $2\frac{1}{2}$; bill at front $\frac{7}{16}$; tarsus $\frac{15}{16}$; hind claw $\frac{3}{8}$, thin, and very slightly curved.

In the yellowish tints on part of this bird, and its slender form there is a marked approach to *Budytes*.

From the synonyms adopted, it will be seen that I consider Hodgson's species, adopted by Horsfield, to be the same as Pallas' bird; and moreover that the *pratensis* of Gould is probably the same bird, as *A. pratensis*, apud Blyth (afterwards *rufosuperciliaris*), certainly is. This Mr. Blyth himself ascertained, though he has not yet published it. I can see no difference in the descriptions of *A. rufogularis* by Temminck, or in the figure in the work on Egypt, from Himalayan specimens, to warrant the separation of the Indian bird; and *cervinus*, Pallas, is given by Bonaparte and others as the same bird. The distinctions between this species and *aquaticus* are obvious.

It has been found on the Himalayas, where it appears to breed; in China; also rarely in Burmah, the Andamans, in Siam, and in Western India, if Mr. Gould's bird be found to be the same. In the Himalayas it frequents the higher elevations chiefly, and the interior of the hills. I did not myself procure it at Darjeeling, but specimens were obtained in Sikhim by Lieutenant Beavan; and Mr. Hodgson procured it in Nepal. Out of India, it occurs in various parts of Asia, the East of Europe, and Northern Africa.

It is quite possible that *A. pratensis* may also be found in the Western parts of India, and, if so, must be introduced into the Indian Fauna. *A. Cecilii*, Aud., from Southern Europe, is separated by some authors, but apparently without sufficient cause. The allied species, *A. aquaticus*, Bechst. (*spinoletta*, L., apud Bonap.), of Europe, occurs chiefly in mountainous regions far inland. Adams, No. 115 of his List of Birds from India,[*] has an *Anthus* from Ladakh, similar to *trivialis*, but with the throat and neck mouse-brown. This corresponds so well to *A. aquaticus*, also figured by Savigny, Egypte, pl. 5, f. 5, that I have very little doubt that it is the same. it may cross the frontier and be found within our limits, but I shall not include it at present. *A. obscurus*, found on the sea coasts of Europe, belongs to restricted *Anthus*.

The next form was considered at first to be of a somewhat anomalous character, and its affinities with the Pipits were not recognised.

Gen. HETERURA, Hodgson.

Char.—Bill deep and strong; culmen regularly arched; feet and legs robust; wings with the first five primaries subequal; tail-feathers attenuated to a point at the tip; tarsus and feet strong; hind toe long, claw not equal to it, slightly curved.

This genus was ranged by Sir W. Jardine near *Malacocercus* and *Megalurus*; but its pointed wing and general structure are quite against that view. It is, in fact, essentially a thick-billed Pipit, and the character of the tail-feathers given above is also shown in *Pipastes*. The plumage is thick about the nape, and its figure is somewhat more robust than in the other Titlarks. In its habits it is monticolous.

606. Heterura sylvana, HODGSON.

Jard., Contr. Ornith. pl.—BLYTH, Cat. 751.

THE UPLAND PIPIT.

Descr.—Above streaked brown, the feathers having broad, dark, brown medial lines, edged with pale rufous brown; the tail brown,

---

* P. Z. S. 1858, p. 485.

the central feathers edged pale brown; the outermost white for about a third, the next with a small terminal white tip, and usually the antepultimate also with a slight white tip; supercilium, and entire lower parts, dull earthy albescent, the feathers all black shafted, forming very faint dark lines.

Bill dusky above, yellowish beneath; legs pale cinereous; irides brown. Length not quite 7 inches; wing 3; tail $2\frac{7}{8}$; bill at front $\frac{1}{2}$; tarsus $\frac{7}{8}$; hind toe and claw nearly $\frac{4}{8}$.

This bird is, says Mr. Hodgson, "exclusively monticolous, being found in the uplands of the central region of Nepal; feeds on grylli, other insects and seeds; its nest is made loosely of grass, and the eggs bluish, thickly spotted." It appears to occur throughout the Himalayas, apparently taking the place there of *Pipastes montanus* of the Neilgherries. Adams records that it is common on the grassy hill sides of the lesser ranges southwards of the valley of Cashmere.

The genera *Seiurus* and *Muscisaxicola* of America are by some placed among the Wagtails, though they differ structurally by their more rounded wing. There are however one or two undoubted species of *Anthus* (or *Corydalla*) in North America; and several from South America.

Fam. AMPELIDÆ.

Syn. *Pipridæ*, Vigors and Horsfield.

Tarsus short or moderate; feet fitted for perching, in some groups strong and scansorial; wings moderate; tail short or moderate; bill various, usually strong, somewhat conic; often of bright, showy, and variegated plumage.

In this, the last dentirostral family, we have an assemblage of birds considerably varied in their structure and coloration; but, as a general rule, of brighter and richer plumage than the majority of dentirostral birds; the *Pittæ* and short-legged Thrushes alone approach them in this respect, and some of these latter are very similarly colored.

The majority of this family appear to be peculiar to America, but, in the Old World, there are several representatives, one group, the *Parinæ*, or Titmice, being found throughout the Old Continent and North America. Some of them are strictly fruit-eaters, others feed readily on buds, and many chiefly live on insects, though freely partaking of vegetable matter. I differ much from Gray and various other Ornithologists, in the extent of this group, in which strangely, as it appears to me, the *Dicrurinæ* and the *Artaminæ* are placed, and, perhaps, with more show of justice, the *Campephaginæ*, one group of which does evince considerable affinities for some of the *Ampelidæ*.

Gray divides them into *Pachycephalinæ*, including many Indian forms with a few Australian; *Piprinæ*, *Ampelinæ*, and *Gymnoderinæ*, the last three strictly American (except the Malayan *Calyptomena*); and the three sub-families above, which I have placed among the Shrikes. I include in it, besides the American sub-families *Ampelinæ*, *Piprinæ* and *Vireoninæ*, the *Muiotiltinæ*, Gray, the Oceanic *Pachycephalinæ* (with *Pardalotus*), the Asiatic *Leiotrichinæ*, the *Parinæ*, and *Accentorinæ*.

Nearly all, with the exception of one group of doubtful location, are strictly arboreal, and some of them have large strong feet, well fitted for clinging to branches. A few of them approach the Shrikes, from which they may be distinguished by their mixed diet, and more variegated colors; and some, chiefly American, resemble the short-legged Thrushes; many are very similar to Warblers, with which they probably unite, but are recognizable by a more conic and pointed bill, in general a peculiar mode of coloration, and stronger feet, with shorter tarsus; some few have been placed as Fly-catchers, but differ by their mixed diet and much stouter bill; and, lastly, the *Accentors* evince some affinities for the Finches and Larks, some of the members of the same family also approximating the Thrushes.

Sub-fam. LEIOTRICHINÆ.

Bill usually short, more or less wide at the base, lengthened and slightly curved in a few, entire in some, notched in others; tail short or moderate, even or slightly rounded; tarsi short, stout; feet strong, claws moderately curved, sharp.

This family, allowed by all Ornithologists to belong to the *Ampelidæ,* is, according to our views, composed chiefly of birds confined to Himalayas, and the hill ranges to the South-east, extending through Burmah. There are, however, a few exceptions.

One genus is found in the Palæarctic regions and North America; and the Australian *Pardalotus* probably enters this sub-family; Bonaparte, indeed, placing it next to the *Leiotrichinæ*, though in a separate sub-family. Two or three of the Indian genera have a somewhat wider distribution than that stated above, being found in the Malayan Archipelago. This group is so closely related to the *Parinæ* that the limits of each are difficult to define.

The plumage is very varied, in most cases the markings on the wing are prominent, and many are brightly coloured; a few only with dull plumage. The majority are of small size, one or two attaining the size of Thrushes; and some of them are very small. Several are highly crested, and most of them have the feathers of the head more or less elongated. They feed on buds, seeds, fruits, and insects, nidificate on trees, and the eggs of the few known are white, with a few reddish spots. They may be sub-divided into the Blue Thrush-tits (*Cochoeæ*); the Hill-tits *Leiotricheæ*; and the Flower-peckers, (*Iэulæ*.)

1st.—Blue Thrush-tits, *Cochoeæ*.

Gen. COCHOA, Hodgson.

Syn. *Oreias*, Temm. ?

Char.—Bill short, wide at the base, depressed, straight, the tip slightly bent and notched; nostrils large and advanced, with a few short hairs incumbent over them; wings rather long, somewhat pointed, 1st quill minute, 2nd and 3rd graduating, 4th quill longest, 5th sub-equal; tail moderate, nearly even, the outer feathers slightly graduating; tarsi rather short and stout; feet moderate; middle toe and hind toe long; claws short, moderately curved. Head moderately crested; of large size, bigger than a Thrush; colors rich blue, purple, and green.

This genus is placed by Gray in the sub-family *Ampelinæ*, all the others of that group being American. Bonaparte places it next to *Irena* in the *Edoliinæ*. Blyth, too, places it at the end of the *Ampelidæ*, but says of doubtful location, and affined to *Pteruthius*. Concurring in this last view of its affinities, I have withdrawn it from the New World family, and placed it next to *Pteruthius*, in the Leiotrichine Group, of which it forms a separate division, distinguished by its large size, and partially terrene habits. *Horsfield* classes it next to *Bombycilla* (which certainly belongs to this sub-family), but in his *Toaidæ*, a fissirostral group.

607. Cochoa purpurea, Hodgson.

J. A. S., V. 359—XII., 450 (with figure)—Gould, Birds of Asia, pt. i, pl. 13—Blyth, Cat. 1175—Horsf., Cat. 631—*Cocho, Nepal.—Lho nyum-pho,* Lepch.

The Purple Thrush-Tit.

Descr.—Head lavender-blue grey; lores, eyebrows, and ear-coverts black; upper plumage ashy purple; wings light purple or soft grey blue, more or less purpurascent; the primaries black with a broad pale lavender band at their base; primary coverts and primaries black, and the secondaries broadly tipped with pure black; the tail light purple with black tip; plumage beneath brownish purple.

The female is reddish brown where the male is purple; and the upper part of the wings also is brown; wing spot and tail as in the male, but duller. The young bird is dusky black above, the head whitish with black edgings, and beneath red brown with dusky bands.

Bill and legs black; irides dark brown. Length nearly 11 inches; extent 17; wing $5\frac{1}{2}$; tail $4\frac{1}{2}$; bill at front $\frac{5}{8}$; tarsus 1.

This elegantly-plumaged bird has only been procured in Nepal and Sikhim. I found it very rare near Darjeeling, and only obtained one specimen, which was shot at a considerable elevation, above 8,000 feet. Hodgson says " They are common to all the three regions of Nepal. They are shy in their manners, adhere exclusively to the woods, live solitarily or in pairs, breed and moult but once a year, nidificate on trees, and feed almost equally on the ground and on trees. I have taken from their stomachs several sorts of stony berries, small univalve Mollusca, and sundry kinds of aquatic insects." Hodgson further adds, "The tongue is simple, flat, with a subjagged tip, and the stomach is muscular, with a tough grooved lining."

608. Cochoa viridis, Hodgson.

J. A. S., V. 359—Blyth, Cat. 1174—Gould, Birds of Asia, pt. 1, pl. 12.

THE GREEN THRUSH-TIT.

Descr.—Head, nape, and back of neck, fine cobalt blue, clearest on the forehead; lores, and narrow supercillia, black; ear-coverts blue black; a small nude space behind the eye, as in Thrushes; body above dull blue green; lesser wing coverts green with black lunules; median coverts green tipped black; greater coverts pale blue externally, green on the inner web, with black tips; primary coverts blue at the base, black tipped; primaries and secondaries black, with a pale blue band at their base; tail dull cobalt blue, with a black tip; beneath green, as on the back, tinged bluish on the throat and lower abdomen.

In one specimen, perhaps a female, the secondaries are olive-brown in place of blue, and the colors generally are paler.

Bill black; legs fleshy brown; irides brown. Length 11 inches; wing 5⅞; tail 4¾; bill at front ¾; tarsus 1 inch.

Hodgson states that the back of the young bird or the female is much lunated with black, and that the soft blue of the wings is smeared with brownish yellow.

This species appears more rare even than the last, and I did not procure a specimen whilst at Darjeeling. It has only been obtained in Nepal and Sikhim. Major Tickell informs me that he procured one specimen in winter, near Kursiong; but in summer it apparently keeps to great elevations, not being found in general below 8,000 feet.

2nd. Hill-tits, *Leiotrichcæ*.

This division comprises *Pteruthius* with some allied forms, and *Leiothrix*. They are birds of small or moderate size, usually with strongly marked, variegated colours; are arboreal in their habits, and most of them associate in small flocks, feeding on insects, fruits and buds; and some of them have a pleasing song. The bill is varied, short in most, in some strong and Shrike-like, in others more slender.

Gen. PTERUTHIUS, Swainson.

Syn. *Allotrius*, Temm.

Char.—Bill short, stout, curved at the tip, and hooked, moderately wide at the base, not compressed, notched; nares basal, apert, but overlaid by a few bristles; wings moderate, 3rd, 4th, and 5th quills about equal and longest; tail short, somewhat rounded, or nearly even; tarsus rather short; toes moderate, with the laterals equal and much syndactyle; hind toe long, claws well curved.

This genus, formerly placed among the *Laniadæ*, and still retained there by Horsfield, is properly referred here by Swainson, Gray, and others. It comprises the largest species of this peculiar group, and the bill attains its maximum in depth and strength, being, indeed, very Shrike-like

609. Pteruthius erythropterus, VIGORS.

Lanius, apud VIGORS.—GOULD, Cent. Him. Birds, pl. 11—BLYTH, Cat. 507—HORSFIELD, Cat. 227—GOULD, Birds of Asia, pt. VIII., pl. 8.

THE REDWINGED SHRIKE-TIT.

Descr.—Male, head black; rest of the upper plumage a light plumbeous grey; wings black; tertiaries chesnut-red internally, fulvous without, and black-tipped; a white superciliary stripe; tips of the primary quills, and the body beneath, white; tail black, and some of the extreme feathers of the upper tail-coverts also edged black.

The female has the head grey, the back, wings, and tail, grey, with a green smear on the rump and upper tail-coverts; wings pale olive-green, dusky externally; primaries tipped white, and the primary coverts black; beneath dingy white, tinged with reddish ash; tail, as the wings, with the central feathers, tipped with whitish.

Bill black; legs pale fleshy; irides dark brown. Length 7 inches; extent 11; wings $3\frac{1}{4}$; tail $2\frac{1}{2}$; bill at front $\frac{9}{16}$; tarsus $1\frac{1}{10}$.

The red-winged *Pteruthius* is found throughout all the Himalayas from the N. W. to Bootan, extending also into the hill ranges of Assam. At Darjeeling it frequents the zone from 2,500 feet to nearly 6,000 feet; lives in small flocks, flying from tree to tree with a lively mellow call, and feeding at times on fruit, at other times on soft insects.

610. Pteruthius rufiventer, BLYTH.

J. A. S., XI. 183 and 945—BLYTH, Cat. 506—HORSFIELD, Cat. 228—GRAY, Gen. of Birds, pl. 66—GOULD, Birds of Asia, pt. VIII., pl. 9.

THE RUFOUS-BELLIED SHRIKE-TIT.

Descr.—Male, the head above and nape deep black; back and upper tail-coverts dark chesnut; wings and tail shining black, the latter tipped ferruginous, as are the secondaries, and the longest of the tertiaries; lores, ear-coverts, and below the eyes, deep black; throat, foreneck and breast pure ashy, the rest of the under parts from the breast, pale brownish cinereous with a patch of golden yellow on each side of the breast, bordering the gray; and the flanks ferruginous. The female differs in having the upper parts, wings, and middle of the tail feathers, green; and only the rump and upper tail-coverts ferruginous; sides of the head grey.

Bill black; length 7½ inches; wing 3½; tail 3⅜; bill at front ⅝; tarsus 1⅛.

I did not procure this species myself, but it was originally sent from Darjeeling, and has since been found by Hodgson in Nepal. It differs from the last structurally by its more slender and less hooked bill.

Allotrius flaviscapis, Temm., from Java, appears to be a typical *Pteruthius.*

The next form differs in its small size.

Gen. ALLOTRIUS, Temm. (restricted).

Char.—Of small size; the bill strongly hooked and notched; tarsus longer than in *Pteruthius*; tail nearly even.

This form differs but slightly from the last, and is barely worthy of separation, but the genus is adopted by some Ornithologists. Its mode of coloration is somewhat different.

611. **Allotrius œnobarbus,** TEMMINCK.

Pl. Col. 589, f. 2—Pt. melanotis, (the male) and P. xanthochloris (the female), HODGSON—BLYTH, Cat. 1883—HORSF., Cat. 226—GOULD, Birds of Asia, pt. VIII., pl. 11 and 12 —*Ku-er-pho*, Lepch.

THE CHESNUT-THROATED SHRIKE-TIT.

Descr.—Male, above vernal green with the forehead yellowish, and the nape slaty; ear-coverts mixed black and yellow; wing coverts blue grey externally, dusky black within, and with whitish edges to the tips; tail with the central feathers green, the outer pair pure white, the rest tipped white, and the pair next the central pair just edged with white; beneath, the chin, throat, and top of breast, are bright chesnut; the rest of the body bright yellow, greenish on the flanks and under tail-coverts. The female has the top of the head bright slaty, the rest of the plumage above vernal green, as in the male; tail tipped yellow; throat white, the rest of the body beneath bright yellow.

Bill plumbeous; legs fleshy white; irides light brown. Length $4\frac{3}{4}$ inches; wing $2\frac{1}{2}$; tail $1\frac{3}{4}$; bill at front $\frac{3}{8}$; tarsus $\frac{13}{16}$.

This curious little bird has been found in Nepal, Sikhim, Bootan, and the Khasia Hills. I got several specimens from the neighbourhood of Darjeeling, though I did not myself observe it there; but I have since seen it abundant near Cherra Poonjee. It associates in small flocks, is lively, and hunts the extreme branches of trees. I found remains of fruits and seeds in some which I examined, but others had only eaten insects.

Gen. CUTIA, Hodgson.

Syn. *Heterornis*, Hodgs.

Char.—Bill moderately long, strong at the base, higher than broad, slightly arched throughout, compressed, barely emarginate; culmen keeled; nares broad, lunate, sub-basal; rictus nearly smooth; wings moderate, firm, the first three graduated; 4th and 5th quills longest; tail short, nearly square, firm; tarsus moderate, strong, almost smooth; feet strong, lateral toes unequal, middle toe not long; hind toe large and strong; nails moderately bent.

This genus is placed by Horsfield in the *Timalinæ*, between *Alcippe* and *Timalia*. Blyth puts it next to *Pteruthius*, as does Bonaparte. Gray makes it a Starling, near *Saraglossa*. From its mode of coloration and habits, I have no hesitation in placing it here.

612. Cutia nipalensis, HODGSON.

J. A. S., V., 774—BLYTH, Cat. 505—HORSFIELD, Cat. 331—GOULD, Birds of Asia, pt. VIII, pl. 10—*Khatya* of Nepal—*Rabnoon* or *Rapnun-pho*, Lepch.

THE YELLOW-BACKED SHRIKE-TIT.

Descr.— Male, top of head and nape slaty; a black band from the base of the bill through the eyes and over the ear-coverts, meeting at the nape; back, rump, and the very long upper tail-coverts, brilliant deep rusty-yellow; wings and tail jet black, and the former with more or less white on their inner webs; a large central portion of the wings, purplish slaty; the scapulars olive-yellow; and most of the quills, and lateral tail-feathers, tipped with white; below, from chin to the legs pure white; from the middle of the abdomen to the under tail-coverts, flavescent, the flanks broadly barred with black. The female is a trifle smaller, her mantle is paler and more flavescent, and variegated with black longitudinal drops, and her cheek-band is brown instead of black.

Bill blackish above, plumbeous beneath; legs orange yellow; irides brown. Length 7 inches; extent 11; wing $3\frac{3}{4}$; tail $2\frac{1}{2}$; bill at front $\frac{5}{8}$; tarsus $1\frac{1}{10}$; hind toe and claw $\frac{3}{4}$.

This bird has hitherto only been procured in the S. E. Himalayas, from Nepal to Bootan. I found it not very common at Darjeeling, usually from 6,000 to 8,000 feet and upwards. It frequents very high trees in small flocks, and lives both on fruit and insects.

Gen. LEIOPTILA, Blyth.

Char.—Bill somewhat lengthened. slender and slightly curved, the tip of the upper mandible slightly bent over, and feebly emarginate; nostrils long, narrow; rictal bristles fine and inconspicuous; wings rather short, rounded, 4th and 5th quills equal and longest; tertiaries broad, almost truncated; tail moderately long, the outer ones graduating, the central feathers equal.

This genus was considered by Blyth to connect *Sibia* with *Yuhina*, with affinities for *Actinodura*, *Sibia* being according to him one of the *Garrulacinæ*, and *Yuhina* a Leiotrichine bird. Gray puts *Leioptila* among the short-winged Thrushes. I unhesitatingly place it in the present group, so far agreeing with Blyth in its affinities for *Yuhina*. Its relations to *Actinodura*, I believe, to be those of analogy merely. Its coloration resembles both *Pteruthius* and *Cutia*, and the Lepchas call them both by the same name. It is in reality, nothing but a slender-billed *Cutia*.

613. Leioptila annectans, BLYTH.

J. A. S., XVI., 450—*Rabnun-pho*, Lepch.

THE SLENDER-BILLED SHRIKE-TIT.

Descr.—Head, neck, and ear-coverts, black, with some white about the nape; back, rump, and upper tail-coverts, bright rufo-ferruginous (as in *Cutia*); wings and tail black; the greater wing-coverts broadly tipped, and the tertiaries edged externally at the base with white, and bordered with white round their broad tips; feathers of the tail white-tipped, especially the outer ones; throat and breast pure white; scapulars, flanks, and under tail-coverts, weak ferruginous.

Bill black, base of lower mandible yellow; legs pale fleshy brown; irides brown. Length 7¼ inches; wing 3⅜; tail 3½; bill at front ⅝; tarsus nearly 1 inch.

I only got a single specimen of this curious bird, when at Darjeeling, and did not myself observe it. Judging from analogy, the female probably differs. I am unable to say anything of its habits, but it was shot at about 5,000 feet of elevation.

The next group is that to which the name of *Leiothrix* was given by Swainson. It comprises, however, several distinct forms, which were well distinguished by Hodgson, and classed by him among the *Parinæ*: although not adopted by Blyth and Horsfield in their respective Catalogues, they are as well worthy of separation as many other genera universally adopted. As a whole, they may be recognized by a moderately short, more or less conic bill, rather short and rounded firm wings, the first four or five primaries being graduated, and the 5th, 6th, and 7th longest and sub-equal; the tail is rather short in most, even or slightly forked; the tarsus rather short, with short, strong, flat toes, the outer toe much syndactyle, and the claws strong and well curved.

"In all the species of *Leiothrix*," says Hodgson, "the tongue, without being elongated, is pointed, rather deeply forked, and more or less jagged on the edges, and, in all, the stomach has a good deal of muscular power, being almost mediate between the typical Finches and Tits. In conformity with this structure, the food is Pariano-fringillidan, consisting almost equally of insects, their nests, larvæ and pupæ, and of seeds. Berries are also frequently taken, but I never found gravel except in the stomach of *L. luteus*. They creep and climb among the foliage

2 I

and flowers of shrubs and trees, and explore opening buds so diligently that they might be termed bud-hunters. Their frontal plumes are in consequence frequently agglutinated by the pollen and viscid juices of plants and trees. They make half pensile or semi-globular nests, well compacted, at a moderate height in leafy trees and shrubs."

All the species dwell in forests, and, as far as we know, are peculiar to the Himalayas and the neighbouring hills in Assam. They are monticolous, never being found in the plains, and most of them are very brightly coloured. In their habits they may be said much to resemble the Tit-mice. The plumage is soft, puffy, and more or less decomposed. The young, in those which I have observed, closely resemble their parents.

Gen. LEIOTHRIX, Swainson.

Syn. *Bahila* and *Mesia*, HODGS.—*Furcaria*, Lesson.

Char.—Bill short, strong, wide at the base, compressed at the tip, which is bent over, and slightly notched; culmen moderately curved; a few long rictal bristles; tail slightly forked, 4th quill very little shorter than the 5th and 6th.

614. Leiothrix luteus, SCOPOLI.

Sylvia, apud SCOPOLI—BLYTH, Cat. 509—HORSF., Cat. 585—Parus furcatus, TEMM., pl. col. 287, f. 1—GOULD, Birds of Asia, pl.—Bahila calipyga, HODGSON, postea Calipyga furcata—*Nanachura*, of the Dehra Dhoon—*Rapchil-pho*, Lepch.

THE RED-BILLED HILL-TIT.

Descr.—Above and flanks olive-green, tinged with yellowish on the crown; lores pale yellow, and a dark line from the base of the lower mandible to the ear-coverts, which are somewhat dusky-green; orbitar feathers whitish; beneath, dark yellow, deepest on the breast, and passing to pale yellowish towards the vent; outer margin of all the primaries, and the base of the secondaries, deep yellow; the last three primaries edged with sanguine towards the tip, forming a conspicuous bar on the wings; the rest of the alars, and the tail black, the inner webs of the tail-feathers being dark slaty.

Bill coral-red; legs fleshy brown; irides brown. Length 6¼ inches; extent 9; wing 2¾; tail 2½; bill at front $\frac{7}{16}$; tarsus 1$\frac{1}{16}$. The green of the back soon fades to a greyish, and the bright yellow to buffy yellow.

The red-billed *Leiothrix* is one of the most common birds about Darjeeling. It usually associates in small parties of five or six, frequenting the dense thickets and underwood that springs up wherever the forest is partially cleared. It is a shy bird, and avoids observation in general. Its food consists of berries, fruits, seeds, and insects. Now and then, during the winter, I have seen a party of them alight on a road for a few seconds, apparently pick up some gravel, and then hurry off into the jungle again. Its usual note is a chattering call, but in the spring the male has a very pleasing song. I got the nest and eggs repeatedly; the nest made chiefly of grass, with roots, fibres, and fragments of moss, and usually containing three or four eggs, bluish white, with a few purple and red blotches. It is generally placed in a leafy bush, at no great height from the ground. Gould, quoting from Mr. Shore's notes, says that the eggs are black spotted with yellow. This is of course erroneous. I have taken the nest myself on several occasions, and killed the bird; and, in every case, the eggs were colored as above. This species appears to spread over all the Himalayas; is found from 5,000 to 8,000 feet, and higher. It is common on the Khasia Hills, and other hill ranges to the south-east; and is said to occur also in China. I have seen it caged, and it is a lively and amusing pet.

The next species differs so slightly in structure, and in its mode of coloration, that I think it barely separable. Hodgson makes it the type of his genus *Mesia*, subsequently *Philocalyx* and *Fringilliparus*. It has the bill a trifle longer and less curved, the tail more lengthened and even, with the outermost feathers slightly shorter.

615. Leiothrix argentauris, Hodgson.

Mesia, apud Hodgson,—*Dang rapchil-pho*, Lepch.

THE SILVER-EARED HILL-TIT.

Descr.—Top of the head black, also the lores, and a streak from the lower mandible; back slaty, strongly tinged with green, and a golden fulvous bar round the nape; some feathers at the base of the bill golden yellow; outer edge of the primaries, and of the lateral tail-feathers, yellow; upper and lower tail-coverts, and a large patch at the base of the primaries (except on the first two) and secondaries, sanguineous-red; throat and breast bright gamboge-yellow, with a red tinge, and the rest of the under parts are slaty-green, tinged with yellow. The colours fade to slaty, with a faint tinge of green, and paler beneath.

Bill yellow; legs fleshy-yellow; irides brown. Length 7 inches; wing $3\frac{1}{16}$; tail 3; bill at front $\frac{1}{2}$; tarsus 1.

The female is said by Hodgson to differ in the tail-coverts being fulvous yellow instead of red, but I found them precisely similar, the young only having those parts coloured as above.

This Hill-tit is not so common at Darjeeling as the last species, and inhabits a lower zone, from 3,000 to 6,000 feet, occasionally ascending higher. Its manners are very similar, and the nest has been brought to me, with the eggs very like those of the last, but with the spots less numerous. It is found chiefly in the S. E. Himalayas, from Nepal to Bootan, and I also found it on the Khasia Hills.

Gen. Siva, Hodgson.

Syn. *Hemiparus* and *Ioropus*, Hodgson.

Char.—Bill more Parian, short, somewhat conic, compressed, gently curved, tip entire; some weak rictal setæ; wings and tail less firm than in the preceding; the tail longish, with the four central feathers square, the others graduated, all broad; feet short, hind toe rather long; claws well curved.

This form is very distinct from the last, and is marked by its longer, broad tail, and Parian bill; the head too is somewhat crested.

616. Siva strigula, Hodgson.

BLYTH, Cat. 510—HORSF., Cat. 587—Muscicapa variegata, DELESSERT, Mag. Zool. 1846, pl. 19—and Souv. d'un Voyage, pl. 8—Leiothrix chrysocephala, JAMESON—*Megblim*, Lepch.

THE STRIPE-THROATED HILL-TIT.

Descr.—Head fully crested, dull orange; lores and cheeks whitish or yellowish; the body above slaty, smeared with green; wings black, the quills edged with yellow; the coverts olive-green; edges of the middle alars fiery red; the outer webs of the secondaries pale grey, tipped whitish; tail black, with the two central feathers deep chesnut at the base, and for two-thirds of the outer web; the next pair tipped yellow-white; and the rest with pale yellow on the outer webs and tips, increasing in extent to the outermost, which is almost entirely pale yellow: beneath, the chin is orange-yellow; the throat whitish or pale yellow, with black lunules or bands, and a black moustachial line bordering it; the rest, from the throat to the vent, yellow. In some the head is greenish instead of being orange, but I do not think that it is a mark of sex, rather of nonage.

Bill bluish grey; legs pale brown; irides brown. Length $6\frac{1}{4}$ inches; extent 9; wing $2\frac{3}{4}$; tail $2\frac{3}{4}$; bill at front $\frac{3}{8}$; tarsus 1.

This species extends throughout the whole Himalayas to the hill ranges of Assam. It is tolerably common in Sikhim, frequenting forests from 3,000 to 7,000 feet, most common perhaps in the upper portion of that zone. It goes in large flocks, keeping at a moderate height on trees, diligently searching there for insects, and every now and then uttering its monotonous call. The Lepchas call this and the two next by the same generic name, specifying this one the yellow " Megblim."

617. Siva cyanouroptera, Hodgson.

Blyth, Cat. 511—Horsf., Cat. 588—Leiothrix lepida, McLelland—Megblim adum, Lepch.

The Blue-winged Hill-tit.

Descr.—Above yellowish brown, passing to blue grey towards the head, which is blue, and rufescent on the rump; visible portion of the closed wing and tail cobalt blue; the secondaries, tertials, and tail tipped with white, and the outer tail-feathers white internally; beneath whitish, with a reddish-lake tinge, fulvescent on the flanks; under tail-coverts pure white, forehead with a few faint black streaks.

Bill dusky yellow; legs fleshy; irides brown. Length $6\frac{1}{4}$ inches; wing $2\frac{1}{2}$; tail $2\frac{1}{2}$; bill at front $\frac{1}{2}$; tarsus $\frac{7}{8}$. The tail is even, with the outer feathers $\frac{1}{4}$ inch shorter.

This very pleasingly plumaged *Leiothrix* is found in the Himalayas from Nepal to Bootan, and also in the hills of Assam. It is common near Darjeeling, from 3,000 to 6,000 feet, and has similar manners to the last, being found in considerable flocks, with a hurried and lively manner, flying from tree to tree, alighting about the middle, and then hopping and climbing up to the topmost branches, hunting for minute insects with a lively chirrup.

Siva nipalensis, Hodgson, is now referred to *Alcippe*, Blyth; and *Siva occipitalis*, Blyth, to the next group.

Gen. MINLA, Hodgson.

Syn. *Certhiparus*, Hodgson.

Char.— Bill somewhat lengthened, slender, depressed at the base, very slightly curved, tip strongly notched, rictus nearly smooth ; tail rather short, slightly rounded ; tarsus moderate ; toes moderate, slender, basally much connected ; hind toe very large ; claws much curved and compressed.

These birds, says Mr. Hodgson, have a quasi-Certhian structure, as shown both in bill and feet, and less so in the tail. They are excellent climbers ; partake of seeds less than the previous species, and are very like the Tits in their habits.

618. **Minla ignotincta,** HODGSON.

BLYTH, Cat. 512—HOUSF., Cat. 589—Leiothrix ornata, McLELLAND—*Minla*, Nep.—*Megblim ayene*, Lepch, *i. e.* the Red *Megblim*.

THE RED-TAILED HILL-TIT.

Descr.—Head and nape black, with a broad superciliary white band, and, beneath this, another black band through the eye ; mantle luteous-olive, tending to vinous on the back of the male ; wings and tail black, broadly margined with crimson on the tail and primaries, which are also tipped with the same ; the other wing-feathers are edged with white ; throat white ; the rest beneath bright yellow.

The female is white beneath, and the colours somewhat duller.

Bill blackish ; legs horny yellow ; irides brown   Length 5½ inches ; extent 7¾ ; wing 2⅝ ; tail 2¼ ; bill at front $\frac{6}{16}$; tarsus $\frac{13}{16}$.

This very pretty bird is tolerably common about Darjeeling, ranging from 5,000 to 8,000 feet. It may be seen in Darjeeling station, often in company with the common Hill-tit, *Parus monticolus*, in small parties of five or six, hunting about the extreme branches of trees, clinging round and under them, diligently searching for insects. Its nest has been brought to me, of ordinary shape, made of moss and grass, and with four white eggs, with a few rusty red spots. It has been found from Nepal to Bootan, and extending into the hill ranges of Assam. I found it far from rare at Cherra Poonjee.

619. Minla castaniceps, Hodgson.

BLYTH, Cat. 514—Horsf., Cat. 590—*Prong-samyer-pho*, Lepch.

THE CHESNUT-HEADED HILL-TIT.

Descr.—Above olive-brown, with a bright chesnut head, the feathers streaked with white, and a white superciliary streak extending to the nape; ear-coverts dusky, mixed with white; a narrow moustachial band black; quills dusky slaty; middle of the wing edged deep rusty, forming a band; the first two outer primaries hoary; tail olivaceous externally, dusky on the inner webs; beneath, the chin and throat white, also the middle of the belly, the sides of the breast and abdomen lutescent.

Bill dusky brown; legs fleshy; irides brown. Length 5 inches; wing $2\frac{1}{4}$; extent 7; tail $1\frac{3}{4}$; bill at front $\frac{5}{16}$: tarsus $\frac{7}{8}$.

This species is found in the South-east Himalayas, from Nepal to Sikhim, extending to the Khasia Hills. It is tolerably common near Darjeeling, inhabiting a slightly lower zone than the last, and its habits much resemble those of that species. In its coloration it shows an approximation to some of the next group.

620. Minla cinerea, Blyth.

J. A. S., XVI. 449.

THE DUSKY-GREEN HILL-TIT.

Descr.—Greyish green above, the feathers of the head broadly margined with black, with a pale yellow supercilium, and, above this, a black one; cheeks mingled dusky and white; secondaries edged with yellowish, and the tertiaries edged grey; beneath pale yellow.

Some birds (females?) differ in being somewhat more cinereous above, and whitish beneath.

Bill dusky; legs fleshy yellow; irides brown. Length $4\frac{1}{2}$ inches; wing $2\frac{1}{4}$; tail $1\frac{3}{4}$; bill at front $\frac{6}{16}$; tarsus $\frac{3}{4}$.

This species is not common in Sikhim, but appears to be more so in Nepal. I only got one specimen at Darjeeling, but I have since obtained it on the Khasia Hills.

Gen. PROPARUS, Hodgs.

Bill entire, quite parian; head crested; wings short, bowed; tail narrow and cuneate; tarsus rather long; feet moderate; hind toe long, its claw very long; nails all large, moderately curved.

This name was at first bestowed on the *Siva* group, but subsequently transferred to this place. The two species at present composing the genus are very distinct in aspect, though agreeing somewhat in their structural characters. The first has the more typical coloring of the group.

621. **Proparus chrysœus**, HODGSON.

GRAY's Zool. Misc. 1844—P. chrysotis, HODGSON, apud BLYTH, J. A. S., XIII. 938—BLYTH, Cat. 516—HORSF., Cat. 592— *Prong-samyer-pho*, Lepch.

Descr.—Head and throat fine dark silvery ash-grey, paler on the throat; rest of the upper plumage olive-green, passing to yellowish on the rump; ear-coverts silvery ash; a longitudinal band of rich orange-yellow on the wings, formed by the margins of the secondaries; the outer primaries edged yellow; the inner edge of the tertiaries margined with white, and the secondaries have also a white spot at their tip; the basal two-thirds of the tail feathers (except the central pair) are edged with orange yellow; plumage beneath bright yellow. The female differs in having the colours less bright, the lower parts ashy white, merely tinged with yellow, the yellow of the wings and tail also being much fainter, and the green above more ashy. The green of the back has a tendency to fade to ashy, even in the male.

Bill plumbeous; legs pale fleshy; irides brown. Length $4\frac{1}{4}$ inches; extent 6; wing 2; tail 2; bill at front not $\frac{5}{10}$.

This pretty little bird is not very common in Sikhim, and I did not myself observe it. It is also found in Nepal, but I did not procure it on the Khasia Hills.

622. Proparus vinipectus, HODGSON.

Siva, apud HODGSON.—BLYTH, Cat. 515—HORSF., Cat. 593.

THE PLAIN BROWN HILL-TIT.

Descr.—Head crested; plumage above and ear-coverts brown, passing into rusty in the rump; wings and tail dusky black, with the outer webs of some of the quills rusty, and the base of the caudals the same; the first four primaries with hoary edges; a white eyebrow extending to the nape; beneath, dirty white, tinged with vinous on the breast, and somewhat brownish towards the vent.

Bill and legs fleshy brown. Length $4\frac{3}{4}$; wing $2\frac{1}{8}$; tail not quite 2; tarsus $\frac{15}{16}$.

This bird was originally described by Hodgson as a *Siva*, and afterwards *Proparus*. Bonaparte has made it a *Pœcila* of Kaup among the true *Pari*. Hodgson remarks of it "distinguished by its perfectly Parian bill without a trace of a notch, and by its long, but not very falcate nails."

Besides its strong affinities for *Parus*, it also tends in its coloration towards the next group. It has hitherto only been sent from Nepal and the N. W. Himalayas.

3rd.—Flower-peckers (*Iculeæ*).

These birds have the bill more slender and lengthened, and slightly curved in some. They are, like the last, mostly social in their habits, frequent the extreme branches of trees, especially searching flowers for the minute insects harboured there. Most of them are of plain and sombre plumage; one genus only having somewhat bright colours.

Gray places them in his *Mniotiltinæ*, next to the *Parinæ*. Horsfield classes most of them in the *Pycnonotinæ*, one alone, *Erpornis*, in the *Timalinæ*. Bonaparte locates them in the *Melliphaginæ*; and

Blyth considers that *Zosterops* belongs to that group, but places the first three genera with the *Leiotrichinæ*. I think that there can be little doubt, but that this is their proper location. The near affinity of some of the species for *Siva* and *Minla* is patent to all; and, although there may be some doubts about *Zosterops* and *Erpornis*, yet most Ornithologists have classed the former genus along with *Yuhina*.

Gen. IXULUS, Hodgson.

Char.—Bill short, straight, slightly curving at the tip, and notched; a very few minute rictal setæ; wings moderate, the first three quills graduated, the three next sub-equal; tail moderate, even or slightly forked; tarsus moderate, stout; toes rather short, stout, slightly unequal, syndactyle at the base; hind toe larger and broad; claws tolerably curved.

This genus differs from *Yuhina*, with which it was at first classed by Hodgson, in its shorter bill, simple tongue, and some few other points.

These are birds of plain and sombre plumage, with the head furnished with a full crest. They are strictly arboreal in their habits, and cling to the minute twigs and flowering branches, or even climb up the larger boughs. They feed both on fruits, buds, and insects, and are particularly fond of searching flowers for small insects and larvæ. The tongue is simple or nearly so.

623. Ixulus flavicollis, HODGSON.

Yuhina, apud HODGSON, As. Res. XIX., p. 167—BLYTH, Cat. 518—HORSF., Cat. 402—*Siripchong-pho*, Lepch.

THE YELLOW-NAPED FLOWER-PECKER.

Descr.—Above dull pale brown, with a dusky tinge; head pure rich brown; cheeks and nape paler brown; back of the neck rusty yellow, continued in a demi-collar round the sides of the neck; a dark brown moustache; primaries edged externally with white on the outer webs; lining of wing also white; chin and throat white; rest of the body beneath pale yellow, the sides shaded with brownish.

The female is usually nearly white beneath, or with the yellow very dilute.

Bill fleshy brown; legs fleshy yellow; irides brown. Length 5¼ inches; extent 7¼; wing 2½; tail 2¼; bill at front $\frac{7}{16}$; tarsus ¾.

This was originally described by Hodgson as a *Yuhina*, but, on subsequent examination, referred to a new genus.

This is a very common and abundant bird about Darjeeling. It associates in large flocks, is very active, incessantly on the move, and diligently hunting among the foliage of bamboos, and various other trees, for minute insects and larvæ, and keeping up a continual twittering the whole time. I have repeatedly had the nest brought to me. It is large, made of leaves of bamboos, carelessly and loosely put together, and generally placed in a clump of bamboos. The eggs are three to five in number, of a somewhat fleshy white, with a few rusty spots. It inhabits the whole Himalayas from Mussooree to Bootan, from 5,000 feet (perhaps lower in the winter) to 9,000 feet, and upwards. It keeps its crest generally elevated when feeding, showing very distinctly the rusty-yellow nape.

624. **Ixulus occipitalis**, BLYTH.

Siva, apud BLYTH, J. A. S. XIII., 937—BLYTH, Cat. 517— HORSF., Cat. 676—*Temgyeng-pho*, or *Turringing-pho*, Lepch.

THE CHESNUT-HEADED FLOWER-PECKER.

Descr.—Crown and nape ferruginous brown; the coronal feathers elongated, and showing a full, but not lengthened or pointed crest, some white on the occiput and nape; rest of the upper plumage dull brownish olive-green; the shafts of the dorsal and scapulary feathers pale; beneath, like the back, but much paler, and rufescent; the throat white, and lower tail-coverts brownish ferruginous.

Bill black; legs pale yellowish brown; iris brown. Length 5¼ inches; wing 2¾; tail 2⅛; tarsus ⅞; bill at front ⅜.

This is also a very common bird about Darjeeling: has similar habits to the last, and constructs a like nest.

A very closely allied species has been described by Horsfield in his Catalogue, No. 677, *Ix. castaniceps*, said to have been brought from Affghanistan by Griffiths, but more likely from Assam; and indeed, since the above was penned, I procured it on the Khasia Hills.

625. **Ixulus striatus**, BLYTH.

J. A. S. XXVIII. p. 413.

THE STRIATED FLOWER-PECKER.

Descr.—Above, the whole plumage dull earthy brown, the feathers all with white shafts; quills dark brown; tail the same, with all except the central feathers tipped white; beneath albescent, sullied on the abdomen.

Bill dusky brown, fleshy yellow at the base; legs pale brown; irides light brown. Length 5 inches; wing $2\frac{1}{2}$; tail $2\frac{1}{4}$; bill at front $\frac{3}{8}$; tarsus $\frac{3}{8}$.

Mr. Blyth described this species from a specimen sent from Tenasserim. I obtained one specimen at Darjeeling and another on the Khasia Hills, which I shot at about 4,500 feet of elevation.

Gen. YUHINA, Hodgson.

Syn. *Polyodon,* Hodgs.

Char.—Bill moderate or rather long, slender, much compressed beyond the nares; tip of the upper mandible slightly inclined, with three minute teeth on each side (nothowever always distinguishable); a few weak rictal bristles; wing as in the last; tail moderate, nearly even, or divaricate; legs and feet strong, slender, hind toe and claw very large; claws well curved.

This genus differs from the last by its longer bill, somewhat brushed tongue, and, in its habits, it is still more a Flower-hunter. The head is more or less crested; the tongue is deeply cleft, filamentous and brushed. Hodgson says " They adhere exclusively to the wild uplands, preferring the lower and more umbrageous to the higher and barer trees, and seem to procure no portion of their food from the ground. They are usually found in small flocks, and have a monotonous feeble monosyllabic note. They feed on viscid, stony berries and fruits, and tiny insects that harbour in the cups of large deep flowers. such as the Rhododendrons, and to which the birds cling with their strong feet."

626. Yuhina gularis, Hodgson.

As. Res. XIX. 166—Blyth, Cat. 519—Horsf., Cat. 399—
Fugi-pho, Lepch.

The Stripe-throated Flower-pecker.

Descr.—Above, with tertiaries and tail, obscure olive-brown ; cap
with a full, soft, somewhat recurved crest, darker and purer brown;
primaries and secondaries black, the former with a narrow edging
of hoary; the latter with a broad one of orange-brown, the lining
of the wings and inner margin of the quills, towards their bases,
albescent ; tail dusky internally ; chin, throat, and breast, obscure
rufous wood brown, albescent on the chin and throat, which are
spotted longitudinally with blackish, and bounded laterally by a
longitudinal stripe of the same hue ; the rest of the body below
bright orange-rusty.

Bill fleshy brown with dusky culmen ; legs deep orange; irides
brown.   Length $6\frac{1}{2}$ inches ; extent $8\frac{3}{4}$: wing 3 ; tail $2\frac{1}{2}$; bill at
front $\frac{9}{16}$; tarsus not quite $\frac{11}{16}$.

This is a very common and abundant bird near Darjeeling, and,
according to the season, is to be found from 4,000 to 10,000 feet,
and upwards.   It associates in large flocks, sometimes fifteen,
twenty, or more : these fly from tree to tree, alighting on the middle
branches, and thence climbing sometimes over the mossy trunk,
and hopping from branch to branch, they gain the summit,
hunting all the while most carefully for small insects and larvæ.
In winter they feed a good deal on small berries of various kinds.
In April, when the Rhododendrons were in flower on Mount
Tongloo, at 10,000 feet, I found them in immense numbers,
on the very summit of the mountain, feeding on the minute
insects harbouring in the flowers.   This species is found from
Nepal to Bootan.

627. Yuhina occipitalis, Hodgson.

As. Res. XIX.—Blyth, Cat. 520—Horsf., Cat. 400.

The Slaty-headed Hill Tit.

Descr.—Top of the head (which is well crested), and back of
the neck, dull slaty brown, with hoary stripes : the forehead narrowly

tinged with rusty ; the back of the crest and nape bright rusty ; the rest of the upper plumage, with the tertiaries, and outer webs of the larger quills, and of all the tail-feathers, dull olive or rufescent brown ; quills and tail feathers dusky on the inner webs ; quills beneath, near the base, pale buff ; lining of wings white ; ears, chin, lower neck, and breast, vinous buff ; an indistinct black moustachial line ; the lower belly, and under tail-coverts, deep rusty ; middle of the abdomen rusty white or greyish, tinged with rusty.

Bill fleshy red ; legs orange buff ; irides brown. Length $5\frac{1}{4}$ inches ; extent $7\frac{1}{2}$; wing $2\frac{1}{2}$; tail 2 ; bill at front $\frac{1}{2}$; tarsus not $1\frac{3}{16}$.

This bird is rare at Darjeeling, and I only procured one or two specimens ; one that I examined had eaten berries. It is found in the Himalayas, from Nepal to Bootan.

628. Yuhina nigrimentum, HODGSON.

J. A. S. XIV. 562—HORSF., Cat. 401—BLYTH, Cat. 1934.

THE BLACK-CHINNED FLOWER-PECKER.

Descr.—Head (crested) and nape, slaty grey ; back and rump dull olive-green ; quills and tail dusky, edged with the same ; tip of chin and lores black ; cheeks grey ; ear-coverts whitish ; throat white, the rest of the lower parts fulvous or rufescent, slightly darker on the lower tail-coverts.

Bill dusky above, lower mandible red ; feet reddish yellow ; irides brown. Length $4\frac{1}{4}$ inches ; extent $6\frac{1}{2}$; wing $2\frac{1}{8}$: tail $1\frac{1}{2}$; bill at front $\frac{3}{8}$; tarsus $\frac{5}{8}$.

This is a somewhat rare bird. I found some seeds and some small insects in the stomach of one I examined. Its forehead was powdered with pollen. A nest was once brought me which was declared to belong to this species ; it was a very small, neat fabric, of ordinary shape, made with moss and grass, and contained three small pure white eggs. The rarity of the bird makes me doubt if the nest really belonged to it. It has as yet only been found in Nepal and Sikhim. The two last species of *Yuhina*, though not well known, apparently, to the Shikarees, were called by them *Turringing-pho*, the name properly applied to *Ixulus occipitalis*.

The next bird differs from the rest of this group by its bright plumage, and the scale-like feathers of the head.

Gen. Myzornis, Hodgson.

Char.—Bill rather long, slightly curved, slender, entire: nostrils almost closed by an impending scale; gape with a few fine vibrissæ; wings much graduated; 4th, 5th, 6th, and 7th quills sub-equal and longest; tail short, even: tarsus moderate; outer toe much syndactyle; claws moderately curved; hind claw large. Plumage soft, dense, and copious, very puffy over the rump; feathers of the head scale-like; tongue brushed.

This genus is unhesitatingly placed by all modern Systematists in the situation now given to it. It has some of the characters of the *Nectariniæ*, *viz.* the scale-like character of the feathers of the head and its bright plumage; but the white tips to the quills, and the red bar on the wing are characters which point out its relation to this sub-family.

629. **Myzornis pyrrhoura**, HODGSON.

J. A. S., XII. 984—BLYTH, Cat. 521—HORSF., Cat. 403— GOULD, Birds of Asia, pt. VIII. pl. 7.—*Lho sagrit-pho*, Lepch. *i. e.* the Mountain Honeysucker.

THE FIRE-TAILED FLOWER-PECKER.

Descr.—General colour fine lively grass-green, becoming bright emerald green on the forehead and crown, the feathers of which have black centres; lores deep black, which color is continued through the eyes; under parts paler, with a slight rufous cast on the throat and upper part of breast; lower tail-coverts yellow; wing-coverts and tertiaries green, like the back; primaries black, the first eight with white tips, and mostly edged white; the secondaries edged red and white, and with a white spot on their tips; tail with the central feathers green, faintly edged externally with red, and tipped dark; the other all dusky internally, red on their outer webs, and black-tipped.

Bill dusky brown; legs fleshy ; irides brown. Length 5¼ inches; wing 2¾ ; tail 2 ; bill at front ⅓ ; tarsus ⅞.

This very beautiful bird is rare at Darjeeling, and I only shot one, myself, close to the station. It was clinging at the time to the trunk of a large tree, not very far from the ground, on which it had flown from a shrub near at hand. Another which I procured had been shot by a pellet-bow in the station, on a shrub close to the road. It apparently keeps to the higher elevations, from 6,500 feet and upwards. One I examined had eaten small insects. It has only hitherto been found in Nepal and Sikhim.

The next form is also a somewhat anomalous one, both as regards structure and coloration, and, like the last, is founded on a single species.

Gen. ERPORNIS, Hodgson.

Char.—Bill moderate or rather long, conic, compressed, strong, straight, pointed; tip of the upper mandible longer and notched, nostrils exposed; wings moderate, round, 5th quill longest; the first small; tail bifurcate, simple; legs and feet moderately strong.

This genus is placed by Gray and Horsfield next to *Stachyris* among the *Timalinæ*. Bonaparte locates it with the *Pycnonotinæ*. Blyth places it where I have done, but with the remark '*incertæ sedis.*'* In its coloration, as in the form of its bill, it is related to *Zosterops;* by the structure of the feathers of the head to *Myzornis;* and it has also some affinity or analogy to *Iora*.

630. Erpornis xantholeuca, HODGSON.

J. A. S. XIII. 380—BLYTH, Cat. 528—HORSF., Cat. 343—
Dang-pu-pho, Lepch.

THE WHITE-BELLIED FLOWER-PECKER.

Descr.—Above light green, beneath dull milky-white; coronal feathers elongated and spatulate.

Bill pale horny-brown; legs fleshy red; irides light-brown. Length barely 5 inches; extent $7\frac{3}{4}$; wing $2\frac{1}{2}$; tail $1\frac{3}{4}$; bill at front $\frac{1}{2}$; tarsus $\frac{5}{8}$.

This is not a very common bird at Darjeeling, and I had not an opportunity of observing its habits. It is found from 2,000 feet or less, to 5,000 feet.

---

* We have here a remarkable instance both of the difficulty of arranging aberrant members of any group, and at the same time of the intricate relations that appear to exist among the outlying species of allied families.

It extends from Nepal, through Sikhim to Arrakan, and even to the Malay Peninsula. This extended geographical distribution, I may remark, is, in some degree, in favor of its relationship to *Zosterops*.

The next genus differs from the preceding ones in having a wide geographical distribution, and comprising numerous species.

Gen. ZOSTEROPS.

Char.—Bill somewhat conic, stout, acute at the tip, slightly but distinctly notched; culmen slightly curved; rictus smooth; eyes surrounded by close-set white feathers; nostrils lengthened, exposed: wings moderate, 3rd and 4th primaries about equal and longest; 1st a little shorter than 2nd; tail short. even; tarsus moderate; toes strongish, two laterals nearly equal, outer syndactyle; hind toe strong; claw well curved.

Horsfield classes *Zosterops* in his *Pycnonotinæ*, between *Myzornis* and *Iora*; Gray in his *Mniotiltinæ* next to *Yuhina*; and Bonaparte and Blyth in *Melliphaginæ*. Some of the species extend from India, through the isles, to Australia even, the head quarters of the Honey-eaters; but also to the Mauritius, Madagascar, and Africa; this distribution in Africa is against the view of its being a really Melliphagous genus; and, as it undoubtedly has affinities with the birds with which it is placed here, I prefer keeping it in this group.

631. **Zosterops palpebrosus**, TEMMINCK.

Sylvia, apud TEMM., Pl., Col. 293 f. 3—Z. Maderaspatana, Auct. BLYTH, Cat. 1333—HORSF., Cat. 406—JERDON, Cat. 128.

THE WHITE-EYED TIT.

Descr.—Above light siskin green, with a circle of close white feathers round the eye; throat and upper breast canary yellow; belly bluish white; leg feathers, lower tail-coverts, and some of the feathers on the abdomen, tinged with pale yellow.

Bill blackish. horny at the base beneath; legs reddish horny; irides light yellow-brown. Length $4\frac{1}{2}$ inches; wing $2\frac{3}{10}$; tail $1\frac{7}{10}$; bill at front $\frac{7}{10}$; tarsus $\frac{3}{4}$; extent $6\frac{1}{2}$.

This bird is spread throughout the whole of India, from the Himalayas to the extreme south, and extends to Assam, Arrakan,

Tenasserim and Ceylon. Towards the south it is somewhat rare, and only found at high elevations; but, as you get further north, it becomes more common, but chiefly occurs in hilly regions, and it is not found in Lower Bengal. It is very abundant on the Neilgherries, both in the woods and in gardens; and there it may be seen clinging to flower stalks, extracting the minute insects that infest flowers, by the pollen of which its forehead is often powdered. It associates generally in small flocks, is lively and brisk in its movements, and keeps up a continual feeble twitter. In the plains it is found in well-wooded districts, or jungly places, only, I think in the cold weather. It breeds on the Neilgherries, and makes an exceedingly neat deep cup-shaped nest of moss, lichen, hair, &c., not suspended, in those I have seen, but fixed in the fork of two small branches, in a Barberry or other low bush. I found two eggs only in several nests, of a very pale blue, almost like skimmed milk. Hutton found at Mussooree that it generally suspended the nest by some fibres, hair, or silk. He describes the eggs as whitish green. He further says that they are often mixed up with the flocks of *Parus erythrocephalus*, and that they appear to feed greedily upon the small black berries of a species of *Rhamnus* common in these localities. They depart for the Dhoon about the end of October, and they do not ascend higher than about 5,000 feet. This bird is rare at Darjeeling, and is only found in the warmer valleys.

Numerous species of *Zosterops* are recorded from Africa, Madagascar, Mauritius, the Malayan Archipelago, and Australia, with Oceanica.

The next two forms are by Gray and Blyth included in the *Parinæ* or true Tits, but, from their mode of coloration, and more slender bill, perhaps better associate with the members of this group.

Gen. SYLVIPARUS, Burton.

Char.—Bill short, conic, straight, very slightly depressed at the base; nostrils concealed by tufts of hairs and plumes; rictal setæ wanting; wings long, 1st primary small, 2nd shorter than the 3rd, which nearly equals the 4th and 5th; tail rather short, or moderate, even, or somewhat emarginate; tarsus moderately long, stout; feet small; hind toe long; claws well curved.

This genus, by its plumed nares, evidently grades directly to the true Tits; and both this and the next genus have some affinity for *Regulus*, and may be said to connect the Warblers with the Tits.

632. **Sylviparus modestus**, Burton.

P. Z. S., 1835, p. 154—Blyth, Cat. 552—Horsf., Cat. 373—Parus sericophrys, Hodgson—Parus minutus, Jerdon, Cat. 132.

The Yellow-browed Flower-pecker.

Descr.—Above light olive-green; beneath yellowish; a pale yellow supercilium; forehead yellow-green; wings and tail dusky, edged externally with bright greenish yellow.

Bill and legs plumbeous; irides light brown. Length $3\frac{3}{4}$ inches; extent $7\frac{1}{4}$; wing $2\frac{5}{10}$; tail $1\frac{3}{8}$; bill at front $\frac{1}{4}$: tarsus $\frac{1}{2}$.

This small Tit is found throughout the Himalayas, extending, perhaps in the cold weather only, to the plains; but it is not common anywhere. I procured one specimen near Ajunteh at the edge of the Northern Ghats; and have since obtained it at Darjeeling. It hunts in small flocks about the foliage and flowers of high trees, feeding chiefly on minute insects.

Gen. Cephalopyrus, Bonap.

Syn. Ægithalus, Vigors.

Char.—Bill like that of *Sylviparus*, but more lengthened, conic, and pointed; nostrils apert; wings very long, pointed; tarsus short, stout; feet very small; lateral toes unequal; hind toe moderately long; claws well curved.

This chiefly differs from *Sylviparus* by its exposed nares, evincing less affinity to the Tits.

633. **Cephalopyrus flammiceps**, Burton.

Ægithalus, apud Burton, P. Z. S., 1835, p. 153—Dicæum sanguinifrons, A. Hay, J. A. S., XV. 44.

The Flame-fronted Flower-pecker.

Descr.—Above yellowish green, brightest on the rump and upper tail-coverts; forehead, top of head, and chin, rich shining orange-red; wings dusky, edged with green; and with two light bars on the wing-coverts; beneath golden yellow, paling on the lower abdomen and under tail-coverts. The female has no red, and is a duller yellow beneath.

Bill plumbeous; legs leaden brown. Length 4 inches; wing $2\frac{1}{2}$; tail $1\frac{3}{8}$; tarsus not quite $\frac{1}{2}$; bill at front 8 mill.

This pretty little bird has hitherto been found only in the North-West Himalayas, extending to Cashmere.

Stachyris chrysœa, antea, p. 22, appears to me to have some relation with the present bird, both in structure and colors. *Acanthiza* is also nearly connected, though Gray places it with the *Accentorinœ.* It is an Australian group, extending to the Malayan Archipelago.

Among the *Leiotrichinœ,* ought to be placed *Bombycilla,* or the Wax-wings, of which *B. garrula,* L., is the type; and there are other well marked species in Japan and North America. It most resembles *Leiothrix,* or it may be said to be intermediate between it and *Pteruthius. Moquinus albicaudus,* Bonap., of Africa, placed by its describer among the Fly-catchers, appears to me, simply judging from the figure, to have a very Pteruthian aspect. *Falcunculus, Pachycephala,* and *Eopsaltria,* of Australia, are by some referred to *Parinœ,* but they appear to be better arranged with the *Leiotrichinœ,* the former genus, by its stout Shrike-like bill, much resembling *Pteruthius.* Gray, indeed, in his List of Genera arranges them here. One species of *Eopsaltria* by its grey and white plumage, appears to tend towards the *Sylviinœ.*

The *Pardaloti,* also of Australia, appear very nearly related to some of the smaller Leiotrichine genera, such as *Minla.* They are diminutive birds with lengthened wings; the head more or less crested; a gay and variegated plumage, with bright markings on the wings; and they breed in holes of trees, in which they more resemble the *Pari.* Among the more slender billed group are placed *Ægithalus,* founded on the *Parus peadulinus* of Southern Europe, noted for its beautiful purse-like nest. *Acanthiza* is chiefly an Australian group, extending to the Malayan isles, of somewhat plain plumage, resembling the *Regulus* group; they are said to construct domed nests, and to lay fleshy-white eggs, with brown, red, or yellowish specks. These two last genera are very close to *Sylviparus* and *Cephalopyrus*. *Ephthianura* is considered by Gray to belong to the *Motacillinæ*, but one species, *E. aurifrons*, Gould (like *Stachyris chrysæa*, in its own group), appears to belong to a distinct type, grading towards *Ægithalus*.

Sub-fam. PARINÆ.

Bill typically rather short, conic, stout, entire ; the nares tufted; wings moderate, somewhat rounded; tail short or moderate, long in a few; tarsus and feet short, stout; hind toe long, claws well curved.

The Titmice or Tits are, typically, a strongly marked group of small birds found chiefly in the Old Continent, a few occurring in the more Northern parts of America. They are most abundant in temperate districts, one or two preferring cold climates, and a good many inhabiting the hilly districts of the tropical or juxta-tropical regions. In India they are chiefly confined to the Hima-layas, only three species extending to the hilly regions of Central and Southern India. They do not appear to be migratory.

The Tits are characterized by a strong, somewhat acute, and conic bill, and stout legs and feet. They differ from most of the Warblers by having their nares protected by tufts of reflected feathers and hairs, and by their conical, entire bill, which led to their being placed in the *Conirostres*, by Cuvier and other. Undoubtedly they have a considerable resemblance to some Coni-rostral groups, especially to the *Garrulinæ*, and they are indeed very like Jays in miniature. This resemblance to conirostral families is exhibited by others of this, the last dentirostral family ; to wit, the *Accentorinæ* to the Finches, and the *Miotiltinæ* to the Tanagers ; and it is probably a real affinity, for it extends, in some cases, to the internal structure, the stomach being thick, and muscular. But their relation to other tooth-billed genera, such as *Pteruthius*, and *Falcunculus*, cannot be ignored, and they thus form part of the last and most aberrant division of the *Dentirostres*.

In their colours they are mostly sober, compared with the *Leio-trichinæ*, black, gray, and white, varied in a few with rufous, and in others pleasingly blended with blue, green, and yellow. Many are crested.

In their habits they are strictly arboreal, active, climbing about and clinging to the twigs and flowering branches of trees and shrubs, with a loud, and reiterated chirp. They are very omnivorous, feed equally on seeds, fruits, and insects ; and they pierce hard seeds or nuts with their strong conical bill, holding it with their feet, and thus extract the kernel. They are excessively bold and even ferocious, the larger ones occasionally destroying young and sickly birds, both in a wild state, and in confinement. They are very social. They nidificate mostly in holes of trees, or even in walls, occasionally on the ground, lining their nest profusely with hair and feathers ; and they lay very numerous eggs, usually white with red spots. A few build pendulous nests like the Ægithaline group.

Of late they have been divided into several genera, varying chiefly in the mode of coloration, crest, and length of tail, but also in the length and strength of the bill. I shall adopt some of these genera in accordance with my previous practice, for, though not very well marked, structurally, they each comprise several nearly allied species.

The first of these is a well marked group, admitted by all.

Gen. ÆGITHALISCUS, Cabanis.

Syn. *Orites* Mœhr.—*Psaltria*, T., and *Paroides*, Brehm, apud Auct. (in part) *Acanthiparus*, apud Gould.

Char.—Bill short, small, conic ; tail somewhat lengthened, of small size ; plumage mixed with rufous, not crested.

The following birds have been usually classed under *Orites*, but the type of that genus, *P. caudatus*, or the long-tailed Tit of Europe, has naked orbits, a still shorter beak, much longer tail, and is very distinct in form and habits.

634. Ægithaliscus erythrocephalus, Vigors.

Parus, apud Vigors, P. Z. S. 1831—Gould, Cent. II. Birds, pl. 30, f. 1—Blyth. Cat. 550—Horsf., Cat. 606—Gould, Birds of Asia, pt. 7, pl. 11, *Pyion j-samyi*, Lepch.

The Red-headed Tit.

Descr.—Head above and nape rufous ; back of neck, back, and rump, cinereous, tinged with reddish on the rump and upper tail-coverts; wings and tail dusky cinercous; superciliary stripe, and outer webs of the outermost tail-feathers, white; the rest with a white tip; a broad black eye-stripe, extending through the eye and ear-coverts to the nape; the throat black, with a white line between it and the eye-streak; chin white, the rest of the body beneath rufescent white, or pale vinous, deepest on the flanks and lower abdomen.

Bill black; legs fleshy yellow; irides brown. Length 4¾ inches; extent 6; wing 2; tail 2; bill at front $\frac{7}{16}$; tarsus ⅝.

This little Tit is found throughout the Himalayas, from the far North-West to Bootan. It is very common at Darjeeling about the Station, at 7,000 feet of elevation, and is found up to 10,000 feet. It associates in small flocks, frequenting shrubs, hedges, and high trees, and lives chiefly on insects. Hutton describes the nest as being 'a round ball, with a small lateral entrance, composed of moss, and well lined with feathers. The eggs are five, white, with a pinkish tinge, sparingly sprinkled with lilac spots, and with a well defined lilac ring at the large end. The nest is placed on a bank, or among creepers twining round the trunk of a tree.'

635. Ægithaliscus iouschistos, Hodgson.

Parus, apud Hodgs., J. A. S., XIII. 942—Blyth, Cat. 549—Horsf., Cat. 608—Gould, Birds of Asia, pt. 7, pl. 15.

THE RUFOUS-FRONTED TIT.

Descr.—Above ashy, slightly tinged with olive; winglet, and coverts of primaries black; a broad streak over the eye black; the central line of head, and sides of head, reddish fawn color; the outer tail-feathers more or less tipped and edged externally with whitish; under parts reddish fawn or rufescent.

Bill black; legs yellow brown; irides brown. Length 4¼ inches; wing 2⅛; tail 2; bill at front ⅜; tarsus ⅝.

This Tit has the three outer tail-feathers graduated, with the middle pair ¼ inch shorter than the next pair, and its bill is something longer, and more slender than in *erythrocephalus*. It is an evident link to the true *Pari*, and Bonaparte includes it in the genus *Pœcila*, of which *P. palustris* is the type.

I did not procure this bird at Darjeeling, but it has been found both in Nepal and Bootan.

636. Ægithaliscus niveogularis, GOULD.

Orites, apud GOULD, MOORE, P. Z. S. 1854, p. 140—GOULD, Birds of Asia, pt. 7, pl. 14.

THE WHITE-THROATED TIT.

Descr.—' Forehead white, passing to buff-brown on the back of the head, nape, and fore-part of the back, and thence to the tail grey, tinged with isabelline on the rump; lores, over the eyes and ear-coverts, black, passing into brown on the nape; ear-coverts blackish anteriorly, brownish-buff posteriorly, and somewhat striped longitudinally with white; base of lower mandible, chin, throat, forepart of breast, and sides of the neck, to the nape behind the ear-coverts, snowy-white, contrasting with the brownish band which runs from the nape across the middle of the breast; the lower part of the breast with the abdomen pale pinky-isabelline, passing to white in the middle of the belly; wings brown, margined with greyish-white; coverts and scapulars blackish; tail dusky-black, margined externally with greyish-white; its outermost feathers white on the outer web.

Bill black, longish, and slender as in *A. ionschistos*, Hodgson; feet yellowish. Length 4½ inches; of wing 2½; tail 2⅝, its outermost feather ½ inch shorter; bill to frontal plumes $\frac{3}{10}$ to $\frac{5}{10}$; tarse $\frac{7}{12}$ of an inch.

Hab. N. India. In the collection of John Gould, Esq.'

A species nearly allied to the three last Tits has been lately described from Affghanistan, *Orites leucogenys*, Moore, Horsf., Cat. 607; which may occur in our extreme North-western limit; and Gould has *O. glauco-gularis*, from China.

Moore remarks that *niveo-gularis*, with *ionschistos*, form one and group; and *erythrocephalus*, with the species from Affghanistan mentioned above, form another. To these Mr. Gould, in his Birds of Asia, has respectively applied the names *Acanthiparus*, and *Psaltria*, but he has placed *O. glaucogularis* under *Mecistura*.

Parus trivirgatus, Temm., Faun. Japan, pl. 34, is placed by Bonaparte next *O. caudatus* of Europe. This last bird, the well known Bottle-tit of Europe, builds a beautiful oval nest with a hole in the side, and lays from ten to twelve eggs, plain white, or with a few red specks. The genus *Psaltria*, Temm., to which these birds have been referred by Gould, is founded on a Japanese bird of a very distinct type, according to Bonaparte.

Gen. LOPHOPHANES, Kaup.

Head crested; bill rather slender; tail moderate; plumage black, grey, and white.

This genus is founded on the *P. cristatus* of Europe, and *P. bicolor* of N. America, which last however is now separated as *Bæolophus*. The Indian species probably differ in type, but I have no means of ascertaining to what extent they do so.

The first species differs considerably from the others, and perhaps forms a distinct group, tending towards some of the *Leuleæ*.

637. **Lophophanes dichrous**, HODGSON.

J. A. S. XIII. 943—HORSF., Cat. 600—GOULD, Birds of Asia, pt. XI., pl. 13.

THE BROWN-CRESTED TIT.

Descr.—Above uniform brownish grey; occiput with a somewhat recurved long crest; forehead and cheeks dirty white; beneath ochreous white, passing to rufescent brown.

Bill dusky bluish; feet plumbeous; irides brick red.

Length $4\frac{1}{2}$ to 5 inches; wing $2\frac{3}{4}$; tail $1\frac{7}{8}$; bill at front not quite $\frac{3}{8}$; tarsus $\frac{3}{4}$.

This appears a rare bird in Nepal. Adams obtained, apparently, the same bird at Simla, No. 77 of his List of Birds of India, and 61 of the Birds of Cashmere. This last he shot on ' the oak-covered slopes of one of the lesser ranges near the valley of Cashmere.'

638. **Lophophanes melanolophos**, VIGORS.

Parus, apud VIGORS—GOULD, Cat. Him. Birds, pl. 30, f. 2—BLYTH, Cat. 542—HORSF., Cat. 599—GOULD, Birds of Asia, pt. XI., pl. 16.

THE CRESTED BLACK-TIT.

Descr.—Above dark iron grey; head (with a long recurved crest) black; a large white spot on the cheeks, from the base of the lower mandible, and including the ear-coverts; a spot on the nape also white, and the wing-coverts spotted with white; quills and tail dusky; chin and throat black; the rest beneath grey, with a slight rufous tinge; axillaries and under tail-coverts rusty.

Bill blackish; legs plumbeous. Length 4¼ inches; wing 2¾; tail 1¾; bill at front 10 mill.

This pretty little Tit is found chiefly in the N. W. Himalayas; it is common at Simla and Mussooree, and spreads into Affghanistan. It is not found in the S. E. Himalayas, where it is replaced by the following very closely allied species. Adams states that in Cashmere it is seen in flocks, in the forests of the valley, and the lesser ranges towards the South, and that it sometimes associates with *Ægithalus flammiceps*.

639.　**Lophophanes rubidiventris,** BLYTH.

Parus, apud BLYTH, J. A. S. XVI. 445—BLYTH, Cat. 543— HORSF., Cat. 600—P. melanolophos, apud HODGSON—GOULD, Birds of Asia, pt. XI., pl. 14.

THE RUFOUS-BELLIED CRESTED-TIT.

Descr.—Above pale rufescent grey, with a strong tinge of ferruginous on the rump; head and crest black; cheek spot as in the last; wings not spotted with white; the black on the throat is of less extent than in *melanolophos*, which it closely resembles in size; but it is a somewhat larger bird, the wings measuring 2⅝; the feet also are stronger; the black on the breast is of less extent; and the bill is conspicuously larger, being 12 mill. long, and much thicker. This species has hitherto only been found in Nepal, and I did not procure it in Sikhim.

The next two birds are very similar in coloring, but are distinctly larger.

640.　**Lophophanes rufonuchalis,** BLYTH.

J. A. S. XVIII. 810—BLYTH, Cat. 541—GOULD, Birds of Asia, pt. XI., pl. 15.

The Simla Black-Tit.

Descr.—Dark grey, with a rufous tinge on the back and belly; the nape white, ferruginous in some; crown of head, (with crest) chin, throat and breast, black; ear-coverts and sides of the neck white; axillaries and lower tail-coverts ferruginous.

Bill black; legs and feet plumbeous; irides brown. Length 5½ inches; wing 3; tail 2¼; bill at front ½; tarsus ⅝.

This species of Tit was procured by Hutton, near Simla, high up towards the snow line.

641. Lophophanes Beavani, Blyth.

Parus, apud Blyth, in Mus. As. Soc.—*Lho tasso,* Lepch.

The Sikhim Black-Tit.

Descr.—Very similar to the last; the grey on the upper parts purer, and less mixed with rufous: the black on the throat is of much less extent, the bill is shorter and more slender, and there is no trace of rufous on the white nuchal spot; axillaries and lower tail-coverts rufous, as in all the group.

Length 5 inches; wing 2⅞: tail 2⅛; bill at front 10 mill.

This is so close to the last that I did not myself discriminate it. I procured it on Mount Tonglo, in Sikhim, at 10,000 feet elevation, where I observed it on bushy ground, in small scattered flocks. Lt. Beavan procured it in the same locality, and Mr. Blyth, on seeing his specimens, considered it to be distinct from the previous bird.

These last four species, it may be observed, closely resemble each other in colors, and chiefly differ in the extent of the black on the throat, and the strength of the bill; the two former species being moreover much smaller than the two last; and, strange to say, with a corresponding difference in the size of the bill in both cases.

Under the next genus, restricted *Parus,* I have placed all the non-crested Tits, except those classed under *Ægithaliscus.* This arrangement appears to bring together all the nearly related species, and the first two on the list closely resemble, in coloration, the species of Lophophanes.

Gen. PARUS, L., (restricted).

Form typical; head not crested; bill usually stout and moderately short; tail rather short.

There are two or three types in this genus, even as now restricted, each of which is represented in India. The first is that *Parus ater* of Europe; the second that of *P. major;* and the third, without a representative in Europe, that of my *P. nuchalis,* is allied, apparently, to the African group *Melaniparus.*

642. **Parus œmodius,** HODGSON.

J. A. S. XIII. 943.

THE HIMALAYAN COLE-TIT.

Descr.—' Very closely allied to P. *ater* of Europe, but the bill decidedly more slender and compressed; the black also descends more upon the breast, and spreads laterally, circumscribing the sides of the neck; and the back is less tinged with olivaceous, while the belly would appear to be more rufescent than its European representative. Nepal.'

Such is the description given. There is no specimen of this bird in the Museum of the Asiatic Society, nor in that of the India House.

P. ater has the head, chin, and throat, black, with a broad white cheek spot, and a nuchal spot of the same color; the back and wing-coverts bluish grey, the latter with white spots, forming two bars; wings and tail brownish grey, the former edged with green; the breast dull white; belly, flanks, and under tail coverts fawn colour, tinged with green; the upper tail-coverts also greenish fawn. Bill and feet black. Length $4\frac{1}{4}$ inches, wing $2\frac{3}{8}$.

643. **Parus Atkinsoni,** JERDON.

THE SIKHIM COLE-TIT.

Descr.—Whole head, chin, and throat, black, with the white nuchal spot and white cheek band as in *ater;* upper parts dark leaden-grey, darker on the wings and tail, the former of which is totally without white spots; beneath, from the throat, dull grey, slightly tinged with rufescent; under tail-coverts ferruginous.

Bill black; legs dark plumbeous. Length 4¼ inches; wing 2⅜; tail 1⅞; bill at front 9 mill. ; tarsus ₁₆⁶.

This apparently new species differs from *P. ater* in the black of the throat only descending a short distance, not beyond the white neck spot, and, in this point, differs still more from *æmodius*. It also wants the greenish tinge of *ater*, the lower parts are much darker; and the white bars on the wings, and tips of the tertiaries are totally wanting.

This Tit was procured by Mr. Atkinson, Secretary to the Asiatic Society, in the interior of Sikhim, at a considerable elevation, not far from the snows.

The next bird is somewhat of the type of *P. major*, of Europe.

644. Parus monticolus, VIGORS.

P. Z. S. 1831, 22—GOULD, Cent. II. B., pl. 29. f. 2—GOULD, Birds of Asia, pt. X. pl. 5—BLYTH, Cat. 536—HORSF., Cat. 595—*Sarak-chak-pho*, Lepch.

THE GREEN-BACKED TIT.

Descr.—Above, the head black; cheeks, and a nuchal mark, white; back and rump olive-green ; wings with the lesser coverts grey, the median and greater coverts black, edged blue, and tipped with white, forming two wing bars; quills black, edged with blue at the base, and with white terminally, and the secondaries and tertials broadly tipped with white ; tail black, bluish externally and tipped white ; neck, throat, breast, and middle of the abdomen, black ; rest of the lower parts yellow.

Bill black; legs dark plumbeous ; irides brown. Length 5½ inches ; wing 2¾ ; tail 2¼ ; bill at front 8 mill. ; tarsus ₁₆¹¹.

This is the most common species of Tit in the Himalayas, not descending lower than about 5,000 feet, and it extends to the hill ranges of Assam, being common on the top of the Khasia Hills, though not found near the station of Cherra Poonjee. It is a common and familiar bird about Darjeeling, coming into gardens ; is active and sprightly, hunting over trees, bushes, and hedges, and carefully searching the foliage, buds, and flowers, and occasionally the bark of trees, for various small insects and larvæ. I have had the nest brought me, from a hole in a tree, a loose mass of feathers and moss, containing five eggs, white, with numerous small red spots.

P. viridescens, Swinhoe, from China, and *P. minor*, Gould, appear to belong to the crestless Asiatic Tits.

The next two Tits, with one of the succeeding group, are the only species found apart from the Himalayas. The first one, as far as general form and the abdominal black stripe, is much of the same type as the last bird, but differs in its plainer coloration.

645. **Parus cinereus**, VIEILLOT.

BLYTH, Cat. 537—HORSF., Cat. 596—P. atriceps, HORSF., L. T. XIII—TEMM., Pl. Col. 287, f. 2—GOULD, Birds of Asia, pt. X., pl. 3—SYKES, Cat. 95—JERDON, Cat. 129—P. nipalensis, HODGSON—P. cæsius, TICKELL—*Ram gangra*, Beng. (B. Hamilton.)

THE INDIAN GREY-TIT.

Descr.—Head, chin, throat and breast, and a line along the abdomen, black; large cheek spot white; plumage above bluish cinereous; greater coverts white-tipped, forming a conspicuous wing-band; quills dusky black, edged with pale blue, and the secondaries and tertials edged white; beneath albescent, with a tinge of rufescent ashy, purer white on the under tail-coverts.

Length nearly 6 inches; wing $2\frac{8}{10}$; tail $2\frac{6}{10}$; bill at front $\frac{7}{10}$; tarsus $\frac{3}{4}$.

This Tit extends throughout the Himalayas, from Nepal to Bootan, Assam, and through Central India, to the Neilgherries and Ceylon; also to Java, and other Malayan isles. I have procured it on the Neilgherries, and it extends all along the range of Western Ghats north to Candeish. I have also obtained it in the hilly regions of Nagpore, and at Saugor, and Tickell got it at Chaibassa in Central India, but it does not occur in Bengal, nor to the eastward. It is a very familiar and abundant bird on the Neilgherries, with the usual habits of the tribe, entering gardens, and feeding on various small insects, and also on seeds. I once found its nest in the deserted Bungalow at Rallia, in the corner of the house. It was made chiefly of the down of hares

(*Lepus nigricollis*), mixed with feathers, and contained six eggs, white spotted with rusty red.

The next species differs remarkably in its mode of coloration, and in this respect approaches the African black Tits, formed into the genus *Melaniparus*, Bonap.

646. Parus nuchalis, JERDON.

2nd. Suppl. Cat. 129 bis—JERDON, Ill. Ind. Orn. pl. 46—*Nalla patsa jitta*, Tel.

THE WHITE-WINGED BLACK TIT.

Descr.—Above black, with a white nuchal mark: a white band across the wing, and the tertiaries broadly margined and tipped with white; tail with the outer feathers nearly white, the next with the outer web only, and the third with the outer web white only at its base and tip; cheeks, sides of neck, sides of breast, and belly, and under tail-coverts, white, with a black mesial stripe from the throat to vent.

Bill black; legs plumbeous; irides red brown. Length 5 inches; wing $2\frac{6}{10}$; tail 2; tarsus $\frac{7}{10}$; bill at front $\frac{1}{10}$.

I obtained this well-marked species of Tit from the Eastern Ghats, west of Nellore. The Shikarees who brought it to me said that it was very rare. It has since been obtained by Dr. Stewart from a tope of trees near Bangalore, so that it probably will hereafter be found in suitable localities on the Southern portion of the great Table-land.

We lastly arrive at a group of black and yellow crested Tits. Three species from India have been determined, which were all formerly referred to *P. xanthogenys*; and there is another in Burmah.

Gen. MACHLOLOPHUS, Cabanis.

Char.—Structure typical; plumage much mixed with yellow and green; head crested. Peculiar to the Indian region.

647. Machlolophus xanthogenys, VIGORS.

Parus, apud VIGORS, P. Z. S. 1831—GOULD, Cent. Him. Birds pl. 29 f. 1—GOULD, Birds of Asia, pt. IX pl. 14—BLYTH, Cat. 538—HORSF., Cat. 597—P. aplonotus, BLYTH, J. A. S. XVI. 444.

THE YELLOW-CHEEKED TIT.

Descr.—Head, fully crested, wings and tail black, the latter tipped white, and the tertiaries laterally edged throughout with white; nape, posterior part of crest, and a small superciliary stripe, bright yellow; back, scapulars, and rump, light olive-green, the scapulars with a few black marks; wing-coverts tipped with pale yellow; the outer primaries white-edged, and with a white bar near their base, the others bluish externally; tail dusky grey, white-tipped; cheeks, sides of neck, sides of breast and abdomen, and under tail-coverts yellow, passing to greenish on the flanks and under tail-coverts; lores, a stripe on each side of the neck from the eye, chin, throat, and middle of breast and abdomen, black.

Bill black; legs plumbeous; irides light brown. Length $5\frac{1}{4}$ inches; wing $2\frac{3}{4}$; tail $2\frac{1}{8}$; bill at front 11 mill.; tarsus $\frac{5}{8}$.

This handsome species extends from the North-western Himalayas to Nepal, but not further east, being replaced in Sikhim by the next species. Hutton says that "it is common at Mussooree throughout the year. It breeds in April; the nest was constructed of moss, hair, and feathers, and placed at the bottom of a deep hole in the stump of an oak tree."

648. **Machlolophus Jerdoni**, BLYTH.

Parus, apud BLYTH, J. A. S. XXV., p. 445—GOULD, Birds of Asia, pt. IX. pl. 16—P. xanthogenys, apud SYKES, Cat. 96—JERDON, Cat. 130.

THE SOUTHERN YELLOW-TIT.

Descr.—Very similar to the last *(xanthogenys)*, but conspicuously larger; has the back less tinged with yellow, being dull green with a slaty tinge; the yellow portion of the plumage not so intense in hue, and the yellow sincipital streak short, and not continued forward over the eye.

Bill black; legs plumbeous; irides light brown. Length 6 inches; wing 3; tail $2\frac{1}{2}$; extent 10; tarsus $\frac{11}{16}$; bill at front 9 mill.

This, the southern representative of the Yellow-cheeked Tits of the Himalayas, is found on the Neilgherries, at a lower elevation than *P. cinereus*, never exceeding 6,000 feet; also in Coorg,

Wynaad, and all along the range of Ghâts; also in the Saugor territories, in the Vindhyan range of mountains near Mhow, and in the jungles South-east of Nagpore. It usually frequents open forest, and has the usual manners of its tribe.

649. **Machlolophus spilinotus**, BLYTH.

Parus, apud BLYTH, J. A. S. XVIII.—BLYTH, Cat. 539—HORSF., Cat. 598—JARD., Contrib. Orn. p. 49, with figure—GOULD, Birds of Asia, pt. IX. pl. 15.—P. xanthogenys, apud BLYTH, J. A. S. XVI. 445—*Muchetink-pho*, Lepch.

THE BLACK-SPOTTED YELLOW TIT.

Descr.—Very similar to *P. xanthogenys*, but the back with broad, black, longitudinal spots, the yellow generally more vivid, and the posterior feathers of the crest broadly tipped with yellow; a well marked yellow supercilium over the eye, extending to the base of the bill; lores yellow; black neck stripe not so broad; the black of the throat and front of the neck also not so broad, nor extending to the gape, as in the other species; the white edging to the tertiaries less conspicuous, and white tips of the tail also are narrower.

Bill black; legs plumbeous; irides light brown. Length $5\frac{1}{2}$ inches; wing 3; tail $2\frac{1}{4}$; bill at front 11 mill.; tarsus $\frac{3}{5}$.

This species of Tit is found in Eastern Nepal, Sikhim, and the Khasia Hills of Assam. It is not very common about Darjeeling, and is chiefly found from 4,000 to 5,500 feet; I observed nothing peculiar in its habits.

An allied species of this group occurs in Burmah, *Parus subviridis*, Tickell.

The last species to be noticed is perhaps the finest of all, and is the giant of the group. It associates very naturally with the last species, but has been separated, on account of its large size, different plumage of the sexes, and slightly different style of coloring.

Gen. MELANOCHLORA, Lesson.

Syn. *Crataionyx*, Eyton.

Char.—Of large size; highly crested; bill somewhat lengthened; sexes differ considerably in colours.

650. Melanochlora sultanea, Hodgson.

Parus, apud Hodgson, Ind. Rev. 1836—Horsf., Cat. 594—
P. flavocristatus, Lafresn., Mag. Zool. 1837, pl. 80—Blyth, Cat.
534—Melanochlora Sumatrana, Lesson, Rev. Zool.—Crataionyx
flava, Eyton.—*Bon tylia-pho*, Lepch.

The Sultan Yellow-Tit.

Descr.—Head above (with a long and pointed crested) yellow ;
rest of the upper parts, with the throat, neck, and breast, glossy
green-black ; abdomen bright yellow, paling on the under tail-
coverts. The female has the parts black that are in the male,
blackish or rifle-green, and the yellow less vivid.

Bill black ; legs slaty ; irides dark brown. Length 8 inches ; extent
13½ ; wing 4 ; tail 3¼ ; bill at front ⅝ ; tarsus ¾.

This magnificent Tit is only found in the warmer valleys of
the Himalayas, extending into Assam, and through Burmah to
the Malayan peninsula, and even to Sumatra. It has not, I believe,
been found in the N. W. Himalayas. Near Darjeeling it is common in the valley of the great Rungeet, about 1,200 feet, and thence
extends to about 4,000 or so. It frequents the tops of high trees,
in small flocks, feeding on insects chiefly, and has a rather loud
note. The Lepchas told me that it bred in holes in high trees, but
did not bring the nest or eggs.

Hodgson says " it is found in the Central and Northern region
of the hills, passing into the Southern in winter: is exceedingly
fond of caterpillars, and occasionally takes pulpy berries.

There are several other *Pari* from Asia, chiefly from Japan and
China. Numerous species of Titmice occur in Europe and Africa.
The Blue-Tits have been separated as *Cyanistes*, Kaup; they are the
prettiest of the tribe. The Marsh-Tit, *P. palustris*, is the type of
Kaup's genus *Pœcila*, in which Bonaparte classes my *P. nuchalis*,
Proparus vinipectus, and the species placed by me under *Ægitha-
liscus*; also a species from Kamtschatka. The African Tits are
placed under *Melaniparus*, Bonap., and *Parus;* and the American
Tits under *Lophophanes* and *Pœcila.*

The bearded Tit of Europe, *Calamophilus biarmicus* (*Panurus*,
Koch), differs remarkably from all the other Tits, and is considered

by Blyth to have some affinity with the *Fringillidæ*, and especially with the *Estreldæ*. It appears to me to have relations with the Timaline group, near *Pyctornis*; and the Australian genus *Xerophila*, formerly referred to the *Timalina* (*vide* p. 10,) is also placed here by Gray. Other genera placed in this family are *Certhiparus*, Lafr., from New Zealand; and *Parisoma*, Swains., an African group, already alluded to, (*vide* p. 74). The former probably belongs to the last sub-family; and *Anthoscopus*, founded on *Sylvia minuta*, Shaw, perhaps belongs to the slender-billed Tits, or Flower-peckers, in the last sub-family, near *Sylviparus*.

Sub-fam. ACCENTORINÆ.

Bill straight, stout, somewhat conic, high at the base, entire, or slightly notched at the tip, which is barely bent down; nostrils exposed; wings moderate, more or less rounded; tail moderate or somewhat short; legs and feet stout, fitted both for walking and perching.

The birds composing this group offer a most perplexing task to the systematic Ornithologist, both as to the position they should occupy in the natural system, and as to the extent of the division. I have placed it here as the last group of the Dentirostral tribe, and as a sub-family of the most aberrant and quasi-Conirostral family of the tooth-billed Perchers, partly because it really appears to have affinities for some of this series; and partly because I know not where else to locate it satisfactorily. Vigors and Horsfield class it as a sub-family of the Warblers, between the Pipits and their *Pipridæ*, our *Ampelidæ*. Swainson places it among the Tits, with the *Mniotiltinæ*. Gray locates it between the *Saxicolinæ* and *Parinæ*. Bonaparte formerly, in his Conspectus, placed it between the *Pratincolæ* and the *Sylvicolinæ*, but, latterly, considered it to be a sub-family of the Thrushes. Blyth in his Catalogue located it between the Buntings and the Larks; and others also look upon its nearest allies as being the Finches. It will thus be seen that most systematists have allowed it to have some near relations with the Tits, or their allies of the *Ampelidæ*, with a tendency towards some Saxicoline and Motacilline forms. Bonaparte and Blyth may be said to represent the extreme views, on each side.

The Accentors may be said to have somewhat the bill of a Tit-lark, but straighter and stouter; and the plumage of the restricted Accentors is much that of certain Finches; in others it is various shades of rufous brown, either plain, or streaked above, and, almost in all cases, with some decided marking on the throat. They are chiefly terrestrial, a few climbing well on rocks; they nidificate both in bushes or hedgerows, and on the ground; and the eggs, of some, at least, are unspotted blue. They feed on various insects, worms, and seeds. They frequent bushy ground, hedgerows, and the like, or rocky mountains. They are sedentary, occasionally familiar, and some of them sing nicely. On the whole, their habits may be said to be a sort of mixture of that of the Finches, with certain Warblers and Tits. Of the extent of the group, there is great diversity of opinion. Gray includes in it *Seiurus, Acanthiza, Sericornis, Gerygone*, and *Pyrrholæmus*, all Australian forms. Bonaparte (with whom Blyth is in accord on this point) considers that *Cinclosoma* of the same region is its nearest ally; and also that *Origma* is another typical form, these composing his section *Accentoreæ* of this sub-family; whilst his *Acanthizeæ* comprise the above last named four genera, with which he has badly associated *Smicrornis*, (*vide* vol. I. p. 376). Swainson also considers that *Seiurus* of America, and some of its allies, grade with the Accentors; this form being usually considered to belong to the *Motacillinæ*. *Orthonyx spinicaudus*, of Australia, appears nearly allied to *Cinclosoma*, and is probably another Accentorine type, showing, by the structure of its tail, an affinity for the *Certhiæ*.

I am not sufficiently acquainted with many of these forms to enable me to form a decided opinion, but, judging from what I do know of them, I consider that the Australian *Cinclosoma* is very nearly related to *Accentor*, and that *Orthonyx, Origma, Pyrrholæmus, Chthonicola*, and perhaps other Australian forms, do form part of the same group; but that some of the others such as *Gerygone* belong to the *Acanthizeæ*, a division of the *Mniotiltinæ*, some of which, it may be remarked, exhibit the markings of the neck and throat, which appear to be conspicuous in most members of this family. *Origma* was formerly considered (*vide* vol. I. page 508) to belong to the Dippers, and, indeed, there is an apparent leaning towards that family among the Accentors, as shewn in the bill of *Accentor* and *Cinclosoma*. *Seiurus* of America also, and its immediate allies, perhaps ought also to enter this as a sub-division, rather than the *Motacillinæ*.

On the whole, taking into consideration the several groups of birds believed to associate naturally with it, we may look on this family as an aberrant group of birds having affinities with certain Thrushes, Saxicolines, and Wagtails on the one side, with more distant analogies for *Certhia*; and, on the other side, with the *Mniotiltinæ*; and, like other of the *Ampelidæ*, showing a marked tendency towards some of the conirostral families.

With such varied forms, and numerous affinities and ana- logies, perhaps the present place is about as appropriate as any other; but, from these very circumstances, it probably ought to form a distinct family, placed between *Motacillinæ* and *Mniotiltinæ*.

The only Indian member of this family is *Accentor*, the type of which is the Hedge-sparrow of Britain, *A. modularis*. In this country they are entirely confined to the Himalayas, and several species have been lately described. Most of them frequent the higher elevations, one species only, in winter, descending to a level of 5,000 feet, in the vicinity of Darjeeling.

Gen. ACCENTOR, Bechstein.

Char.—Bill straight, conic, sharp, of moderate length, high, rather wide at the base, notched at the tip, which is very slightly bent down; wings moderate, the 3rd quill the longest; tail moderate, even; feet and legs stout; hind toe somewhat elongated and stout.

The Dunnocks, as they are called by some, frequent bushy ground, hedge-rows and the like, a few affecting rocky ground among high mountains. They feed much on the ground, on various insects, worms, and seeds. They have of late been sub- divided into several genera, which I shall not here adopt.

The first species noticed is the only Indian one with unstreaked plumage, and, in its coloration, we see a distinct approach to a Leio- trichine type, in the wing-coverts and pale wing band.

651. Accentor immaculatus, Hodgson.

P. Z. S., 1845—A mollis, BLYTH, J. A. S., XIV. 581—
BLYTH, Cat. 729—HORSF., Cat. 579—GOULD, Birds of Asia, pt.
VII. pl. 5.

THE MARONNE-BACKED ACCENTOR.

Descr.—Head and neck dark ashy; upper back and scapulars
maronne, passing into reddish brown in the lower back and upper
tail-coverts; frontal feathers to above the eye, margined with white;
lores blackish; wings with the secondary-coverts pure dark grey;
those of the primaries, with the winglet, black, as are the primaries,
these last having their unemarginated portion externally bordered
with pale grey, forming a conspicuous wing-spot; tail greyish
dusky; entire under parts deep brownish ashy, as far as the vent,
which is pale and mixed with ferruginous; under tail-coverts, and
flanks posteriorly, dark ferruginous.

Bill blackish; feet pale. Length about 6 inches; wing $3\frac{1}{4}$; tail
$2\frac{1}{2}$; bill at front $\frac{7}{16}$; tarsus $\frac{7}{8}$.

This species has hitherto only been sent from Nepal and Darjeeling.

652. Accentor nipalensis, Hodgson.

J. A. S., XII. 958—BLYTH, Cat. 724—HORSF., Cat. 573—
A. cacharensis, HODGSON.—GOULD, Birds of Asia, pt. VII.
pl. 4.

THE LARGE HIMALAYAN ACCENTOR.

Descr.—Head, neck, and ear-coverts uniform dark grey; back,
rump and upper tail-coverts, greyish brown, with dark centres to
the feathers; wings dusky black, edged ferruginous; wing-coverts
black with white spots; tail brownish black, with a terminal spot
on the inner web of each feather, and the whole tip, whitish or
rusty; chin and throat white with black spots; breast brownish
grey; belly and flanks dark ferruginous; under tail-coverts dusky,
tinged with rusty, and edged with white.

Bill dusky, yellow on the lower mandible; legs reddish brown.
Length 7 inches; wing $3\frac{3}{4}$; tail $2\frac{3}{4}$; bill at front nearly $\frac{1}{2}$;
tarsus $\frac{16}{16}$.

This, the largest of the Indian Accentors, appears to represent *A. alpinus* of Europe, in the higher regions of the Himalayas. Its European representative occasionally visits England, and is recorded as having been seen climbing adroitly round the buttresses of a building.

653. Accentor altaicus, BRANDT.

A. variegatus, BLYTH, J. A. S. XII. 958—BLYTH, Cat. 725—HORSF., Cat. 574—A. Himalayanus, BLYTH,—A. alpinus, apud VIEILLOT, Gal. pl. 156, (fid. MOORE)—GOULD, Birds of Asia, pt. X. pl. 14.

THE HIMALAYAN ACCENTOR.

Descr.—Forehead, crown, occiput, neck, shoulders, and rump, uniform dingy brownish grey ; back, scapulars, and tertiaries, rufous brown, mottled with large black spots ; a light grey or whitish eye streak ; wings with the primaries dusky, pale edged, and the secondaries edged with brown, and pale tipped ; tail dusky, each feather with a white spot at the tip of the inner web ; chin, throat, and foreneck white, with some small black spots on the chin ; a narrow brown pectoral band or gorget, beyond which is rufous, bright on the breast, and the latter edged with white, increasing on the lower abdomen ; lower tail-coverts white, with brown streaks.

Bill black ; legs reddish brown. Length about 6 inches ; wing $3\frac{1}{2}$; tail $2\frac{1}{4}$; bill at front $\frac{7}{10}$; tarsus $\frac{7}{8}$.

This species, which is also allied to *alpinus,* has been found throughout the Himalayas, from Sikhim to the far North-West, and is said to be common at Kussowlee in winter

654. Accentor strophiatus, HODGSON.

J. A. S. XII. 959—BLYTH, Cat. 726—HORSF., Cat. 576—GOULD, Birds of Asia, Pt. VII. pl. 7—*Phooching-pho*, Lepch.

THE RUFOUS-BREASTED ACCENTOR.

Descr.—Above reddish brown, streaked with dark brown ; a broad eye streak, the first portion of which is white to the middle of the eye, surmounting a ferruginous streak continued backward to the occiput, and above this again is a black streak, forming the

side of the head ; a semi-circle of white also surrounds the dusky
ear-coverts ; wings dusky, margined with dark ferruginous, and an
albescent spot at the tip of each covert; tail brownish, with dull
rufous outer margins ; throat white, with a few dusky spots, forming
a line descending from each angle of the lower mandible ; breast
deep ferruginous ; abdomen and lower tail-coverts with dusky
brown streaks.

Bill black ; legs reddish brown; irides dark brown. Length
$5\frac{1}{2}$ inches ; wing $2\frac{3}{4}$; tail $2\frac{1}{4}$; bill at front $\frac{3}{8}$; tarsus $\frac{7}{8}$.

This Accentor has been found both in Nepal and Sikhim. It
was the only species I obtained when at Darjeeling, and that in
winter.

655. Accentor Huttoni, MOORE.

A. atrogularis, HUTTON, apud BLYTH, J. A. S. XVIII. 811—
BLYTH, Cat. 727—HORSF., Cat. 577—GOULD, Birds of Asia, pt.
X. pl. 13.

THE BLACK-THROATED ACCENTOR.

Descr.—Above brown, the feathers centered dusky, rufescent on
the back, but greyish on the nape, rump, and upper tail-coverts ;
the crown darker brown ; a broad line above the white superciliary
streak, with the ear-coverts and throat, dusky black, the latter
divided from the ear-coverts by a pale line proceeding from the
base of the lower mandible, and this, with the entire supercilium
and the breast, of an uniform light rufescent sandy hue ; belly
whitish, the flanks streaked with dusky ; wing-coverts tipped
albescent, forming slight cross-bands.

Bill dusky, yellowish towards the gape ; feet pale ; irides
brown. Length 6 inches ; wing $2\frac{7}{8}$; tail $2\frac{1}{2}$; bill at front $\frac{7}{16}$;
tarsus $\frac{3}{4}$.

The Black-throated Accentor has been found in the North-
west Himalayas, near Simla, in the Punjaub Salt range, and
also in Affghanistan. Moore considers it distinct from *atrigularis*
of Brandt.

656. Accentor rubeculoides, HODGSON.

MOORE, P. Z. S. 1854—HORSF., Cat. 578.—GOULD, Birds of
Asia, pt. VII. pl. 6.

THE ROBIN ACCENTOR.

Descr.—Forehead, crown, nape, ear-coverts, and chin brown; infra-orbital feathers tipped with whitish; throat, sides of neck, and shoulder of wings, dingy grey brown, the feathers of the throat blackish at the base; back and rump ferruginous, centered with dusky; wings dusky, margined exteriorly with ferruginous; lesser and greater coverts tipped with white; tail dusky, margined exteriorly with pale ferruginous: breast and forepart of flanks ferruginous, the latter streaked with dusky; belly white, tinged with ferruginous on the flanks posteriorly, vent, and margins of the under tail-coverts, the latter centered dusky.

Bill blackish; feet pale reddish. Length 6 inches; wing 3; tail $2\frac{1}{2}$; bill at front $\frac{4}{10}$; tarsus $\frac{3}{4}$.

This species has hitherto only been sent from Nepal by Mr. Hodgson. It is most nearly allied to *strophiatus.*

Other species recorded, besides the two European species, are *A. rubidus*, Temm., from Japan; *atrigularis*, Brandt (if distinct from *Huttoni*), from North Asia; *A. montanellus*, Pallas, from Eastern Siberia, the type of *Spermoleyus*, Kaup; and *A. Temminckii*, Brandt (*montanellus*, apud Temminck), from Eastern Europe and Siberia. *A. modularis* is the type of Kaup's genus *Tharrhaleus;* and *alpinus* is the type of restricted *Accentor.*

The Australian genus, *Cinclosoma*, comprises several very prettily marked birds, the size of a small thrush, of a bright rufous colour, more or less streaked, with the throat black, or white with black markings; the wing-coverts usually white-spotted, and the tail white-tipped; one species with unstreaked plumage, *C. castanotus*, Gould, having a marked resemblance to *Accentor immaculatus*. *Orthonyx* very closely resembles *Cinclosoma* in its plumage, but has the tail feathers ending in a point or spine.

The remaining families of the *Ampelidæ* are all American. They comprise the *Mniotiltinæ, Piprinæ, Ampelinæ* and *Gymnoderinæ* of Gray. The MNIOTILTINÆ, or Bush-creepers, are the *Sylvicolinæ* of Bonaparte, and are usually placed next the Titmice. They are peculiar to America, where they take the place of the Warblers of the Old Continent. They are very varied in their plumage, some being coloured like the *Phylloscopinæ*, others like *Zosterops;* and

some are mottled with black and white. They have a moderately
long, straight, sharp, and conical bill, lengthened wings, a short tail,
and a moderately long tarsus. They associate in small flocks,
feeding on various insects chiefly ; and nidificate either on the
ground, or on trees and bushes. They have no regular song. On
the whole their habits are much those of the Tits, and they evidently grade into *Acanthiza*, *Zosterops*, and others of the slender-
billed section of the *Leiotrichinæ*, some of which are, indeed, placed
by Gray in this sub-family, in defiance of geographical distribution.

The PIPRINÆ or Manakins are mostly small birds, with a short,
thick, well-curved bill, with the nares concealed, a short tail, and
the tarsi rather long, with the outer toe much joined to the middle
one. They are said to asssociate in flocks, feed both on insects
and on fruits, are very active in their movements ; and many
are adorned with rich colours. They are somewhat akin to the
Pardaloti. The beautiful Cock of the Rock, *Rupicola* of South
America, belongs to this sub-family, and is said to breed in holes
in rocks or caverns, and to lay white eggs. This last trait approximates it to some of the *Eurylaimi* ; and the pretty *Calyptomena
viridis* of Malacca and Java, which has been found lately in
Tenasserim, is usually placed next the South American genus.
(*vide* vol. I, p. 239.) If this last is not a type of the *Eurylaimidæ*,
it perhaps ought to be placed near *Cochoa*. (*vide* p. 242).

The AMPELINÆ, Gray, (*Cotinginæ*, Bonap.) are peculiar to
America, and chiefly to the more tropical parts of that Continent.
They are very varied in form and colour, but mostly have a
moderately short, rather broad bill, with a wide gape devoid of
bristles, and often notched at the tip ; nostrils usually exposed ;
long and pointed wings ; a short tail and short tarsus, with feet
fitted for perching. They live much on fruit, and some appear not
a little to resemble the eastern Bulbuls, whilst others rival or excel
in brilliancy of plumage our Orioles and Blue-birds (*Irena*): such
are the Cotinga and Pompadour chatterers, and their allies, clothed
in glistening blue and purple, a few of which are not unlike some
of the *Eurylaimi*.

GYMNODERINÆ of Gray, comprise some very remarkable birds of
rather large size, some having the face or neck bare, whilst one of

them, the celebrated Umbrella bird. *Cephalopterus ornatus*, has the most gorgeous crest of any known bird, and of which Wallace has given a good account from life. A second species has been lately made known to science. Another remarkable type is the *Arapunga*, or Bell-bird of Guiana, of a pure white colour, and having a clear bell-like note, capable of being heard at a great distance.

These Fruit-crows, as they are sometimes called, are quite arboreal, and feed chiefly on fruit, occasionally, it is said, on insects. They appear to have distant affinities for some of the Crows and Starlings.

Perhaps the *Vireoninæ* should enter this family rather than the Fly-catchers, with which they are usually associated.

Tribe CONIROSTRES.

Bill usually entire at the tip, thick, more or less conic, with the lower mandible deeper than in most of the preceding tribe; wings more generally lengthened; tail usually moderate or short, even or emarginate, rounded in a few; feet fitted for walking on the ground, as well as for perching.

The Conirostral birds, as a general rule, can be readily distinguished from the birds of the last tribe by their comparatively thick bill, with the lower mandible of more equal proportions with the upper (*i. e.* conic), than in most of the Dentirostres, rarely notched at the tip, or bent down over the lower mandible. They are mostly ground-feeders, and while some may be said to be omnivorous, others feed almost exclusively on grain. Their nidification is varied, most building in trees, a few on rocks or buildings, some in holes in banks, or of trees; one family on the ground. The majority of birds composing this tribe are of plain, though, in some cases, pleasing plumage, one family alone being adorned with rich and gaudy colours. They are usually of great intelligence; many are fine songsters, and our most familiar birds belong to this tribe. Their anatomy is similar to that of the Dentirostres; but the stomach or gizzard of many is thick and more muscular, and many of this tribe are in the habit of constantly swallowing small pieces of stone or gravel to assist them in triturating the hard grains on which they feed.

The Conirostres are divided into the following families :   1st,
Corvidæ, comprising Crows and Magpies ; 2nd, *Sturnidæ*, the
Mynas and Starlings ; 3rd, *Fringillidæ*, the most numerous of all,
comprising Sparrows, Weaver-birds, Amaduvads, Buntings, and
Rose Linnets ; 4th, *Tanagridæ*, or the Tanagers ; and lastly the
Alaudidæ or Larks.   All of these are represented in India except
the Tanagers, which are confined to America.

Fam. CORVIDÆ.

Bill strong, more or less compressed, usually entire, rarely
notched at the tip ; nostrils thickly clad with stiff incumbent
bristles ; tarsus stout ; feet strong, and claws well curved : of large
size mostly.

This family comprises the Crows, Choughs, Magpies, and Jays.
They are of large size compared with others of this tribe, or the
Dentirostral perchers.   They are the most omnivorous of all birds,
and, indeed, with the Starlings and some other birds, not now
referred to this tribe, they constitute Temminck's order,
Omnivora.   They vary a good deal in the length and strength
of their bill, length of wing and tail, and also of tarsus.
Many feed habitually on the ground, others on trees, and, as
Temminck's name signifies, they eat all kinds of food from
carrion to grain.

They are divided into the following sub-families : *Corvinæ*,
Garrulinæ, *Dendrocittinæ*, *Fregilinæ*, and *Streperinæ* ; the last
only occurring in Australia and Oceanica.

Sub-fam. CORVINÆ,   Crows and Magpies.

Bill very stout, long, straight, with the ridge more or less
curved ; wings long, somewhat pointed ; tail variable ; tarsus stout,
strongly scutate ; claws well curved.

The Crows are birds of large size and robust form, usually
black, or pied with grey or white, and are too well known to require
any further details.   They are undoubtedly the most highly
organized and intelligent of birds, they possess the most varied
powers, and can live on all kinds of food.   They fly well, walk
with ease, climb adroitly ; and may be seen eating carrion with the
Vultures ; catching winged Termites with Fly-catchers and Bee-

eaters; fishing with Gulls and Terns at the wake of a ship; plucking fruit with green Pigeons and Cuckoos; or eating grain with Sparrows and Weaver birds. They are familiar and bold, if undisturbed, but excessively wary if danger approach them; they are domesticated readily, have great powers of imitation, and, in their habit of pilfering and hoarding up articles of different kinds, they exhibit great cunning and intelligence. Lastly, the most typical species occur in almost all climates habitable by man, and are, therefore, found all over the world, except in that exceptional country, Australia.

Gen. CORVUS, Linnæus (in part).

Char.— Bill long, very strong and thick, straight; the culmen more or less elevated; nares protected by very long and rigid bristles; wings long and pointed, 1st quill short; 2nd a little shorter than the 3rd and 4th, and the 5th usually sub-equal to them; tail moderate, even, or somewhat rounded; tarsus very stout, of moderate length, with strong scutæ; feet moderate; lateral toes about equal; claws sharp and strongly curved.

The Crows have of late been sub-divided into several sub-genera, but, with Horsfield, I shall only separate the Jackdaws generically. The crows may be sub-divided into Ravens, Carrion Crows, Rooks, and Crows.

1st.—Ravens, restricted *Corvus*, apud Gray; *Corax*, apud Bonaparte.

They are of large size, have very stout beaks, are solitary in their habits, and very predacious and carnivorous.

657. Corvus corax, LINNÆUS.

GOULD, Birds of Europe, pl. 223—BLYTH, Cat. 447—HORSF., Cat. 829.—*Dom-kak*, and *Doda*, H. in the N. W.

THE EUROPEAN RAVEN.

Descr.—Wholly glossy black; the feathers of the chin and throat lanceolate; tail rounded; the ridge of the upper mandible much arched towards the tip; the wings reach to about 3 inches from the end of the tail.

Bill and legs black; irides dark brown. Length 25 to 26 inches; wing $16\frac{1}{2}$; tail $9\frac{1}{2}$; bill at front 3; height of bill $1\frac{3}{16}$, tarsus $2\frac{1}{2}$.

The Raven of Europe is stated to occur in the Punjab, about Ferozepore, on this side of the Indus, and also in Upper Sindh, during the cold weather only, migrating to Affghanistan and the neighbouring hills to breed, which it is said to do in the N. W. Himalayas, and in the neighbourhood of Cashmere. Dr. Stewart states that at Wuzeerabad (in the Punjab) it is as common and as impudent as *Corvus splendens;* and that it appears to replace *C. culminatus* entirely in the Punjab. Hutton, on the contrary, says that he never saw it in India, but that it is common in Affghanistan. Adams confirms Dr. Stewart's statement, and says that it "is an inhabitant of the Northern countries of India, commencing at Upper Sindh; it is found all over the Punjab, at every season of the year, where they frequent camps and cantonments with Govind Kites, and Egyptian Vultures." Many interesting accounts of the docility and intelligence of Ravens are to be found in all popular treatises on Ornithology, and it is considered to imitate the human voice as perfectly as any known bird.

658. Corvus tibetanus, Hodgson.

Ann. Nat. Hist. n. s. III. p. 203—Horsf., Cat. 830—C. bactrianus, Bonap.

The Tibet Raven.

Descr.—Nearly allied to *C. corax,* but somewhat larger in size, and the bill appears to be somewhat higher at the base, and stronger than in the bird of Europe; wings and tail also longer. Length fully 26 inches; wing 19; tail $11\frac{1}{2}$; bill at front 3; height $1\frac{5}{16}$. The wings reach to within 2 inches or so of the end of the tail.

Horsfield keeps this species apart from the Raven of Europe, and I have followed him in so doing, but I am not fully convinced of their being quite distinct, and a larger series of specimens from different regions should be examined more critically. If it really be distinct, it will probably be found to inhabit all Eastern and Central Asia, with China; in fact, to replace the European species in the east of the Old Continent. Bonaparte considered it a good species, but Adams states that he considers those which he obtained and named *corax*, to be identical with Hodgson's *tibetanus*. It has been found in Ladakh, Kumaon, and other sites on the more eastern part of the Himalayas. I never saw it in Sikhim.

Other Ravens are found in various part of the World.

2nd.—Carrion crows, *Corone*, Kaup and Gray.

659. Corvus corone, Linnæus.

Gould, Birds of Europe, pl. 221—Horsf., Cat. 831—Adams, List of Birds of Cashmere, No. 13.

The European Carrion Crow.

Descr.—Plumage black, highly glossed ; feathers of the throat short, ovate, lanceolate, compact ; tail very nearly square ; the bill, compared with that of *culminatus*, more rounded on the culmen, more gradually curved, and altogether weaker, with the nareal bristles perhaps longer.

Bill and legs black. Length 19½ inches; wing 13; tail 7; bill at front 2⅛; tarsus 2¼.

On the authority of Dr. Adams, I insert the Corby or Carrion Crow of Britain among the birds of India, for it is not in Blyth's Catalogue, nor in that of Horsfield, as from India; but the latter naturalist has it from Affghanistan, where it was obtained by Griffith. Adams says that it is very common in Cashmere.

660. Corvus culminatus, Sykes.

Cat. 117—Blyth, Cat. 448—Horsf., Cat. 833—C. macror-hynchos, apud Jerdon, Cat. 158—C. corone, var. Franklin—C. corax, apud Royle—C. enca, apud Sundevall—C. orientalis, Eversman—Gray and Hardwicke, Ill. Ind. Zool. 2, pl. 36, f. 2. —*Dhar* or *Dhal kowa*, H., on the North, *Dheri-kowa* H. in the South—*Karrial* of some Falconers—*Dad-kag*, Beng.—*Kaki*, Tel. —*Kaka*, Tam.—*Ulak-pho*, Lepch.—*Ulak*, Bhot.—*Raven* of some Europeans in India.

The Indian Corby.

Descr.—Above glossy black, dull black beneath; tail slightly rounded; wings reach nearly to the end of the tail; bill straight at the base and high, culmen raised, curving strongly towards the tip.

Bill and legs black; irides dark brown. Length 21 inches; wing $13\frac{1}{2}$; tail $7\frac{3}{4}$; bill at front $2\frac{4}{10}$; tarsus $2\frac{1}{2}$.

The common Carrion Crow of India is found throughout the whole country, from the extreme south and Ceylon, to the Himalayas as far west as Cashmere; and, eastward, it occurs in Assam, Burmah, and the Malayan Peninsula. Adams states that it is not found in the Punjab. Though not nearly so numerous as *C. splendens*, this Crow is yet very abundant and generally spread, less affecting the neighbourhood of man, and often found in the most wild and unfrequented spots, in dense forests or bleak mountains. In the south of India, as at Madras, the Neilgherries, and elsewhere, it is almost as familiar and impudent as the common Crow, but, towards the north, it is perhaps less seen about towns and villages. It is eminently a Carrion Crow, and Mr. Blyth remarks that it " especially frequents the vicinity of the great rivers." It is often the first to discover the carcass of any dead animal. Like the rest of its tribe, however, it will partake of any kind of food, and Sundevall states that he found nothing but larvæ and butterflies in those that he examined. Its voice is the usual harsh *caw*, but hoarser and shorter than that of the European Crow, according to Sundevall. It is very destructive, in some places, to young chickens, pigeons, &c., and, I am informed, will occasionally destroy a young kid. It also pilfers the eggs and nestlings of many birds, on which account, perhaps, the King Crow *(Dicrurus macrocercus)* pursues it more relentlessly than it does the common Crow.

It breeds, according to the locality, from April to June, or later, generally on some isolated tree, making the usual nest of sticks, which is, sometimes, in colder countries. lined with hair. (*Vide* Hutton, Oology of India, J. A. S. XVII. pt. 2, p 9). The eggs are three or four, dull green, thickly spotted with dusky brown. Occasionally the Koel (*Eudynamys orientalis*) drops an egg in the nest of this Crow, in place of that of the common Crow (*vide* vol. I. p. 343). I have often heard it called the Raven by Europeans in Bengal.' Occasionally the Luggur is flown at it, but in general it makes such a stout resistance, and shows such fight, that Falconers do not like slipping their Hawks at it.

661. Corvus intermedius, ADAMS.

P. Z. S. 1859, p. 171, No. 14, Birds of Cashmere.

THE BLACK HILL-CROW.

Descr.—' Uniform metallic black ; tail wedge-shaped ; tertials mucronate at their tips, as are the tail-feathers also. Intermediate between the Carrion Crow (*corone*) and the Jackdaw, smaller than *corone*, not larger than the Indian Jackdaw (*C. splendens*). It is gregarious, feeds on offal and carrion ; its flight is strong and rapid, and it is often seen tormenting kites and other large birds. It is familiar in its habits, and is generally seen feeding in villages or around the hill stations ; is abundant on the mountains round the Valley of Cashmere, and, eastward, on the ranges near the stations of Dugshai and Simla, also on the lesser Himalayan ranges.' This is evidently the black Hill-Crow of Theobald, J. A. S. vol. XXIII., p. 601.

3rd Crows—restricted *Corvus.*

662. Corvus tenuirostris, MOORE.

HORSF., Cat. 840.

THE SLENDER-BILLED CROW.

Descr.—' Above glossy purple black, palest on the head, neck, back, and body beneath, and there having an ashy cast ; forehead jet black, contrasting with the ashy cast of the plumage of the crown.

Length 18 inches ; wing $12\frac{1}{2}$; tail 7 ; bill at front $2\frac{1}{2}$; its height at the base $\frac{9}{10}$; tarsus $2\frac{1}{4}$.

From Bombay, from Major Kittoe's collection.'

We have no further information where this Crow was obtained. I at one time thought that it might have been one of the dark races of *C. splendens*, which it evidently much resembles in the contrasting

hue of the forehead and the crown, &c., but its bill and tarsus
are longer, the former apparently more slender, and it appears to
be altogether a larger bird. Is it possible that it is the last-mentioned Hill-crow, *C. intermedius*?

Corvus sinensis, Gould, is nearly related to *C. macrorhynchos*;
and *C. pectoralis*, Gould, also from China, is recorded in Horsfield's
Catalogue. *C. enca*, Horsfield, from Java, is a small, rather slender-
billed Crow. Adams states that he thinks he has observed *C.
cornix*, or the Hooded Crow, in Ladakh, but he did not obtain
specimens. It has, however, been procured in Affghanistan.

663. **Corvus splendens**, VIEILLOT.

TEMM., Pl. Col. 425—SYKES, Cat. 118—JERDON, Cat. 157—
BLYTH, Cat. 451—HORSF., Cat 842—C. monedula indica, BUCH.
HAMILTON, MSS.—C. impudicus, HODGSON—C. dauricus, apud
PEARSON—*Kowa, Pati-kowa* and *Desi-kowa*, H. in various districts.
Kag or *Kak*, Beng.—*Manchi kaki*, Tel.—*Nalla kaka*, Tam.

THE COMMON INDIAN CROW.

Descr.—Forehead, sinciput, and lores, glossy black; occiput,
nape, hind neck, and sides of neck, purplish ashy; back, wings, and
tail, black, with rich purple and steel-blue reflections; chin, throat,
and sides of the neck, in part, black, with steel reflections; breast
ashy, tinged dark; middle of abdomen dull black, slightly tinged
with steel blue.

Length varies from 15 to above 18 inches; of one of the latter
dimensions the wing $11\frac{1}{4}$; tail 7; bill at front $2\frac{1}{8}$; tarsus $1\frac{7}{8}$.
Of one 15 inches long, the wing was 10; tail $6\frac{1}{4}$. The wings
reach to less than 2 inches from the end of the tail. Bill and
legs black; irides deep brown.

The common Crow of India is found from the foot of the
Himalayas to Ceylon, and eastwards in Assam and part of Arracan.
Adams states that it occurs in the Valley of Cashmere, and it
is found in Nepal, but it does not extend into the interior of the
hills, and is at present quite unknown in Sikhim. It is one of
the best known and familiar birds in India, being found in vast
numbers in every city, town, village, and cantonment or camp;
and the scientific traveller in India often regrets that such an

inappropriate specific name should have been applied to this species, for it tends to bring into ridicule, among the unscientific, the system of nomenclature.

This Crow, though eminently social, is not strictly gregarious, but it roosts in company in vast numbers, and there are certain spots near all large towns or stations, where they nightly congregate for this purpose, coming from a distance varying from three to ten miles of radius. Great is the clamour in selecting a spot, and numerous are the squabbles, and prolonged to a late hour, before all are settled for the night; and this noise is increased by the swarms of Parrakeets, Mynas, and other birds, that all have their night's lodgings together.

Very early in the morning, the Crows are on the alert, occasionally before daylight, but generally shortly afterwards; and, after a considerable amount of cackling and flying hither and thither, probably to compare notes of yesterday's success in foraging, perhaps to propose an interchange of locality for the day, they disperse in parties, varying from two or three to twenty, thirty, or more; those that have a distance to go, starting early, and those whose hunting grounds are at hand, taking it more leisurely, chatting with their neighbours, or making themselves smart by a little extra pruning of their feathers.

The food of this Crow is greatly varied; but, as a rule, it may be said that it lives on the crumbs that fall from the food of man. Many natives eat habitually out of doors, and the remnants of boiled rice or other grain are thrown away, whilst, in those that feed within doors, the fragments are pitched out at certain stated intervals, well known to the Crows of the vicinity, who proceed from house to house, warned by some watchful member of their community when the feast is at hand. So well known is the process of cooking, that a small fire, or rather its attendant smoke, even in some unusual spot, far away from their daily haunt, will at once attract one or two hungry Crows, who, if the symptoms of food are favorable, remain for the expected leavings. In the intervals between the meals of mankind, some betake themselves early in the morning to some plain that has perhaps been flooded, to pick up a crab, a frog, a fish, or insect. Others hunt for grubs in

ploughed lands, or in pastures, along with cattle, and others may
be seen ridding cattle of the ticks or other insects that infest them ;
some betake themselves to the side of a river or tank ; a few, in
the vicinity of large rivers or creeks, follow vessels, and hunt with
the gulls and terns ; and not a few, about Calcutta and other large
cities, find a plentiful repast on the corpse of some dead Hindoo,
or on that of a dead bullock. A banian tree, a peepul, or other
tree with ripe fruit, will always be visited by many Crows ; and,
if a flight of winged termites takes place, morning or evening,
there are the Crows to be found in abundance, and adroitly catching
them in company with Bee-eaters, Kites, King-crows, and, mayhap,
Bats. In the hot weather the Crows take a long siesta, and evidently
feel the mid-day heat much, as they may be seen seated with open
beaks, gasping for a mouthful of cool air. When their daily
avocations are over, they retire, as they issued forth, in various sized
parties, picking up stragglers by the way from small hamlets or
single huts.

The Crow breeds from April to July, according to the locality,
and, occasionally, two or three build in the same tree, though, in
general, there is not more than one. Now and then they select a
corner of a house or some convenient nook, but generally build in
trees, making a moderate fabric of sticks, occasionally thinly lined
with some softer materials. An instance is recorded by Mr.
Blyth, where a pair of Crows, in Calcutta, had built their nest of
the wires taken off from soda-water bottles, which must have been
purloined from some native slop-seller. The eggs are usually four
in number, and are greenish blue, spotted and blotched in various
degrees with brown. They are figured in Jardine's Contrib. to
Ornithology. As related under the head of the Coel, vol. I.
p. 343, this Crow's nest is almost exclusively selected by that
Cuckoo, to deposit her eggs in. In defence of her young the
Crow is very bold, and I have been struck on the head by
one for carrying off a young bird that had fallen from the
nest. The young are fed by their parents for long after they quit
their nest.

The flight of this Crow is easy and moderately quick, but, when
pursued by a Brahminy Kite or a Luggur, it is capable of con-

siderable speed, and exhibits wonderful activity and cleverness in dodging its pursuer. The cunning, familiarity, and intelligence of these birds is so great, that pages could be filled with anecdotes about them, but my space forbids me to prolong this account. Their great abundance and familiarity is one of the first objects that strike the attention of the stranger on landing in India, and they often enter rooms through open windows, and carry off food, or any object that attracts them. With a very little encouragement they may be induced to enter a room in numbers, and take food almost from the hand. " About large towns," says Mr. Blyth, " they walk and hop like domestic birds, just stepping aside out of the way of the passers-by, and regardless of the ordinary throng ; but they still retain all the craft and wariness of their tribe, and are ever vigilant, making off on the least suspicious movement, or even on the fixed glance of a stranger. Their noise is incessant, and if any thing, as the sight of a dead crow, excites them, is most uproarious and annoying. Eager, bustling, and busy, their flight is always singularly hurried, as if time were a matter of some consequence to them ; and in short every trait of the Crow tribe is prominently developed in this species. The report of a gun excites a grand commotion among the community of crows ; they circle and cross rapidly to and fro overhead, for the most part out of range, cawing lustily, and dodging when the gun is pointed at them, whilst others sit observantly on the neigbouring house-tops, &c., all launching on the wing on the next discharge with clamourous outcry, and then by degrees returning to their place of observation."

The Crow appears to possess the element of fun, for it may often be seen, evidently in sport, to make a swoop at one of its own kind, or some other bird, and then fly off, when it has alarmed the bird, with loud caws of success at the joke. Many anecdotes of the cunning of this Crow are to be found in the notes of Sykes, Tickell, Burgess, Layard, and Philipps.

A melanoid variety or race occurs throughout Burmah, southwards from Akyab, which Blyth is inclined to consider distinct. *Vide* J. A. S., 1863, p. 76.

Rooks. *Frugilegus*, Lesson and Gray.

The Rooks have the bill straighter, more slender and pointed than the Carrion-crows, and less bent at the tip; the face of the adult is denuded of feathers up to the eyes. They are, perhaps, worthy of generic separation.

664. Corvus frugilegus, LINNÆUS.

GOULD, Birds of Europe, pl. 224—BLYTH, Cat. 453—HORSF., Cat. 838.

THE ROOK.

Descr.—Black, finely glossed with purple throughout.

Length 19½ to 20 inches; wing 13; tail 7¼; bill at front 2¼; tarsus $1\frac{8}{10}$; wings reach to within 1 inch or so of the end of the tail.

This Rook is found in the Punjab in the cold weather, and also in Cashmere. Dr. Saunders of the Bengal Army first informed me of this, and it has been subsequently confirmed by several observers. It is also a winter visitant to Affghanistan. As in England, it feeds chiefly on ploughed lands.

A nearly allied Rook is found in China and Japan, *C. pastinator*. Gould.

Gen. COLÆUS, Kaup.

Syn. *Lycos*, Boie—*Monedula*, Brehm.

Char.—Bill shorter than in *Corvus;* colours mixed black and grey. Associate in large flocks, and nidificate on rocks or high buildings.

The Jackdaws are separated generically from *Corvus* on account of their much shorter bill, smaller size, and other characters.

665. Colæus monedula, LINNÆUS.

Corvus, apud LINNÆUS—GOULD, Birds of Europe, pl. 223 —BLYTH, Cat. 454—HORSF., Cat. 843—ADAMS, Birds of Cashmere, No. 15.

THE COMMON JACKDAW.

Descr.—Forehead and top of head black, glossed with purple; hind head, ear-coverts, back, and sides of the neck, silvery grey;

wings and tail black, moderately glossed; lower parts dull black, not so deep as the upper parts, and only slightly glossed.

Length about 15 inches: wing $1\frac{3}{4}$; tail $5\frac{1}{2}$; bill at front $1\frac{1}{4}$; tarsus $1\frac{3}{4}$. The wings reach to within an inch or so of the end of the tail.

The Jackdaw is tolerably abundant in Cashmere and in the Punjab, in the latter country in the cold weather only. It builds in Cashmere in old ruined palaces, holes in rocks, beneath roofs of houses, and also in tall trees, laying four to six eggs, pale bluish green, dotted and spotted with brownish black. It has not been noticed in any other part of India, but inhabits all Europe and Western Asia.

A second species of true Jackdaw, *C. dauricus*, Pallas, is found in China and Central Asia.

Many species of Crows are found in all parts of the world, except in Australia; some from Africa, very remarkable for their large size and strong vulturine bills, are rightly separated as *Corvultur*. The habits of some of the African Hornbills are described as being not unlike those of Carrion-crows (*vide* vol. I. p. 241), and the Darwinian might venture to theorize that the high-ridged bill of the Crows above alluded to was inherited by them in right of descent from these African Hornbills.

The next birds are the Nut-crackers, comprising only three known species, found in the temperate parts of the Old Continent, and the Himalayas: one bird, differing slightly in type, but by some referred to this division, *Corvus columbianus*, Wilson (now *Picicorvus*, Bonaparte), occurs in North America.

Gen. NUCIFRAGA, Brisson.

Syn. *Caryocatactes*, Cuv.

Char.—Bill straight, subulate, longish; the tip blunt, not hooked, dilated at the base, and dividing the frontal feathers; short incumbent bristles at the base of bill, concealing the nostrils; wings with 4th and 5th quills sub-equal and longest; tail moderate, or rather long, slightly rounded; tarsus and toes moderate, lateral toes nearly equal, hind toe longish; claws slightly curved.

The Nut-crackers are birds of generally brown color, and spotted plumage, and feed chiefly on seeds and nuts, but also on insects

and small birds. They breed in holes in trees, which they excavate,
or enlarge, with their powerful Woodpecker-like bills, and, like that
tribe, they are said to climb well, and to peel the bark off trees, to
get at insects. They are a sort of link between the Crows and
the Starlings.

666. Nucifraga hemispila, Vigors.

P. Z. S., 1830— Gould, Cent. Him. Birds, pl. 36—Blyth,
Cat. 455—Horsf., Cat. 845—*Lho-kariyo-pho*, Lepch.

The Himalayan Nut-cracker.

Descr.—Light umber brown ; the top of the head, wings, and
tail blackish, all the feathers of the tail, except the two centre
ones, broadly tipped with white ; under tail-coverts pure white ;
ear-coverts, chin (and forehead in some), back, and sides of
neck, interscapulars, breast, and upper part of the abdomen, spotted with white.

Length 15 inches ; wing 9 ; tail $6\frac{1}{2}$; tarsus $1\frac{1}{2}$; bill at front $1\frac{3}{8}$
to $1\frac{3}{4}$; height $\frac{9}{16}$.

The bill is shorter and stouter at the base than in the European
Nut-cracker, and approaching that of the Jays. The wings reach
to within $1\frac{1}{2}$ inch or so of the end of the tail.

The Himalayan Nut-cracker is found throughout the Himalayas,
chiefly frequenting the pine forests. In Sikhim it is rare, and
I only got one specimen, on Mount Tonglo, 10,000 feet high. It is
said to be more abundant in the interior, where pine forests are
more prevalent, and occur at lower levels than in British Sikhim.
Dr. Adams says that it has a loud discordant cry, like that of
the Magpie ; that it is generally seen at high elevations, and lives
among the topmost branches of the pine trees.

667. Nucifraga multimaculata, Gould.

Gould, Birds of Asia, pl.

The Larger Spotted Nut-cracker.

Descr.—General colour chocolate-brown ; wings and tail glossy
black, the whole body, except the head, including the wing-
coverts, with long and large blotches of white ; primaries with

a minute white speck at their tip; secondaries and tertials largely spotted at the tip; tail broadly tipped white, except the two central tail feathers; under tail-coverts pure white.

Bill horny brown; legs black. Length nearly 15 inches: wing $8\frac{1}{4}$; tail $6\frac{1}{2}$; tarsus $1\frac{1}{2}$; bill at front $1\frac{3}{4}$; height $\frac{1}{2}$. In this species the bill is much more slender than in the last, and the wings reach to within 2 inches of the end of the tail, which is much rounded.

This fine species of Nutcracker has only been found on the hills of the North-western Himalayas, and Cashmere.

The next group is that of the true Magpies, which differ much in their long and highly graduated tail, and pied plumage.

Gen. PICA, Brisson.

Syn.—*Cleptes*, Gambel and Gray.

Char.—Bill much as in *Corvus*, but more slender; wings long; 1st quill spurious; 3rd nearly equal to 4th and 5th, which are longest; tail long, graduated; legs and feet strong. Of black and white plumage.

The Magpies are smaller birds than the Crows, and of slighter build. They are very omnivorous, cunning, and wary; and they build large domed nests of sticks with the entrance at one side, and lined with mud. They are chiefly inhabitants of the temperate and Northern portions of both Continents. One species inhabits the confines of the Himalayas, just coming within our limits.

668. **Pica bottanensis**, DELESSERT.

Rev. Zool. 1840—BLYTH, Cat. 459—HORSF., Cat. 827—P. megaloptera, BLYTH, J. A. S., XI. 193—P. tibetana, HODGS.

THE HIMALAYAN MAGPIE.

Descr.—Glossy black, with the scapulars, abdomen, and inner webs of the primaries (except at the tip) pure white.

Length 18 to 20 inches; wing $9\frac{1}{4}$ to 10; tail $10\frac{3}{4}$; bill at front $1\frac{5}{8}$; tarsus $2\frac{1}{8}$.

This Magpie has been found in Bootan, and in various parts of the extreme limit of the Indian region bordering on Tibet.

The wing is longer, the tail not so long as in the European Magpie, and the grey band across the rump of the latter is absent; the bill too is also slightly longer.

Adams states that this Magpie inhabits the wildest parts of Ladakh, and, says he, "it is strange that a bird whose near ally is so fond of fertile localities in Europe, should prefer the wastes of little Tibet to the cultivated and wooded mountains of Cashmere, but such is the case; and the Magpie is the same crafty and familiar bird among his Tartar friends, as with Englishmen."

Pica bactriana, Bonap., from Affghanistan, is said to be distinct from the Indian bird, more like the European Magpie, and chiefly differing in its longer bill; but Adams believes it to be identical with the present species. *Pica sericea*, Gould, (*media*, Blyth,) from China, is another closely allied Asiatic species. This bird, says Swinhoe, roosts in company, sallies out for food, and returns at night cackling, curveting, and with sundry antics. The Magpie of Europe, as is well known, is celebrated for its ability to imitate the human voice, and for its thieving propensities. Besides the species above referred to, there is one from Africa, and one or two from North America.   •

The next two families differ from the true *Corvinæ* by their more rounded wings, and colours; comprising various shades of brown, fawn, blue, and green, with black and white in some. They are all more arboreal than the last.

Sub-fam. GARRULINÆ, Jays.

Bill short and conic in some, longer and less conic in others; the tip often bent down and emarginate; nares usually tufted; wings moderate or short, rounded; 5th quill usually longest; tail moderate or very long and graduated; tarsus moderate; feet arboreal, toes rather long.

The Jays comprise several distinct types, the European Jay being the typical one; and others, approaching the Magpie in form and length of tail, are found in Asia and America. They are noisy birds, wander about a good deal, and feed on various kind of insects and fruit, occasionally robbing other birds' nests of their eggs or young.

Gen. GARRULUS, Brisson.

Char.—Bill rather short, thick, compressed, conic, slightly notched and bent at the tip ; lower mandible, with the gonys, equally curved towards the tip ; commissure straight ; nostrils oval, basal, covered with incumbent plumes and bristles ; wings moderate, rounded, 5th and 6th quills sub-equal, 5th usually longest, 7th equal to the 4th ; tail moderate, slightly rounded, or nearly even ; legs moderate ; lateral toes slightly unequal.

The Jays are moderate-sized birds, of pretty plumage, a well marked and highly coloured speculum or wing-spot, being found on most. They are peculiar to the Old World, being chiefly found in the more temperate climates, and, in India, are confined to the Himalayas. They are more frugivorous than most of the *Corviæ*, but they will also eat insects, worms, eggs, and even small birds. They have a varied voice, and great powers of imitation. Their nests are made of sticks lined with roots, and the eggs are greenish or grey, more or less spotted.

669. **Garrulus bispecularis**, VIGORS.

P. Z. S. 1830—GOULD, Cent. Him. Birds, pl. 38—HORSF., Cat. 863—G. ornatus, GRAY, HARDW., Ill. Ind. Zool. 1, pl. 23, f. 2—BLYTH, Cat. 476—*Lho-karrio-pho*, Lepch.

THE HIMALAYAN JAY.

Descr.—General colour light fawn brown or bay ; a black stripe from the gape below the eye and ear-coverts ; upper tail-coverts white ; greater wing-coverts and quills black, the primaries edged externally with whitish on their outer web, gradually diminishing in extent ; two pale sky-blue spots with black bars on the wing, formed respectively by the winglet, and the greater part of the outer web of the secondaries ; tail black ; beneath paler fawn ; vent and under tail-coverts white.

Bill dusky horny ; legs dull yellowish ; irides red brown. Length 12 to 13 inches ; wing 6¼ ; tail nearly 6 ; tarsus 1½ nearly ; bill at front 1 to 1⅛. The wings do not reach to end of tail by 3 inches or nearly so, and the tail is barely rounded.

The Himalayan Jay is found throughout the Himalayas, common towards the North-west, rare in the South-east. I only got one

specimen at Darjeeling, and the natives were not well acquainted
with it. It is probably more common in the interior of Sikhim,
where pine forests abound. Adams states that it is common in the
lower ranges of the Himalayas, but not in Cashmere ; and that its
cry is loud and harsh.

670. Garrulus lanceolatus, VIGORS.

P. Z. S. 1830.—GOULD., Cent. Him. Birds, pl. 39, 40--HORSF.,
Cat. 864--G. gularis, GRAY, HARDW., Ill. Ind. Zool. 1, pl. 10.
--BLYTH, Cat. 477--G. Vigorsii, GRAY, Ill. Ind. Orn. pl. 9 (the
young bird)--*Ban-sarrah* of Hillmen at Simla.

THE BLACK-THROATED JAY.

Descr.--Whole head, with crest, face, and ears, black ; neck
behind, and back, pale vinous bay ; wings black, the quills with
a large and broad blue band, black-barred, on the outer web,
the outer edges light, and tipped white ; the coverts of the primaries white, the feathers black at their base, and the two outer
ones blue-banded on the outer web ; the tertiaries the same as
the back, with a broad black terminal band, tipped white ; tail blue,
narrowly barred with black, and with a terminal white band ;
chin, throat, and upper part of the breast, black, ending in iron
grey, the feathers lanceolate, and centred or shafted pure white ;
belly the same colour as the back, but more reddish.

The young bird has a vinous tinge, and the white shafts of the
throat are not developed. The wings reach to about 4 inches from
the end of the tail, which is much rounded or graduated.

Length 13 inches ; wing 6 ; tail 6½ ; tarsus 1¼ to $1\frac{5}{10}$; bill
at front ⅞.

This handsome Jay is found only in the N. W. Himalayas,
extending to Nepal. It is not known in Sikhim. Hutton says that
it is one of the commonest birds of the hills about Simla, usually
appearing in small parties of five or six. It breeds in May and
June. The nest is made of twigs, roots, and fibres, loosely put
together. The eggs, three or four in number, are greenish stone
grey, freckled, chiefly at the larger end with dusky, and a few
black hair-like streaks not always present.

Other true Jays, besides *G. glandarius* of Britain, are *G. japonicus*, Schlegel, from Japan; *G. melanocephalus*, Bonelli; *G. krynicki G. Brandti*, and *G. Lidthi*, apud Bonap., all from Western Asia, the first occasionally occurring in Eastern Europe; and *G. cervicalis*, Bonaparte, from North Africa.

A vast number of Jays are found in America, some crested, others not, and many of very beautiful blue plumage. *Cyanopica*, Bonap., has been instituted for some blue jays, one of which *C. Cookii*, is not rare in Spain; and two others are from Central and North-eastern Asia. *Perisoreus* of Bonaparte contains the curious *Lanius infaustus* of Linnæus, from the North of Europe and Asia, whose habits appear to be much those of some of the Babbling Thrushes; and another species from North America.

The next genus is peculiar to the hilly regions of India and China, and the species are remarkable for their beautiful blue plumage, and very long, graduated tails. They were formerly classed with some American Jays under *Psilorhinus*, but have lately been justly separated.

Gen. UROCISSA, Cabanis.

Syn. Calocitta, Bon.—*Psilorhinus* Rüpp.

Char.—Bill stout, broad at the base, moderate or rather long, straightish, culmen gently curved and hooked, obsoletely toothed at the tip; gonys nearly straight; rictus with a few weak bristles; nostrils basal, lateral, open, but impended by a few soft lengthened bristles; wings rounded, 4th and 5th quills sub-equal and longest, 6th about equal to the fourth; tail very long, graduated, with the two central feathers much elongated; tarsus moderate; lateral toes unequal, claws strong.

These are beautiful birds of large size, with the bill more slender and longer than in the true Jays, either bright red or yellow; usually solitary, of wandering habits, noisy, and bear confinement well. Three species only are known.

671. Urocissa sinensis, LINNÆUS.

Cuculus, apud LINNÆUS—Pl. Enl. 622—HORSF., Cat. 860—Psilorhinus occipitalis, BLYTH, Cat. 471—Pica erythrorhyncha, GMELIN—GOULD, Cent. Him. Birds, pl. 41—Psil. albicapillus,

BLYTH (the young bird)—*Nil-khaut*, at Mussooree—*Dig-dall*, of the Hillmen at Simla.

THE RED-BILLED BLUE MAGPIE.

Descr.—Whole head, neck, and breast, deep black, with a lengthened occipital white band extending from the back of the head down the whole neck, gradually shading to bluish; some of the feathers of the crown tipped white; mantle and scapulars ashy cobalt blue, upper tail-coverts the same, with broad black tips; wings fine rich cobalt blue; the quills black on their inner webs, and all tipped white; the tail blue, the central feathers tipped white, and all the others with a black and white tip; beneath, from the breast whitish, with a tinge of purplish ash.

Bill coral red; legs orange; irides fine red. Length 26 inches, wings 8; tail 17 to 18; tarsus not quite 2; bill at front 1¼.

This splendid bird is found in the Himalayas, from the far north-west to Nepal, replaced towards the east by the next species. It is found chiefly on the lesser ranges of the hills. Adams states that it is pretty common on the ranges round Simla, Kussowlee, and to the westward, till replaced by *U. flavirostris*. It is also said to be found in parts of China. It breeds at about 5,000 feet, making, says Hutton, a loose nest of twigs, externally lined with roots. The nest is built on trees, sometimes high up, at others 8 or 10 feet from the ground. The eggs are from three to five, of a dull greenish ash-grey, blotched and spotted with brown dashes, confluent at the larger end. It is very terrene in its habits, feeding almost entirely on the ground. Several of these Magpies will often follow a Leopard for more than a mile, perching on the trees and bushes above it, and keeping up a continual screeching. (Ind. Sport. Rev. 1856.) It is sometimes caged, and bears confinement very well. It will eat raw meat, young or small birds, insects, and, indeed, almost any kind of food.

672. **Urocissa flavirostris**, BLYTH.

Psilorhinus, apud BLYTH, J. A. S., XV. 28—BLYTH, Cat. 472—HORSF., Cat. 861—*Tying-jongring*, Lepch;—*Pianging jabbring*, Bhot.

THE YELLOW-BILLED BLUE MAGPIE.

Descr.—Whole head, neck, and breast, deep black, with a narrow transverse white occipital band; upper plumage and scapulars purplish ashy ; upper tail-coverts, with some small black spots ; wings and tail dull cobalt blue, with an ashy tinge ; the quills black on their inner webs, and white tipped, and the tail feathers broadly tipped black and white, except the centre pair which are only tipped with white ; beneath, from breast whitish, with a strong tinge of purplish ashy.

Bill yellow ; legs orange yellow ; irides brownish red. Length 24 inches ; wing 7½ ; tail 16 ; tarsus 1¾ ; bill at front 1¾.

This species differs from the last in its generally duller hue, yellow bill, and small occipital mark ; the legs, too, are shorter, and not so strong.

The Yellow-billed Magpie is found throughout the Himalayas, but confined to certain localities. It is found in Cashmere and at Jummoo, in Kumaon, in parts of Nepal, and in Sikhim, where it is the only species. It occurs about Darjeeling from 6,000 feet to 10,000 feet or so ; wanders about a good deal, generally flying low, and alighting on low trees and shrubs, sometimes on a stone, or the stump of a tree. It lives chiefly on large insects, grass-hoppers, locusts, &c., and it has a loud ringing call which the natives attempt to imitate in the names given above. I had the nest and eggs brought me once. The nest was made of sticks and roots ; the eggs, three in number, were of a greenish fawn colour, very faintly blotched with brown.

Another species of *Urocissa* is found in Burmah, *U. magni-rostris* of Blyth, exceedingly similar to *U. sinensis*. I obtained it at Thayet Myo. Bonaparte, in his Conspectus, has two long-tailed Jays with black bills from Eastern Asia, which he classes under *Cyanurus*.

The next genus is also exclusively Indian, and there are only three known species.

Gen. CISSA, Boie.

Syn. Corapica, Lesson—*Kitta*, Temminck—*Citta*, Wagler—*Chlorisoma*, Swainson.

Char.—Bill strong, robust, compressed, moderately long, gently curved and hooked, and slightly notched at the tip ; gonys curving upwards ; nostrils basal, impended by short bristles and feathers; rictus slightly bristled; wings rounded; tail lengthened, cuneate; feet strongish, moderate; lateral toes unequal, inner toe much shorter, outer much joined to middle one; claws strong, well curved; hind toe and claw large.

673. Cissa Sinensis, Brisson.

Galgulus, apud Brisson—Pl. Enl. 620—Horsf., Cat. 859— Kitta venatoria, Gray, Ill. Ind. Zool. 1, pl. 2—Cissa venatoria, Blyth, Cat. 468—Corvus speciosus, Shaw—*Sirgang*, Beng.—*Chapling-pho*, Lepch—*Rabling-chapu*, Bhot.

The Green Jay.

Descr.—General color beautiful pale chrysophrase green, fading to bluish or bluish green, yellowish on the head, the feathers of which are lengthened, forming a crest; a black streak from the lores through the eyes to the nape, meeting the opposite one, and forming the lower part of the crest; wing-coverts and quills fine dark red, fading to rufous brown, or greenish brown in old specimens; the secondaries tipped pale blue-green, broadly edged above with black; tail with the central feathers tipped white, the outer ones tipped black and white.

Bill and legs coral red; irides dark red brown; orbits vermilion. Length 15½ inches; expanse, 8 inches; wing 6; tail 8½; bill at front 1⅜; tarsus 1⅞.

This lovely bird is found in the South-eastern Himalayas; also in the hill ranges of Assam, Sylhet, Arracan, and Tenasserim. It is not rare in Sikhim from 1,200 feet to 5,000 feet or nearly so. It wanders about from tree to tree, and picks various insects, grasshoppers, locusts, mantides, &c., off the leaves and branches. It has a rather loud, not unpleasant call, besides the usual harsh cry of the Jays and Magpies. They are frequently tamed and caged, and become, says Blyth, " very tame and fearless, are very amusing and imitative; sing lustily a loud and screeching strain of their own, with much gesticulation, and are highly carnivorous in their appetite. The Shrike-like habit, in confinement, of placing a bit of food between the bars of their prison, is in no species, more strongly exemplified than in this."

Buch. Hamilton states that it is said to be trained in Tipperah to hunt like a hawk, and catch small birds.

Another very closely allied species, *Cissa thalassina*, Temminck, is found in Sumatra ; and a beautiful species has lately been found in Ceylon, *Cissa ornata*, Wagler, (*C. puella*, Blyth,) which has a chesnut head, neck and wings; the rest of the body bright cobalt blue.

The next sub-family have still shorter and more rounded wings, and are, perhaps, still more arboreal.

Sub-fam. DENDROCITTINÆ.

Syn. Calleatinæ, Gray—*Glaucopinæ*, Swainson and Horsfield.

Bill short, with the culmen much elevated and curved, quite entire at the tip, gonys straight ; commissure curved ; nares protected by dense, velvety, short feathers ; wings short, rounded ; tail long, graduated ; tarsus short, stout ; feet arboreal with the lateral toes slightly unequal.

The Tree-crows or Magpies differ from the Jays by their still shorter, more curved beaks, more rounded wings, and strictly arboreal habits. They frequent forests in the hills, and well-wooded districts, and several are peculiar to the Himalayas. others to the hill ranges of Southern India. one only being found throughout the plains. They feed both on fruit and insects, and occasionally even capture young and sickly birds. They only take short flights, have loud chattering notes, and are mostly confined to the Indian province, one genus only being African, for I exclude the Australian birds generally placed here by Gray and others, *Glaucopis* and *Struthidea* (*vide* page 10).

Gen. DENDROCITTA, Gould.

Char.—Bill short or moderate, compressed, well curved from the base ; nostrils small, basal, concealed by short incumbent feathers; wings short, rounded, 5th and 6th quills longest, 4th, sub-equal ; secondaries nearly as long as the primaries ; tail elongate, wedge-shaped, with the two central feathers produced ; feet moderate or short, arboreal ; middle toe short, lateral toes unequal, hind toe and claw rather large.

This is a peculiarly Indian group, one or two species only extending into the Malayan countries.

674. **Dendrocitta rufa,** Scopoli.

Corvus, apud Scopoli—Blyth, Cat. 463—Horsf., Cat. 848—
Pica vagabunda, Vieillot—Gray and Hardw., Ill. Ind. Zool. 1,
pl. 25—Gould, Cent. Him. Birds, pl. 42—Jerdon, Cat. 159—P.
rufiventris, Vieillot—*Maha-lat,* H. *i. e.,* Large Shrike—*Kotri,*
H. in Bengal—*Takka-chor,* Beng., *i. e.,* Rupee thief—also *Handi-
chacha,* Beng., *i. e.,* Pan-scraper, imitative of its cry—*Mahtab* and
Chand, Sindh—*Gokurayi,* Tel., vulgo, *Konda-kati-gadu,* Tel.

THE COMMON INDIAN MAGPIE.

Descr. Whole head, neck, and breast, sooty brown, or blackish,
deepest on the forehead, chin, and throat, and passing into dusky
cinereous; scapulars, back, and upper tail-coverts dark ferruginous;
wing-coverts, and the outer web of the secondaries, light grey,
almost whitish in some; rest of the quills black; tail ashy-grey,
the feathers all broadly tipped with black, least so on the centre
feathers; beneath, from the breast, ferruginous or fulvous.

Bill black; irides blood-red; legs dark slaty. Length 16 inches;
wing 6; tail 10; bill at front through the frontal bristles 1⅜,
height ½ inch; tarsus 1¹²₁₀.

The Indian Magpie is found throughout all India, from the extreme south to the foot of the Himalayas on the east; but in the
North-west ascending apparently to some height. It extends to
Assam and even to China. Adams says that it is found in Cashmere,
and that it is common on all the lesser ranges of the North-western
Himalayas.* In the plains it is most common in well-wooded
districts; and, in the Carnatic, and bare table land, it is only
found occasionally about the larger towns, and in hilly jungles;
but, as you go further north, it is to be seen in every grove
and garden, and about every village. It occurs singly occasionally, very frequently in pairs, and now and then in small
parties. It flies from tree to tree with a slow undulating flight.
At times it feeds almost exclusively upon fruit, but at other times
on insects, grasshoppers, locusts, mantides, and caterpillars. The
natives always assert that it destroys young birds and eggs, and

* But these birds should be compared with *D. pallida.*

consider it of the Shrike genus. Mr. Smith says, " he has known
this bird enter a covered verandah of a house, and nip off half a
dozen young geraniums, visit a cage of small birds, begin by
stealing the grain, and end by killing and eating the birds, and
repeating these visits daily till destroyed." Mr. Buckland informs
me that he has known it enter a verandah and catch bats. It has
a variety of notes; the usual harsh cry of the Magpie; a clear
whistling, somewhat metallic call, which Sundevall syllabizes into
Kohlee-oh-koor, or *Kohlee-oh*; the Bengalees into '*Kotree*'; and it has
also a feeble indistinct note at the pairing season, which the male
utters, and the female responds to in a sort of chuckle. When
several pairs are together, they have a curious guttural call, which
the Revd. Mr. Philipps, as quoted by Horsfield, says, 'sounds
like *kakak* or *keke-kak*, repeated several times.' It builds a large
nest of sticks, generally on lofty trees, and lays three or four eggs
of a light greenish fawn colour, sometimes with a few indistinct
pale brown blotches.

Buch. Hamilton says:—" The Bengalese women imagine whenever they hear this bird calling, that it forebodes the approach of
religious mendicants, who, by partaking of the fare prepared for
the family, will clean the pots used in cooking; from which
circumstance, its native name is derived" (Pan-scraper); hence
he called it *Corvus mendicantium*, or the Beggar's Crow.

675. Dendrocitta pallida, BLYTH.

J. A. S. XV. 30—BLYTH, Cat. p. 336—HORSF., Cat. 849.

THE PALE MAGPIE.

Descr.—Plumage as in *D. rufa*, but altogether much paler; the
back and scapularies isabelline, with a shade of dusky, but devoid
of any decided rufous tinge; rump paler; the belly, and lower tail-
coverts pure isabelline, or buffy cream colour. "The hue of the
lower parts," says Blyth, "approaches that of the young of *D. rufa*,
but the much firmer structure of the plumage, indicative of
maturity, at once distinguishes it from that species."

Length 15 inches; wing $5\frac{1}{2}$; tail $8\frac{3}{4}$; bill at front 1; tarsus $1\frac{1}{8}$.

This species, if really distinct from the last, has only been
found in the extreme North-west Himalayas, bordering on

Affghanistan. It is perhaps Adams' species referred to *D. rufa*, as found in Cashmere.

676. Dendrocitta Sinensis, LATHAM.

Corvus, apud LATHAM—GRAY and HARDW., Ill. Ind. Zool. 1, pl. 26—GOULD, Cent. Him. Birds, pl. 43—BLYTH, Cat. 464—HORSF., Cat. 850—JERDON, Cat. 461—*Kokia-kak* at Mussooree—*Karrio-pho*, Lepch —*Karriah-ban*, Bhot.

THE HIMALAYAN MAGPIE.

Descr.— Forehead, lores, and patch over the eye, black; chin, throat, and ear-coverts sooty-brown; top of head, nape, and hind neck, bluish ashy; mantle and scapulars earthy brown; rump and upper tail-coverts cinereous; wings (with their coverts) black, with a white spot, formed by a bar across the base of the primaries; tail with the two centre feathers cinereous, passing into black at the tip, all the others black; lower parts, from the throat, reddish cinereous, paling on the lower abdomen and thigh-coverts; under tail-coverts rich chesnut.

Bill horny black; legs dusky black; irides red brown. Length 16 inches; wing 5½; tail 8½; tarsus 1⅛; bill at front 1¼, less strongly curved and hooked than in the last two.

This Magpie is found throughout the Himalayas, and occurs very rarely on the hills of Southern India. I got a specimen, said to have been killed on the Eastern Ghâts, and fancied that I saw it on the Segoor pass of the Neilgherries. Horsfield also has one specimen from Madras. On the Himalayas it is very abundant from 2,000 feet up to 7,000 feet, mostly so perhaps from 4,000 to 6,000 feet. It is found in the more open parts of the forest, and near cultivation and villages. Like its congeners it is a noisy bird, and has a variety of notes, similar in character to those of *D. rufa*. It usually feeds on trees, on insects and fruit. I have, however, seen it on the ground eating grain. I have had the nest and eggs brought me at Darjeeling frequently. The nest is made of sticks and roots, and the eggs, three or four in number, are of a pale dull greenish fawn colour, with a few pale reddish brown spots and blotches, sometimes very indistinct. Hutton, who got the eggs at Mussooree, describes them as dull greenish ash, with brown blotches and spots, somewhat thickly clustered at the larger end. It is doubtful if it is also an inhabitant of China, as its name would imply.

677. Dendrocitta frontalis, McLelland.

P. Z. S. 1839—D. altirostris, Blyth, Cat. 465—Horsf., Cat. 851—*Hamshi-bon*, Lepch.—*Kolio-ko*, Bhot.

THE BLACK-BROWED MAGPIE.

Descr.—Forehead, top of head, ear-coverts, throat and foreneck, deep black; wings and tail also black; wing-coverts (except those of the primaries) pure ash grey; the occiput, rest of the neck, breast and belly, whitish grey; the back, scapulars, upper and lower tail-coverts, vent and flanks, bright ferruginous or chesnut; the tibial feathers mixed grey and rufous.

Bill and feet black; irides brown red. Length 15 inches; wing $5\frac{1}{4}$; tail $9\frac{1}{4}$; bill at front 1, $\frac{3}{4}$ deep; tarsus 1. The bill is somewhat shorter, and much deeper than in the other species; the claws too are longer.

This Magpie is found only, in our province, in the South-eastern Himalayas, in the east of Nepal, and in Sikhim; it also occurs in Assam, where the original specimens were obtained. I found it near Darjeeling at from 3,000 to 5,000 feet of elevation. It is somewhat rare, though well known to the natives, and the Bhotia name, which is intended to represent the call, is curiously similar to the call of the *D. rufa*, as syllabized by Sundevall. It lives both on fruit, and on insects of various kinds.

678. Dendrocitta leucogastra, Gould.

Trans. Zool. Soc., vol. 1., p. 89., pl. 12—Blyth, Cat. 462—Horsf., Cat. 852—Jerdon, Cat. 160.

THE LONG-TAILED MAGPIE.

Descr.—Forehead, face, ears, sinciput, throat, neck, and breast, black; back of head and neck, white; wings black, with a white bar in the middle, formed by a band on the primaries; scapulars, back, and rump, bright chesnut bay; upper tail-coverts whitish; tail black, with the two outer feathers ashy grey, broadly tipped black, as is the half of the 5th pair, and the base of the 4th; belly white; lower tail-coverts pale chesnut; bill short, not so deep as in the last; tail very long.

Bill black; legs and feet dark plumbeous; irides blood red. Length 19 inches; wing $5\frac{3}{4}$; tail 12; bill at front 1; tarsus $1\frac{3}{10}$.

This long-tailed Magpie, the handsomest of the tribe, is only found in some of the jungles of the Malabar Coast. I have seen it most abundant in the Wynaad; on the slopes of the Neilgherries up to 5,000 feet and upwards; also in Coorg and Travancore. Those which I killed had eaten fruit only. It has a loud call like others of the genus.

Another species, *D. rufigastra*, has lately been described by Gould from Southern Asia; and *D. occipitalis*, Müll., from Sumatra, is recorded in Bonaparte's Conspectus. Others of this family are *Temia varians*, from Burmah, with ten tail feathers, the central pair enlarged at the tip, and somewhat curled up as in the Drongos; also a new species of the same genus found by myself in Upper Pegu, *Temia cucullata. Glaucopis leucopterus*, Pl. Col. 265; *Gl. temnurus* Pl. Col. 337, both from Malacca; and *G. aterrimus*, Temm., from Borneo, are nearly related. *Ptilostomus*, from Africa, with two species, is referred here by Gray and others.

Sub-fam. FREGILINÆ, Swainson.

Syn. *Pyrrhocoracinœ*, Gray.

Bill more or less lengthened, slender and arched, slightly notched at the tip in some, and brightly coloured; nares covered with dense silky plumes; wings long and pointed; tail moderately long; tarsi stout, and lateral toes equal.

This sub-family contains only two genera, both of which are European. but are also found in the higher slopes of the Himalayas. In their habits they closely resemble Crows and Jackdaws, are more or less gregarious, and nidificate in rocks, or on high buildings. They are nearly related to the Crows, into which they appear to grade, and should properly have followed them.

Gen. FREGILUS, Cuvier.

Char.—Bill long, slender, arched, compressed; the tip entire; nostrils covered with setaceous plumes; wings long, somewhat pointed; 4th and 5th quills longest; tarsi strong, robust; tail square.

679. Fregilus Himalayanus, Gould.

P. Z. S. 1862—F. graculus, apud Blyth, Cat. 458—Horsf., Cat. 822.

The Himalayan Chough.

Descr.—Black, finely glossed with purple and green; wings and tail black.

Bill and feet coral red. Length 15½ inches; wing 12¾; tail 6¾; tarsus 2¼; bill at front 2¼.

It differs from the European species in its larger size and longer bill. It is found on the Himalayas in flocks, near the snows; some of them migrating, (with the Jackdaws) to the plains of the Punjab in winter. Its call is rough and harsh. Adams found it on the mountains of Cashmere; and it has also been sent from Nepal. Its wild excited flight, and still wilder cry, says Adams, attract the sportsman's attention.

Gen. Pyrrhocorax, Vieillot.

Char.—Bill moderate or rather short, stronger than in *Fregilus*, and less curved, subulate; the tip of the upper mandible toothed; feet robust ; claws strong, well curved.

This genus, with *Glaucopis* and those very peculiar New Zealand birds, *Creadion* and *Neomorpha*, once referred by Bonaparte to this sub-family, are now separated by him as a distinct group of his *Curvirostres*, leading to the Crows.

680. Pyrrhocorax alpinus, Vieillot.

Corvus pyrrhocorax, Linn.—Gould, Birds of Europe, pl. 218 —Blyth, Cat. 457—Horsf., Cat. 823.

The Alpine Chough.

Descr.—Brilliant black with iridescent tints ; wings long, nearly reaching to the end of the tail.

Bill yellow; legs bright red. Length 16½ inches; wing 11¼; tail 7 ; bill at front 1⅜; tarsus 1⅝.

The Alpine Chough is found in the higher ranges of the Himalayas. It lives in flocks, feeds on various fruits, especially on the mulberry; and it breeds in holes in rocks. In Europe it is found on the Alps and Apennines; and it is noted by Powys as 'a curious, fearless, chattering bird.'

One allied species, *Fregilus leucopterus*, Vigors and Horsfield, is found in Australia, since separated generically as *Corcorax*.

Podoces Panderi, a remarkable bird of Northern Asia, is placed by Bonaparte in this sub-family, but by Gray in his *Garrulinæ*, and it appears to have decided affinities or analogies for the *Timalinæ*.

The only sub-family of *Corvidæ*, not represented in India, is the STREPERINÆ or Piping Crows, from New Holland, New Guinea, and adjacent islands. Their bill is straight, long, compressed, broadish at base and advancing on the forehead; the tip sometimes notched, and the nostrils are linear, quite exposed, pierced in the bill. They are noisy birds, with lively manners and omnivorous habits. By their bill they appear to lead the way to the next family, the *Sturninæ*; and, at the same time, some of them have the habits of the Shrikes, whose place indeed, they partly take in Australia; most of them are coloured black, or black and white.

Fam. STURNIDÆ, Starlings.

Bill straight, or very slightly curved, longish, compressed, subulate, often angulated at the base, slightly notched at the tip or entire; wings long, rather pointed; tail moderate or short; tarsi stout, moderate; lateral toes about equal.

The Starlings are, typically, birds of moderate size, with straight pointed bills, generally dividing the feathers at the base of the bill, which advance to the nostrils on each side. They have long pointed wings, fly well, and mostly walk on the ground, like Crows, which they much resemble in habits, being often gregarious, and feeding alike on grain, fruit, and insects. They nidificate in holes of trees or in buildings, a few constructing large nests in trees. In captivity they are docile and intelligent and can be taught to imitate the human voice well. In most there is little or no difference between the sexes.

They are divided into *Sturninæ*, Starlings and Mynas; *Lamprotornince*, glossy Mynas, or Grakles; *Buphaginæ*, Ox-peckers; *Quiscalinæ*, Boat-tails; *Icterinæ*, Hang-nests; and *Agelainæ*, Maizers. The first three are peculiar to the Old World; the last three to America.

The Starlings may be said to grade from the Crows through the Australian Piping-crows, some of which much resemble large Starlings. On the other side they pass into the Finches, through the shorter-billed *Agelainæ*, or Maizers of America, such as *Dolichonyx* and others.

Sub-fam. STURNINÆ.

Bill moderately long, compressed, straight, or slightly curved, entire in most; commissure usually angulated, or bent down towards the base: frontal plumes soft, dense, covering the base of the bill, which is prolonged backwards between the plumes; wings with the 2nd primary usually longest; the tail short, even, or slightly rounded; tarsus moderately long, stout.

This family comprises the Starlings of the Old Continent, and the Mynas of India, a group considerably developed throughout the Indian region. They are all more or less familiar, sprightly in their habits, loquacious, and easily domesticated.

The first group is that of the true Starlings, which are limited in number, and comprise two forms, the one distinguished by its nearly black color, and the other by its pied plumage, combined with some slight details of structure.

The typical Starlings are a very limited group, comprising only two species, one of which has but lately been discriminated, and is not very satisfactorily distinct. Both the European species occur in India, Northern Africa, and Western Asia.

Gen. STURNUS, Linnæus.

Char.—Bill long, straight, subulate, slightly depressed at the base; the culmen convex; tip obtuse, barely deflected; nostrils basal, partly closed by a vaulted membrane; wings with 1st quill minute; tail even, short; tarsus moderately long; lateral toes nearly equal; hind toe long.

681. Sturnus vulgaris, Linnæus.

GOULD, Birds of Europe, pl. 210—BLYTH, Cat. 580—HORSF., Cat. 800—S. indicus, HODGSON—S. splendens, TEMM.—*Telia-maina*, Hind.—*Tilora*, at Ghazeepore—*Nakshi-telia*, at Agra.—*Tilgiri*, in Cashmere.

The Common Starling.

Descr.—Glossy black, with a pale whitish or brownish tip to each feather, giving the bird a pretty speckled appearance; all the clothing feathers long and lanceolate. In very old birds the specks are said to disappear altogether, or nearly so. The young bird is dull brown.

Bill brown at first, for several moults, finally becoming rich yellow; legs yellow; irides brown. Length about 9 inches; wing 5; tail 3; bill at front through the feathers 1¼; tarsus 1⅝. The clothing feathers become longer and more pointed at each moult.

The common Starling is found, during the cold weather only, in the North-western Provinces of Bengal, as low down as Monghyr, South of the Ganges, and perhaps still lower; and as far as Purneah, at least on the North bank of the Ganges. It is, however, much more common further to the North-west, and I have never seen it out of the valley of the Ganges. It associates in large flocks, feeding both on grain, and on insects among cattle, associating with the common and Bank Mynas, and roosting on high reeds at night. Theobald found it breeding in Cashmere, in holes of bridges, of tall trees, &c.; the eggs pale clear bluish-green.

682. **Sturnus unicolor,** Marmora.

Gould, Birds of Europe, pl. 211—Blyth, Cat. 581.

The Glossy Black Starling.

Descr.—Glossy black, never having any white specks to the feathers; the clothing feathers still more elongated than in the common Starling. Length 9½ inches; wing 5½; tail 1¾; bill at front 1.

This Starling, (found in the South of Europe; particularly in Sardinia, in Africa, and Western Asia,) is said by Adams to be common in Sindh, the Punjab, and in Cashmere, and to build in holes of decayed trees. It is possible that Theobald may have been referring to this species, when he describes the breeding of the former bird, but Adams says that *St. vulgaris* is also common in Cashmere.

Gen. STURNOPASTOR, Hodgson.

Syn. *Psarites*, Cabanis.

Char.—Bill nearly straight, slightly curving, more so than in *Sturnus*, deflexed at the tip, more depressed than in *Sturnus*, and stronger; base of the bill plumed to the nostrils, but ascending in the middle; orbits bare; wings shorter; tarsus and toes strong.

This genus chiefly differs from *Sturnus* by its bare orbits and pied plumage; and, as its name implies, is a sort of link between the true Starlings and Mynas.

683. **Sturnopastor contra**, LINNÆUS.

Sturnus, apud LINNÆUS—JERDON, Cat. 162—BLYTH, Cat. 579—HORSF., Cat. 801—EDWARDS, Birds, pl. 187—S. capensis, LINN.—P. jalla, HORSF.?—*Ablak maina*, H.—*Ablaka gosalik*, Beng., also *Guia-leggra*,—*Venda gorinka*, Tel.

THE PIED STARLING.

Descr.—Head, neck, and upper part of breast, glossy black; ear-coverts white, extending in a narrow line to the nape; back, wings, and tail, black, slightly glossed; upper tail coverts white, as also an oblique bar on the wing, caused by the lesser coverts and outer portion of the scapulars; beneath, from the breast, white, tinged with reddish-ash; under tail-coverts pure white. The young bird is more brown than black, and the colors are less defined.

Bill red at the base, yellow at the tip; legs yellowish; irides brown; nude skin and orbits orange yellow. Length 9 inches; wing $4\frac{3}{4}$; tail $2\frac{3}{4}$; bill at front $1\frac{1}{8}$; tarsus $1\frac{1}{4}$.

The *Ablaka* is found throughout a considerable part of India, but absent in the South and South-west. It is found throughout Bengal up to the foot of the Himalayas, extending as far as Allahabad at all events; towards the South it is found all along the Northern Circars to near Masulipatam, thence inland to Hyderabad, but no further South nor West, except perhaps a straggler here and there; thence it is found in Nagpore sparingly, more abundantly at Saugor, and through Bundelkund to Allahabad. It is unknown in the West Coast, in the Deccan, and at Mhow in Central India. According to Philipps it is found also in the Upper Provinces of India.

The Pied Starling is more abundant in the Northern Circars than anywhere else where I have seen it. It here associates in vast flocks of many hundreds, feeding among cattle. In general, it is only found in small parties. It feeds like the others on grain fruit, and insects. It is a familiar bird, feeding close to houses, and breeding on trees near houses, sometimes, as at Saugor, in the midst of the town ; though as Mr. Blyth says, "it does not venture into the streets in Calcutta." It makes a large nest of sticks, grasses, and feathers, usually about 8 or 10 feet from the ground, and lays three or four eggs of a clear greenish blue. It breeds from April to June or July, according to the locality. It is very often taken young and caged ; has a pleasant song, and is a great imitator of other birds.

Tytler observed a caged specimen of a uniform black colour which he believed to be a distinct race, and named *St. Moorii*, but Mr. Blyth, I know, did not consider it distinct. Birds from Assam, Burmah, and the eastwards generally, differ slightly from Indian birds by a distinct white supercilium, and some streaks of white on the forehead ; this race has been named *S. superciliaris*, Blyth, J. A. S., 1863. It however should be compared with *Pastor julia* of the Malayan region. *Pastor tricolor*, Horsf. (*melanoptera*, Dandin), from Java ; *P. temporalis*, Wagler, from China, and, perhaps, *Sturnus cineraceus*, Temm., from Japan, belong to this genus. *P. temporalis*, like *S. contra*, builds a large round nest on high trees ; and the Japanese bird is aberrant, grading towards *Temenuchus*.

We next come to the true Mynas, which have a rather shorter bill, slightly curved on the culmen, and a dull or slightly glossed plumage. The first group comprises the typical Mynas, a form peculiarly characteristic of the Indian province. They are birds of somewhat massive form and dull plumage, and feed chiefly on the ground, often associating with cattle. They prefer insect food, but will also eat grain, and, indeed, are almost as omnivorous as the Crows

Gen. ACRIDOTHERES, Vieillot.

Syn. *Gracula*, Cuvier.

Char.—Bill rather short, stout, compressed ; culmen gently curving and deflected : gonys slightly sloping upwards : nostrils

almost concealed by the frontal plumes, which extend above
them their whole length; tail rounded : tarsus stout ; feet strong ;
toes lengthened : the laterals nearly equal; claws moderately
curved. The head is more or less crested, and some of them
have a naked space behind and under the eye.

684. Acridotheres tristis, LINNÆUS.

Paradisea, apud LINNÆUS—BLYTH, Cat. 574—HORSF., Cat. 806
—Pastor, apud SYKES, Cat. 113, and JERDON, Cat. 163—Gracula
gryllivora, DAUDIN—Maina tristoides, HODGS.—*Maina, H.*—*Desi-
maina*, also in the north— *Salik*, Bengal, and *Bhat-salik*—*Bemni*,
or *Saloo*, in Chota Nagpore—*Salonka*, Mahr.—*Gorwantera*, Can.
—*Goranka* or *Gorinka*, Tel.

THE COMMON MYNA.

Descr.—The whole head, with moderate occipital crest, neck,
and breast, glossy black ; the rest of the plumage quaker or snuff
brown,* darkest on the back and wing-coverts, and lightest beneath ;
primaries black with a white spot at their base, forming a conspicuous wing-spot; tail black with a white tip, successively broader
from the centre pair ; lower abdomen, vent, and under tail-coverts
white.

Bill and orbits deep yellow ; legs dull yellow ; irides red brown
with white specks. Length about 10 inches; wing 5¼; tail 3½:
bill at front ⅞ : tarsus 1⅜.

Some specimens are much darker colored than others, and
those from Ceylon appear to be always darker.

The common Myna is found throughout India, extending into
Assam and Burmah. It is one of the commonest birds in the
country, affecting towns, villages, and the neighbourhood of man
rather than the jungles. It roosts generally in large numbers,
in some particular tree in a village or cantonment, and, morning
and evening, keeps up a noisy chattering concert. Soon after
sunrise the birds disperse, and in parties of two, four, six or
more, wing their way in different directions, to their various
feeding grounds. Some remain about villages and cantonments,

* Hence probably Linnæus' name *tristis*, the ' sad colour' of our forefathers.

looking out, like the Crows, for any fragments of cooked rice that may be thrown out by the side of a house, or even coming into a verandah for that purpose; others attend flocks of cattle, which they follow while grazing, picking up the grasshoppers disturbed by their feet; while some hunt for grain or fruit. The Myna walks well, nodding his head at each step, and hops occasionally. Its flight is strong, direct, and tolerably quick. It has a great variety of notes, some of them pleasing and musical, others harsh; some have a resonant metallic sound. One of its notes has been syllabized as *praikh, praikh;* another, when flying, as *twee, twee.*

The Myna is a household bird, breeding almost exclusively in nooks and caves of houses, under the roofs, in holes in walls, or in pots hung out for that purpose by the natives. Mr. Smith, in his Notes, says: "It has several broods during the year." I have not, however, found this to be the case in general. Hutton says that at Mussooree, where it is a summer visitant, it breeds in holes in trees; Layard says the same of it in Ceylon; and doubtless many do so also in Bengal, and in other parts of India. The eggs are four or five in number, pale bluish green.

The Myna is very commonly caged and domesticated, and becomes very tame and familiar, often following its master about the house like a dog. It is a good imitator, and soon learns to pick up words and sentences. It is sacred to *Ram Deo,* on whose hand it sits.

This bird was introduced into the Mauritius from India, to destroy the grasshoppers, and is perfectly naturalized there.

685. **Acridotheres ginginianus,** LATHAM.

Turdus, apud LATHAM—BLYTH, Cat. 575—HORSF., Cat. 807—
Pastor gregicolus, HODGS.—P. Mahrattensis, apud ROYLE.—
Gangu maina, H —*Gang salik,* or *Ram salik,* Beng.—*Bardi-maina,*
in Nepal—*Luli,* Sindh—*Gilgila* of the Upper Provinces.

THE BANK-MYNA.

Descr.—Head, with rather short occipital crest, lores, ear-coverts, and nape, glossy black; the rest of the plumage dull cinereous or inky black, paling beneath ; wings black, with the wing-spot ferruginous; tail black, tipped dull ferruginous ; middle of abdomen, of vent, and the under tail-coverts, pale ferruginous. The frontal feathers are slightly erectile, and those on the sides of the head, are directed towards the median line.

Bill red, yellow at the tip ; nude eye spot reddish ; feet dull yellow. Length $8\frac{1}{2}$ inches; wing 5 ; tail $3\frac{1}{4}$; tarsus $1\frac{1}{4}$; bill at front nearly $\frac{7}{8}$.

The Bank Myna is found throughout Bengal, the Upper Provinces, and Sindh, extending into Central India as far as the Nerbudda and the Mahanuddy. I got it at Mhow and Saugor, though rare, and on the banks of the Nerbudda. It is also found in the lower Himalayas, extending, it would appear, into Affghanistan, as Horsfield has one specimen from Griffith, stated to be from Candahar, but it is possible there may be some mistake about this, especially as Adams says that it is not found in the Punjab, nor in the Himalayas. It also extends into Assam and Burmah. It certainly does not occur in Southern India, notwithstanding its specific name taken from Gingi, south of Madras. It is especially abundant in the Gangetic provinces, not occurring, says Mr. Blyth, so low down the Hooghly as Calcutta, but abounds as soon as the banks of the river become of sufficient height for it to burrow in with tolerable security. It has the usual habits of the group, feeding much with cattle, and partaking alike of insects, grain, and fruit. It breeds in holes in river banks, usually in large societies ; also in holes in wells, as I saw commonly at Ghazeepore and neighbouring country ; and lays, according to Theobald, as many as seven or eight eggs of the usual greenish blue colour.

The next bird has the same bulky form, but no naked space on the face, and the frontal feathers form a short, erect, narrow crest.

686. **Acridotheres fuscus,** WAGLER.

Pastor, apud WAGLER—JERDON, Cat. 164—HORSF., Cat. 810 —P. Mahrattensis, SYKES, Cat. 114—A. griseus, apud BLYTH, Cat. 577—Maina cristatelloides, HODGS.—Gracula cristatella, apud SUNDEVALL—*Pahari maina,* H.—*Jhonti maina,* H. in Bengal—*Jhont salik,* Beng.

Descr.—The whole head, small frontal crest, and ear-coverts, glossy black; the upper plumage fuscous black, or blackish brown, with a vinous tinge; primaries black, with a white spot near their base; tail also black, white-tipped, most broadly on the outer feathers; beneath, the throat and breast dull cinereous blackish; abdomen reddish cinereous, paling in the centre, whitish on the vent, and the under tail-coverts pure white; the secondaries are glossed with bronze towards their end.

Bill orange yellow; irides greyish white in the South of India, yellow in the North; legs yellow. Length $9\frac{1}{2}$ inches; wing 5; tail 3; bill at front $\frac{7}{10}$; tarsus $1\frac{1}{10}$.

This Myna takes the place of the last in hilly and jungly districts throughout India. I have found it on the Neilgherries, in the Wynaad, in parts of Mysore bordering on the Ghâts, and along the crest of the Western Ghâts, also in some of the jungles of Central India and Bundelkund. It is also found in Nepal, the more jungly parts of lower Bengal, Assam, and Burmah.

It is very remarkable that this species should have grey eyes in the South and yellow ones in the North, but such is certainly the case. At one time I thought that there must be two distinct species, but specimens from both localities are barely distinguishable from each other. Those from the south of India have the color of the upper surface, perhaps somewhat lighter and more brown than in specimens from Bengal, and are a trifle smaller. These differences, with the fact of the eye being white instead of yellow, perhaps should constitute this a distinct species or race, in which case it would bear Sykes' name. *Mahrattensis.*

This bird has almost the same habits as the common Myna, like it often attending cattle, but also frequently seen in gardens, as at Ootacamund, eating seeds and fruit of various kinds; and it is very often seen clinging to the tall stem of the large *Lobelia* so common on the Neilgherry hills, feeding on the small insects (bugs chiefly) that infest the capsules of that plant. It is most abundant on the Neilgherries, where it is a permanent resident, breeding in holes in trees, making a large nest of moss and feathers, and laying three to five eggs of a pale greenish-blue colour. From what Hodgson says it is probably also a permanent

resident in Nepal, where, he says · perpetually associating with
.1. tristis, every large flock of which has many individuals of this
bird among them.' At Mussooree, Hutton says that it is only a
summer visitant, breeding in holes in trees there. He further says,
" it does not appear to visit Simla, but is to be found in some of
the valleys below it to the south; when the young are hatched
they betake themselves to the Dhoon in July." Captain Tytler says
that at Dacca this bird builds in the old temples and houses about
the Sepoys' huts.

.1. cristatellus of China is nearly allied to this bird, as is
.1. javanicus, Cabanis, of Java, (griseus, apud Horsfield). The
former is said by Swinhoe to breed in holes of trees in general,
but sometimes to make a large oval nest on high trees.

The next birds differ from the previous group in their smaller
size, less massive form, lighter and more elegant plumage, more
arboreal habits, and more or less grey plumage.

Gen. TEMENUCHUS, Cabanis.

Syn. Sturnia, Lesson—Heterornis, Gray.

Char.—Bill short, compressed, less stout than in Acridotheres,
barely deflected at the tip, often parti-coloured; wings moderate,
1st and 2nd primaries sub-equal; tail nearly even; tarsus short;
lateral toes slightly unequal; claws more curved. Head usually
crested.

This genus comprises several nearly allied species from India
and Burmah. The first noticed differs from all the others in the
black head, and it is, at the same time, more terrestrial in its habits.

687. Temenuchus pagodarum, GMELIN.

Turdus, apud GMELIN—JERDON, Cat. 165—SYKES, Cat. 116—
BLYTH, Cat. 588—HORSF., Cat. 803—Pastor nigriceps, also Maina
sylvestris, HODGSON—Popoya maina, H., vulgo Bamuni maina—
Pahaia, H. in the Upper Provinces—Monghyr pawi, Beng.—Pabiya
pawi at Muttra—Papata gorinki, Tel.—Papata pariki, also Rawan-
ati, Tam.—Brahminy Myna of the English.

THE BLACK-HEADED MYNA.

Descr.—Head and long pendent crest black; body above grey;
beneath and ear-coverts bright fulvous buff, with some mesial

pale streaks; wings blackish, with a white edge near the shoulder; tail dull black.

Bill blue at the base, then greenish, yellow at the tip; irides greenish white; legs bright yellow. Length $8\frac{1}{2}$ inches; wing $4\frac{2}{10}$; tail 3; bill at front $\frac{6}{16}$; tarsus $1\frac{1}{10}$.

The Brahminy Myna is found more or less throughout all India, but much more abundant in some localities than in others. It is most numerous in the Carnatic, as about Madras and Trichinopoly, and in the Southern portion of the Northern Circars; rare on the Malabar Coast, only seen in the Deccan at the end of the cold weather, and a casual visitant in lower Bengal at the same time. It is found in the lower regions of Nepal, in Cashmere, and also in the lesser ranges of Cashmere, and, it is stated, more or less throughout the North-western Provinces, though only for a short time. Dr. Adams, however, who saw it in Cashmere, says that he never saw it on the plains in the North-western Provinces. It occurs also, though rarely, in Assam, and Arracan, and, in Ceylon, only towards the North.

At Madras it feeds chiefly on the ground, among cattle, in company with *Acridotheres tristis*, picking up grasshoppers and other insects. It also feeds on trees on various fruits, berries, and flower-buds, and occasionally insects. Adams says that in Cashmere, it feeds on the seeds and buds of Pines. When the silk cotton tree comes into bloom, is always to be found feeding on the insects that harbour in the flowers. I observed this at Jalna, and Blyth remarked the same at Calcutta. At Madras, it breeds about large buildings, pagodas, houses, &c., and lays three or four greenish-blue eggs. Mr. Philipps records it as building in holes of trees. It has a variety of calls, and a rather pleasing song. It is frequently caged and domesticated, is docile and hardy, and will imitate any other bird placed near it. Like the others of its tribe, it is lively in its manners and actions, and has a steady swift flight.

688. **Temenuchus malabaricus,** GMELIN.

Turdus, apud GMELIN—BLYTH, Cat. 587—HORSF., Cat. 804—Pastor cinereus, apud JERDON, sub. No. 166—JERDON, 2nd Suppl. Cat. 166, bis—P. caniceps, P. Blythii, and Maina affinis,

HODGSON—P. pagodarum, female, apud WAGLER and McLELLAND
—*Puwi*, H. and *Desi-pawi*, Beng. *Pali palisa*, Tel.

THE GREY-HEADED MYNA.

Descr.—Upper parts grey ; the forehead and throat whitish, the
feathers being centred white, and the former, occasionally, pure
white; entire under parts, from the foreneck, ferruginous buff (some
of the feathers of the breast also centred with whitish), deep coloured
in old males, faint in young and in females; quills black ; the inner
web deep brown ; the primaries slightly glossed and faintly tipped
with grey; the middle tail feathers grey, the rest dusky, successively more broadly tipped with deep ferruginous. The colors fade
much by abrasion, and become more nearly uniform.

Bill blue at the base, greenish in the middle, and yellow at the
tip; irides greyish white ; legs dull yellow. Length 7½ inches;
wing 4 ; tail 2½ ; bill at front $\frac{6}{10}$; tarsus 1.

The young birds are nearly all grey, lighter beneath, and with
rufous tips to the outer tail-feathers.

The Grey-headed Myna is found throughout India, but somewhat
locally distributed. It is most common in the North of India,
in lower Bengal, extending to the Upper Provinces and Central
India, but in smaller numbers. In the South of India, it is only
a cold weather visitant. It extends to Assam, and Tenasserim.

It feeds chiefly on trees, on various fruit and seeds, also on
insects, and lives in small flocks; has the usual chattering notes of
the Mynas, and a pleasant song. Tytler says that they build in
the hollows of trees.

689. **Temenuchus Blythii,** JERDON.

Pastor, apud JERDON, 2nd Suppl. Cat. 166—P. Malabaricus,
apud JERDON, Cat. 166—JERDON, Ill. Ind. Orn., pl. 22—BLYTH,
Cat. 586—HORSF., Cat. 805—

THE WHITE-HEADED MYNA.

Descr.—Whole head with long crest, neck, throat, and breast,
silky-white ; back and scapulars grey ; belly and under tail-coverts
deep rufous ; wing-coverts and outer web of most of the quills, and

all the tertiaries also grey; quills black, grey tipped; central tail-feathers dark grey, blackish at the base, the outer feathers deep ferruginous brown, dusky towards the base.

Bill blue at base, greenish in centre, yellow at the tip; irides greyish white; legs reddish yellow; claws pale yellow. Length $8\frac{1}{2}$ inches; wing $4\frac{2}{10}$; tail 3; bill at front $\frac{7}{10}$; tarsus 1.

This pretty Myna is only found in the Malabar forests, both near the level of the sea, and up to a level of 2,000 feet or so in the Wynaad and the slopes of the Ghâts. It is found from the extreme south of the Malabar coast to about North Lat. 15° or 16'. It is entirely arboreal, living in small flocks, and keeping to the tops of high trees, feeding on various insects and larvæ, small shells (*Bulimi*), and occasionally on fruit. Its usual cry is neither so loud nor so harsh as that of the Mynas in general, and it has a very pleasing song. Its nails are well curved, and it climbs about the trunk and branches of trees with great facility. It is said to nidificate in holes of trees.

Other species of *Temenuchus* from neighbouring countries are *T. erythropygia*, Bl., from the Nicobars; and a nearly related race from Burmah, *T. nemoricolus*, Jerdon. *T. sericeus*, Latham, from China, by its larger and straighter, bill somewhat approximates the Starlings; and *T. burmannicus*, Jerdon (Ibis, vol. 4), is a nearly allied species from Pegu. This last bird feeds much on the ground like the true Mynas, and perhaps, with *sericeus*, ought to form a separate section. Both have red beaks. *T. sinensis*, Gmel., (*elegans*, Lesson,) approaches *Calornis*. Layard (Ann. Mag. Nat. Hist. 1854) has *Sturnia albofrontata*, from Ceylon. Bonaparte has *Pastor senex*, Temm., from Bengal, perhaps the same as Blyth's *erythropygia*, or, as Layard suggests, with his species quoted above.

Gen. PASTOR, Temm.

Char.—Bill short, compressed, curving from the base, very slightly hooked at the tip; gonys straight; nostrils partially concealed by fine frontal plumes; wings long, pointed; 1st quill longest, 2nd sub-equal, 3rd a little shorter; tail nearly even; tarsus rather short; lateral toes slightly unequal; head adorned with a long pendent, occipital crest.

This genus, which is composed of but a single species, with somewhat the form of *Temenuchus*, has the gregarious habits of the true Starlings and Mynas, and is more a grain and fruit eater perhaps than others of this family.

690. Pastor roseus, LINNÆUS.

Turdus, apud LINNÆUS—GOULD, Birds of Europe, pl. 212—SYKES, Cat. 115—JERDON, Cat. 167—BLYTH, Cat. 593—HORSF., Cat. 811—*T.* suratensis, GMEL.—*Golabi maina,* H. in the North—*Tilyer,* H. in the South—*Pariki-pitta,* Tel.,—*Palisa,* Tel., of some *Sura kurari,* Tam.—*Bya,* in Sindh—*Cholum bird* of Europeans in Madras.

THE ROSE-COLORED STARLING.

Descr.—Whole head, with crest, neck, and breast, fine glossy black, with purple reflections ; wings and tail black with a green gloss ; rest of the plumage pale salmon or light rose color.

Young birds have the rose color much dashed with pale brown and fuscous, and the head not so glossy ; and the young of the year are more or less earthy brown, paler beneath, and without a crest.

Bill orange yellow at the base, then pinkish, and brown at the tip ; irides deep brown ; legs dusky reddish. Length $9\frac{1}{2}$ inches ; wing $5\frac{1}{4}$; tail 3 ; bill at front $\frac{15}{20}$; tarsus $1\frac{2}{10}$. The tongue is bifid at the end and somewhat fringed.

The Rose-colored Starling is found throughout the greater part of India, most abundant in the South and South-west, rare towards the North and North-east, and, apparently, not known in Assam and Burmah, unless *P. Peguanus,* Lesson, be the immature state of this bird.

It usually makes its appearance in the Deccan and Carnatic about November, associating in vast flocks, and committing great devastations on the grain fields, more especially on those of the Cholum or Jowaree (*Andropogon sorghus*), whence its familiar name in the South. Mr. Elliot, in his MSS. Notes, quoted in my Catalogue, says : "Is very voracious and injurious to the crops of white Jowaree, in the fields of which the farmer is obliged to station numerous watchers, who, with slings and a long rope or thong, which they crack dexterously, making a loud report, endeavour to drive the depredators away. The moment the sun appear above the horizon they are on the wing, and at the same instant, shouts, cries, and the cracking of the long whips, resound from every side. The Tillyers, however, are so active that if they are able to alight on the stalks for an instant, they can pick out several grains. About 9 or 10 o'clock A. M., the exertions of the watchmen cease, and the Tillyers do not renew their plundering till evening. After sunset they are seen in flocks of many thousands retiring to the trees and jungles for the night. They prefer the half ripe Jowaree whilst the farinaceous matter is still soft and milky." When they can no longer get grain, they feed on various grass and other seeds, flower-buds, fruit, and also on insects, seeking them on the ground, but rarely seen with cattle in India. Their Telugu name is derived from the name of a plant whose fruit they are particularly fond of. Mr. Blyth remarks that " they visit the neighbourhood of Calcutta only at the end of the cool season, when flocks of them are not unfrequently observed upon the arboreal cotton tree then in bloom."

Burgess states that he has seen them busily feeding on the flowers of the leafless Caper, a shrub very common in the Deccan on the banks of the larger rivers. Dr. Adams says that " it is very abundant in the Punjab, committing great havoc on the grain there." In the North-west of India, and in Affghanistan, they devour large quantities of Mulberries in spring, hence called the ' *Mulberry-bird*' in the North-west, disappearing afterwards. They at times, however, feed much on insects, and are called the ' locust-eater' in Persia, according to Chesney. They do not breed in this country, quitting the South of India in March, but lingering in the North a month or so longer. It is ascertained that they breed in vast numbers in Syria, and other parts of Western Asia, in rocky cliffs. Burgess states his belief that they breed in India somewhere, and was informed by a native that they do breed in the Ghâts. This however is, doubtless, totally without foundation. Mr. Layard states that one year he saw large flocks of these birds in July, that they remained only a week and then disappeared. They were entirely

STURNINÆ. 335

unknown to the Natives. Burgess also states that in 1850,
towards the end of August, he saw a large flock of the Rose-colored Starlings feeding on insects in an open field. These intances of
their appearing so early are very unusual, and more especially their
occurrence in Ceylon in July, by which time the young could only
have been just fairly fledged. Most of the birds met with in
India are, of course, young birds in imperfect plumage.

Sub-fam. LAMPROTORNINÆ, Grakles or Hill Mynas.

Syn. *Ptilinorhynchinæ*, Gray and Horsfield—*Eulabetinæ*, Horsf.
—*Graculinæ*, apud Gray.

Bill somewhat stout, the ridge more or less curved and hooked,
and the tip notched; nostrils more or less hidden by the close set
frontal plumes; wings long or moderate, and pointed; tarsus short
and stout.

The Grakles are birds of usually glossy plumage, found in the
warm regions of the Old Continent. Many are found in Africa,
a few in India and Malayana. They are more or less gregarious,
live chiefly on fruit, and nestle, in general, in holes of trees or in
rocks. Many feed habitually on the ground, associating with
cattle; others are more arboreal.

The glossy Mynas of India comprise two very distinct forms,
one with rather slender bill, of delicate conformation, consisting of
a single species; the other of robust make, with strong beaks, and
furnished with prominent wattles, the Hill Mynas. They are both
strictly arboreal in their habits, living, in forests, on fruit, and nidificating in holes of trees. In his List of Genera, Gray places these
birds respectively under *Juidinæ* and *Eulabetinæ*, the first including
Saraglossa, Calornis, and some other Eastern forms, and all the
African Mynas; the second our Hill Mynas and one or two allied
genera. G. R. Gray in his Genera included the former (together
with the Bower birds of Australia), under his *Ptilinorhynchinæ*, and
the latter under *Eulabetinæ*. The Indian members of this group do
not appear to associate very well with the African ones, in spite of
some resemblance of plumage, and perhaps ought to form a distinct
division. They evidently grade to the true Mynas through
Calornis.

Gen. SARAGLOSSA, Hodgson.

Char.—Bill rather long, straight at the base and depressed, compressed at the tip; culmen ridged, curved, and slightly hooked; gonys
nearly straight; nostrils apert, but the frontal plumes descending over
the base of the bill, which does not divide the frontal plumes; wings
pointed, the first three nearly equal; tail firm, short, sub-furcate or
nearly even; legs and feet strong and arboreal; nails acute and
well curved.

The founder of this genus states that he considered it to be a
'Sturnideous bird with Melliphagous adaptations,' and compares
its bill with that of *Phyllornis*. It is generally classed among the
Lamprotorninæ, but appears to be a somewhat anomalous form of
this sub-family.

691. **Saraglossa spiloptera**, Vigors.

Lamprotornis, apud Vigors, P. Z. S. 1831—Gould, Cent.
Him. Birds, pl. 34—Blyth, Cat. 582—Horsf., Cat. 816—*Puli*
at Mussooree.

The Spotted-winged Stare.

Descr.—Above pale plumbeous, the feathers tipped with dusky,
giving it a speckled and Stare-like appearance; upper tail-coverts
tinged with rufescent brown; quills and primary coverts glossy
green black, with a white spot at the base of the primaries; tail
deep brown; beneath, the chin and throat, deep chesnut rufous;
some of the feathers tipped with glossy grey, the rest white, deeply
tinged with rufous on the abdomen and flanks.

Bill dusky horny; legs brown; irides white. Length 8 inches,
wing 4$\frac{3}{4}$; tail 2$\frac{1}{2}$; bill at front $\frac{3}{4}$; tarsus $\frac{7}{8}$.

This bird is found only in the Western and Central Himalayas.
It is not known in Sikhim. It frequents the valleys about Simla and
Mussooree, up to 6,000 feet, lives in small flocks of five or six; its
note and flight, says Hutton, " are very much like those of *Sturnus
vulgaris*, and it delights to perch on the very summit of the forest
trees. I have never seen it on the ground, and its food appears to
consist of berries. It nidificates in the holes of trees, lining the
cavity with bits of leaves cut by itself; the eggs are usually three

to five, of a delicate pale sea green, speckled with blood-like stains, which sometimes tend to form a ring near the larger end. Dr. Adams says that it frequents rice fields, or the sides of mountain streams, and that it is shy and timid.

Turdus madagascariensis, Gmel., figd. P. E. 557-1, is referred here by Gray, but evidently belongs to a very different family (*vide* page 79).

The next birds are the glossy or Hill Mynas of India, comprising four distinct races, one from the south of India, another from Ceylon, a third from the Himalayas and Burmah, and the last from Malayana.

Gen. EULABES, Cuvier.

Syn. *Gracula*, L. (in part), and Swainson—*Mainatus*, Lesson—*Maina*, Hodgson.

Char.—Bill short or moderate, stout, compressed; culmen gradually curved; tip notched; nostrils basal, lateral, placed in a plumed fossa; under mandible with the base broad and dilated; frontal feathers short, velvety, advancing on base of bill; head with naked wattles; wings long, 4th quill longest, 1st short; tail short, even; feet strong; tarsus equal to the middle toe; outer toe slightly longer than inner one; claws well curved; hind toe and claw large.

The Hill Mynas are well known birds of fine glossy plumage, and with prominent yellow wattles. They are readily tamed, and can be taught to repeat words very distinctly. They are entirely frugivorous in their habits. They progress on the ground by hopping only, not by alternate steps as the true Mynas.

692. Eulabes religiosa, LINNÆUS.

Gracula, apud LINNÆUS—JERDON, Cat. 168—BLYTH, Cat. 571—HORSF., Cat. 796—EDWARDS. Birds, pl. 17 (the upper figure) —Eul. indicus, CUVIER—Gracula minor, JERDON, 2nd Suppl. Cat. 168—*Kokui maina*, H. in the South—*Konda yorinka*, Tel.

THE SOUTHERN HILL MYNA.

Descr.—General plumage glossy purplish black, with green reflections on the lower back and upper tail-coverts; beneath less

2 U

brightly glossed; wings and tail coal black without reflections; a
white spot on the first seven primaries, forming a conspicuous
wing-spot.

The wattles on the head commence below each eye, are crossed
at the lower posterior angle of the eye by a triangular patch of
minute feathers, pass beyond the ear, where they form a rather
large loose flap, or lappet, and then return in a narrow stripe
to the top of the head. There is also a small nude patch below
the eye.

Bill orange; wattles deep yellow; irides dark brown; legs deep
yellow. Length 10 inches; extent $18\frac{1}{2}$; wing $5\frac{6}{10}$; tail $2\frac{8}{10}$; bill
at front 1; height $\frac{3}{8}$; tarsus $1\frac{2}{10}$.

The Hill Myna of Southern India is found in the forests of
Malabar from Travancore up to North Lat. 16° or 17°, most abundant
parhaps on the Gháts, and especially in the Wynaad, Coorg, and
other elevated districts, up to 3,000 feet or so. It also occurs in
the thick forests of the Northern Circars, as far as Goomsoor,
extending west into the wooded portion of the Nagpore territories.
It is stated also to be found in Ceylon, where, however, another
species occurs. It is somewhat locally distributed, the birds
appearing to congregate in certain spots. It is found at times in
small parties of five or six or more, sometimes in large flocks; and,
during the cold weather, at all events, they appear to roost in
company, in great numbers, especially on bamboos along the
edges of mountain streams. It appears, as far as I have observed,
in a wild state, to feed exclusively on fruit and berries of various
kinds. The song of this bird is very rich, varied and pleasing;
but it has some harsh notes also. It breeds in holes of trees,
but I never saw the eggs, though I have had the young brought to
me in the Wynaad. It is occasionally taken when young and
caged, but less frequently than would be the case were it a
denizen of Northern India, the birds in confinement being
usually those of the next species brought from the North. It was
most probably by confounding it with *Acridotheres tristis,* that
Linnæus was led to call this bird *religiosa,* for I never heard of its
being held at all sacred.

693. Eulabes intermedia, A. Hay.

Gracula, apud Hay, Madras Journal, XIII. 156, and J. A. S. XV. 32.—G. religiosa, apud Sundevall—Blyth, Cat. 570— Horsf., Cat. 797.—*Paharia-maina*, H.

The Nepal Hill Myna.

Descr.—Larger than the last, but the colors similar. The bill is larger, deeper, and stronger, and much wider at the base, and less flattened; the naked skin is broader where it begins below the eye, and the patch of feathers is differently shaped; the loose flap too is smaller, and it is not continued back to the top of the head.

Bill deep orange; wattles bright yellow; irides dark brown; legs dusky yellow. Length $10\frac{1}{2}$ inches; wing $6\frac{1}{2}$; tail not quite 3; tarsus $1\frac{1}{4}$; bill at front 1; height $\frac{1}{2}$.

The Hill Myna of Northern India is found all along the lower ranges of the Himalayas, extending into Assam and Burmah, as far as Tenasserim certainly. It does not ascend to any height on the Himalayas, keeping to the Terai, and the warmer valleys. Its habits and manners do not differ from those of the last. It is taken, when young, in large numbers, in the Nepal Terai, and other parts, and sold at Monghyr and elsewhere. It is easily tamed, and learns to speak with great facility and accuracy.

E. ptilogenys, Blyth, from Ceylon, differs in only having the loose flap of skin, the rest of the cheeks being feathered. *E. javanensis* is found in the Nicobars, Malacca, and the islands. It is still larger than the Nepal bird, and has a stronger bill, about $\frac{11}{16}$ inch deep, with the wattles less developed, but the lappets larger.

Bonaparte has *Grac. venerata*, Temm., from Sumbava, with a lengthened and slender bill. An interesting form, nearly related, is found in Burmah, *Ampeliceps coronatus*, Blyth. It has the top of the head and throat yellow, as well as the wing-spot.

Other allied forms are *Mino*, from New Guinea, barely distinct from *Eulabes*; and *Gymnops*, from the Philippines; and those very remarkable birds, *Enodes erythrophrys*, and perhaps *Scissirostrum*

Pagei, the former from Java, and the latter from Celebes, appear to belong to this sub-family. *Basilornis*, or the crested Mynas, from Malayana, are usually placed near the Hill Mynas. *Calornis* may be said to be the Malayan representative of the African *Lamprotornis*. One species, *L. cantor*, Gmel. (*chalybæus* Horsf.— *affinis*, Hay) is recorded, from Tipperah, Burmah, and Malacca. Another species, *Calornis dauricus*, Pallas, is quite intermediate, both in color and structure, between the glossy Mynas and the grey Mynas (*Temenuchus*); it extends from Malayana into China and Central Asia; and *Heterornis pyrrhogenys*, Müll., and *Pastor ruficollis*, Wagler, are nearly allied species from Borneo, Japan, and the Philippines. Several others allied to *cantor* are recorded from the Malayan isles and Oceanica.

The rest of this sub-family are chiefly African. They are showy birds, with rich glossy plumage, of moderate size, and often with lengthened tails. They live in flocks, eat both fruit and insects, and often perch on the backs of cattle. One of these birds, *Amydus Tristrami*, figured by Gould, Birds of Asia, XI. pl. 9, occurs in Palestine.

Buphaginæ, or the Oxpeckers, are a purely African tribe, whose position has been a subject of much doubt. They are a singular group, comprising only two species, with short, stout, somewhat curved bills, short but stout feet, with strongly curved claws. They are of plain and sombre plumage, and perch a good deal on the backs of cattle, camels, and rhinoceros, &c.; and are said to extract the larvæ of botflies and ticks from the skins of those animals.

The remaining families of the *Sturvinæ* are strictly American. Some, *Quiscalinæ*, have long graduated tails, with the sides curved upwards, whence called Boat-tails. Their bill is long, straight, with the nostrils placed in triangular grooves, pointed wings, and a long hind toe, with curved claw; their plumage is usually glossy black, mixed with chesnut. They live in troops, feeding alike on grain and insects, and nestle in society, forming nests of mud, lined with grass and hair.

The *Icterinæ*, or Hang-nests, chiefly differ from the last in wanting their boat-like tail; they are often adorned with yellow and black colors, and build long pendulous nests, open at the top, in company.

Another group, the *Agelaianæ*, or Maize-birds, are usually clad with orange or scarlet and black. They are of smaller size, have shorter bills than the last family, are very destructive to grain, and evidently grade into the *Fringillidæ*. Among them is the celebrated Cow-bird of the United States, the only bird besides the Cuckoos that lays its eggs in the nests of other birds. It is the *Molothrus pecoris*, Auct.

Certain birds of New Zealand and Oceanica, *Aplonis*, Gould, and *Creadion*, Vieillot, are generally considered, and, perhaps correctly, to belong to the Starling family ; but the Bower-birds of *Australia, Ptilinorhynchinæ*, placed here by some, are very doubtful members of this division, and, perhaps, belong to a particular section of the Birds of Paradise, as suggested by Blyth, which, as already noticed, used to be placed among the Conirostres, and are so still by many. These Bower-birds and Satin-birds, *Chlamydera* and *Ptilino-rhynchus*, are birds about the size of a Myna, and are noted for the remarkable bower-like structure they make, and adorn with shells, pebbles, small bones, and feathers ; and which does not appear to serve for nidification, but simply for amusement, or a place of resort for both sexes, which run through and around the bower in a sportive and plaintive manner.

Fam. FRINGILLIDÆ.

Bill short, thick, and conic ; wings usually long, pointed ; tail moderate, even, forked in most ; tarsus moderate or short ; feet suited both for perching and terrestrial habits ; of small size.

The Finches comprise a very large number of small birds, with thick conical bills, which live for the most part on seeds, and many are well known and familiar birds. They exhibit a great variety of structure, varying much in the strength and thickness of the bill. The tongue is somewhat more fleshy than in most *Insessores* (except Parrots), but horny at the tip. The bill is usually entire, more or less notched in one sub-family. The œsophagus is dilated into a craw or crop, in which the food is allowed to remain awhile, and undergo maceration, before passing into the powerful and muscular gizzard, required in these birds that live so much on hard grain. They are usually very active on the wing, with a strong jerking flight, and they hop on the ground. Many of them are social, or even gregarious in winter, and most of them construct neat, and, in some cases, elaborate nests.

They are perhaps more abundant in northern and temperate regions than in tropical countries, and, in India, if we except the Sparrows, the Munias and the Weaver-birds, most are migratory and only winter visitants.

They are divided into numerous sub-families, concerning the extent of which there is much disagreement among Ornithologists. I shall, with Blyth, divide them into *Ploceinæ, Estreldinæ, Passerinæ, Emberizinæ, Fringillinæ*, and *Alaudinæ;* besides the great group of American Tanagers, *Tanagrinæ*, the most aberrant of the family.

The first two sub-families are well distinguished from the others by possessing a minute first primary.

Sub-fam. PLOCEINÆ, Weaver-birds.

Bill strong, conic, slightly lengthened ; the culmen arched, and the ridge continued back upon the forehead ; wings somewhat rounded, first primary very minute ; tail short in most ; legs and toes very strong and robust, the latter lengthened, especially the hind toe, and the claws well developed.

The Weaver-birds form a well marked group of Finches, peculiar to the tropics of the Old World, and nearly so to Africa, for there are only four Asiatic species. They are eminently social and gregarious, nidificating in society, making most ingenious and elaborate nests, and the Indian species, at least, laying pure white eggs. They have a double moult, the males of most putting on a gay plumage in spring, which is yellow in the majority, red in a few. They have a remarkable similarity, both in colours and habits, to some of the American *Icterinæ* and *Agelainæ*. They do not sing, but the flocks keep up a continual chirping. They are readily domesticated, and will, it is stated, breed in confinement.

Horsfield classes the Weaver-birds among his *Fringillinæ*, and Swainson in his *Coccothraustinæ;* but these differ, as already stated, in wanting the first small primary.

There is only one genus of this sub-family in India.

Gen. PLOCEUS, Cuvier.

Syn. *Euplectes,* Swainson (in part.)

Char.—Bill thick at the base, laterally compressed, pointed at the tip; culmen smooth, broad, rounded, and produced backwards on the forehead to a point; commissure nearly straight; nostrils basal, partly concealed; wings moderate or somewhat short, with the first quill small, about one third of the next four or five, 2nd a little shorter than 3rd, which is usually longest; tail short even, or very slightly rounded; feet large, hind toe and claw strong, all the claws lengthened.

This genus comprises the four Indian species, and many African. In all the Indian birds the crown of the head, in the males, becomes bright yellow in the breeding season. In winter the sexes are alike, or nearly so. All build nests of strips of leaves or grass interwoven together, from June to August, and have pure white, rather long-shaped eggs.

Of three Indian species found within our limits, one is widely diffused, and the other two are more locally distributed. They are often called Tailor-birds in India.

694.   Ploceus baya, BLYTH.

J. A. S. XIII. 945— HORSF., Cat. 785—P. Philippinus, apud SYKES, Cat. 106—JERDON, Cat. 169—BLYTH, Cat. 614—P. atrigula and passerinus, HODGSON (m. and f.)—Fring. bengalensis, SUNDEVALL—*Baya,* H.—*Chindora,* H. in Bengal—*Bawi,* or *Talbabi,* Beng.—*Parsupu-pitta,* Tel.—*Manja-kuravi,* Tam.

THE COMMON WEAVER-BIRD.

Descr.—Old males, in breeding plumage, have the crown of the head bright yellow, the rest of the upper plumage with the wings and tail, dull brown, edged with pale fulvous brown, some of the feathers in the middle of the back edged yellow; rump and upper tail-coverts pale rufous brown ; primaries with a narrow edging of pale yellow ; lores, ear-coverts, chin, and throat, blackish brown ; breast bright yellow ; belly and lower tail-coverts dull white ; the flanks and under wing-coverts and thigh-coverts pale rusty or buff.

Bill black ; irides dusky brown ; legs brownish fleshy.

Younger males in the breeding plumage have the breast pale rusty instead of yellow, and the yellow edging of the interscapulars is wanting. The females, and males in winter dress, totally want the yellow head, the crown being brown with dark streaks, have pale rufous supercilia, and the chin and throat are whitish.

Bill pale horny brown ; Length about 6 inches ; extent $9\frac{1}{2}$; wing $2\frac{8}{10}$; tail not quite 2 ; bill at front $\frac{6}{10}$; tarsas $\frac{8}{10}$; spread of foot $1\frac{3}{4}$.

The common Weaver-bird is found throughout the whole of India from Cape Comorin and Ceylon to the foot of the Himalayas, and extending into Assam, Burmah, and Malayana. It is most abundant in the well wooded parts of the country, and in the bare table land of the Deccan you may travel for days without seeing one. It appears to wander about in some localities, for some observers have stated that it is migratory, but it is certainly a permanent resident in most parts of the country ; and their roosting places on certain trees are well known. Grain of all kinds, especially rice and various grass seeds, form the chief food of the Weaver-bird, and I never observed it feeding on fruit, as Sykes asserts he has known it do on the fig of the Banian tree. Whilst feeding, particularly, as well as at other times, the whole flock keeps up a perpetual chirruping. I have seen it feeding in grain fields in company with flocks of *Emberiza melanocephala;* and Sykes relates that he has seen it associate with the common Sparrow.

The Baya breeds during the rains, according to the locality, from April to September, but I am not aware if they ever have more than one brood. Its long retort-shaped nest is familiar to all, and it is indeed a marvel of skill, as elegant in its form, as substantial in its structure, and weather-proof against the downpour of a Malabar or Burmese Monsoon.

It is very often suspended from the fronds of some lofty Palm-tree, either the Palmyra, Cocoanut, or Date, but by no means so universally so as Mr. Blyth would imply, for a Babool (*Acacia arabica*, or *Vachellia Farnesiana*), or other tree will often be selected, in preference to a Palm-tree growing close by, as I have seen within a few miles from Calcutta on the banks of the canal. Very often a tree overhanging a river or tank, or even a large well is chosen, especially, as Tickell says, if it have spreading branches and scanty foliage. In India I have never seen the Baya suspend its nests except on trees, but in some parts of Burmah, and more particularly in Rangoon, the Bayas usually select the thatch of a bungalow to suspend their nests from, regardless of the inhabitants within. In the cantonment of Rangoon, very many bungalows may be seen with twenty, thirty, or more of these long nests hanging from the end of the thatched roof, and, in one house in which I was an inmate, that of Dr. Pritchard, Garrison Surgeon there, a small colony commenced their labors towards the end of April, and, in August, when I revisited that station, there were above one hundred nests attached all round the house! In India, in some localities, they appear to evince a partiality to build in the neighbourhood of villages or dwellings; in other places they nidificate in most retired spots in the jungle, or in a solitary tree in the midst of some large patch of rice cultivation.

The nest is frequently made of grass of different kinds plucked when green, sometimes of strips of plantain leaf; and not unfrequently of strips from the leaves of the date palm, or cocoanut; and I have observed that nests made of this last material are smaller and less bulky than those made with grass, as if the little architects were quite aware that with such strong fibre less amount of material was necessary. The nest varies much in the length both of the upper part or support, and the lower tube or entrance, and the support is generally solid from the point whence it is hung for two or three inches, but varies much both in length and strength. When the structure has advanced to the spot where the birds have determined the egg compartment to be, a strong transverse loop is formed, not in the exact centre, but a little at

one side. If then taken from the tree, and reversed, the nest has
the appearance of a basket with its handle, but less so in this than
in the next two species, which have seldom any length of support
above. Various authors have described this loop or bar as peculiar
to the male nest, or sitting nest, whereas it exists primarily in all,
and is simply the point of separation between the real nest and
the tubular entrance, and, being used as a perch both by the old
birds and the young (when grown sufficiently), requires to be very
strong. Up to this time both sexes have worked together indiscriminately; but when this loop is completed, the female takes up
her seat on it, leaving the cock bird to fetch more fibre and work
from the outside of the nest, whilst she works on the inside, drawing
in the fibres pushed through by the male, re-inserting them in their
proper place, and smoothing all carefully. Considerable time is spent
in completing this part of the nest, the egg chamber being formed
on one side of the loop and the tubular entrance at the other;
after which there appears to be an interval of rest. It is at this
stage of the work, from the formation of the loop to the time that
the egg compartment is ready, that the lumps of clay are stuck on,
about which there are so many and conflicting theories. The original notion, derived entirely, I believe, from the natives,* was
that the clay was used to stick fire-flies on, to light up the apart-
ment at night. Layard suggests that the bird uses it to sharpen its
bill on; Burgess that it serves to strengthen the nest. I of course
quite disbelieve the fire-fly story, and doubt the other two sugges-
tions. From an observation of several nests, the times at which
the clay was placed in the nests, and the position occupied, I am
inclined to think that it is used to balance the nest correctly, and
to prevent its being blown about by the wind. In one nest lately
examined, there was about three ounces of clay in six different
patches. It is generally believed that the unfinished nests are built
by the male for his own special behoof, and that the pieces of clay
are more commonly found in it than in the complete nests. I did not
find this the case at Rangoon, where my opportunities of observing

---

* See the interesting and almost unique Natural History by a native, Akbar
Ali Khan of Delhi, of the *Baya*, in the Asiatic Researches, vol. 2.

the bird were good, and believe rather that the unfinished nests are
either rejected from some imperfect construction, weak support, or
other reason, if built early in the breeding season ; or, if late, that
they are simply the efforts of that constructive faculty which appears, at this season, to have such a powerful effect on this little
bird, and which causes some of them to go on building the long
tubular entrance long after the hen is seated on her eggs.

I have generally found that the Baya lays only two eggs, which
are long, cylindrical, and pure white, but other observers record a
larger number. Sundevall states that he found three in one nest.
Layard says from two to four ; Burgess six to eight ; Tickell six
to ten. Blyth thinks that four or five is the most usual number.
From many observations, I consider two to be the usual number,
but have found three occasionally. In those exceptional instances,
where six or more eggs have been found, I imagine they
must have been the produce of more than one bird. The
Baya, is stated not to use the same nest for two years consecutively, and this I can quite understand, without having actually
observed it.

The Baya is frequently taken when young, tamed, and taught
to pick up rings, or such like articles, dropped down a well ;
or to snatch the Ticca mark off the forehead of a person point-d
out. It is also taught occasionally to carry a note to a particular
place, on a given signal. Mr. Blyth, in an unpublished paper,
has the following interesting account of some of this bird's perfor-
mances : "The truth is that the feats performed by trained Bayas
are really very wonderful, and must be witnessed to be fully
credited. Exhibitors carry them about, we believe, to all parts
of the country ; and the usual procedure is, when ladies are
present, for the bird, on a sign from its master, to take a cardamom
or sweetmeat, in its bill, and deposit it between a lady's lips, and
repeat this offering to every lady present ; the bird following the
look and gesture of its master. A miniature cannon is then
brought, which the bird loads with coarse grains of powder one by
one, or more commonly with small balls of powder made up for
the purpose ; it next seizes and skilfully uses a small ramrod ;
and then takes a lighted match from its master which it applies

to the touch-hole. All this we have personally witnessed in common with most persons who have resided in or even visited India; and we have seen the little bird apply the match five or six times successively before the powder ignited, which it finally did with a report loud enough to alarm all the crows in the neighbourhood, while the little Baya remained perched on the gun, apparently quite elated with its performance." Captain Tytler mentions also "the twirling of a stick with a ball of fire at each end. This the bird turns in several ways round its head, making luminous circlets in imitation of a native practice; the stick being held by the beak in the middle."

In an ordinary cage or aviary, they will employ themselves constantly, if allowed the chance, in intertwining thread or fibres with the wires of their prison, merely gratifying the constructive propensity, with apparently no further object; unless, indeed, the sexes are matched, when they breed very readily in captivity; of course, provided they are allowed sufficient room, as in a spacious aviary.

This bird has currently passed as *P. philippinus*, Auct., but on a reference to the figure in the Pl. Enl. of Buffon, the type of that species, I am convinced that it refers to the species named *hypoxantha* by Daudin.

695. **Ploceus manyar**, HORSFIELD.

Fringilla, apud HORSFIELD—BLYTH, Cat. 615—HORSF., Cat. 783 —JERDON, 2nd Suppl. Cat. 170—Euplectes flaviceps, SWAINSON —E. striatus, BLYTH,—E. bengalensis, JERDON, Cat. 170— *Bamani baya*, H. in the Deccan—*Telia baya*, Beng.--*Bawayi*, in Rungpore.

THE STRIATED WEAVER-BIRD.

Descr.—The male in full breeding dress has the crown of the head intense yellow; lores, cheeks, ear-coverts, chin, throat, and neck, brownish black; back, wings, and tail, brown; the feathers of the back with a mesial dark streak, those of the primaries and tail edged with yellowish; rump streaked like the back; upper tail-coverts rufescent; beneath, from the throat whitish, tinged with fulvous, and streaked on the breast and flanks with dusky black.

Bill black; irides light brown; legs fleshy. Length about $5\frac{0}{10}$ inches; extent 9; wing $2\frac{3}{4}$; tail $1\frac{3}{4}$; bill at front $\frac{9}{16}$; tarsus $\frac{3}{4}$; stretch of foot $1\frac{3}{4}$.

The male in winter dress is clad like the female, and has the head brown, streaked like the back, a pale yellow supercilium, and a small yellow spot behind the ear-coverts; the chin and throat are whitish, and the streaks on the lower surface less developed. The bill is pale horny fleshy.

This species of Weaver-bird is found in suitable localities, throughout all Northern India, spreading into Central India, and more rarely to the Deccan. It does not appear to occur in the N. W. Provinces. It is also found, and perhaps more abundantly, in Assam, Burmah, Malacca, and some of the Islands. It chiefly frequents long grass and reeds on the banks of rivers and jheels, and was hence named by Buchanan Hamilton *Loxia typhina*. It invariably breeds among high reeds, and usually in places liable to be inundated; and, as the breeding season is during the rains, the nest is thus unassailable except from the water. The nest is fixed to two or three reeds, not far from their summit, and the upper leaves are occasionally turned down and used in the construction of the nest, which is, in all cases that I have seen, made of grass only. The nest is non-pensile, that is to say, it is fixed directly to the reeds, without the upper pensile support that the nest of the last species has; and, in some cases, the eggs are laid before any tubular entrance is made, a hole at the side near the top forming the entrance. This, however, is often, but not always, completed during the incubation of the female; and, in other cases, a short tubular entrance is made at first, in a very few, prolonged to a foot or more. I have found the eggs in this case, as in the last, to be generally two in number, three in a few; and in one nest I found five.

696. **Ploceus Bengalensis**, LINNÆUS.

Loxia, apud LINNÆUS—BLYTH, Cat. 616—HORSF., Cat. 784—
Euplectes flavigula, HODGSON—E. albirostris, SWAINSON—P.

aurcus, LESSON—*Sarbo baya*, H.—*Shor baya*, and *Kantawala baya* in Bengal.

THE BLACK-THROATED WEAVER-BIRD.

Descr.—The male in breeding plumage has the crown brilliant golden yellow, with, in some instances, a slight inclination to flame color; back dusky brown; rump dingy grey brown; wings and tail dark brown, the former with very slight pale margins to some of the feathers; the throat white; the cheeks, ear-coverts, and sides of the neck white, more or less suffused with dusky on the ear-coverts and throat; a broad, brownish black pectoral band; the rest of the lower plumage sullied or fulvous white, brownish on the flanks. In some the pectoral band is broad and entire, in others narrower, and divided along the middle.

The female has the head streakless dusky brown, the feathers of the back edged with pale rufous brown; a pale yellow supercilium, and a spot of the same colour behind the ear; also a narrow moustachial stripe; throat white, yellowish in some, and usually separated from the yellow moustache by a narrow black line; pectoral band less developed. Males, after the autumn moult, resemble the females, but the breast and flanks are more rufescent; the pectoral band is frequently wanting, or rather concealed by pale fulvous deciduary edgings.

Bill always pearly white; irides light brown; legs dusky carneous. Length 5½ inches; extent 9¼; wing 2¾; tail 1¾.

This very pretty Weaver-bird is more locally distributed than either of the preceding. It is found in various parts of Lower Bengal, extending into Assam, Tipperah, and parts of Burmah. It appears unknown in Central India and the N. W. Provinces. I found it abundant near Purneah, also in Dacca, building in low bushes, in a grassy churr overflown during the rains. The nest was non-pensile, and had either no tubular entrance or a very short one, made of grass, and more slightly interwoven than either of the others. Though a good many pairs were breeding in the neighbourhood, the nests were, in no instance, close to each other, rarely indeed two on the same bush.

The figure in Pl. Enl. 393, f. 2, usually quoted for this species, appears to me more applicable to *manyar*, but, in either case, is barely recognisable.

The only other eastern species of *Ploceus* is *P. philippinus*, (*hypoxanthus*, Daudin) *vide* p. 348, recorded from Java, and various parts of Malayana, perhaps extending to the Philippines. I found this very pretty Weaver-bird at Thayet-myo in Upper Burmah, rare; in Rangoon, where observed also by Mr. Blyth; and frequent in swampy ground near the mouth of Rangoon river, where I also found its nest, solitary, in a thick thorny bush, very similar to that of *P. bengalensis*.

Africa is the head quarters of this tribe, and there are many species very similar to our Indian birds; others are clad in black and red, or flame color. Most of them build pensile nests of grass, but the eggs are described as being bluish-white, or greenish-blue, in some instances speckled. They are referred to several genera. One remarkable species, *Philæterus socius*, builds in society, constructing a common roof or shed, beneath which their nests are placed contiguously. The Whidah birds, *Vidua*, during the breeding season, develop tails of extraordinary length and form, and, in one instance, a ruff. It is supposed by some that these birds are polygamous.

Sub-fam. ESTRELDINÆ.

Of small size; bills large in many and bulged, more slender in others; wings short, rounded; feet large; tail rounded or cuneiform.

The Munias or Amadavads closely resemble the Weaver-birds in many particulars, and perhaps, with these, should form one group. They inhabit Africa, India, Malayana, and Australia, in which country they are the sole representatives of the *Fringillidæ*. The first primary is minute, as in *Ploceinæ*, and, like them, they are often social, even during the breeding season, but they do not construct such elaborate nests. The eggs of all known are pure white, as in our Indian Weavers; many are very pleasingly colored, and some of them are very beautiful. In general they do not sing, but one of the Indian species has a rather pleasing song,

The sexes are usually alike; in a few that moult in spring, the male is more richly colored than the female. They inhabit grassy or reedy ground, bushy jungle, and open spaces in forests, occasionally being found in immense flocks. There are two forms found in India, one the Munias, with a thick tumid bill; the other the Amadavads, (*Estrelda*), with a more slender, conic, and waxy red bill.

Gen. Munia, Hodgson.

Syn. *Lonchura*, Sykes—*Spermestes*, in part, Swainson.

Char.—Bill very thick and at the base as deep as long, compressed at the tip; culmen arched, flattened, prolonged backward to a point on the forehead; gape strongly angulated; nares round, sunk and free; wings short; 1st primary minute, the three next nearly equal; tail moderate or short, rounded or wedged; tarsus stout, moderate; toes long. slender; claws long.

The birds appertaining to this genus are found in India, Malayana, and Australia, and almost all have the large beak of a pale glaucous lead color. They are of small size, but larger than the next group; and build large, loosely-constructed nests of grass. They feed much on rice, as well as on grass seeds; are readily domesticated; and the young of most are light brown.

697.   **Munia Malacca,** Linnæus.

Loxia, apud Linnæus—Edwards, Birds, pl. 355, f. 2— Blyth, Cat. 623—Horsf., Cat. 773—Jerdon, Cat. 174—*Nakalnur* H. *Nalla jinawayi*, Tel.

The Black-headed Munia.

Descr.—Whole head, neck, and breast, rich black; back, wings, and tail, pure rich cinnamon red; upper tail-coverts brighter tinged, and with a glistening lustre; beneath, from the breast, white, with the middle of the abdomen and vent black.

Bill bluish, yellowish at the tip; irides dark brown; legs plumbeous. Length $4\frac{1}{2}$ inches; wing $2\frac{6}{10}$; tail $1\frac{1}{2}$. The young bird is pale cinnamon brown above, whitish below, dusky about the head and neck.

The Black-headed Munia is chiefly found in Southern India and Ceylon, a few stragglers occurring in Central India, and even in Bengal occasionally. It is very abundant in parts of Southern India, especially on the Malabar coast, frequenting long grass by the sides of rivers and tanks, occasionally dry grain fields, and very commonly sugar-cane fields. It often associates in very large flocks. The nest is usually placed among reeds, in tanks, or in the beds of rivers; occasionally in long grass in the bunds of paddy-fields. It is a rather large, nearly round or oval nest, neatly but loosely made of grass, with the hole at one side, this in general being very artfully concealed by the interlacing of the fibres of grass, so that I have been puzzled for a few moments to discover the entrance; and the eggs, four to six in number, are pure white.

698. **Munia rubronigra,** Hodgson.

As. Res. XIX. 153—Blyth, Cat. 622—Horsf., Cat. 774—Lox. malacca, var., Latham—Lonchura melanocephala, McLelland.

The Chesnut-bellied Munia.

Descr.—Head, neck, and breast, black; rest of the plumage deep chesnut or cinnamon, passing to glistening maronne on the upper tail-coverts, and tinged with fulvous on the tail; a stripe down the middle of the belly, vent, and under tail-coverts, black.

Bill and feet plumbeous; irides dark brown. Length $4\frac{1}{2}$ inches; wing $2\frac{1}{8}$; tail $1\frac{1}{2}$; bill at front $\frac{1}{2}$; tarsus $\frac{9}{16}$. The young are brown above, paler brown below; head and breast somewhat infuscated.

This very closely allied species, which differs from the last only in having the belly chesnut in place of white, replaces it in the north of India, being found throughout Lower Bengal, and all along the foot of the Himalayas as far as the Dehra Doon; and also in some of the more wooded adjacent districts, but it would appear to be rare in the open country of the N. W. Provinces. I have seen specimens from the Eastern coast north of Madras, and Mr. Layard procured it in Ceylon, but it is certainly rare in Southern

India. It is much more common in the countries to the eastward,
Assam, and Burmah as far as the Tenasserim provinces, southwards of which it is replaced by *M. sinensis*, which wants the
black abdominal stripe altogether.

According to Mr. Frith the nest is ordinarily placed in a
Baubul tree in Lower Bengal, solitarily, and is composed of a large
ball of the tufts of *Saccharum spontaneum*. I have always found
its nest fixed to reeds or long grass, and suspect that Mr. Frith
must have been mistaken in the identity of the owner of the nest
above noticed, the more so because that is exactly the character,
both as to materials and site, of the nest of the next species
noticed.

699. Munia undulata, LATHAM.

Loxia, apud LATHAM—BLYTH, Cat. 624—HORSF., Cat. 772—
M. lineoventer, HODGSON—Amadina punctularia, apud PEARSON
—Lonchura nisoria, apud SYKES, Cat. 109—JERDON, Cat. 172—
EDWARDS, Birds, pl. 40—*Telia munia*, H. in the North—*Sing-baz*
or *Shin-baz*, H. in the Deccan, and at Mussooree—*Shubz munia*,
Beng.—*Kakhara jinuwayi*, Tel.

THE SPOTTED MUNIA.

Descr.—Above ruddy brown, deeper on the head and neck,
inclining to whitish on the rump, and the upper tail-coverts and
margins of the lateral tail-feathers, glistening fulvous ; quills
chesnut externally, dusky within ; beneath, the chin and throat,
with the face and ear-coverts, rich chesnut ; breast and flanks
white, with numerous zig-zag cross bars of black ; lower abdomen,
vent, and under tail-coverts, whitish, unmarked.

Bill and legs plumbeous ; irides brown. Length $4\frac{1}{2}$ inches ;
wing $2\frac{2}{10}$; tail $1\frac{1}{2}$; bill at front $\frac{1}{10}$; tarsus $\frac{13}{20}$. The two central
tail-feathers are very slightly elongated. The young are rufous
brown above, paler below.

The Spotted or Barred Munia is found throughout India and
Ceylon, somewhat rare in the extreme south, common in the north,
and spreading into Assam, and Burmah as far as Tenasserim. It is

somewhat local in its distribution, but, where met with, is there
tolerably abundant. I have seen it on the edges of the Neilgherries, and in various parts of the Carnatic and Central India,
as well as in Bengal, but it does not occur in the Malabar Coast.
It is occasionally found in grassy or bushy ground, and Buchanan
Hamilton states it to live in thickets of Hugla grass (*Typha
elephantina*), near villages where small grains are sown; but more
frequently it occurs near cultivated ground, affecting mangoe groves,
or patches of tree jungle. It builds in thorny bushes, chiefly
about fields, and makes a large nest of very fine grass, or not
unfrequently of the flowering tufts of some *Saccharum*, which I
have often seen it conveying to its nest; and I have always found
the nest solitary, contrary to Mr. Layard's observations, who states
that he has seen thirty or forty nests in one tree, and that in one
instance he found one structure containing several nests. The
eggs, of course, are pure fleshy white, usually four to six in number.
At Thayet-myo I found it building in a hole in the thatch of my
bungalow. Blyth states that this bird, which is very commonly
caged, is known in Bengal as the Nutmeg-bird from the peculiar
mottling of its breast.

The nearly allied *M. punctularia* (*nisoria* of Temminck), occurs
in the Malayan provinces.

700. **Munia pectoralis,** JERDON.

Spermestes, JERDON, Suppl. Cat. 173 bis.

THE RUFOUS-BELLIED MUNIA.

Descr.—Head, neck, and back, brown, the shafts of the feathers
pale; upper tail-coverts dark brown, the feathers tipped with
glistening yellow; wings and tail dark brown; face, forehead,
throat, and breast, dark brown, strongly contrasting with the sides
of the neck; lower parts from the breast, reddish-fawn colour;
under tail-coverts dark brown with pale shafts.

Bill plumbeous; legs plumbeous brown; irides dark brown;
Length $4\frac{1}{2}$ inches; wing $2\frac{2}{10}$; tail $1\frac{7}{10}$; tarsus $\frac{6}{10}$. The central
tail feathers are barely longer than the next pair.

This species occurs only, that I have observed, in Wynaad and Coorg ; but most probably may be found all along the crest of the Western Ghats. I found it associating in small flocks, in bushy and jungly ground near rice fields.

A nearly allied species *M. Kelaarti* Blyth, occurs in Ceylon, with the lower parts, from the breast, mottled black and dull white.

The three next species have the tail feathers successively more elongated.

701. **Munia striata**, Linnæus.

Loxia, apud Linnæus—Blyth, Cat. 628—Horsf., Cat. 779—Fringilla leuconota, Temm. Pl. Col. 500, f. 1—Sykes, Cat. 111—Jerdon, Cat, 173—*Shakari munia*, Beng.

The White-backed Munia.

Descr.—Plumage above rich dark brown, deepest on the head, and the feathers white shafted ; rump white ; tail almost black ; beneath from chin to breast uniform deep blackish brown ; belly, flanks and vent white ; under tail-coverts and thigh-coverts brown.

Bill bluish ; legs dark slaty ; irides brown. Length $4\frac{1}{2}$ inches ; wing $2\frac{1}{10}$; tail $1\frac{3}{8}$. The middle tail feathers exceed the outermost by nearly half an inch.

This species is most abundant in the Malabar coast, where it is occasionally to be seen in vast flocks feeding in the rice fields. It also occurs sparingly in other parts of India, in the Northern Circars, in lower Bengal, Arrakan, and Ceylon ; but is replaced in the lower Himalayas. and throughout the Burmese province, by the next species. It is also stated to occur in Java.

In Malabar it is a familiar bird, being constantly seen on the road side, about houses, and in stable yards ; and it builds in gardens and orchards, solitarily, making a large loosely constructed nest of grass, and laying four or five white eggs during the rains.

702. **Munia acuticauda**, Hodgson.

As. Res. XIX. 153—Horsf., Cat, 778—M. molucca, apud Blyth, Cat. 626—*Samprek-pho*, Lepch. *Namprek*, Bhot.

The Himalayan Munia.

Descr.—Above deep brown, blackish on the forehead and sides of the face, all the feathers white shafted; rump white; upper tail-coverts black, tipped brown; tail deep black; throat and breast brown black, the throat almost black, the feathers of the breast pale-shafted, and with whitish edges (more or less); belly dull white, with narrow hastate marks of dusky brown; under tail-coverts and thigh-coverts brown; the lining of the wings buff.

Bill and legs slaty blue; irides dark brown. Length 4½ inches; extent 6½; wing 2; tail 1¾; the medial tail feathers are much elongated, exceeding the outermost by ¾ inch.

This species, which differs chiefly from the last in the lower parts being lineolated, in place of pure white, is found, within our province, only in the Himalayas; but extends into Assam, parts of Burmah and Malayana; and is perhaps identical with the birds said to be from the Moluccas, named *L. moluccæ*, Lin., and figured Pl. Enl. 139 f. 2.

In the Sikhim Himalayas it ascends to at least 5,000 feet, and is tolerably abundant near cultivated lands. Its nest is of the usual structure, large and loosely made of fine grass, and there are generally five or six white eggs. I found it far from rare on the Khasia Hills, whence it had not been previously sent, and it probably will be found all through the intervening country to Mergui (where Blyth obtained it), in suitable localities.

The next species has the central tail feathers still more lengthened, and Sykes made it the type of his genus *Lonchura*, but, as already seen, there is a regular gradation in this respect.

703. **Munia Malabarica,** Linnæus.

Loxia, apud Linnæus—Blyth, Cat. 630—Horsf., Cat. 776—Jard and Selby, Ill. Orn. 2nd ser. pl. 34—Lox. bicolor, Tickell, —Lonchura cheet, Sykes, Cat. 110—Jerdon, Cat. 174—*Chorya*, H. in the North—*Charchara*, in the N. W. P.—*Piddari* in Southern and Central India—*Sar-munia*, Beng.—*Jinuwayi*, Tel.

THE PLAIN BROWN MUNIA.

Descr.—Upper plumage pale earthy brown, slightly rufescent
on the head, and darker towards the forehead; wings and tail
blackish; the tertiaries slightly bordered with whitish at their
truncated tips; upper tail-coverts white, edged with black externally; cheeks and lower parts white, tinged with pale earthy brown
on the flanks, which sometimes have some faint cross rays.

Bill plumbeous; legs livid carneous; irides deep brown.
Length 5 inches; wing 2⅛; tail 2. The central tail-feathers are
much elongated, being ¾ inch longer than the outermost pair.

This plain coloured Munia is found throughout India, not
entering the hills, nor extending to the countries towards the
east, but very abundant in Sindh and the Punjab. It also occurs
in Ceylon. It frequents bushy jungles, hedgerows, thickets near
cultivation, and groves of trees, often entering gardens, and is
to be met with, in the south and in Central India, near every
village; it is more rare in Malabar and other well-wooded districts, and generally so indeed in forest country. Like all the
others it associates in small flocks, and feeds on grass seeds and
grains. The nest is a large, loosely constructed fabric, of fine
grass, with an opening at one side, which, says Theobald is "sometimes prolonged into a short deflected neck, partially closed by
the elasticity of the long spikes of grass forming it." The eggs
are numerous, small and white. Sykes took ten from one nest;
Burgess never more than six; I have usually found from five to
eight. Theobald on one occasion took "twenty-five in different
stages of incubation from one nest, but he has satisfactorily
accounted for this by showing that two pairs of birds" (if not more)
"are frequently, if not usually, employed in the construction of
one nest, and the two hens lay consecutively in it." The same
observer states that "sometimes the nest is a simple platform
of grass, open at each end, but the grass ends curved over to meet
at the top. It is much to be doubted if the eggs found occasionally in October and December are often hatched." With
Mr. Blyth, I consider that the nest last described was not intended
for incubation. Col. Sykes states that they "frequently take

possession of deserted nests of the Weaver-bird; and that the
cry of this bird is "*cheet, cheet, cheet,*" uttered simultaneously by
flocks in flight."

" This bird is very commonly tamed, and a pair," says Buchanan
Hamilton, " always being kept in the same cage, each bird has a
small cord fastened round its body, and the owner, holding one
bird by the cord, throws up the other, which always returns and
sits by its companion."

Besides the Asiatic species already referred to, there are several
others from Malayana. *M. maja,* L., from Malacca and the isles;
M. ferruginosa, Latham, from Java, both with white heads, but
otherwise like *M. rubronigra ;* and *M. leucogastra,* Blyth, from
Malacca, is another species. *Donacola,* an Australian group, is
very close to *Munia* in structure and mode of coloration. The well
known Java sparrow, *Oryzivora leucotis,* Blyth, Pl. Enl. 388, has
the bill more lengthened than in *Munia,* but still very thick, and
bright cherry red, thus leading to the next group. So many birds
of this species have escaped from cages at Madras, that, I am informed it is to be seen wild in the neighbourhood.

The next birds have the bill more slender, and waxy red.

Gen. ESTRELDA, Swainson.

Char.—Bill much more slender than in *Munia* ; the culmen
less arched and flattened at the base, more compressed throughout,
deep red color; tail soft and graduated ; feet moderate. Of still
smaller size, and more delicate conformation.

In the form of their beak the Wax-bills, as Blyth calls them,
deviate towards the Finches and Linnets, as the Munias do towards
the Grosbeaks. There are two Indian species, one or two in
Australia, and many in Africa.

704. Estrelda amandava, LINNÆUS.

Fringilla, apud LINNÆUS—SYKES, Cat. 105—JERDON, Cat. 175
—BLYTH, Cat. 637—HORSF., Cat. 706—Amaduvade Finch,
EDWARDS, Birds, Pl. 355, f. 1—*Lal* (the male), *Munia* (the female,)
H.—generally called *Lal munia*— *Yerra jinuwayi,* Tel.—*Amaduvad*
of Europeans.

THE RED WAX-BILL.

Descr.—The male in full summer plumage is more or less crimson, darkest on the throat, breast, supercilia, cheeks, and upper tail coverts; tail black, the outer feathers more or less white tipped; wings brown; a range of minute white feathers beneath the eye, and the wing, flanks and sides of breast, with numerous round white spots, and a few smaller specks on the back; abdominal region infuscated; lower tail-coverts black.

Bill deep red, the upper mandible black above; irides crimson; feet fleshy. Length about 4 inches; wing $1\frac{3}{4}$; tail $1\frac{3}{8}$.

The female is olive-brown above, with the lores blackish, bounded by a whitish semi-circle below the eye; a few white specks occasionally on the back; rump and upper tail-coverts tinged with crimson; beneath paler brown, the abdomen strongly tinged with fulvous yellow; the lower tail-coverts dull white. The young is brown above, paler beneath, whitish on the throat and belly, tail blackish, and a few small white specks on the wings. After breeding the males assume, by moulting, a plumage similar to that of the female.

The Amaduvad (*par excellence*) is found throughout all India, more rare in the South, abundant in the North. In the south of India, I have seen it tolerably frequent on the lower hills of the Neilgherries, in Mysore, here and there throughout the Carnatic, but rare in the Deccan and the bare table-land generally. It is more common in Central India, and abundant in Oudh and in Lower Bengal, extending into the lower ranges of the Himalayas, as well as to Assam and Burmah.

It frequents bushy ground, gardens, and especially sugar-cane fields, and long grass, associating in large flocks, except towards the end of the rains, at which season it breeds. The nest is large, made of grass, and placed in a thick bush, or occasionally in long grass or reeds, and the eggs, six to eight in number, are very small, round, and white. This species moults twice a year, the male after breeding assuming the plumage of the female. Large numbers are taken in many parts of the country and caged. The male has a pleasant little song, and it is also said to fight with much spirit, for which purpose it is kept by the natives. The popular name of *Amaduvad* was originally applied to this species, and Mr. Blyth has shown that this word took its origin from the city of Ahmedabad, whence it used to be imported into Europe in numbers.

A nearly allied species, *E. punicea*, Horsfield, inhabits Java and other Malayan isles.

705. Estrelda formosa, LATHAM.

Fringilla, apud LATHAM—BLYTH, Cat. 638—*Harre lal*, II., or *Harre munia—i. e.*, the green Munia.

THE GREEN WAX-BILL.

Descr.—Above light olive-green, quills and tail dusky, the former edged with green; beneath very pale yellow, somewhat darker on the lower belly and under tail-coverts, and with broad transverse dashes of dusky on the flanks and sides of the abdomen.

Bill waxy red; feet plumbeous brown; irides pale brown. Length barely 4 inches; wing 1¾; tail 1¾.

This very pretty little bird is chiefly found in Central India. I have seen it in the jungles north of Nagpore, on the high land near Seonee, on the Pachmarri range of hills, rather abundant, and on the Vindhian range of hills near Mhow. It has also been found at Omerkantak, near the source of the Nerbudda, and in other parts of Central India, and I am told that it occurs in Oudh, and other parts of Northern India, in the Pindoon Dhoon according to Col. Tytler. It is occasionally caught and caged at Kamptee, Saugor, and Mhow. It associates in tolerably large flocks, with a low chirping note, and keeps much to the woods.

Blyth indicates, from a drawing, a plain colored species from Assam. This group is greatly developed in Africa. Among the Eastern species especially deserving notice here, is the very beautiful *Erythrura prasina*, from Sumatra and Java, with three or four allied species from the oceanic region; and there are one or two similarly colored Australian species, *viz. Poephila Gouldiæ*, and another, which resemble Parrots in the gaudiness of their plumage.

The remaining sub-families want the minute first primary of the two preceding groups.

2 z

Sub-fam. PASSERINÆ, Sparrows.

Bill stout and strong, somewhat tumid, slightly compressed towards the tip; the culmen broad, convex; commissure straight; wings moderate, the first three primaries about equal, the fourth nearly as long; tail moderate, nearly square, or very slightly forked; tarsus moderate; feet formed both for hopping on the ground and perching; lateral toes about equal.

The sparrows comprise a small group only found in the Old World, none occurring in America nor in Australia, and only one species is known in Malayana. They are social in their habits, and many species evince a marked predilection for the neighbourhood of man, even living in the midst of crowded cities. They breed either in suitable spots and nooks in buildings, or in holes of trees, and occasionally on trees. Their nests are a large loose mass of grass, or any soft material, usually copiously lined with feathers; and their eggs are white, speckled with dusky or olive brown. They chiefly live on grain, but will also eat insects, and many feed their young chiefly on the latter food. Their plumage is plain, usually more or less chesnut brown above, and the sexes differ in some species, but not in others.

Gen. PASSER, Brisson.

Syn. *Pyrgita*, Cuv. and Swainson.

Char.—Those of the family, of which it is the only genus.

There are several types of form and colour among the Sparrows, but none so well marked as to constitute a distinct genus.

Two species are found throughout the greater part of India, one affecting the neighbourhood of man, the other chiefly confined to open forests, or well wooded districts; and there are a few other species with a limited geographical distribution in India.

706. **Passer indicus**, JARD. and SELBY.

Ill. Orn., pl. 118—BLYTH, Cat. 642—HORSF., Cat. 761—P. domesticus, apud SYKES, Cat. 112—and JERDON, Cat. 176—*Gouriya*, H. in the North—*Churi* and *Khas churi*, H. in the South—*Charia* or *Chata*, Beng.—*Uri-pickike*, Tel.—*Adiki lam kuravi*, Tam.

THE INDIAN HOUSE SPARROW.

Descr.—Male, head above and nape dark grey ; a deep chesnut patch behind the eye, widening on the nape ; wing-coverts, scapulars, and mantle, dark chesnut, the scapulars and back with brown stripes or dashes ; a white band on the tip of the lesser coverts ; quills dusky, with their outer edges rufous, more broad on the secondaries, and tipped pale ; rump and upper tail-coverts ashy brown ; tail dusky, light-edged ; lores, round the eyes, and base of the bill, black ; chin, throat, and breast, black ; ear-coverts and sides of the neck white ; lower parts whitish, ashy on the sides of the breast and flanks.

Bill horny brown ; irides light brown ; legs dusky. Length $5\frac{1}{2}$ to 6 inches ; extent 9 ; wing 3 ; tail $2\frac{1}{4}$.

The female is light brown above, back and scapulars edged with pale rufous ; a pale eye-streak, and the lower parts sullied white ; slightly smaller than the male.

The common Sparrow of India differs very little from that of Europe, but most systematists agree in placing it as distinct. It chiefly differs from *P. domesticus* in the greater purity of its colours and in the female being somewhat paler. It is somewhat smaller too than its European congener, the black of the breast in the male is more extended laterally, and the cheeks and sides of the neck are purer white, as are the lower parts generally, these being distinctly ashy in the European bird.

This Sparrow is generally diffused over all India, from the extreme south and Ceylon, to the foot of the Himalayas, and eastwards to Assam, Arrakan, and Upper Pegu, and also to Siam, according to Crawford. It is less abundant on the Malabar Coast, and, generally, in the very rainy districts, and Quilon is said to be exempt from its society, as well as that of the common striped squirrel (*Sciurus palmarum*), two of the greatest pests of most other stations. It is not found at Darjeeling, but it occurs on the N. W. Himalayas up to a moderate height. Out of India we have no accurate record of its distribution, but it is said to occur in Afghanistan.

The Sparrow builds in thatched roofs, under the eaves of houses, and in similar concealed nooks and cavities, making a nest quite like that of the English bird, and the eggs also are very similar, and much varied in their markings. In various parts of India, and in Ceylon, the natives hang up earthern vessels on trees, and in verandahs, for this bird to build in, which it does very readily.

The note of this sparrow is quite like that of the European one, and, as it familiarly enters rooms (where, indeed, if allowed, it often breeds on the cornices of ceilings), it is quite a nuisance in many parts of the country, especially during the hot weather. I have frequently seen it chase and capture moths in a room.

707. Passer salicicolus, VIEILLOT.

Fringilla, apud VIEILLOT.—GOULD, Birds of Europe, pl. 185, f. 1 —BLYTH, Cat. 644—HORSF., Cat. 764—Fringilla hispaniolensis, TEMM.

THE WILLOW SPARROW.

Descr.—Male, head and back of neck dark chesnut, the feathers edged paler; the mantle blackish, with creamy-white edgings to the feathers; rump and upper tail-coverts pale brown; shoulder of wing chesnut, with white borders to the lesser coverts; the rest of the wing dusky, with broad pale rufous brown edgings, and a whitish bar, formed by the tips of the greater coverts; secondaries edged and tipped whitish; tail dusky with pale edging; lores, cheeks, and a narrow supercilium, white, passing into ashy brown on the ear-coverts; beneath, the chin, throat and breast, black, some of the feathers edged whitish; rest of the lower parts sullied white, the flanks and under tail-coverts with dusky longitudinal streaks.

Length 5¾ inches; wing 3; tail 2. The female resembles that of the common Sparrow, but the striation of the dorsal feathers is less strongly marked.

This Sparrow very closely resembles the last, chiefly differing in the back of the male more resembling that of the female of the common Sparrow, and in the black of the breast being less defined, and passing into dashes on the flanks. It has only occurred, within our limits, at Peshawar and Shikarpore; but it appears to be common further west, in Afghanistan. Out of India it is common in the north of Africa, spreading to the south of Europe and Western Asia. It is said to be common at Kandahar, and to build both in houses and on trees.

708. Passer cinnamomeus, GOULD.

Pyrgita, apud GOULD, P. Z. S. 1835—BLYTH, Cat. 645— HORSF., Cat. 762.

THE CINNAMON-HEADED SPARROW.

Descr.—Male, with the whole upper plumage, including the shoulder and fore part of the wings, bright cinnamon rufous, marked on the middle of the back with black streaks; a small white bar on the wing, formed by the tips of the lesser coverts; wings dusky, the feathers edged and tipped with pale brown; primaries pale brown at their base on the outer webs; plumage beneath, and cheeks, yellowish, with a tinge of grey, albescent towards the vent and under tail-coverts; chin and throat with a narrow central black patch.

The female is light brown above, with a pale supercilium, wants the black throat band, and is dingy brown beneath. Length 5¼ inches; wing 2⅔; tail barely 2.

This Sparrow is found chiefly in the N. W. Himalayas, but also occurs in Nepal, and even in Bootan, according to Horsfield. I never procured it in Sikhim, nor has Mr. Blyth seen specimens from Darjeeling or Nepal. Hutton says that it breeds at Mussooree, and that he suspected it to build in sheds, though he did not actually observe it to do so. It is chiefly a jungle bird, perhaps, and Adams records that it is common in Cashmere, and is seen in flocks, in wooded copses, and round hamlets. Its chirp is stated by Hutton to resemble that of the common Sparrow.

709. Passer pyrrhonotus, BLYTH.

J. A. S. XIII. 946—BLYTH, Cat. 643.

THE RUFOUS-BACKED SPARROW.

Descr.—Male above, head and ear-coverts grey, with a chesnut stripe from the eye to the nape; the rest of the plumage maronne, the feathers of the back centered dark ; wings and tail dusky, the feathers pale edged ; beneath sullied brownish-white ; throat black.

Length 5 inches ; wing 2⅔ ; tail 2.

This Sparrow differs from *P. indicus* by its smaller size ; the rump feathers are dull maronne instead of greyish brown ; and the black of the throat does not descend over the fore-neck and breast. The beak and feet too are conspicuously smaller. It has only been procured at Bahawulpore, in Sindh, and nothing is known of its habits. It appears much to resemble *P. rutilans* of Japan.

The female is at present unknown.

The next Sparrow is remarkable for both sexes being clad alike, in a plumage similar to that of the males of the previous species.

710. **Passer montanus**, LINNÆUS.

Fringilla, apud LINNÆUS—GOULD, Birds of Europe, pl. 184 f. 2—BLYTH, Cat.—647—HORSF., Cat. 763.

THE MOUNTAIN SPARROW.

Descr.—Head above and nape vinous chesnut ; the shoulders of the wings rich chesnut ; the back and wings rusty chesnut, with black streaks ; rump and upper tail-coverts unstriped yellowish-brown ; the quills dusky, edged with rufous, and with the outer webs, near their base, entirely so ; two whitish bars on the wings formed by the tips of the coverts ; tail dusky, narrowly edged with rufous ; the lores, a stripe below the eye, and the posterior edge of the ear-coverts, black, as are the chin and throat ; the anterior parts of the ear-coverts, and the sides of the neck extending towards the nape, white ; beneath pale ashy, albescent on the lower abdomen and under tail-coverts, and tinged with fulvous brown on the breast, flanks, and thigh-coverts.

Sexes alike. Length about 5 inches ; wing 2¾ ; tail 2.

The Mountain Sparrow is found, in India, only on the Himalayas, thence extending to the South-east throughout the hill ranges of Assam ; and finally in Burmah, from Ramree in Arrakan and

Upper Pegu, southwards to Singapore and Java, frequenting the plains, as well as the hills, and, in many places, it is the only species of Sparrow found.* It is also common in China, Afghanistan, and other parts of Asia, in the North of Africa, and all through Europe, being found in Britain, and as far north as Lapland and Siberia. Where it occurs in India, Burmah, in China, and most other Eastern countries, it replaces the common Sparrow, building about the roofs of verandahs and houses, and being quite as familiar as its better known representative, and, indeed, in Eastern Europe, it appears to have the same habits. I have seen it at Darjeeling, where it is the only Sparrow; at Thyet-myo, where it occurs along with *P. indicus* and *P. flaveolus*; and in Rangoon and Moulmein. Its voice is less harsh than that of the common Sparrow, and it is not nearly so noisy nor so troublesome as that bird.

Lesson, in Belanger's Voyage aux Indes Orientales, records a Sparrow from Southern India, said to inhabit the Coromandel Coast, and to be common in the neighbourhood of Pondicherry. I have never been able to procure it, nor do specimens exist in any of our Museums. Mr. Blyth suspects that it may be *P. italicus*; if so its locality is probably incorrectly given, but "more probably it refers to the common Indian Sparrow badly described." I give a brief description of it in case it should be recognised hereafter.

PASSER PYRRHOPTERUS, *Fringilla*, apud Lesson.

Size of the common Sparrow.—Head and neck spotless rufous brown; the mantle bright rufous, with black central streaks to the feathers; shoulder deep maronne, bordered by a small oblique white line; the middle wing-coverts black, edged with rufous and maronne, and the rest of the wing pale ashy externally, and brownish on the inner barbs of the feathers; under parts rufous grey; the throat reddish grey, with a black patch commencing on the lower part of the neck; bill and tarsi yellowish. Female grey brown, above silky brown with central streaks to the feathers; below of a blonde-grey throughout; wings ash grey, with a white ray on the shoulder, but no maronne."

---

* Blyth noticed that Burmese examples were more rufous above, and whiter beneath than birds from Sikim, which are identical with British specimens.

P. flaveolus, Blyth, I found common at *Thyet-myo*, in Upper Pegu, usually building on thorny trees, but occasionally in verandahs. *P. jugiferus*, Temm., from the Philippines, is recorded by Bonaparte.

The only other Sparrows of Europe and Asia not previously alluded to are *P. italicus*, Degland (*cisalpinus*, Temm.), of S. Europe and North Africa; and *P. jagoensis*, Gould, from the Cape de Verde Islands. There are several others from Africa.

The next species has been classed as a *Ploceus* by Sykes, and Hodgson makes it the type of his genus *Gymnoris*, but it scarcely differs, except in its mode of coloration, from some of the preceding Sparrows.

711. **Passer flavicollis,** FRANKLIN.

Fringilla, apud FRANKLIN—BLYTH, Cat. 649—HORSF., Cat. 759—JERDON, Cat. 177—SYKES, Cat 107—*Raji*, H., vulgo *Jangli churi—Adari pichike*, also *Konde pichike*, and *Cheruku pichike*, Tel.

THE YELLOW-NECKED SPARROW.

Descr.—Above ashy brown, beneath dirty or brownish white, more albescent on the vent and under tail-coverts, and white on the chin; a yellow spot on the middle of the throat; shoulders and lesser-coverts chesnut; wings with some white marks on the tertiaries, and two white bands formed by the tips of the coverts.

The female merely differs in the yellow neck-spot, and the chesnut on the wings, being paler than in the male.

Bill black; irides brown; legs cinereous brown. Length $5\frac{1}{2}$ inches; extent 10; wing $3\frac{1}{10}$; tail 2; tarsus $\frac{7}{10}$.

The yellow-necked Sparrow is found over the greater part of India, but does not appear to occur in Lower Bengal, nor in the countries to the eastward; and it does not ascend the Himalayas to any height. It has not yet been observed in Ceylon.

It frequents thin forest jungle; also groves of trees, avenues, and gardens, in the better wooded parts of the country. It lives in small parties, occasionally, during the cold weather, congregating in very large flocks; feeds on various seeds, grains, and flower-buds, and has much the same manners and habits as the common house-sparrow. It has also a very similar note. It breeds in holes in trees, and in some parts of the country, in the roofs of houses, in the hollow bamboos of the roof, and, occasionally, in pots hung out for the purpose. The eggs are three or four, greenish white, much streaked and blotched with purplish brown.

Two allied species are *P. petronius*, Linn. of S. Europe and Afghanistan, which may occur in the extreme N. W. of India; and *P. superciliaris*, A. Hay, from Africa, both of which have the yellow throat spot.

Sub-fam. EMBERIZINÆ, Buntings.

Bill with the upper mandible typically smaller and more compressed than the lower, which is broader, equal in a few; a palatal protuberance in many; commissure usually sinuate; tail moderate, even or emarginate.

The Buntings form a considerable group of birds found in all parts of the world, except in Australia, more abundant in temperate than in tropical climes. Some have unequal mandibles, the upper one small, and furnished internally with a palatal knob or protuberance; whilst others have the mandibles nearly equal, and no trace of the palatal knob. The ridge of the upper mandible is usually straight, or nearly so, and the margins of both are more or less inflected. The legs are of moderate length, and the claws slender. They are not remarkable for beauty of plumage or rich colours; several have more or less yellow, and the head is often marked with supercilia or medial coronal stripes. A few are crested; and, in general, the males are brighter coloured than the females. They do not appear, as a rule, to have a vernal moult, but, in winter, the colours of some are less pure, having pale edges, which wear off towards summer; and a few do put on a richer plumage in spring. They are more or less terrestrial in their habits, and build their nests in low bushes, or in tufts of grass. These are neat, cup-shaped, and the eggs are marked with spots and irregular streaks or dashes. The young are said to be fed chiefly on insects. Some species, in winter, collect in huge flocks and migrate. They have little or no song in general, and are less noisy than many other *Fringillidæ*. They form, with two exceptions, a very inconspicuous part of the Indian Fauna, none of them being permanent residents. Three or four are winter visitants to the plains; and the remainder are almost confined to the Himalayas and adjacent districts, one or two species only occurring in Assam, Burmah, and the countries to the East, and none aparently visiting the Malayan isles. They have been sub-divided into several groups, which however are not very strongly characterized, except in the case of certain American Buntings. They approximate some of the *Fringillinæ*; and the Snow Buntings, by their long hind claw, approach the Larks; but these are by Blyth referred to the *Fringillinæ*. The Indian Buntings may be referred to three groups: the true Buntings; the yellow Corn-Buntings, or *Gundams* of India; and the crested Buntings.

1st. True Buntings.

Gen. EMBERIZA.

Bill of varied strength, and the mandibles more or less unequal, usually somewhat lengthened; wings moderate or rather long, with the 1st quill a little shorter than the second and third, which are longest; tail of moderate length; the outermost feathers more or less marked with white.

The first on the list are the most typical Buntings, to which the yellow ammer of England belongs. They are the restricted *Emberiza* of some.

712. Emberiza pithyornis, PALLAS.

GOULD, Birds of Europe, pl. 180—HORSF., Cat. 728—E. albida, BLYTH, J. A. S. XVIII., and Cat. 705—E. leucocephala and E. dalmatica, GMELIN.

THE WHITE-CROWNED BUNTING.

Descr.—Top of the head white in the male, greyish in the female; upper parts rufescent brown, with central dark-brown streaks, nearly wanting on the back of the neck; rump and upper tail-coverts cinnamon-rufous, edged with pale brownish; wings and tail dusky brown, edged yellowish, and the two outer tail-feathers with a patch of white on the inner web, largest on the outer feathers; beneath, the chin, throat, and a moustachial line, are dark rufous with pale edgings, and there is a triangular patch of white on the middle of the throat; ear-coverts pale brown; breast and sides of abdomen rufous, with pale edgings, and the middle of abdomen, of vent, and the lower tail-coverts white with a few streaks.

Length 6 to 6½ inches; wing 3½; tail 3; tarsus ¾.

This is a typical Bunting, very like *E. citrinella*, but the yellow replaced by white. It has been only found, in India, in the N. W. Himalayas. Hutton found it on the Tyne range, beyond Simla, and Dr. Adams in the same locality; and it has also been procured near Peshawur. It is a native of Siberia and Northern Asia, in summer, occasionally straggling into Eastern Europe.

The next birds have the bill weaker, with the mandibles less unequal, and the palatal knob smaller. They constitute Kaup's genus *Cia*.

713. **Emberiza cia,** LINNÆUS.

GOULD, Birds of Europe, pl. 179—BLYTH, Cat 719—HORSF., Cat. 729.

THE WHITE-BROWED BUNTING.

Descr.—Above rufescent brown with black central streaks, brighter on the rump and tail-coverts, which are unstreaked; crown black, with a pale median line, and a broad white supercilium; a black line through the eye round the pale ear-coverts, meeting another, from the base of the lower mandible; cheeks and chin greyish white, passing into pale ash grey in the neck, throat, and breast, with obsolete dusky spots on the front of the neck; the rest beneath ruddy brown; wings dusky, edged rufescent; the two outer tail-feathers chiefly white.

Bill dusky plumbeous; legs light fleshy yellow. Length 6¾ to 7 inches; wing 3½; tail 3¼; tarsus ¾.

The female has the head and lower parts more weakly and dully colored than in the male; the crown and breast are more or less streaked and spotted with dusky; and, in some, there is scarcely a trace of grey on the crown. In winter the colors are less pure; with somewhat rufous edgings to the coronal feathers, and a tinge of the same on the grey neck.

This well known European Bunting has been killed near Simla, and appears not very rare in the N. W. Himalayas. It extends throughout most of Western and Northern Asia. It is said to nestle in low bushes, and the eggs are whitish, with delicate black lines.

714. Emberiza Stracheyi, MOORE.

P. Z. S. 1855, pl. 112—HORSF., Cat. 730—BLYTH, Cat. p. 337.

THE WHITE-NECKED BUNTING.

Descr.—Allied to *E. cia*; differs in having the markings about the head more broadly developed, and of a deeper black colour, and forming three well defined black bars, as seen laterally; in the throat and sides of the neck being whiter, and ashy on the front of the neck only; the breast, and the rest of the under parts being uniform bright rufous-brown, which colour is also prominent on the back, and especially on the scapulars, rump, and upper tail-coverts.

Length about 6 inches; wing $3\frac{1}{4}$; tail 3; tarsus $\frac{3}{4}$.

This species has been killed in Kumaon. The chief differences from *cia*, are the whiter chin and throat.

EMBERIZA CIOIDES, Temm., is recorded by Adams to be common in the lower ranges of the N. W. Himalayas. It is said to differ from *E. cia*, by the shorter wing and more distinct markings. Adams' Bird, is probably the same as the last bird; but Temminck's species was originally described from Japan, is said to occur in China, and may also be found in the Himalayas.

The next group is that of the European Ortolan, and some nearly affined species of Northern India, and probably of Central Asia, which differ by a peculiar mode of coloration, and, in their structure, approach the African group named *Fringillaria*. They are the *Glycyspiza*, of Kaup. There is considerable confusion about the first two species, and I shall follow Horsfield's nomenclature here, as there are not sufficient materials at my disposal for a thorough examination of these birds.

715. Emberiza hortulana, LINNÆUS.

GOULD, Birds of Europe, pl. 176—BLYTH, Cat. 715—HORSF., Cat. 734—E. Buchanani, BLYTH, J. A. S. XIII. 957 (not XVI. 780)—*Jamjohara*, Hind.

THE ORTOLAN BUNTING.

Descr.—Whole head, neck, and breast, grey, with a green cast; a pale yellow streak from the base of lower mandible, and a broad central stripe of the same colour down the chin and throat; upper parts rufescent brown, with dark central streaks ; wings and tail dingy brown, pale edged ; the outer tail-feathers with a large patch of white on the inner web ; beneath, from the breast, ferruginous, paling posteriorly.

Bill reddish ; feet fleshy yellow. Length $5\frac{3}{4}$ to 6 inches ; wing $3\frac{1}{4}$; tail $2\frac{1}{8}$.

The Ortolan of Europe, considered by Horsfield identical with Blyth's species, formerly named by him *E. Buchanani*, is recorded to have been occasionally found in Western India. It is well known in the south of Europe, where they are caught in great numbers, fattened for the table, and considered a great delicacy. In India the social lark (*calandrella brachydactyla*) and the *Pyrrhulauda grisea* are popularly called Ortolans.

The next bird has the bill somewhat stouter and larger.

716. Emberiza Huttoni, BLYTH.

J. A. S., XVIII., 811—HORSF., Cat. 735—E. Buchanani, BLYTH, J. A. S., XVI., 780.

THE GREY-NECKED BUNTING.

Descr.—Nearly allied to *E. hortulana*, but differing in colour, having the head, neck, throat, and interscapularies, greyish, without marks, but a few traces of striation on the lower part of the back ; orbital feathers whitish ; scapularies, forepart of wing, and margins of the coverts and tertiaries of the same pale rufous buff as the entire lower parts, from the breast inclusive, which is similar to that of the abdominal region, only, of *E. hortulana*.

Bill reddish ; feet pale fleshy brown. Length 6 inches ; wing $3\frac{1}{2}$; tail 3 ; tarsus $\frac{3}{4}$.

From the N. W. Himalayas; found in winter in flocks near shingly and stony hills. Hutton found it at Candahar in summer. It does not appear certain whether this, or the preceding species, is Sykes' *E. hortulana*, Cat. 102 ; no specimen of which appears to exist in the Museum E. I. C. H., but it was most probably this

species, or perhaps *E. fucata*. Mr. Blyth states that I sent a specimen of the present bird to him as my No. 181, which I must have
confounded with that species. If this was the case, it makes it
more probable that the present was Sykes' Ortolan, and in this case
it is probably a rare straggler into Western India.

In the next three the bill is still smaller and more compressed.

717. Emberiza spodocephala, PALLAS.

E. melanops, BLYTH, J. A. S. XIV. 554, and Cat. 716—E.
chlorocephala of Nepal, J. A. S. XV. 39—E. personata, TEMM.
P. C. 580 ?

THE BLACK-FACED BUNTING.

Descr.—Head, neck, and breast, dull green, faintly streaked with
dusky on the crown ; lores, chin, and feathers at the base of the lower
mandible, black ; belly and lower tail-coverts sulphur yellow ; flanks
greenish, with dusky streaks ; scapulars and interscapulars greenish
rufescent, black streaked ; wings blackish, edged rufescent ; rump
plain rufescent-greenish ; tail dusky, outer feathers, with the terminal two-thirds white, also about a third of the inner web of the
next one.

Bill dusky, lower mandible whitish ; legs pale.   Length 6
inches ; wing $2\frac{7}{8}$; tail $2\frac{5}{8}$; bill at front $\frac{7}{16}$; tarsus $\frac{3}{4}$.

This Bunting has been found rarely in Nepal, and extending
through the hill ranges of Assam and Sylhet into Tipperah.   It
appears to correspond better to the description of Pallas' *spodo-
cephala* than to *personata*, which has the whole under parts yellow,
but they are perhaps the same bird.   The former is said to be an
inhabitant of Northern Asia, the latter of Japan, and Swinhoe says
that *E. personata* is the commonest winter Bunting in China.

718. Emberiza Stewarti, BLYTH.

J. A. S. XXIII. 215—E. caniceps, GOULD, Birds of Asia,
pt. VI., pl. 16—HORSF., Cat. 736.

THE WHITE-CAPPED BUNTING.

Descr.—Male, crown greyish-white ; lores, a broad line passing
over the eye to the nape, and the throat, black ; cheeks and
ear-coverts white ; back, scapularies, rump, and upper tail-coverts,

deep reddish-chesnut; wing-coverts dark brown, edged with buffy brown; wings brown, narrowly edged with greyish white; the central tail feathers blackish brown; the two outer on each side blackish brown at the base, and white for the remainder of their length, with the exception of the outer web, which is brown; the whole under surface creamy white, crossed on the chest by a broad band of lively chesnut red.

Bill and feet fleshy brown. Length 6 inches; wing $3\frac{1}{8}$; tail $2\frac{3}{4}$; tarsus $\frac{7}{10}$.

The female has the whole upper surface, wings, and tail, pale olive-brown, with a streak of dark brown down the centre of each feather; a slight tinge of rufous on the upper tail-coverts; under surface pale buffy brown, streaked with dark brown.

This Bunting is said by Adams to be common in Cashmere in fields, near the mountains, with the habits of the yellow Bunting. It was also found by Dr. Royle in the N. W. Himalayas, and in the Salt range of the Punjab by Stewart.

719. Emberiza fucata, PALLAS.

PALLAS, Zoog. Ross. As. pl. 46—GOULD, Birds of Europe, pl. 178—BLYTH, Cat. 717—HORSF., Cat. 741—E. lesbia, apud TEMMINCK—E. cia, apud JERDON, Cat. 181—Putthur-chirta, H.

THE GREY-HEADED BUNTING.

Descr.—Above, head and neck darkish grey, with some darker mesial streaks; scapulars, back, and rump, deep rufous or rufescent brown, also streaked with black, except on the rump and upper tail-coverts; ear-coverts deep rufous; a whitish supercilium; wings and tail dark brown, broadly edged with reddish fawn colour; and the outer feathers of the tail partly white on their inner webs; throat, foreneck, and breast, greyish white; a narrow black streak from each corner of the gape, widening as it descends, and forming a gorget with the opposite one; below this white; then an interrupted pectoral band of rufous; and the belly whitish, tinged with rufous on the flanks, and sides of vent.

Bill dusky reddish; feet dirty yellow; irides dark brown. Length $6\frac{1}{2}$ inches; wing $3\frac{1}{2}$; extent 10; tail $2\frac{1}{2}$; tarsus $\frac{16}{20}$; bill at front barely $\frac{4}{10}$.

In some specimens the pectoral band is more or less imperfect, consisting chiefly of spots, and the sides of the abdomen are streaked with brown. In the cold weather the majority of birds want the mesial streaks to the feathers of the back, the black lines from the gape, and the black pectoral band; and the lower parts are uniformly whitish-cinereous, tinged with rufous on the throat and breast, and passing into reddish-white or fulvous posteriorly. The ashy of the head and neck, too, has a fulvous tinge. The female is said by Blyth to want the cinnamon-colored band, and the colours to be generally duller.

This Bunting appears to be spread sparingly through Northern and Central India, in the cold weather. It has been found in Bengal, near Calcutta occasionally, in some seasons occurring rather plentifully; also in Nepal, and the Dehra Dhoon; and not uncommon about Simla and Mussooree. I have seen it at Jalna in the Deccan, at Mhow and Saugor, and also near Nagpore. In most of these cases it was frequenting rocky and bushy hills in small parties; and I occasionally saw it in the fields, near hedges and trees. Its Hindustani name, which means stone-grazer, is given from being seen so much about rocks and stones; and I see that Buch. Hamilton applies the same name to another Bunting. Out of India it appears to be an inhabitant of Central Asia, visiting the south of Europe occasionally, and common in Greece and the Crimea. Swinhoe records it as frequenting standing cornfields in China.

The next bird, the last of our true Buntings, differs somewhat from the others, and has received distinct generic rank from Hodgson. It has the bill very acute and perfectly conic, culmen and gonys being equally straight, and there is no palatal knob. It somewhat resembles *Emb. schœniclus*, of Europe, the type of *Cynchramus*, Kaup.

720. Emberiza pusilla, PALLAS.

Zool. Ross. Asiat. 2, pl. 47, f. 1.—E. sordida, HODGS., J. A. S. XIII. p. 958.—Ocyris oinopus, HODGSON.—BLYTH, Cat. 718—HORSF., Cat. 742.

The Dwarf Bunting.

Descr.—Male, above streaked with black, rufous, and grey-brown, most rufous on the back and scapulars, supercilium pale rufescent, with a broad black line above; ears, and spot on the nape, rufous; wings dusky, edged with ruddy olive; tail dusky, with a broad oblique white line on the outer feathers, and a narrower one on the penultimate; beneath, whitish, with a dusky throat-band, dusky streaks on the breast and flanks, and two dusky lines on the chin, which meet the throat-band.

Bill horny; legs pale fleshy brown; irides brown. Length 5¼ inches; wing 2¾; tail 2¼; bill at front ¾; tarsus ⅚. The female is dull olive greenish, with a rufous tinge; wing-coverts tipped whitish; beneath whitish-yellow, sullied on the breast, and streaked on the flanks and sides of the foreneck.

This small Bunting is found throughout the whole extent of the Himalayas, during the winter. I procured it at Darjeeling; Hodgson in Nepal; and Adams in the N. W. It frequents bare spots of ground with low bushes, in small flocks. Adams says that it has the habits of a Redpole. Quite recently I shot one near Kolassee, in the Purneah district, frequenting grass and bushes near a small river, and, as it is not a bird likely to be remarked, it will probably be found in similar places throughout the plains in the North of India, during the cold weather.

It is an inhabitant, in summer, of Northern and Central Asia, and has been killed in Europe. Swinhoe saw it in occasional flocks in China, during winter.

2nd.—Yellow Corn-buntings.

Gen. EUSPIZA, Bonap.

Char.—Bill strong, sub-conic, with the mandibles about equal, and scarcely a trace of a palatal knob; wings and tail rather long, firm.

These Buntings visit various parts of India in large flocks, during the winter, and are very destructive to the crops of grain. The two most typical species have no white on the outer tail-feathers.

3 B

721. Euspiza melanocephala, GMELIN.

Emberiza, apud GMELIN—SYKES, Cat. 101—JERDON, Cat.
179—GOULD, Birds of Europe, pl. 172—E. simillima, BLYTH,
J. A. S. XVIII. 811—BLYTH, Cat. 708 and 709—HORSF., Cat.
737—*Gandam*, H.

THE BLACK-HEADED BUNTING.

Descr.—Whole head, including the ear-coverts, black, the
feathers generally (*i. e.* in winter) edged light brown, this disappearing towards spring ; back and scapulars rich chesnut,
passing to yellowish on the rump and upper tail-covert, the
feathers being edged with bright yellow ; wings and tail brown,
with pale edgings to all the feathers; beneath, from the chin to the
vent, bright yellow, passing behind the ear-coverts to the nape;
the side of breast chesnut, continuous with the color of the back.

Length $7\frac{1}{2}$ to 8 inches ; wing $3\frac{8}{10}$ to 4 ; tail 3 ; bill at front $\frac{5}{10}$;
tarsus $\frac{9}{10}$.

The black-headed Bunting is found in India, only in the
North-western Provinces, most abundant in the Deccan, and
thence extending to the Upper Provinces of Hindustan. It makes
its appearance in the Deccan usually about the end of November;
is found in immense flocks, and is very destructive to the crops
of Jowaree, and other grains. It leaves early in March, and
certainly does not breed in any part of India. It is a well known
bird in Asia Minor, and the South-east of Europe, and is
occasionally killed in France and Germany. Tristram states that
it breeds in Corfu, frequenting brushwood on hill sides, and has
an agreeable song. Drummond remarks that it builds often in the
stump of an old vine, and that, in Crete, they seem to be confined
to certain localities where they breed.

Blyth was misled by a small specimen to separate it from the
European species, and Horsfield has followed Blyth in making it
distinct. This latter naturalist now admits its identity with the
European bird.

722. Euspiza luteola, SPARRMAN.

BLYTH, Cat. 710—HORSF., Cat. 738—E. icterica, EVERS-
Gen. Bir ds, pl. 91—E. brunniceps, BRANDT—E.

personata, apud BLYTH (olim)--*Gandam*, H. in Central India.
—*Dalchidi*, Sindh—*Pacha jinuwayi*, Tel.

THE RED-HEADED BUNTING.

Descr.—The whole head, neck, and breast, rich chesnut; back
and scapulars yellowish or greenish-yellow, with dark brown
striæ; rump and upper tail-coverts deep yellow, faintly streaked;
quills and tail brown, the coverts and secondaries broadly edged
with pale whity-brown; quills and rectrices narrowly edged with
the same; beneath, from the breast, including the sides of the
neck, rich yellow.

Bill pale fleshy yellow; legs brown; irides brown. Length
nearly 7 inches; wing 3½; tail barely 3.

The young, and perhaps the females also, want the rich chesnut
head and breast of the adult male; the general colour is brownish
above, fulvous beneath, passing to yellowish on the rump, and on
both upper and lower tail-coverts.

The Red-headed Bunting is found in various parts of India, but
locally distributed. Beginning from the South, I have seen it
rarely in Coimbatore, in Mysore, Cuddapah, and the edges of the
Eastern Ghats. Mr. Elliot obtained it abundant at Dharwar; I
saw it near Nagpore, and tolerably abundant at Mhow and Saugor;
but I never obtained it, nor saw it, that I am aware of, among
the thousands of *E. melanocephala*, that yearly visit the corn-fields
about Jalna. Mr. Blyth has obtained it from Central India,
and from the Upper Provinces, and it occurs also in Scinde and
the Punjab, during the harvest season, but never in the Himalayas.
Out of India it has been found in Affghanistan and other parts of
Central Asia, but not in Western Asia, nor in Europe. Like the
last, it is only a cold weather visitant to India, but does not, in
general, appear in the vast numbers that *E. melanocephala* does in
the Deccan; yet I have observed considerable flocks near Saugor,
and seen them netted there. This Bunting prefers cultivated
land, with bush jungle near, to which it can retreat during the
middle of the day, and it is also frequently seen about hedges.

It appears to breed in Affghanistan, for Hutton says—It arrives
at Candahar the beginning of April, and departs in autumn. Adams
states that it has a sweet and melodious song.

The next species differs from the type of the preceding two by having the outer tail-feathers marked conspicuously with white, and perhaps might be ranked with the true Buntings; but, in its mode of coloration, and its more extensive migrations, as well as in the strong beak, it resembles the last two, which it thus appears to represent in Eastern India. Horsfield and Bonaparte both class it in *Euspiza*; Cabanis separates it as *Hypocentor*.

723. Euspiza aureola, PALLAS.

Emberiza, apud PALLAS, Zoog. Ross. As. pl. 50—GOULD, Birds of Europe, pl. 174—BLYTH, Cat. 711—E. flavogularis, McLELLAND, P. Z. S. 1839—BLYTH, Cat. 712, the female—Passerina collaris, VIEILLOT.

THE BROWN-HEADED BUNTING.

Descr.—In winter plumage, above dark maronne-brown, blackish on the head and interscapulars; the feathers edged lighter on the back, rump, wings, and tail; ear-coverts mixed yellow and grey; eyebrow, chin, throat, breast, and belly yellow; primaries, and tail, dark brown; a large white spot on the lesser wing-coverts, and a white edging to the lower wing-coverts; the two outer tail-feathers, with a wide oblique patch of white, occupying the greater part of feathers; the next with a narrow patch on the inner web close to the shaft. In summer there is a dark brown collar round the throat and upper part of the breast, and the flanks are brownish; the forehead, face, ear-coverts and chin also become black.

The female is light rufescent-brown above, the eye-brows and plumage beneath fulvous yellow, paling posteriorly.

Length about 6 inches; wing 3½; tail 2½.

This Bunting, an inhabitant of Siberia and Central Asia, in winter straggles sparingly into Nepal and the S. E. Himalayas, but is more abundant in Assam, Tippera, and Burmah. It avoids Bengal and the plains of India. It is occasionally found in Europe. Swinhoe found it in China in flocks, in autumn, feeding on the ripening corn.

Emb. rutila, Pallas, of Northern Asia, was lately found by Mr. Blanford in Upper Burmah; and these two appear to be the only Buntings found in Burmah.

3rd.—Crested Buntings.

The next and last Bunting differs remarkably in its black plumage, and crested head.

Gen. MELOPHUS, Swainson.

Char.—Bill compressed, with the upper mandible slightly notched near the tip; wings rather short; tail even; hind claw slightly lengthened; head with an erectile frontal crest; otherwise as in *Euspiza.*

This genus differs but slightly in structure from *Euspiza*, but the coloration is so remarkable, that I shall here keep it as a distinct type. In its habits, too, it differs, never associating in large flocks, and chiefly frequenting hills and ravines. Bonaparte places it among the crested Buntings of America, as does Gray in his List of Genera.

724. **Melophus melanicterus**, GMELIN.

Fringilla, apud GMELIN—JERDON, 2nd Suppl. Cat. 182—HORSF., Cat. 743—Euspiza Lathami, GRAY—BLYTH, Cat. 713—Emb. cristata, VIGORS, P. Z. S., 1831—SYKES, Cat. 103—E. subcristata, SYKES, Cat. 104 (the female)—E. erythroptera, JARD. and SELBY, Ill. Orn. pl. 132—E. nipalensis, HODGSON—*Pathar chirta*, H.

THE CRESTED BLACK BUNTING.

Descr.—Male—The whole body, with crest, glossy blue black; wings and tail dark cinnamon, with dusky tips; tail-coverts at their base black and cinnamon.

Bill fleshy brown; legs red brown; irides dark brown. Length $6\frac{1}{2}$ inches; extent 10; wing $3\frac{1}{4}$; tail $2\frac{3}{4}$.

The female is dusky brown above, the feathers edged light olive brownish; beneath rufescent white, or pale brownish fulvescent, with dusky streaks; quills and tail dull and paler cinnamon than in the male, dusky internally, and on the central tail feathers. She is a little smaller, and the crest not so highly developed.

The Crested Black Bunting is found on the Himalayas, extending into Central and Southern India. I have seen it at Mhow, among the Vindhian Hills; at Saugor, and on the banks of the

Nerbuddah ; also in the Nagpore country. Sykes obtained it in
the Deccan, where he found it on rocky and bushy mountains.   I
found it in similar places at Mhow and Saugor, but also occasionally on hedges and trees near cultivation, not far, however, from
hilly ground.   Hodgson found it on hedgerows and brushwood
on the upland downs in winter ; resorting in summer to the
Northern region, and it is said to be common near Simla and
Mussooree.   It does not, I believe, breed in the plains of
India.

It also inhabits Central Asia and China, and it is figured in Buffon,
Pl. Enl. pl. 224, f. 1 as '' Le Moineau de Macao.'' Swinhoe states
that a few couple only breed in China, but that it is common
in winter. I have had it caged, and it has a rather pleasant
chirping song.

Many other Buntings are found in Central and Northern Asia,
and Europe, but none in the Malayan region. Among them
may be noticed the *E. citrinella* (the yellow ammer), *E. miliaria,
E. provincialis, E. lesbia, E. cirlus, E. schœniclus, and E. pyrrhuloides,* all from Europe ; the two last constituting the *Schœniclus*
of Bonap., or *Cynchramus* of Kaup.

Asia possesses in addition *E. cinerea*, Strickl., and *E. shah,*
Bonap., from Western Asia, *E. elegans*, T., *E. chrysophrys*, Pall.,
E. sulphurata, T., *E. cioides*, Brandt, (not of Temm.,) and *E. rustica,*
Pallas, from Japan and Northern Asia.   Gould has *E. castaniceps,*
and Swinhoe *E. canescens*, both from China.   The African Buntings
are classed under *Fringillaria ;* and the American Buntings form
several natural groups, very distinct from those of the Old
World, and which appear to grade into the *Tanagers.* One
species, the *Gubernatrix cristatella,* a beautiful crested bird, from
South America, deserves especial notice.

The long-clawed or Lark-heeled Buntings, forming the genus
Plectrophanes, Meyer, are peculiar to the Northern portions of
both Continents, and evidently grade into the Larks.

The Tanagers, TANAGRINÆ, are a very numerous group, almost
confined to South America and the more southern part of Central
America. They are very richly colored, and, in general, have
a notch on the upper mandible, from which Cuvier placed them in

the *Dentirostres.* The bill is more or less triangular at the base, and the culmen more or less arched. They feed on fruit and insects, build slight nests on trees, and many have a pleasing song. Sclater has published a valuable Monograph of this family, describing many new species. They may be said to stand in the same relation to the rest of the *Conirostres,* that the *Ampelidæ* do towards the *Dentirostres;* and, indeed, some naturalists hint that the *Sylvicolinæ,* part of our *Ampelidæ,* join the Tanagers (*vide* p. 289).

Sub-fam. FRINGILLINÆ.

Bill varied in size and form, more or less conical and thick, short and bulged in some, slender and more elongate in others; wing moderate or long, 1st primary wanting.

The Finches, as here recognised, constitute an extensive series of birds of considerable variation as regards the form and size of the bill. They are chiefly seed-eaters, cracking small seeds between their mandibles, and rejecting the husk by the joint action of the mandibles and the tongue.

The male is, in general, more brightly colored than the female, and becomes still more so in the breeding season, not by a fresh moult in all, but chiefly by the shedding of the deciduary margins to the feathers, in some, perhaps, by a change of colour in the feathers themselves. The bill, too, of many becomes darker at this season. Many are colored more or less red, a few yellow.

The young of most are fed with vegetable food, not with insects, as in the Sparrows and Buntings. Many sing pleasingly, and they have a peculiar call note. They are more or less gregarious in winter. The nest is generally neatly made, and the eggs are mostly white, with brown spots and dots, never lined as in the Buntings. They are, with a very few exceptions, confined to the temperate and colder regions of the Northern hemisphere; and, in India, with one exception, are confined to the Himalayan region, and in many instances only wintering there.

They may be divided into the following groups, distinguished chiefly by the form of their bill, and mode of coloration, but they intergrade much with each other.

1st. —Grosbeaks ; 2nd.—Bull-finches ; 3rd.—Cross-bills ; 4th.— Rose finches ; 5th.—True Finches.

Bonaparte classes them in *Fringillinæ* and *Loxiinæ*, placing the Grosbeaks, true Finches,and Bull-finches in the former ; while the Cross-bills and Rose-finches, with the Linnets, and the Mountain-finches are classed among the latter.

1st.—Grosbeaks—*Coccothraustinæ* of some.

In these the bill is very large, thick, and conical ; the wings rather long, and the tail somewhat short ; the legs are stout and strongly scutate ; and they comprise the giants of the Finch tribe. They frequent forests, and live chiefly on stony fruit, which they crush with their powerful mandibles. There are only a few species, spread over Europe, Asia, and North America ; and, of these, four species are found in the Himalayas, belonging to two genera.

Gen. HESPERIPHONA, Bonap.

Char.—Bill conic, thick, half as long again as deep, slightly tumid for the basal two-thirds, with the tip of the upper mandible bent a little over that of the lower ; wings with the 2nd, 3rd, and 4th quills sub-equal, 1st rather shorter ; tail rather long, even or sub-furcate.

This genus was founded on a bird from North America, and has a somewhat elongated form compared with other large Grosbeaks. The males are black and yellow, and the females duller. There are two species in the Himalayas.

725. Hesperiphona icterioides, VIGORS.

Coccothraustes, apud VIGORS—GOULD, Cent. Him. Birds, pl. 45—Birds of Asia, pt. III, pl. 13—BLYTH, Cat. 687— HORSF., Cat. 697.

THE BLACK AND YELLOW GROSBEAK.

Descr.—Male, with the head and neck, wings, thigh-coverts, the extreme tail-coverts, and tail, black ; the rest of the plumage rich yellow, inclining to orange on the nape, and paler beneath.

The female is dull olivaceous grey, with the back and rump tinged with fulvous, and the abdomen and under tail-coverts more strongly fulvous, or rusty yellow ; quills and tail black.

Bill yellow; legs fleshy. Length 9 inches; wing $5\frac{1}{4}$; tail nearly 4; bill at front 1. The female is a little smaller.

This handsome Grosbeak has only been found in the N. W. Himalayas, extending into part of Nepal, but it is unknown further East. Hutton says that it is only found in the interior of the hills. Adams states that it haunts the Pine-forests of Cashmere in small flocks, and that its call-note is loud and plaintive.

726. Hesperiphona affinis, BLYTH.

J. A. S. XXIV. p. 179.

THE ALLIED GROSBEAK.

Descr.—Very nearly allied to the last species. Differs in the male having the black portion of its plumage deep and shining instead of dull ashy, black; the black of the head extends somewhat lower down, and the interscapulars and axillaries are also black, and the tibial feathers are yellow, whilst in *icterioides*, the reverse is the case. The female differs more, having the upper parts olive-green, tinged with yellowish on the collar and rump, and more brightly so on the lower plumage; wings and tail black; the coverts, secondaries, and tertiaries broadly margined externally with yellow green; the crown and ear-coverts ashy, passing into pale grey on the chin and throat.

Bill bluish in winter, yellow in summer; feet fleshy yellow. Length not quite 9 inches; wing $4\frac{3}{4}$; tail $3\frac{1}{2}$.

This is a somewhat smaller species than the last, with a slightly smaller bill; the males resemble each other very closely, but the females are very distinct. It has only hitherto been sent from the extreme North-west, *viz.*, the Alpine Punjab.

One or two species of this genus, found in North America, are said by Bonaparte to differ in their somewhat longer wings.

Gen. MYCEROBAS, Caban.

Syn. *Strobilophaga*, Hodgson.

Char.—Bill enormous, very thick, as deep as long, very nearly conic; the upper mandible compressed, and slightly bent over, with a sort of tooth at its base; commissure sinuate; wings rather

long, with the first three primaries nearly equal, the second slightly
longest; tail moderate, emarginate.

In this genus, the plumage of both sexes is black and yellow,
but the coloring differently disposed to what it was in the last.
Mr. Blyth remarks that the typical species manifests a very
remarkable affinity with the diminutive and slender-billed Siskins
of this sub-family, both in plumage and structure of wings and
tail.

727. Mycerobas melanoxanthos, HODGSON.

Coccothraustes, apud HODGSON—GOULD, Birds of Asia, pt.
III. pl. 11—BLYTH, Cat. 685—HORSF., Cat. 695—C. fortirostris,
LAFRESN.—*Maltam-pho*, Lepch.

THE SPOTTED-WINGED GROSBEAK.

Descr.—Male, with the entire parts above, including the head
and neck, dull slaty black; beneath siskin yellow; the base of the
primaries, excepting the first three or four, pure white, forming a
conspicuous spot; some of the greater coverts, the shorter primaries, and the secondaries and tertiaries, with an oval yellowish white
spot on the outer webs at the tip.

Bill and feet plumbeous; irides brown. Length 8½ inches;
extent 15; wing 5¼; tail 3; bill at front ⅞; tarsus ¾.

The female is a little smaller, has the upper parts like the male,
but there is a yellow supercilium, occasionally some of the same
colour on the forehead, crown, and nape, as also on the upper part
of the dorsal plumage; the cheeks, too, are yellow; but the upper
ear-coverts dark; beneath bright yellow, spotted with black, except
on the vent and under tail-coverts; a dark line from the gape, and
another from the base of the lower mandible, enclosing the chin,
which is unspotted; wings as in the male, but the pale spots larger,
especially on the wing-coverts. The young resemble the female,
but the lower parts are whitish, as are the feathers of the crown,
nape, and interscapular region.

This magnificent Grosbeak has been found both in the North-
west and in the South-east Himalayas, but more common in the
latter region, and chiefly at considerable elevations. In winter, a
few descend to a lower region, in which season I got one or two

pairs near Darjeeling. Hodgson obtained it in Nepal, where he says they belong to the Northern region, whence they wander into the central region, even in summer, in search of ripe stony fruits. According to Captain Hutton this species " comes to Mussooree in flocks, during March and April, and remains as long as it can find plenty of cherry stones to crack, after which it disappears. They have a curious chattering note, and love to sit on the tops of the tallest trees. When at work on a wild cherry-tree they are easily detected by the constant cracking sound of the cherry-stones, which they never break, but open most dexterously at the joining of the valves. The ground beneath the trees is strewed with the opened shells."

The next species is not a typical one, and is placed by Bonaparte under *Hesperiphona*, but it does not range satisfactorily with either. The sexes are alike, and the bill is much less bulged than in the last species, perfectly conic, and with the culmen straight, and it somewhat approximates, according to Mr. Blyth, an African genus, *Pyrenestes* of Swainson.

728. **Mycerobas carnipes,** HODGSON.

Coccothraustes, apud HODGSON—GOULD, Birds of Asia, Pt. III. pl. 12—BLYTH, Cat. 686—HORSF., Cat. 696—Cocc. speculigerus, BRANDT.

THE WHITE-WINGED GROSBEAK.

Descr.—Whole head, neck, and breast, sooty brown ; wings and tail dusky, with yellowish edgings, and a white speculum on the wings, as in the last, but larger ; the back, wing-coverts, and terti-aries with some olive yellow spots and stripes ; the lower back and rump greenish yellow; beneath, the abdomen, vent, and under tail-coverts, greenish yellow, the last sometimes dashed with dusky.

Bill and legs fleshy grey; irides brown. Length $8\frac{3}{4}$ inches ; wing $4\frac{5}{8}$; tail $3\frac{1}{2}$ to nearly 4; bill straight to front $\frac{3}{4}$.

This species has hitherto only been procured in Nepal, within our limits; but it is known as an inhabitant of Northern Persia, and parts of Central Asia, and it appears to occur very rarely on the south side of the Himalayas.

Other Grosbeaks are, the Hawfinch of Europe, *Coccothraustes vulgaris*, and a closely allied species or race from Japan; and two other species from China and Japan, *C. melanura*, and *C. personatus*, are now placed under *Eophona*.

The genus *Pyrenestes*, Swainson, consists of some remarkable Grosbeaks from Africa, which are the only birds of this particular division found out of the temperate portion of the Northern hemisphere.

A peculiar tribe of thick-billed Finches inhabits the Galapago islands, off the West Coast of South America, which may be classed near the Grosbeaks. They constitute the *Geospizinæ* of Bonaparte, and, although some of them, by their enormous bills, approach the Grosbeaks, others have that organ lengthened, more slender, and Starling-like. They live on seeds, and much on roots, which they dig up; and they also eat portions of *Cactus* and other vegetables.

The genus *Cardinalis*, containing some fine scarlet plumaged and crested Grosbeaks of North America, is usually placed in this division, but Blyth considers it more strictly to belong to the Bull-finches.

2nd.—Bull-finches, *Pyrrhulinæ* (in part) of some, *Pyrrhulcæ*, Bonap.

The Bull-finches have the bill smaller than in the Grosbeaks, shorter, deeper, and more tumid, with the ridge convex; the wings are more rounded; the tarsi are short, with the lateral toes unequal, and they are tolerably arboreal in their habits. They feed much on the buds of trees, especially in winter. They do not associate in general in large flocks, and they have peculiar and plaintive call-notes. There are very few species known. Bonaparte places them as a sub-division of his *Fringillinæ*, and Gray joins them with the Rose-finches to make a distinct sub-family.

Gen. Pyrrhula, Cuvier.

Char.—Bill short, as high and broad as long, tumid; the tip slightly compressed and overhanging; wings with 2nd, 3rd, and 4th primaries sub-equal and longest, the 1st and 5th shorter; feet formed for perching, rather broad in the sole; tail truncate, emarginate, rather long.

The plumage of the Bull-finches is soft and puffy, the feathers of open texture, and the colors distinct and massed, in this respect approximating the Grosbeaks. Four species are known from the Himalayas.

729. Pyrrhula erythrocephala, VIGORS.

P. Z. S. 1831—GOULD, Cent. Him. Birds, pl. 32—Birds of Asia, pt. IV. pl. 12—BLYTH, Cat. 667—HORSF., Cat. 683.

THE RED-HEADED BULL-FINCH.

Descr.—Male, with the head dull crimson, continued round the sides of the neck, and more or less on the ear-coverts; a narrow band on the forehead, and round the base of the bill black, set off with whitish, passing into the red of the cheeks; back, scapulars, and wing-coverts, dull reddish ashy; rump and upper tail-coverts pure white, the outermost feathers of the latter black; median coverts, wings, and tail, glossy black; the greater coverts ashy, tipped with white; chin whitish; throat, breast, and upper part and sides of abdomen, the same red as the head, but somewhat paler, and tinged with orange; lower part of abdomen pale greyish fawn, passing into white on the lower tail-coverts.

The female has the head and neck dull greenish yellow, the back browner than in the male, and the lower parts pale brown.

Bill black; legs pale fleshy brown; irides light brown. Length about 6 inches; wing $3\frac{1}{8}$; tail $2\frac{3}{4}$.

This Bull-finch has much the form of the European bird, but the tail is slightly longer and more forked. It is found throughout the Himalayas, more common in the North-west, somewhat rare in the South-east. I procured it at Darjeeling, but it is rare there, and only a winter visitant; and Mr. Blyth had not previously seen specimens from Sikim. At Mussooree, Hutton states it to be common in winter, feeding on the ground, as well as on berry-bearing bushes, and it perches high on the top of trees.

730. Pyrrhula erythaca, BLYTH.

J. A. S., 1863.

THE RED-BREASTED BULL-FINCH.

Descr.—A narrow band round the base of the bill, black, edged with white; the whole head, neck, back, and wing-coverts, pure ashy grey, paler on the chin and throat, and edged with black where it joins the pure white of the rump; wings and tail glossy black, the greater coverts pale silvery ashy, forming a conspicuous pale wing-bar; beneath, from the breast, lively red, passing to white on the vent and under tail-coverts.

Bill black; feet fleshy—Length about 6 inches; wing 3¾; tail 3.

This handsome Bull-finch was found by Lieutenant Beavan on Mount Tonglo in Sikim. The female has not yet been observed.

731. **Pyrrhula Nipalensis,** Hodgson.

As. Res. XIX. 155—BLYTH, Cat. 664—HORSF., Cat. 684—GOULD, Birds of Asia, pt. V. pl. 13.

THE BROWN BULL-FINCH.

Descr.—Above pale ashy brown, smeared with slaty cinereous; rump, upper tail-coverts, wings, and tail, glossy black, the former with a white band; the outer web of the last tertiary crimson; and a pale, broad wing-band formed by the greater-coverts; top of the head slightly marked with dusky brown; and a narrow band of the same round the base of the bill; a small white spot under the eye; lower plumage as above, but paler, and passing to white on the lower abdomen, vent, and under tail-coverts.

Bill greenish horny, with a black tip; legs fleshy brown; irides brown. Length 6¼ inches; extent 10½; wing 3⅜; tail 3½; the middle feather ¾ inch shorter.

The female resembles the male, except in being a trifle smaller, and the small tertiary is dull saffron-yellow instead of red.

This plain-colored Bull-finch differs from the typical species by its firmer plumage, longer and more forked tail, the feathers of which are slightly truncated. It has been procured only in the South-east Himalayas, in Nepal, and Sikim, where it is not very rare in winter, in summer seeking the higher elevations.

732. **Pyrrhula aurantiaca,** Gould.

P. Z. S. 1857—ADAMS, Birds of Cashmere—GOULD, Birds of Asia, pt. X. pl. 2.

The Orange Bull-finch.

Descr.—Male, face, wings, and tail, deep purplish black; rump, upper and under tail-coverts white; the rest of the plumage rich reddish orange; apical half of the innermost of the greater wing-coverts also orange; the outer ones slightly tipped with buffy white.

Bill black; feet fleshy; irides dark brown. Length 5¼ inches; wing 3¼; tail 2¾; tarsus ⅝.

The female has a circle round the bill black; head and neck ash-colour; back ashy, tinged with orange red; the lower parts as in the male, but less brilliantly colored.

This Bull-finch was found by Dr. Adams in Cashmere, in the lesser ranges of hills, in thick bushy places, in small societies. Its call is like the chirrup of the Green-finch.

There are two Bull-finches in Europe, differing only in size, *P. vulgaris*, and *P. coccinea.* The former, which is the smaller race, is the only one found in Britain. A nearly allied species occurs in Japan, *P. orientalis,* Temm. and Schlegel. Bull-finches in Europe are taught to whistle whole airs, and fetch a considerable price. These piping Bull-finches, as they are called, are taught by a flute or a bird-organ. Only a few appear to possess a sufficiently fine ear to whistle perfectly in tune.

The following bird is as uniquely coloured in this sub-family, as the crested Bunting is in its own group.

Gen. PYRRHOPLECTES, Hodgson.

Syn. *Pyrrhuloides,* Blyth.

Char. Bill bulged as in *Pyrrhula,* but not so short nor so broad; tip of upper mandible slightly overhanging; lower mandible very thick; wings moderate, 2nd, 3rd, and 4th primaries sub-equal and longest; tail even, or very slightly divaricate; legs more slender than in *Pyrrhula,* and more suited for the ground; claws not much curved.

This genus, which was characterized almost at the same time by Hodgson and Blyth, consists but of one species, a remarkably colored and very handsome bird. "Its bill," says Blyth, as viewed from above, is that of a *Pyrrhula*, whilst viewed laterally, it is like that of a stout *Emberiza*. It appears to lead through *Pyrrhula striolata*, Rüpp., to *Serinus*, and thence to *Chrysomitris*."

733. **Pyrrhoplectes epauletta,** HODGSON.

Pyrrhula, apud HODGSON, As. Res. XIX. 156—HORSF., Cat. 685—Pyrrhuloides, apud BLYTH, J. A. S., XIII. 951 and XXIV. 257—*Lho samprek-pho*, Lepch.

THE GOLD-HEADED BLACK BULL-FINCH.

Descr.—Male, with the top of the head and occiput bright golden orange; the rest of the body brownish black, except a tuft of golden yellow feathers on the axillaries, and the inner webs of the uppermost tertiaries are partially white.

The female is reddish brown, with the forehead and neck grey, and the coronal patch, with the ear coverts, dull greenish saffron; axillaries as in the male; primaries and tail dusky, with the white on the tertiaries, as in the male.

Bill dusky horny; legs brown; irides brown. Length $5\frac{3}{4}$ inches; wing 3; tail $2\frac{1}{4}$; bill at front $\frac{7}{16}$; tarsus $\frac{11}{16}$.

This remarkably colored Bull-finch has only been found in Nepal and Sikim, and is very rare. I got one pair near Darjeeling in the winter. Hodgson says, " inhabits the Northern and Central regions of Nepal, shy, adhering to the forests."

3rd.—Cross-bills—(*Loxiinæ* of some.)

These are a very remarkable group of Finches, somewhat allied to the Bull-finches, with the colors of the Rose-finches, but well distinguished from both by the peculiar structure of their bill. They are stout birds with large heads and strong bills, with the mandibles crossed and overlapping, and they are generally distributed over the northern parts of both Continents, one species only having been found in the Himalayas. Bonaparte, as before mentioned, does not separate them from the Rose-finches.

Gen. LOXIA, Linn. (restricted.)

Char.—Bill somewhat lengthened, strong, compressed towards the tip; the culmen keeled strongly, hooked at the tip, and both mandibles produced, so that the tips cross each other; wings moderately long, the 1st and 2nd quills sub-equal and longest ; tail short, forked ; feet fitted for perching, the lateral toes unequal, the hind toe long, and all the claws well curved. The peculiar structure of the bill of these Finches enables them to extract the seeds from the hard woody cones of Pines, and the ease and rapidity with which they do this, is said to be very wonderful. They are stated also to eat apples and other fruit. They nidificate high up on Pine trees, making a nest of twigs and grass, lined with hair. They somewhat approach the Parrots in the form of their bill, and also in the way in which they climb by the aid of that organ. Pallas, who remarked this, states that were it not for the form of their feet, they could not be distinguished from Parrots.

734. Loxia Himalayana, Hodgson.

J. A. S. XIII. 952—Blyth, Cat. 671—Horsf., Cat. 680— Bonap. and Schlegel, Mon. Lox. pl. 7.—Gould, Birds of Asia, pt. XII. pl. 13.

The Himalayan Cross-bill.

Descr.—The greater part of the head and neck, and the whole body beneath, red, of a hue between roseate and blood-red, and more or less tinged with dusky brown ; the rest of the head, neck, back, wings, and tail, ashy brown, smeared and edged with red.

The female is brown above, the rump tinged with yellow ; pale brownish beneath, tinged on the breast and abdomen with olive yellow.

Length $5\frac{3}{4}$ inches ; wing $3\frac{1}{4}$; tail $2\frac{1}{4}$; bill at front $\frac{1}{2}$.

The Himalayan Cross-bill is only found in the higher regions of the Himalayas, not far from the snows; and even there, says Hodgson, it is rare. It is much smaller than the European species, with the colors somewhat deeper. We have no record of its habitat elsewhere, but it will probably be found in Tibet, and other regions of Central Asia. It does not appear to have been observed in the N. W. Himalayas.

The European species of Cross-bill are *L. curvirostra*, the common Cross-bill; *L. leucoptera*, the white winged Cross-bill; and *L. pityopsittacus*, or the Parrot C., all of which have been observed in Britain; and a fourth species from Eastern Europe is recorded by Bonaparte. Another species, is common in North America, *L. Americana.*

A remarkable bird, *Psittirostra psittacea,* from the Sandwich Islands, is placed next *Loxia* by some systematists. It is green, with the head and neck yellow, thus still more approximating some of the Parrots; and Bonaparte latterly placed near this bird the *Fringilla coccinea,* of the Sandwich Isles, the type of the genus *Hypoloxias,* Lichtenst.

The next two genera might either be placed with the Cross-bills, or the Rose-finches. Bonaparte puts them next the Cross-bills; Gray with the Rose-finches. The coloration of the males is common to both groups, whilst that of the females more approximates the tints of the Cross-bills by its yellow tone. The first noticed has more brilliant red plumage than any of the group.

Gen. HÆMATOSPIZA, Blyth.

Char.—Bill large, longer than deep, moderately bulged; the upper mandible distinctly curved and over-hanging, with a slight subterminal notch; wings with the 2nd, 3rd, and 4th primaries sub-equal and longest, the 5th slightly shorter, and the 1st shorter than the 5th; tail nearly even.

This form, says the founder of the genus, leads from the Grosbeaks to the Bull-finches; its coloring is distinctive and remarkable. Only one species is known.

735.   Hæmatospiza sipahi, HODGSON.

Corythus, apud HODGSON, As. Res. XIX. 151—HORSF., Cat. 681—H. boetonensis, BLYTH, Cat. 663—GOULD, Birds of Asia, pt. IV. pl. 12—*Phanying-pho biu,* Lepch.—*Labbia ma-phoo,* Bhot.

THE SCARLET GROSBEAK.

Descr.—Male, brilliant scarlet, with the wings and tail dusky brown, more or less scarlet edged; the tibial feathers dark brown, and the lower tail-coverts dashed with dusky. The female is dusky brown; the feathers broadly margined with dull greenish-yellow; rump bright yellow; beneath pale olivaceous yellow, with dusky crescentic marks, becoming more albescent on the lower abdomen.

Bill yellow; legs brown; irides hazel brown. Length $7\frac{1}{2}$ inches; extent $12\frac{1}{4}$; wing $4\frac{1}{8}$; tail $2\frac{1}{2}$; bill at front $\frac{1}{2}$; tarsus $\frac{3}{4}$.

This magnificent bird has chiefly been found in the S. E. Himalayas, in Nepal and Sikim; and is unknown in the North-west. It is by no means rare about Darjeeling, and haunts elevations from 5,000 to 10,000 feet, according to the season. I have generally seen it in pairs. It frequents both forest and bushy-ground, feeds on fruits and seeds of various kinds, and has a loud whistling note.

Pr. Bonaparte and Schlegel, as quoted by Gould, state that this bird sings very agreeably, and plays a great part in the mythology of the Hindoos. This of course is quite erroneous, and the common *Tuti* of India, *Carpodacus erythrinus*, was probably intended.

Bonaparte places next this bird a remarkable species from Japan, *Chaunoproctus papa*, which appears to be coloured somewhat like *Pyrrhospiza punicea*.

Gen. PROPYRRHULA, Hodgson.

Syn. *Spermopipes*, Caban.

Char.—Bill as in *Pyrrhula*, but somewhat longer, and the tip of the upper mandible less distinctly prolonged and overhanging; wings shorter and more rounded; plumage as in *Loxia* or *Strobilophaga*.

This form, says Blyth, can only be arranged satisfactorily as a separate division, especially intermediate to *Pyrrhula* and *Carpodacus*. As previously observed, by the coloration of the female, it ranks very naturally in the present group. Bonaparte places it with *Corythus*, the type of the European Pine Grosbeak, *C. enucleator*, L., but states that it approximates the *Carpodaci*. Blyth first applied Hodgson's Manuscript generic name to this species, which Hodgson afterwards gave to another bird, the *Pyrrhospiza punicea*, Bl., (*vide* p. 406).

736. **Propyrrhula subhemachala,** Hodgson.

Corythus, apud Hodgson, As. Res., XIX. 152—Blyth, Cat. 668—Horsf., Cat. 682.

The Red-headed Rose-Finch.

Descr.—Male, the forehead and supercilia, cheeks, and more or less of the throat and breast, fine roseate, brightening to crimson in the breeding season ; crown, back, and wings, olivaceous brown, margined with the same, more or less bright, and often mingled with dull greenish orange, both purer on the rump and upper tail-coverts; primaries and tail hair-brown, margined with red or orange ; lower parts, below the breast, dull brownish grey, tinged with olivaceous on the flanks.

The female has the forehead, and part of throat and breast, bright yellow; the rest of the head, the neck, and the lower plumage plumbeous grey, tinged with greenish. paler and albescent on the vent and under tail-coverts; upper plumage dusky greenish ; wings and tail dusky brown, with yellow edges to the outer webs, slight upon the tail-feathers.

Bill fleshy brown ; legs pale brown ; irides hazel brown. Length about 8 inches; wing 3¾ to nearly 4 ; tail 3.

In winter the rosy hue is more or less wanting, or much mixed with greenish dusky. Young males have little red, except on the forehead and throat.

This fine Rose-finch has only been procured in the S. E. Himalayas, in Nepal and Sikim, during winter. I obtained it near Darjeeling, frequenting the more open parts of the woods in small parties. It has not hitherto been sent from the N. W. Himalayas.

The Pine Grosbeak is found in the northern portion of both Continents, and is quite intermediate in its colours and structure to the Cross-bills and the Rose-finches.

4th. The Rose-finches.

These comprise a number of Finches, varying in the form of the bill, but all agreeing in the males being more or less rosy red, and the females dusky olive, with darker streaks, in some more or less mixed with yellow.

Gen. CARPODACUS, Kaup.

Syn. *Erythrina*, Brehm.—*Hæmorrhous*, Swains.—*Pyrrhulinota*, Hodgs.

Char.—Bill somewhat as in *Pyrrhula*, but longer, distinctly tumid and compressed at the tip; commissure sinuated, or with a notch near its base; wings, with the first three primaries sub-equal and longest; tail distinctly furcate; feet robust; claws well curved.

The members of this genus, says Blyth, have the bill midway between the true Bull-finches and the Linnets. The males are more or less tinged with roseate. becoming crimson in the breeding season, and the females are brown streaked, without any yellow. There are several species in Northern Europe, Asia, and America, and one of this genus is the only Fringilline form that extends its migrations far into the tropical regions of India. Another inhabits Northern Africa. They are distinguished from *Propasser* by a brighter tone of red, and in general a thicker bill.

737. **Carpodacus rubicilla**, GULDENSTADT.

Loxia, apud GULDENSTADT—GOULD, Birds of Asia, pt. IV. pl. 13—HORSF., Cat. 687—Cocc. caucasicus, PALLAS.

THE CAUCASIAN ROSE-FINCH.

Descr.—Male, with the crown of the head, the nape, back, wing-coverts, scapularies, and upper tail-coverts, of a beautiful pale rosy grey, the rosy tint predominating on the margin of the wing and tail-coverts; forehead, ear-coverts, and throat, shining white, bordered with carmine red; chin, breast, and abdomen, carmine red, with a triangular spot of shining white at the tip of each feather, giving it a spangled appearance; under tail-coverts pale carmine red; rump carmine red; primaries, secondaries, and tail, brownish black, narrowly edged with reddish.

The female is pale brown above, still lighter beneath: the feathers of both upper and under-surface streaked down the centre with dark brown ; primaries and secondaries brown, edged with pale brown.

Bill with the upper mandible dark brown, lower one fleshy horn colour; feet dark brown. Length about 8½ inches ; wing 4⅝ ; tail 4 ; tarsus 1.

Latham states that this fine species chiefly occurs in the colder parts of the Caucasian Mountains, feeding principally on the berries of the Sea Buckthorn, *Hippophae rhamnoides ;* that it is frequently seen in large flocks, and that its note is not unlike that of a Bull-finch. It has only been obtained, in India, in the far N. W. Himalayas, Mr. Blyth having received one from the neighbourhood of Pind Dadun-khan, and it has also been found in Cashmere. It varies much in the brightness of its plumage, according to the season. It is probably this species which Adams alludes to in his Birds of Cashmere, No. 68, as being like *Carp. erythrinus,* but larger, and of a brighter red, and only seen in flocks, high up near the snow.

738. Carpodacus erythrinus, PALLAS.

Loxia, apud PALLAS, Zoog. Ross. As. pl. 36—BLYTH, Cat. 658—HORSF., Cat. 686—GOULD, Birds of Europe, pl. 206—Hœmorrhous roseus, apud JERDON, Cat. 195—C. roseus, apud ADAMS, Birds of Cashmere, No. 67—L. totta, GMELIN—Pyrrhulinota roseata, HODGSON—*Tuti,* H.—*Amonga tuti,* in Nepal—*Chota tuti* in Sylhet—*Phulin-pho,* Lepch.—*Yedru-pichike,* or *Yedru-jinowayi,* Tel.

THE COMMON ROSE-FINCH.

Descr.—Male, in winter plumage, has the head, throat, breast, moustachial stripe, rump, and flanks of the abdomen, roseate color, deepest upon the crown, throat, and breast, and paling on the flanks ; upper plumage generally brown, more or less ruddy, brightening towards the rump and on the upper tail-coverts ; the wing-coverts tipped with ruddy brown, forming two pale bars on the wings ; tertiaries margined with pale brown ; quills and tail-feathers with ruddy edgings. In summer the crown, throat, breast, and rump become brilliant crimson. The female is pale

olive brown with dark streaks, the tips of the greater and lesser
wing-coverts whitish, forming two conspicuous bands on the
wings; below paler brown, albescent on the throat, the middle of
the belly, and the under tail-coverts; and darker and somewhat
streaked on the breast and flanks.

Bill yellowish brown; feet horny brown; irides light brown.
Length 5½ inches; wing 3¼; tail 2¼.

The Rose-finch is found as a cold weather visitant throughout
the greater part of India, more rare towards the South, common
in Central and Northern India, and in the Himalayas, chiefly however at the foot of the hills and in the valleys; and it extends into
Assam and Arracan. Out of India it is found over great part
of Central and Northern Asia and Europe. It visits the plains
during October, and leaves in April. In March, many are taken
in fine breeding livery. In the extreme south I have chiefly seen
it in bamboo jungle, feeding on the seeds of bamboos on
several occasions, and so much is this its habit that the
Telugu name signifies ' Bamboo sparrow.' In other parts of the
country it frequents alike groves, gardens, and jungles, feeding
on various seeds and grain; also not unfrequently on flower buds
and young leaves. Adams states that in Cashmere it feeds much
on the seeds of a cultivated vetch. Now and then it is seen in
large flocks, but in general it associates in small parties. It breeds
in Northern Asia. It is frequently caught and caged, and has rather
a pleasing song. Blyth says, "The *Tuti* has a feeble twittering
song, but soft and pleasing, being intermediate to that of the Gold-
finch, and that of the small Red-pole Linnet; the call-note much
resembling that of a Canary-bird."

Perhaps the North American Red-finches, *Fr. purpurea*, Gm.,
and *Fr. frontalis*, Say, with three or four lately discriminated
species from the same Continent, ought to be classed in this genus,
rather than in *Propasser*.

Gen. PROPASSER, Hodgson.

Syn. *Phœnicospiza*, Blyth.

Char.—Bill more elongated, Finch-like, or much as in the
Sparrows, scarcely bulged, the culmen and gonys slightly curved,

and the tip faintly notched; wings rather short; tail slightly forked.

The birds of this genus differ from those of the preceding by the more lengthened and less tumid bills, and by the general tone of the plumage, which is more of a vinous or claret colour than in *Carpodacus*. In some, the first four primaries are about equal; in one species the 3rd and 4th are the longest, and the 1st and 2nd successively shorter. Most of the known species are from the Himalayas, and probably Central Asia.

739. Propasser rodopeplus, Vigors.

Fringilla, apud Vigors, P. Z. S. 1831—Gould, Cent. Him. Birds, pl. 31, f. 1—Blyth, Cat. 658—Horsf., Cat. 689—*Gulabi tuti*, in Nepal.

The Spotted-winged Rose-finch.

Descr.—Male, above dull crimson or ruddy brown, with dusky or blackish median stripes, more brown on the back; superciliary stripe pale glistening roseate; rump, and the tips of the wing-coverts and tertiaries, vinaceous rosy pink; the throat, breast, and body beneath, dull vinous rosy.

The female is deep brown above, with paler lateral margins; beneath light yellowish-brown, with dark central lines; a broad pale supercilium, and another pale line from the lower mandible.

Bill horny brown; legs pale brown; irides brown. Length 6¾ inches; wing 3¼; tail 2¾. Wings somewhat rounded, the 1st being a good deal shorter, and the 2nd something shorter than the 3rd.

This Rose-finch appears to be most abundant about Nepal and the Central part of the Himalayas, being found sparingly at Mussooree, according to Hutton, and it has not been procured in Sikim. Hutton states "that it likes the brushwood best, where it often keeps company with various Accentors."

740. Propasser thura, Bonap.

Bonaparte and Schlegel, Monog. Lox. pl. 23—P. rodopeplus (in part), Hodgson—Moore, P. Z. S. 1855—Horsf., Cat. 690.

THE WHITE-BROWED ROSE-FINCH.

Descr.—Very similar to *rodopeplus;* differs in the male being hair brown above, centred with blackish, and only the lesser range of wing-coverts being tipped with pale crimson; the end of the superciliary streak and the centre of the belly are pure white. The female differs from the female of *rodopeplus* in being paler above, with paler centres to the feathers, and in the colour of the lower parts being more uniform. It is a little smaller too than the last species, and its bill is smaller and more pyrrhuline in its form.

This species was sent from Nepal by Mr. Hodgson, along with *rodopeplus,* and its geographic range is not accurately known.

741. **Propasser rhodochlamys,** BRANDT.

Pyrrhula, apud BRANDT.—GOULD, Birds of Asia, pt. IV., pl. 14 —C. sophia, BON. and SCHLEG.—C. grandis, BLYTH, Cat. 659.

THE RED-MANTLED ROSE-FINCH.

Descr.—Male, the feathers of the supercilium, the cheeks and throat, shining rosy white; upper surface greyish brown, strongly tinged with rosy red; the crown of the head washed with purplish rose colour, and a line of dark brown down the centre of each feather; under surface and rump of a deep rose red; quills and tail-feathers brownish black, margined with greyish red; under wing-coverts rosy white.

The female is brown, somewhat brighter on the lower surface and with a streak of brownish-black down each feather; the wings and tail brown with paler margins, especially on the greater and middle coverts of the wings.

Bill brownish-grey above, yellowish beneath; feet brownish yellow. Length of a female 7 inches; wing $3\frac{1}{2}$; tail $2\frac{3}{4}$. The male is somewhat larger.

This species has been obtained in the Tyne range of mountains between Simla and Mussooree, and in the Publier valley, near the snow, on the Simla side, by Hutton; and it also inhabits Tibet and the Altai mountains. It resembles *Propasser rhodochrous* in its colours.

742. **Propasser rhodochrous**, Vigors.

Fringilla, apud Vigors, P. Z. S. 1831—Gould, Cent. Him.
Birds, pl. 31, f. 2—Blyth, Cat. 661—Horsf., Cat. 691—
Gulabi tuti in Nepal—*Cheerya* by the people of the plains below
Nepal.

The Pink-browed Rose-finch.

Descr.—Male, above brown, edged with reddish; head and
nape dusky or vinous rosy; forehead, superciliary stripe, and rump,
pale rosy; wings unspotted; the wing-coverts reddish brown;
beneath dull vinous rosy.

The female is brown above, the feathers edged with pale
olive brown; beneath pale rufous or rufescent, with brown
streaks. Compared with the female of *rodopeplus*, she is
altogether paler, and the supercilia are therefore less distinct and
contrasting.

Bill pale brown. Length about 6 inches; wing $2\frac{6}{10}$; tail $2\frac{3}{8}$.
The bill is less pyrrhuline, and more linnet-like than in *rodopeplus*.

This species is chiefly a denizen of the more Western
Himalayas; it was procured by Hodgson in Nepal, but has not
been observed in Sikim. Hutton states, "that it is common at
Mussooree, flying in small flocks, often mixed up with Bull-finches
and Siskins. They alight on the ground in search of seeds; and
if disturbed, either fly off with a wheeling flight that brings them
back to the same spot, or they rise up into a tall tree and cluster on
its topmost branches." If Royle is correct, it occurs on the
plains near Saharunpoor, but never far from the foot of the
Mountains.

743. **Propasser pulcherrimus**, Hodgson.

Gray, Zool. Misc. 1844—Moore. P. Z. S. 1855—Horsf.,
Cat. 692.

The Beautiful Rose-finch.

Descr.—Similar to *rhodochrous;* it differs in having the
forehead, superciliary streak, cheeks, throat, and under parts, with

the rump, silvery crimson ; being almost silvery white about the head ; the upper parts, with the crown, are dark brown, with pale crimson edges to the feathers. The female differs from the female of *rhodochrous* in having the under parts dusky white, instead of rufescent, and in the colours above being less rufescent. The size is the same as that of *rhodochrous*, but the wing is somewhat longer.

This species appears to have much the same range as the last, both having been sent from Kumaon and Nepal.

744. Propasser frontalis, BLYTH.

J. A. S. 1863.

THE SIKIM ROSE-FINCH.

Descr.—Broad frontal band, and eyebrow silvery rose pink ; lores, and a narrow band round the base of the bill beneath, crimson ; top of the head, nape, and cheeks, plain dark brown ; back brown with broad central dashes ; wings brown, with the median coverts tipped with pale rosy, forming a prominent band, and the greater coverts and tertiaries narrowly edged with rosy white ; tail brown ; rump and upper tail-coverts pale vinaceous rosy ; beneath, the chin, throat, neck, and breast, rosy with silvery white shafts, and the rest of the plumage of a dull rosy tint.

The female has the whole upper plumage yellowish brown, with black dashes, two pale, very narrow wing-bands ; quills and tail dark brown ; forehead, eyebrow, lores, and face white, with black stripes ; chin, throat, and breast rufous, with black stripes ; belly, vent, and under tail-coverts white, with dark stripes.

Bill horny brown ; legs pale brown. Length 6¾ inches ; wing 3¼ ; tail 3.

The bill is tolerably thick, scarcely elongated, and somewhat tumid. The 3rd and 4th quills are the longest, 1st and 2nd successively shorter.

This handsome species has lately been discovered in Sikim, by Lt. Beavan, at a considerable elevation, on Mount Tonglo I believe. It is very near to *P. pulcherrimus* and *P. thura*, but appears to differ from both.

745. **Propasser Murrayi,** BLYTH.

J. A. S. 1863.

MURRAY'S ROSE-FINCH.

Descr.—A female only of this species is known. Above earthy brown, the feathers of the head edged with white, and a white eye-brow from the eye to the nape ; back very faintly pale edged ; wings with two pale bands, and the tips of the secondaries also pale ; primaries and tail feathers very narrowly edged with pale ; beneath, the chin and throat are albescent, with a few ill-defined dusky spots on the chin, and becoming fulvescent on the throat ; the rest of the lower parts pale earthy brown, passing to rusty on the middle of the belly, vent and under tail-coverts.

Bill horny brown ; legs pale brown.   Length 6 inches ; wing 3 ; tail $2\frac{1}{2}$.

This bird was said to have been procured somewhere in the Gwalior territories, but if so, must have been a straggler from the Himalayas.   It appears to differ from the females of the other known species, sufficiently to warrant its being considered distinct.

I am inclined to think that the *Pyrgita? .concolor* of my Catalogue No. 178, might have belonged to the present group, and in its coloration it much resembles the females of *P. githaginea* and *P. sinaitica ;* but, as it was founded on a single specimen, shot in the Deccan along with a lot of the so-called Ortolan, I shall not record it separately.   It was of a nearly uniform light brown colour, palest beneath, and albescent on the chin and vent.   Length 6 inches ; wing $3\frac{3}{4}$; tail $2\frac{1}{4}$.

Other species of this genus are *P. rosea*, Pallas, from Northern Asia, occasionally visiting Europe ; *P. sinaitica*, Licht. (*synoica,* Temm.,) from Arabia and Eastern Africa; *P. githaginea,* Licht., from Northern Africa and the South of Europe.   The latter is placed by Bonaparte in his genus *Erythrospiza,* but its colors appear to be quite those of this group.   Two other species placed under the same genus, viz., *Fr. obsoleta,* and *F. rhodoptera,* of Lichtenstein, from Central and Western Asia, perhaps belong rather to *Carpodacus.*   Whether the remarkable, long-tailed, small Red-finches of North-eastern Asia, forming the genus *Uragus,* should be placed with these Rose-finches, as Bonaparte has done, or elsewhere, I have no means of deciding.

The next two birds have the bill more Finch-like, and may be said to grade into the true Finches.

Gen. PROCARDUELIS, Hodgson.

Syn. *Pyrrha*, Caban.

Char.—Bill longer and more slender than in *Propasser*, but less acutely pointed and compressed at the tip than in the Gold-finches; wings rather long, with the 2nd, 3rd, and 4th primaries sub-equal, the 1st a little shorter; general form elongated; colours as in *Propasser*, but deeper.

746. **Procarduelis nipalensis,** HODGSON.

J. A. S., XII, 955—As. Res. XIX, 157—BLYTH, Cat. 657—HORSF., Cat. 749—Linota saturata, BLYTH, J. A. S., XI. 192—(the male)—L. fusca, BL., (the female)—*Ka-biya*, Lepch.

THE DARK ROSE-FINCH.

Descr.—Male, above, neck and breast sooty or dusky, strongly tinted with dark sanguineous blossom-red; forehead, a line over the eye to the occiput, chin, throat, breast, and belly, pure blossom red; quills and tail-feathers sooty brown, more or less tinged on the outer margin with the red hue of the upper surface.

Bill brown; irides red brown; legs fleshy brown. Length 6½, to 7 inches; extent 10½; wing 3⅞; tail 2¾.

The female is olive-brown above; below, from the chin to the breast, dirty yellowish; from breast to tail white; wings and tail dusky brown; wing-coverts and tertiaries externally margined and tipped with dirty yellowish.

This fine Finch is found in Nepal and Sikim. Hodgson says that it inhabits the Central and Northern hills of Nepal. It is common at Darjeeling, in the cold weather only, in moderately large flocks, feeding on the roads sometimes, or among the ferns and brush-wood.

The next bird is a somewhat remarkable form, and is slightly allied, in its coloration, to *Hæmatospiza sipahi*, but its more Finch-like bill, and feet fitted for terrene habits, have influenced me in placing it here as a connecting link between the Rose-finches and the true Finches.

Gen. PYRRHOSPIZA, Hodgson.

Char.—Bill conical, elongate, with slightly curved outline both above and below, somewhat compressed, and tapering to the tip as viewed from above; gonys arched; wings long, reaching to more than half the length of the tail, which is also moderately long; first four primaries sub-equal, 2nd and 3rd rather the longest; feet adapted for ground habits; toes rather long, with large and arched claws.

747. **Pyrrhospiza punicea,** HODGSON.

J. A. S., XIII., 953—BLYTH, Cat. 656—HORSF., Cat. 694—Propyrrhula rubeculoides, HODGS., P. Z. S., 1845.

THE LARGE RED-BREASTED FINCH.

Descr.—Male, above nearly uniform dusky brown, the feathers margined with paler; forehead and rump, with the cheeks, ear-coverts, and under parts, except the abdominal region, roseate in winter, brightening to rich crimson in the breeding season, and varying to orange saffron; flanks and abdomen colored like the back.

Bill dark horny; feet dusky black. Length $7\frac{1}{2}$ to 8 inches; wing $4\frac{1}{2}$ to $4\frac{3}{4}$; tail $3\frac{1}{8}$.

The female is devoid of the red, having the forehead, cheeks, fore-neck, and breast, more or less fulvescent, each feather marked with a blackish mesial streak, widening at the tip; belly and lower tail-coverts, dingy brown.

This fine Finch has hitherto only been found in the higher regions of the Himalayas, bordering the Snows. I did not procure it in Sikim. It is probable, however, that this and others of the cold-weather visitants to Nepal and other parts of the Himalayas, are to be met with in the interior of Sikim, towards the Snows, my researches having been limited to British Sikim.

5th. True Finches.

The next bird, though somewhat allied to the preceding, is sufficiently marked to warrant its generic separation. It has been classed as a true *Fringilla*, and as a *Carduelis*. Its colors approximate it to the Rose-finches as well as to the Gold-finches; and Blyth indeed notes that " it is a true *Fringilla*, allied to the Gold-finches, with affinities for the Red-finches."

Gen. CALLACANTHIS, Reichen.

Bill Finch-like, *i. e.* as in *Fringilla*, but somewhat more robust and broader, much shorter and stouter than in *Carduelis*; otherwise as in *Fringilla*, but with a peculiar coloration.

Bonaparte who adopts this genus, says " scarcely a *Fringilla*, by no means a *Carduelis*."

748. Callacanthis Burtoni, Gould.

Carduelis, apud GOULD, P. Z. S. 1837, 90—GOULD, Birds of Asia, pt. I., pl. 15—Fringilla erythrophrys, BLYTH, J. A. S. XV. 38—BLYTH, Cat. p. 337. (App., No. 6).

THE RED-BROWED FINCH.

Descr.—The male has the crown, ear-coverts, wings, and tail, brownish black; the forehead, a broad supercilium, chin, and throat, crimson; the upper plumage ruddy brown, deepest on the rump and upper tail-coverts; wings marked with white, chiefly on the primary and greater coverts, and on the secondary quills; the outer tail-feathers mostly white towards the tip; all the others except the middle pair, white tipped. In summer the whole under parts appear to become more or less crimson.

Bill yellow; legs light brown. Length 7 inches; wing $3\frac{7}{8}$; tail $2\frac{5}{8}$.

The female is plain brown above, darker on the crown, with a bright saffron eye streak, and the forehead ochreous; the back is yellowish brown, and there is less white on the wings than in the male; beneath pale brown, tinged with fulvous.

This remarkable Finch has only hitherto been found in the North-west Himalayas, chiefly in the mountains beyond Simla.

Gen. CARDUELIS.

Char.—Bill lengthened, conic, compressed; the tip attenuated and acute; the gonys straight, ascending; the commissure slightly sinuated; wing lengthened, pointed; the first three quills nearly equal; tail moderate, slightly forked; feet short; hind claw rather long.

The Gold-finches are a very limited group of small birds, distinguished by a bright and variegated coloration; some red about the head and a golden yellow bar on the wings. They sing well, make remarkably neat nests, and the eggs are pale bluish-white, spotted with purple and brown.

749. Carduelis caniceps, Vigors.

P. Z. S. 1831—Gould, Cent. Him. Birds, pl. 32, f. 1—Royle, Ill. of Bot. Himal., pl. 8, f. 2—Blyth, Cat. 675—Horsf., Cat. 751—*Shira*, H.—*Saira* in Cashmere.

The Himalayan Gold-finch.

Descr.—General color above pale whity brown; the rump and upper tail-coverts white; a narrow band on the forehead, continuing round the base of the bill to the chin, scarlet; wings black, with a golden yellow band, and a few white spots on the secondaries; tail black, with the inner webs of the two outer tail-feathers with a large white patch, and the four medial feathers tipped with white; beneath whitish, tinged with brownish ashy on the breast and flanks.

Bill carneous with a dusky tip; legs pale brown; irides brown. Length 5½ inches; wing 3¼; tail 2¼; bill at front ½.

The Himalayan Gold-finch differs from the European species, in wanting the black and white of the head behind the scarlet band, and in being a somewhat smaller bird. It is only found in the N. W. Himalayas, near Simla and Mussooree, extending into Affghanistan and other parts of Central Asia. Adams says that it is common in Cashmere in winter, and that it visits the ranges next the plains. It is perhaps Pallas' variety of the common Gold-finch, figured pl. 38 of his Zool. As. Ross., found in summer on the Jenisei river. Caged specimens are occasionally brought to Calcutta for sale, and its song is said by Adams to be exactly similar to that of its European congener.

Besides the Himalayan and European Gold-finch, there is only one other species, *C. orientalis*, from Siberia and Northern Asia.

Next the Gold-finches come the Siskins.

Gen. CHRYSOMITRIS, Boie.

Char.—Bill very short, broadish at the base, compressed at the tip and acute; the culmen flat; tail forked; otherwise as in *Carduelis.*

The Siskins are a small group, nearly allied to the Gold-finches, but with a peculiar style of coloration and a shorter bill. Their form is short, and their plumage is black or brown and yellow. The only Indian species of the genus has been separated by Cabanis as *Hypacanthis;* but apparently without much reason. This genus is remarkable for including in it several species from South America, which, however, are separated by certain Ornithologists.

750 **Chrysomitris spinoides,** VIGORS.

Carduelis, apud VIGORS—GOULD, Cent. Him. Birds, pl. 32, f. 2 —BLYTH, Cat. 673.—HORSF., Cat. 752—*Saira* in Cashmere— *Phazhiplro,* Lepch.

THE HIMALAYAN SISKIN.

Descr.—Male, forehead, occiput, and back of neck yellow; the rest of the body above olivaceous brown; wings dusky black, with some yellowish spots on the wing-coverts, and a pale but bright yellow band on the primaries; tail dusky, the lateral tail-feathers yellow, except on the shaft and tip, this color diminishing in quantity towards the central feathers; beneath yellow, dashed with olivaceous on the sides of the breast and the flanks.

The female has merely the colours less deep, and both the back and abdomen are striated with dusky olive.

Bill fleshy; legs fleshy brown; irides light brown. Length 5½ inches; extent 9¾; wing 3⅛; tail not quite 2.

This pretty little Siskin is found throughout the Himalayas. It is a somewhat larger and more brightly coloured bird than the European Siskin, and the bill is proportionally much stronger. At Darjeeling it is only a winter visitant, but then, by no means rare. It keeps to the woods, occasionally entering gardens in small parties. Adams says that it is common in the wooded

3 F

districts in the North-west, and that its song is very like that of
the English Siskin. Hodgson says it is more common in the
Central region than in the northern.

Besides the common Siskin of Europe, *C. spinus,* another
species from Siberia, *Ch. pistacina,* Eversman, is recorded by
Bonaparte.

The South American Siskins are numerous, and one with a red
tone of color has been separated by Bonaparte as *Pyrrhomitris.*

The smallest member of this sub-family, perhaps should be
placed next the Siskins.

Gen. METOPONIA, Bonap.

Char.—Bill short, thick, nearly regularly conic, slightly bulging;
the culmen very gently curved; gonys almost straight; wings
long; tarsus moderate; middle toe long, laterals short.

This unique little Finch in some measure recalls the coloring of
the Weaver-birds, and, it represents the Pyrrhuline *Pyrrhoplectes*
among the True Finches, as also, says Bonaparte, a remarkable
American bird, *Catamblyrhynchus diadema.*

751. Metoponia pusilla, PALLAS.

Passer, apud PALLAS, Zool. Ross. As., 2nd vol. pl. —HORSF.,
Cat. 754—Fringilla rubrifrons, HAY, J. A. S. XV. 38—Serinus
aurifrons, BLYTH, Cat. 681.

THE GOLD-HEADED FINCH.

Descr.—Forehead and top of head bright golden yellow;
occiput, cheeks, throat, and foreneck, black, passing to dusky on the
nape and sides of the neck; back dusky, with yellowish lateral
margins to the feathers; rump, towards the tail, deep canary yellow;
shoulder of wing golden fulvous; margins of quills and tail feathers
saffron yellow; under tail-coverts pale canary yellow; the rest of
the lower parts albescent yellow, with dusky central streaks;
axillaries pure white; a pale bar on the wing, formed by the tips
of the greater coverts, and the outer webs of the secondaries near
their base.

The female, or perhaps the young only, has the forehead narrowly reddish, wants the black of the head and throat, and is altogether less brightly colored.

Bill and feet dark. Length $4\frac{3}{4}$ to 5 inches; wing 3; tail $2\frac{1}{4}$.

The Gold-headed Finch has been found occasionally in the N. W. Himalayas, not, it appears, as a regular visitor, for Hutton says, he "observed this bird in 1851-5, at Mussooree, after an interval of many years. It appeared to be always in pairs, and, like our Siskin and Gold-finch, is very fond of alighting upon the tall coarse nettles which abound there." It was found by Speke in Spiti and Ladakh, in summer; and in Affghanistan by Griffith, who observed it "in flocks about cultivation, rather shy; feeds on thistles on which they cling." Adams found it very common in Ladakh, in flocks, with the habits and call note like those of the European Redpole. According to Pallas it is common on the Caucasus, and near the Caspian Sea; and it occurs in Eastern Europe. Pallas' figure is unrecognisable.

Next should come the Linnets and Canary birds. The former comprise a number of small Finches with slender conical bills, which, during the breeding season, acquire more or less a red color on the head and breast, and thus evince an affinity for the Rose-finches. One species, *Linota brevirostris*, Gould, P. Z. S. 1855, has been found in Ladakh, and may occur within our limits.

The Canary birds, *Serinus*, with somewhat thick bills, are chiefly from Africa, and the neighbouring islands; and the Lutinos (as Blyth calls them) of *S. canaria*, are the well known song birds. The Canary bird, as is well known, will inter-breed both with the Gold-finch and Siskin. Some other African Finches are placed in the genera *Alario*, *Auripasser*, *Citrinella* and *Buserinus*. *Crithagra*, a South American group, with somewhat thick bills, and more or less yellow plumage, ought also to be placed along with the Serins.

The true Finches are chiefly Northern birds, two species occurring in the most Northern portion of our province, belonging to different genera.

Gen. FRINGILLA, Linn. (as restricted.)

Char.—Bill forming a perfect and somewhat lengthened cone, both mandibles being of nearly equal thickness, the upper one slightly notched near the tip; commissure about straight; wings lengthened, pointed, with the first four primaries sub-equal, the first rather shorter; tail moderate, forked ; legs slender ; feet adapted for perching.

The common Chaffinch of Britain, *Fr. cœlebs*, L., is the type of this form.

752. **Fringilla montifringilla**, LINNÆUS.

GOULD, Birds of Europe, pl. 188—BLYTH, Cat. 653--HORSF., Cat. 746.

THE MOUNTAIN FINCH.

Descr.—In summer, the male has the head, lores, cheeks, sides of neck, back, and rump, blackish, with pale white edges to the feathers of the rump; the shoulders and lesser-coverts rufous, edged with white ; secondary coverts also margined with whitish, and a white spot on some of the quills ; these and the tail black, edged with brownish yellow; the outer tail-feathers margined at their base with white ; beneath, from the chin to the breast, and the flanks, rufous, passing into pale cinereous on the belly. In winter the upper parts are black, the head and back edged with rufous, and the rump pure white ; the sides of the head and the nape much tinged with grey. The female differs, in having the head grey, and less rufous on the breast.

Length 6 inches; wing 3¾; tail 2½.

This Finch, chiefly an inhabitant of the temperate and northern parts of Europe and Asia, has been occasionally found in the N. W. Himalayas during the cold weather. It was sent from Affghanistan by Griffith, and Blyth has seen specimens from Simla and Cashmere. At Mussooree, Hutton observed it as " a rare winter visitant, though it may be common higher up. I have only seen it in the flocks of *Propasser rhodochrous*."

Besides the well-known Chaffinch of Europe, there are two or three allied species from the north of Africa and adjacent isles.

The Green-finches, *Ligurinus*, Koch, (*Chlorospiza*, Bonap.) include, beside the well known Green-finch of Britain, two or three species common in China and Northern Asia, *Fr. sinica*, and *Fr. kawariba*, Temm., which, by their colours, may be said to connect the Siskins and their allies with the plainer coloured Finches.

Two species of *Montifringilla* are found in Ladakh, and may stray within our limits. The type of the genus is the *M. nivalis*, and it is distinguished from Fringilla by its slightly curved and lengthened claws, and the 3rd primary is shorter than the first two. It is somewhat related to *Plectrophanes*, which indeed Blyth places here rather than with the Buntings.

Montifringilla hæmatopygia, Gould, P. Z. S., 1851, and figured in his Birds of Asia, pt. III. pl. 15, has the upper plumage light, with the lower back and rump tinged with crimson. Adams found it common on the mountains surrounding the Chimourarec lake, in small flocks, feeding on the seeds of a worm-wood.

M. Adamsi, Moore, said to be very like *M. Gebleri*, is ashy above, white below and on the upper tail-coverts, with the wings black, with white-coverts. Adams found it " a native of the barren wastes and mountains of Ladakh, in small flocks, terrestrial in its habits ; and, in its call note, and mode of progression on the ground, very similar to the true Larks. The nest is composed of dried grass, and usually placed in dykes and stony places by the way side."

Other species are *M. brunneinucha*, Brandt., from North-eastern Asia ; *M. griseinucha*, Br., from North America ; *M. arctous*, and *M. Gebleri*, from Northern Asia, probably extending in winter into Central Asia.

The next form is a somewhat anomalous one, though related to the last by the long hind claw.

Gen. FRINGILLAUDA, Hodgson.

Char.—Bill short, conic, somewhat tumid ; commissure gently curved ; wings very long, pointed ; the first three primaries longest and sub-equal ; tarsus somewhat lengthened, slender ; feet formed for ground habits ; claws slender, hind claw long, slightly curved.

This remarkable genus has some affinities for the Larks, both by its coloration and structure. Blyth latterly referred it to the genus *Leucosticte*, Sw., which is usually considered the same as *Montifringilla*. Bonaparte considers that it has analogies for the Sparrows.

753. Fringillauda nemoricola, Hodgson.

As. Res. XIX. 158—Fr. longipennis, Bonap. MSS.—Bonap. and Schleg., Mon. Lox, pl. 47—Horsf., Cat. 748—Montifringilla, apud Blyth, Cat. 652.

The Himalayan Lark-finch.

Descr.—Above dusky brown, edged with rufous on the back and scapulars, as in the Larks; quills and tail dusky with pale edgings; the long wing-coverts and tertiaries have a broad edging of pale rufous or whitish; upper tail-coverts blackish with white tips; beneath, the plumage is light earthy grey, pale and albescent on the vent and lower tail-coverts, which are white with dusky centres.

Bill and legs fleshy-brown; irides red brown.

Length $6\frac{1}{2}$ inches; extent $11\frac{1}{2}$; wing $3\frac{3}{4}$; tail $2\frac{3}{4}$.

This curious Lark-like Finch is found throughout the Himalayas, most common towards the North-west. Hodgson states that its habits are very like those of the arboreal Larks; and that it feeds on the skirts of the forests. Adams says that they are seen in large flocks feeding round the margin of the melted snow, and coming to the lower ranges in winter. "Their stomach," says Hodgson, "is a powerful gizzard, and their food consists of kernels and hard seeds, which they digest by means of trituration with gravel." I did not obtain this bird in Sikim, but it is noted in Horsfield's Catalogue as having been procured at Darjeeling by Dr. Pearson.

Those remarkable birds, the Plant-cutters of South America, *Phytotoma*, are placed among the Finches by Gray and others as a separate sub-family, but they perhaps belong to the great group of the Tanagers. They have the margins of the bill serrated.

Sub-fam. ALAUDINÆ, Larks.

Bill typically longer and more slender than in most *Fringillidæ*, short and thick in many ; wings broad ; tertiaries elongated, pointed ; claws slightly curved ; hind toe and claw typically long; plumage brown, more or less striated.

The Larks form a very distinct group of small ground-birds, chiefly frequenting open lands, and which rise singing into the air. Their form is robust, their wings are large and very broad, to sustain them in their hovering flight, whilst singing ; and the tertiaries are usually much developed, as in the *Motacillidæ*, and in some other tribes, viz., the Plovers and Snipes, among the Waders. The bill varies much in thickness, from that of a stout, short and Finch-like bill, to a long, slender, and slightly curved beak ; the culmen is generally more or less curved, and the tip blunt, not notched. Their feet are fitted for running on the ground, which they do with alternate steps, not hopping, and they rarely perch on trees. In some, the hind claw is very greatly elongated and nearly straight. The tail is short or moderate, nearly even, or very slightly forked. The plumage is plain colored, usually brown, with medial dark streaks more or less developed; and the sexes, in most, resemble each other. In a few there is some black on the lower surface.

The young have pale margins to the feathers of the upper surface. Most have the coronal feathers more or less lengthened, and some are crested. They moult once a year, but the general tone of colour alters somewhat according to season, by the abrasion of the feathers ; in some, by a natural shedding of the tips of the feathers. The Larks do not wash, but dust themselves, like the Gallinaceous birds. They feed partly on grains, and much on grasshoppers and insects; nidificate on the ground, and their eggs are dusky greenish with numerous speckles. Many sing well, and are highly imitative. They are almost confined to the Old World, one form only occurring in North America, and they are very sparingly represented in Malayana and Australia. The Larks may be said to grade to the Finches on the one hand, through *Montifringilla* and *Plectrophanes*; and, on the other, into the Pipits through *Corydalla*.

The Larks may be sub-divided into the Bush-larks, the true Larks, and the long-billed or Desert-larks.

1st. Bush-Larks.

These have the bill stout, with the nostrils not concealed by feathers; the wings more or less rounded, and the tail short. They are squat, heavy looking birds, which prefer more bushy places than the true Larks, and seek concealment.

Gen. MIRAFRA, Horsfield.

Char.—Bill stout, thick, compressed; the culmen curved and convex; the tip slightly deflected; commissure gently curving; wings rather short, 1st quill short, 2nd shorter than the 3rd, 4th, 5th, and 6th, which are nearly equal; tail very short, even; legs rather long; hind claw moderately long.

The Bush-larks, as they may be called, are distinguished by their rounded wings, short tail, and they have usually more or less ferruginous on their wings. The edges of the mandibles are often worn away about or beyond the middle. They are found in India, including Malayana, Australia, and in Africa.

754. Mirafra assamica, McLelland.

P. Z. S. 1839—BLYTH, Cat. 746—HORSF., Cat. 720—Plocealauda typica, HODGS.—*Aggia* H.—(*Bhatal* at Muttra ?)—*Bhiriri* at Bhagulpore.

THE BENGAL BUSH-LARK.

Descr.—Above ashy brown, with an olive tinge; feathers of the crown, interscapulars, and scapulars, with dusky brown centres; wings and tail dusky, the outer webs of the primaries, and the edges of the secondaries, with the whole under surface, bright ferruginous, fainter beneath; under-parts fulvescent white, whiter on the throat, and spotted on the breast; a light superciliary streak, and the ear-coverts speckled with dusky; outer tail-feather, with the exterior web, ferruginous, the others edged with the same.

Bill dusky above, fleshy whitish beneath; legs pale fleshy brown; irides hazel brown. Length $5\frac{1}{2}$ to $5\frac{3}{4}$ inches; extent $10\frac{1}{2}$; wing $3\frac{1}{4}$; tail $1\frac{7}{8}$; bill at front $\frac{6}{10}$; tarsus not quite 1.

This species, which may be at once distinguished from the others by the prevalent ashy hue, has a very thick, stout form; the bill is very thick, and is often much worn away at the edges; the 2nd primary is about equal to the 6th; and the tail is very short.

The Bengal Bush-lark is found throughout all Northern India to the Nerbudda, extending eastwards into Assam. It is stated also to occur in the N. W. Provinces, and in the Deyra Doon, but I think that doubtful. Gray states this to be the same as *Javanica* of Horsfield, but the description of that bird is very different, and more like that of another Indian species, *M. erythroptera*. It is a tolerably familiar bird, feeding in gardens and bushy places, squatting when watched, and then taking a short flight; and it appears to have the propensity to hide itself more than any of the other Indian species. It frequently perches on bushes. Mr. Philipps, as quoted by Horsfield, says that " in the morning and evening, it may be observed, perched on a naked bank, and there pouring out its song, which consists of about eight notes, the first six quickly repeated, the last two slowly ;" but, as before stated, I am inclined to doubt if this bird really occurs in the N. W. Provinces, and I imagine that Philipps' remarks apply to another species.

Mr. Blyth says that 'in captivity it is a heavy inactive bird, prone to hide itself from observation, and that its song is pleasing, but of no power.' It appears to be more common in long grass than in bushy ground; and I have only observed it myself in lower Bengal, Dacca, and Sylhet. The nest is described by Tickell as like that of *Ammomanes phœnicura*; but one which I obtained in Dacca in June, was distinctly domed, or covered in by turning the stems of grass over, and was very artfully concealed. The eggs are dull greenish white, with numerous grey and brown spots.

755. Mirafra affinis, Jerdon.

Ill. Ind. Orn. (under M. erythroptera, Pl. 38)—2nd Suppl. Cat. 189—Blyth, Cat. 743—Horsf., Cat. 718—*Eeli-jitta*, Tel.— *Leepee* in Central India—*Chirchira*, H.

3 G

THE MADRAS BUSH-LARK.

Descr.—Plumage above dusky brown, with pale rufous edges to the feathers, and a pale supercilium; ear-coverts pale rufous, tipped with dusky; beneath white, faintly tinged with fulvous, and with the breast marked with large oval brown drops; quills dusky brown, rufous on the outer web of all (except the first two) to near the tip, and with the inner webs rufous at the base, that color obliquely margining them to near the tip; the four central feathers of the tail pale brown, the others darkish brown, the two outermost edged with yellowish white on their outer webs.

Bill dusky, fleshy beneath; legs fleshy; irides brown. Length $5\frac{3}{4}$ to 6 inches; wing $3\frac{1}{4}$; tail $1\frac{3}{4}$; bill at front $\frac{7}{10}$; tarsus $\frac{9}{10}$; hind toe and claw $\frac{3}{4}$. 1st quill above 1 inch long, 2nd about $\frac{2}{10}$ shorter than the next three; tail very short; bill moderately thick.

This Bush-lark is found on the Malabar Coast, in the Carnatic, in Mysore, and the southern part of the table-land, extending North to Goomsoor and Midnapore. Col. Tytler states that it occurs at Barrackpore, but it is certainly very rare in Bengal. It is also found in Ceylon, and I lately found it abundant at Thayet-myo in Upper Burmah.

It is a tolerably familiar bird, entering gardens, and coming close to houses, and does not care so much, as some others of the genus, to conceal itself from observation, for it simply squats, in general, close to the ground, and does not hide itself. It frequently perches on shrubs or even on trees, and takes short flights in the air, descending again with outspread wings. It breeds on the ground, making a loose nest of grass, under the shelter of a bush or tuft of grass, and lays three or four eggs, greenish grey, with spots and stains of brown and dusky. It has a pleasant little song which it utters during its short flights, or occasionally from the ground. Specimens from the Carnatic have a redder tinge than others from Midnapore and Ceylon.

756. **Mirafra erythroptera,** JERDON.

JERDON, Ill. Ind. Orn. pl. 38—BLYTH, Cat. 744—HORSF., Cat. 717—M. Javanica, apud JERDON, Cat. 189.—*Jungli aggia*, H.—*Chinna celi-jitta*, Tel.

THE RED-WINGED BUSH-LARK.

Descr.—Upper parts streaked, the centres of the feathers being dusky brown, and the edges light fulvous brown, rufescent on the head; coronal feathers lengthened; a whitish eyestreak; ear feathers rufescent-brown : beneath, the throat is pure white, and the rest of the plumage pale fulvescent-whitish; the breast marked with large oval blackish spots; primaries and secondaries ferruginous on both webs, except towards the tip, the dusky portion gradually increasing to the outermost feather; tail blackish, the four middle feathers brown and the outermost only whitish on its outer web.

Bill horny fleshy; feet fleshy; irides dark brown, Length $5\frac{1}{2}$ inches; wing $3\frac{2}{10}$; tail 2; bill at front $\frac{5}{10}$; tarsus $\frac{17}{20}$; hind claw $\frac{3}{10}$; the bill is thick; the 1st quill $\frac{3}{4}$ inch long; the 2nd $\frac{1}{8}$ of an inch shorter than the 3rd, 4th, and 5th, which are about equal.

This species, though very similar to the last, is readily distinguished from it by its smaller size, and by the rufous colour extending over the whole of the primary quills; also by the longer tail.

The Red-winged Bush-lark is found in the table-land of the Deccan, extending south to the edges of the Carnatic, and it is found also in the hilly district of Monghyr, where I lately procured it, but I did not observe it in the intermediate Saugor district, nor at Mhow in Central India. Buch. Hamilton appears to have observed it, for it is figured among his drawings. It is very common about Jaulnah, in low jungle. I saw it once only in the Carnatic, at the foot of the Eastern Ghâts, inland from Nellore; and here I found it within a mile or so of the preceding species, *M. affinis*, but neither encroaching on the other's ground. It never frequents the open plains, nor does it enter gardens and enclosures like the last one, but it keeps almost exclusively to low scattered jungle. It frequently perches on shrubs, whence it occasionally rises a short distance in the air, and descends again with outspread wings, its bright rufous quills glittering in the sun. Like the others, it is found single or in pairs, never congregating; is a shy and wary bird, and, when observed, hides itself behind a bush; and, if followed, soon contrives to conceal itself.

757. Mirafra cantillans, JERDON.

J. A. S. XIII. 960, and 2nd Suppl. Cat. 185—BLYTH, Cat.
745—HORSF., Cat. 719—Alauda chendoola, apud JERDON, Cat.
185—*Aghun* or *Aghin*, H.—*Burutta pitta*, Tel., also *Aghin
pitta*, Tel.

THE SINGING BUSH-LARK.

Descr.—Above dusky brown, the feathers laterally margined
with rufescent brown; wings and their coverts strongly margined
with rufous brown; a pale eyestreak; throat and below the ear-
coverts white, and the rest of the under parts pale rufescent,
darker on the breast, with a few indistinct small breast spots; outer
tail feathers nearly all white, the penultimate white on the outer
web only.

Bill dusky horny, fleshy beneath; legs fleshy brown; irides
dark brown. Length $5\frac{1}{2}$ inches; extent 10; wing $2\frac{7}{8}$; tail 2;
bill at front, $\frac{7}{16}$; 1st primary $\frac{3}{4}$ inch; the four next equal, or the
2nd and 5th a trifle shorter; bill not very thick; feathers of head
elongated.

This species is distinguished from the other Bush-larks by the
less amount of rufous on the wings, and this, with its more
slender bill, led me, from seeing a caged specimen, to consider it
a true Lark. It is very closely allied to *M. Horsfieldi*, Gould,
from New South Wales.

The Aggun Bush-lark is generally spread throughout India,
but not very common, except in some localities. It is most
abundant in the Carnatic, the Northern Circars, and in some
parts of Mysore; more rare in the table-land. It is found in
Bengal also, but rare; common in Behar, according to Buch.
Hamilton, and in Central India, according to Tickell. It chiefly
frequents meadows and grass land near cultivation; and it is said
to rise higher in the air than other *Mirafræ*; thus, in its colours,
habits, haunts, and song, it is more Lark-like than any other
Mirafra. It is often caged, and much prized by the natives for
its pleasant little song, which is very sweet. It also imitates the
notes of other birds, though perhaps not so well as the *Chandul,
Galerida cristata*.

M. Jaranica is found in Java, and in some of the other islands of Malayana, and appears to be the only species of this group known throughout the Malayan Archipelago. *M. Horsfieldi*, Gould, from Australia, has been already alluded to. There are, perhaps, several of this genus found in Africa, but some that are referred to it by Dr. Smith, appear to belong to the genus *Megalophonus* of Gray (*Brachonyx*, Swains), as well as some of the *Alauda* of Smith. This merely differs from *Mirafra* in having weaker bills.

2nd The True Larks.

These have the nostrils covered with a tuft of incumbent bristle-like feathers. They frequent more open ground than the Bush-larks, and do not endeavour to conceal themselves further than by squatting close to the ground. There are several forms among the true Larks, some of them having their bills nearly as strong as in *Mirafra*.

The first two genera have their plumage nearly uniform, and, scarcely, if at all, striated; their bills are thick and Finch-like, and were it not for their tufted nostrils, they might be ranked with the *Mirafræ;* and, indeed, two of them were described under that generic appellation.

Gen. AMMOMANES, Cabanis.

Char.—Bill short, thick, compressed, arched at culmen, acute at the tip, which is slightly bent over; gonys ascending; wings long, straight, 1st quill minute, 2nd not so long as the 3rd and 4th, which are the longest, and 5th is nearly equal; tertiaries not elongated beyond the secondaries; tail rather long, slightly emarginate; tarsus and feet moderate; hind claw large. These birds have a remarkable rufous coloration on the back, tail, and under parts; frequent open bare fields and plains, and do not congregate.

758. Ammomanes phænicura, FRANKLIN.

Mirafra, apud FRANKLIN, P. Z. S. 1831—SYKES, Cat. 100—JERDON, Cat. 188—BLYTH, Cat. 747—HORSF., Cat. 722—*Aggiya*, H.—*Reytal*, H., of some—*Ambali-jori-gadu*, Tel., sometimes *Dowapitta, i. e.* Road bird.

The Rufous-tailed Finch-lark.

Descr.—Plumage above ashy brown with a rufescent tinge ; rump, base of tail, the inner webs of the quills, and the tail-feathers, dark rufous or dull ferruginous ; the quills and tip of the tail dark brown ; lower parts the same ferruginous hue, but paler on the throat and lower tail-coverts, and with a few dusky streaks on the breast ; extremity of the lower tail-coverts with a dusky spot.

Bill horny brown above, fleshy at the base beneath ; legs fleshy ; irides brown. Length $6\frac{1}{2}$ inches ; wing $4\frac{2}{10}$; tail $2\frac{4}{10}$; bill at front $\frac{9}{10}$; tarsus $\frac{6}{10}$; hind toe and claw $\frac{6}{10}$.

The Rufous-tailed Lark is found throughout the southern part of India, as far North, at all events, as the Nerbudda on the West, more rare however towards the North. I have seen it North of the Nerbudda, at Mhow and Saugor, but rare ; and Tickell appears to have met with it in Central India. It is unknown on the Malabar Coast, in Bengal and in the N. W. Provinces. It is most abundant in the bare table-land of the Deccan, frequenting open plains, ploughed lands, stubble fields, and dry beds of rivers. It frequently ascends suddenly in the air by a few interrupted strokes of its wings, and uttering at the same time a pleasant loud whistling note, something like *too-whee* ; it then descends with a sudden fall, changing its note to a low lark-like warbling ; when close to the ground, it again repeats this, and so on for several times. It occasionally, though very rarely, perches on low trees or bushes. It feeds on seeds of various kinds, and hard insects ; and it makes its nest on the ground, of grass and other light material, generally under the shelter of a clod of earth, or tuft of grass, laying three or four eggs, dirty greenish-white, with numerous small brown spots. It breeds about Jaulnah in February and March. Tickell found it breeding in Central India in June.

759. Ammomanes lusitanica, Gmelin.

Alauda, apud Gmelin—A. deserti, Lichten.—A. isabellina, Temm, Pl. Col. 244. f. 2.—Gould, Birds of Europe, pl. 163— Mirafra phœnicuroides, Blyth.—Horsf., Cat. 723.

THE PALE-RUFOUS FINCH-LARK.

Descr.—Allined to *A. phœnicura*, but the general hue is less rufescent; upper parts dull sandy grey-brown; the wing-coverts dark-shafted; the under parts fulvous grey, or isabelline, albescent on the throat, and with a few faint dusky streaks on the breast; tail brown, faintly rufescent at its extreme base, and on the outer web of the outermost feather; broad margins to the inner webs of the primaries and secondaries, with the axillaries, also pale rufescent.

Bill dusky above, yellowish beneath; feet pale yellow-brown. Length about 6 inches; wing 4; tail $2\frac{3}{4}$; tarsus $\frac{7}{8}$; hind claw above $\frac{5}{16}$.

This species inhabits Affghanistan and Central Asia, but spreads into Cashmere and the Punjab Salt range, where procured by Mr. Theobald. Griffith states that it frequents rocks and stony places, and that the claws are usually much worn. It is chiefly an inhabitant of Arabia, Northern Africa, and Southern Europe, especially in the south of Spain and Portugal.

It is much paler and less rufous than the last; of which it may be supposed to have the habits. Tristram found its nest in Africa, and describes the eggs as cream colour, blotched with red and brown.

Other species of this Finch-lark are *A. cinnamomea*, Bonap., and *A. pallida* of Ehrenberg. It does not seem that the Indian examples have been accurately compared with *lusitanica*, and Horsfield, in his Catalogue, gives both these last species with a query, as perhaps the same as our bird.

The next genus is chiefly developed in Africa, one species only occurring in India.

Gen. PYRRHULAUDA, A. Smith.

Char.—Bill short, very stout, sides compressed; tip entire; culmen strongly arched; commissure straight; wings moderately long, broad, and well developed, and the tertiaries lengthened; first quill very small, the four next equal and longest; tail moderate, slightly forked; tarsus short; toes small; hind claw slightly lengthened and curved.

This genus of small Larks was formerly classed among the
Finches by some naturalists. With much of the structure of the true
Larks, it differs remarkably by its short stout bill ; and the sexes
differ in colour, the males having some large patches of black on
their under parts.

760. Pyrrhulauda grisea, Scopoli.

Alauda, apud Scopoli—Blyth, Cat. 718--Horsf., Cat. 724—
P. crucigera, Temm. Pl. Col. 269-1—Sykes, Cat. 108—Jerdon,
Cat. 194—Alauda gingica, Gmel.—*Diyora*, H. *Duri*, H. of some,
commonly called *Dabhak churi*, i. e., Squat Sparrow—*Jothauli*, of
Hindu bird-dealers (Buch. Ham.)—*Chat-bharai*, and *Dhula chata*,
Beng.—*Poti-pichike* or *Piyada pichike*, Tel., i. e., Short Sparrow
or Ground Sparrow. *Ortolan* of some Europeans in the south
of India.

The Black-bellied Finch-Lark.

Descr.—Male, above pale brownish grey, the feathers slightly
centred darker, somewhat rufescent on the back ; forehead and
cheeks whitish; wings and tail brown, the feathers all pale edged; and
a deep brown or black band from the base of bill through the eyes,
continued to the occiput ; chin and throat, sides of neck (extending
at right angles behind the ear-coverts, and thus taking the form
of a cross, whence Temminck's specific name), breast, and lower
parts deep chocolate brown or black ; sides of breast, of abdomen,
and the flanks, whitish, bordering the dark colour.

Bill pale; legs fleshy ; irides dark brown. Length about 5
inches ; extent 10 ; wing 3 ; tail nearly 2 ; bill at front not ¾.

The female wants the black on the lower parts, the plumage
is darker, and more rufescent above ; the breast faintly streaked
with brown, and earthy on the flanks, sides of breast, and neck.
She is a smaller bird, measuring about 4¾ inches

This curious little bird is common throughout all India, from
Ceylon to the foot of the Himalayas, except on the Malabar
Coast, and it does not ascend the Himalayas at all. It is
especially abundant in Western India, in Sindh, and the Punjab, and extends thence to Arabia. It frequents the open
plains, and ploughed or fallow fields, and prefers the barest spots,

and especially roads, where it may often be seen dusting itself. It is remarkble for the sudden ascents and descents of its flight, mounting up some height by a few flappings of its wings, and then descending almost perpendicularly, till it nearly reaches the ground, when it again rises as before, and repeats this several times. In general, it takes but a short flight, and, on alighting, squats close to the ground, and will almost allow itself to be ridden over before it rises. It occasionally may be seen seated on the house-top, but I never saw it perch on a tree except on one occasion, when I observed about twelve or fifteen of them perched on a low tree close to cantonment in the hot weather. It makes its nest, from January to March, in the Deccan, later further north, on the ground in a slight hollow, with grass, thread, pieces of cloth, &c., and lays two or three eggs of a light greenish grey tint, with small brown spots, chiefly at the larger end. The young birds are plumaged like the true larks. Sundevall says that he heard it singing in the air like a lark, with expanded wings. This I have not witnessed.

It remains the whole year in India, and, in the cold season, sometimes collects in large flocks, and is then often shot for table as the ' *Ortolan.*' Layard says, that it visits Ceylon in flocks, in the cold weather, but does not breed there.

Several species of this genus occur in Africa, and have been figured in Dr. Smith's Zoology of South Africa.

In the next group, the wings are much lengthened, the 1st primary rudimentary, or even wanting in some. To this belongs the *Calandra* Larks, and *Calandrella*, in which the bill is still thick and short, and the plumage plain, not strongly streaked ; and, in *Calandra* there is a patch of black on the breast, assimilating them to the preceding birds.

Gen. CALANDRELLA, Kaup.

Syn. *Coryphidea*, BLYTH.

Char.—Bill short, sub-conic, moderately compressed ; wings long, straight ; first primary minute, the next three primaries about equal ; tertiaries elongated ; feet small, with shortish toes, and moderately short, but straight hind claw.

This form has more the aspect of a Bunting than a Lark.

3 н

761. Calandrella brachydactyla, Temminck.

Alauda, apud Temminck—Horsf., Cat. 714—Al. calandrella,
Bonelli—Blyth, Cat. 736—Alauda dukhunensis, Sykes, Cat.
99—Jerdon, Cat. 187—A. arenaria, Stephens—Emberiza baghaira, Franklin—E. olivacea, Tickell—*Baghaira*, or *Bag-*
heyri or *Baghoda*, H.—*Ortolan* of Europeans in India.

The Short-toed or Social Lark.

Descr.—Upper parts pale rufescent sandy, streaked with dusky;
a stripe over the eye, and the whole under parts, fulvous-white,
tinged with earthy brown on the breast, which is spotless in some,
in a few slightly spotted; wings dusky brown, with fulvous edgings, broader and deeper-colored on the tertiaries, and on the
tips of the coverts, and with a whitish edge to the first developed
primary; tail dusky, the penultimate feather having the outer web
white-edged, and the outermost feather with the outer web wholly
white to near the base, and also some of the inner web.   In old or
worn plumage the dusky tinge prevails on the back, the breast has
some narrow dusky streaks, and a patch of the same appears on
each side of the lower part of the foreneck; this is also slightly
observable in newly moulted specimens.

Bill whitish horny, dusky on the ridge of upper mandible; legs
brownish, darker at the joints; irides dark brown.   Length $6\frac{1}{4}$
inches; wing 4; tail $2\frac{1}{4}$; tarsus $\frac{8}{10}$; hind toe with claw about $\frac{6}{10}$.

This species is widely distributed throughout Asia, Europe, and
Africa, and has even been once killed in Britain.   It is found
throughout India, more rare to the extreme south, and it has not
been observed in Ceylon, but numerous in the Deccan, and thence
northwards to the foot of the Himalayas, but not in the countries
to the eastward.

The short-toed Lark appears in India in October and November,
in flocks, frequenting the bare grass downs, frequently damp spots
near tanks, also grain fields and ploughed land, and it almost
always retires to cornfields or grass for shelter during the heat of
the day, whence it does not in general issue again till next morning, for they are seldom seen flying about or feeding in the
afternoon or evening.   It feeds almost entirely on seeds; both

runs and hops on the ground, and has a call note like that of the real Larks. Towards the end of March in the south, April in the north of India, different flocks often unite into vast troops, containing many thousand birds, and quite darkening the air, so close do they keep together, even when flying. Great numbers are netted in some parts of the country, or taken by bird-lime, or shot; for when feeding, they keep close to each other. On one occasion, on the cavalry parade-ground at Kamptee, I bagged twelve dozen birds after discharging both barrels, and many wounded birds escaped. They get quite fat about this time, and are really very excellent eating, and they are always called Ortolan by Europeans in India. They leave the north of India about the end of April, or beginning of May, and they breed in the steppes of Central Asia, Eastern Russia, and also in Northern Africa, placing their nest on the ground at the edge of a scrub or bush, and laying four to six eggs, usually marked with grey and rufous spots, but sometimes, it is said, unspotted yellow brown.

Alauda leucoptera, Pallas, from North Asia, is placed as a *Calandrella* by Bonaparte. The Calandre Larks (*Melanocorypha*, Boie) are large species, with very thick convex bills; wings with the first primary very minute or wanting, and the tertiaries not elongated. The hind claw is straight and of moderate length. They are chiefly inhabitants of Northern and Central Asia, the South and East of Europe, and of Africa. Their habits are said to be that of the last bird, and of *Alauda*, but that they keep aloof from cultivation. One species, *M. torquata*, Blyth, *M. bimaculata* of Menetries, is the Bokhara Lark of some Europeans in the North-west, the *Jull* of the natives. It is a favorite song bird of the Affghans, and is often brought to the Punjab, Cashmere, and even to Calcutta. It is very like *M. calandra*, but is considered generically distinct by Blyth, and named *Calandrina*, having a longer and less robust bill. Its general color is much as in *Cal. brachydactyla*, but with a large blackish patch on each side of the breast above, tending to meet across; beneath whitish, upper parts dusky, with pale sandy edgings. Length about $7\frac{1}{2}$ inches; wing $4\frac{1}{2}$; tail $2\frac{1}{4}$. It is quite possible that this Lark may yet be found in the extreme North-west Provinces, it being

common in Affghanistan. To this genus also belong *Al. tartarica,*
Pallas, of North Asia, almost entirely black in summer dress,
(occasionally killed in Europe); and *A. mongolica,* Pallas. *Al.
clot-bey,* Temminck and Bonaparte, belongs to the same group; but,
from its very thick and deeply notched bill, has been separated as
Ramphocoris, Bonap.

The next form is not unlike the preceding one, but smaller, and
less social in its habits.

Gen. ALAUDALA, Blyth.

Char.—Bill more lengthened and slender than in the preceding
genera, but still rather short and thick, and slightly curved ; wings
moderate, with no rudimentary first primary, and the first three
quills longest; tail even; feet very small; hind claw about the
length of the toe, nearly straight. Of small size.

This genus may be said to combine the general form (including
the bill) of *Alauda,* with the feet and plumage of *Calandrella.*
There is only one species known, the smallest of all the
Indian Larks.

762. **Alaudala raytal,** Buch. Hamilton.

Alauda, apud B. HAMILTON—HORSF., Cat. 773—Cal. raytal,
BLYTH, Cat. 737—Al. pispoletta, PALLAS ?—*Retal,* H., *i. e.* Sand-
bird.

THE INDIAN SAND-LARK.

Descr.—General hue of the upper parts light brownish-ashy,
with narrow dark centres to the feathers ; lower parts white, faintly
tinged with fulvous on the breast, where obscurely marked with
small spots ; wing-coverts and tertiaries margined with pale
fulvescent or whitish ; the outermost tail-feathers white, except
the inner half of the inner web, and the next one is white along
the marginal half of its outer web only ; a whitish line through the
eyes.

Bill pale horny ; legs fleshy yellowish ; irides brown. Length
$5\frac{1}{4}$ inches; extent 8 ; wing 3 ; tail $1\frac{3}{4}$ to 2 ; tarsus $\frac{7}{10}$; hind toe and
claw not $\frac{1}{2}$; bill at front $\frac{3}{8}$; spread of foot 1.

This little Sand-lark is found on the banks of the Hooghly, Ganges, Indus, and Bramapootra; also, as I lately had the opportunity of observing, abundant on the banks of the Irrawaddy in Upper Burmah. It frequents the sand dunes, the colour of which its own plumage strongly approximates. During the height of the flood of the Irrawaddy, I observed it feeding on the roads and plains in the station at Thayet-myo in small parties. "It occasionally," says Blyth, "ventures short snatches of song, frequently without rising from the ground, and I never saw it mount high."

It is also found in Central Asia, and has been considered the same as *A. pispoletta* of Pallas, which name will stand, if it be identified with that bird. The description applies pretty fairly, but the measurements given do not correspond, the wing being given as 3.8½ inches, and the tail as 2·3. Blyth has seen specimens from Ladakh.

The birds next noticed comprise a very distinct form, and it is the only one which has been observed in the American Continent. They are easily recognised by their sincipital crests, and a peculiar coloration. They are mostly inhabitants of cold or temperate regions, and the following species are probably confined, in India, to the Himalayas.

Gen. OTOCORIS, Bonap.—Crested-Larks.

Syn. *Phileremos.* Brehm.

Char.—Bill moderately short, slender, somewhat conical; the culmen distinctly arched; wings moderately long; no minute primary, and the first three sub-equal and longest; tail long, even; toes short; claws rather long and nearly straight; head with a double, erectile, sincipital crest.

The crested Larks differ from the two last forms, in their shorter wings and longer tail, as well as in the double crest, and there is always some black on the head and breast.

763. Otocoris penicillata, GOULD.

Alauda, apud GOULD, P. Z. S. 1837—BLYTH, Cat. Appendix, p. 337—HORSF., Cat. 709—O. scriba, BON.—GRAY. Gen. Birds, pl. 92.

THE HORNED-LARK.

Descr.—Head, neck, and back, streakless vinaceous ashy, passing to purer grey on the wings; narrow frontal band, lores, ear-coverts, and the sides of the neck, meeting as a gorget across the breast, purple black; the crown and the pointed sincipital tufts also black ; forehead, supercilia, continued round the ear-coverts posteriorly, throat, and below the breast, white, the latter tinged with yellow; primaries fuscous-ashy, the first, externally, white; the tail blackish, except the medial feathers, which are colored like the back, and the outermost and penultimate, which have white margins.

Bill and feet black.   Length about 8 inches ; wing $4\frac{1}{2}$; tail 3 ; bill at gape $\frac{2}{3}$; tarsus 1.

This is the description of the summer dress ; in winter, probably, judging from the analogy of *O. alpestris*, the colors would be much concealed by deciduary grey edgings, and the black would be less intense and not so deep. The males differ from the females in being of a brighter colour, and in having the black feathers on the top of the head much more distinctly marked. The yellow gorget in winter is bright, and in summer remarkably faint, while the black on the nape is *vice versâ*.

The Horned-lark is an inhabitant of the cold regions of Northern Asia, in winter descending to the plains, and coming South.   It has been found in Nepal, Kumaon, and other parts of the Himalayas ; also in Cashmere.   Either this, or the next species, was observed by Adams on the lower Himalayan range (Birds of India, under No. 111).

Messrs. Dickson and Ross, who observed it in Western Asia, say, that they are driven to the plains in winter in search of food, which consists of the grain found in the dung of cattle.   They fly in companies of from three to twelve birds ; are very familiar, especially in winter, when they may be killed easily with an ordinary whip.   They run on the snow with surprising rapidity, and, as soon as the snow has melted on the plains, they return to the mountains.

This Lark is said to sing well, mounting into the air, like a true *Alauda*.

764. Otocoris longirostris, GOULD.

MOORE, P. Z. S., 1855, with figure—HORSF., Cat. 710.

THE LONG-BILLED HORNED-LARK.

Descr.—Allied in colour and in the black markings of the head and breast to *O. penicillata*, but differs in its larger size, considerably more lengthened bill, wings, and tail, in the thicker toes, and in the feathers of the back being broadly centred with brown.

Length $7\frac{3}{4}$ inches; wing 5; tail $3\frac{3}{4}$; bill at front $\frac{6}{10}$; tarsus $\frac{10}{12}$; hind toe and claw $\frac{7}{10}$.

This species has lately been described, and is said to have been procured in the neighbourhood of Agra, but most probably was from the Himalayas. Judging solely from the figure in the P. Z. S., it appears very close to the last, of which perhaps it is only a large specimen. The black on the neck is not continuous with the band from the eye, as in *penicillata*, but the resemblance is very close. Nevertheless, as Mr. Gould is familiar with the previous one, I shall, for the present, give it a place as a distinct species.

Otocoris alpestris is found in Europe, frequenting the sea shores, and has been killed on the English coast; and *O. bilopha*, Temm., Pl. Col. 241, f. 1, much smaller than the preceding, is found in North Africa, and Arabia Petræa, and may occur in the extreme west of Sindh and the Punjab. Several species occur in America, being the only Larks found in the New Continent, and some of these have been separated by Sclater as *Neocorys*.

Gen. SPIZALAUDA, Blyth.

J. A. S. XIV. 258.

Char.—Bill as in *Alauda*, *i. e.*, with the nostrils protected by bristles, but thicker and *Mirafra*-like in its form; wings long, with the 1st quill minute, the next four about equal and longest, as in the true Larks; tertiaries lengthened; hind toe and claw moderately developed; claws longer than in *Mirafra*; coronal feathers lengthened, and forming a pointed crest.

This is simply a thick-billed and highly crested *Alauda*.

765. **Spizalauda deva**, Sykes.

Alauda, apud Sykes, Cat. 98—Mirafra Hayi, Jerdon, 2nd
Suppl. Cat. 188 bis.—J. A. S. XIII. 959—Blyth, Cat. 742—
Horsf., Cat. 721—*Chinna chandul*, Tel.

The Small Crested Lark.

Descr.—Upper part, including the crest, isabelline or rufous
brown, with black mesial streaks ; upper tail-coverts rufescent
without streaks; the first long primary broadly edged with rufescent, and the outermost tail-feather and most of the penultimate of
the same hue ; superciliary streak continued round the back of the
head, and lower parts of a similar or isabelline hue, with a few
dusky striæ on the breast, and paling on the throat.

Bill horny brown, yellowish below; feet fleshy brown ; irides
dark-brown. Length $5\frac{1}{2}$ to $5\frac{3}{4}$ inches; wing $3\frac{3}{8}$; tail about 2, a
trifle longer ; bill at front $\frac{7}{16}$; tarsus $\frac{3}{4}$; hind toe and claw $\frac{11}{16}$. The
short first primary is about $\frac{1}{2}$ an inch long ; the crest has its longest
feathers about $\frac{3}{4}$ inch long; and the mesial dark streak of each is
strong and contrasting.

This small crested Lark is found throughout Southern India,
chiefly on the table-land, rare in the Carnatic. Sykes procured it
in the Deccan, where also I observed it, at Jaulnah, and I obtained
examples from the top of the Eastern Ghâts, and from Mysore.
It frequents grass-land, and has quite the habits of a true Lark, and
not at all those of a *Mirafra*, with which, from its thicker bill,
I at first classed it. It is frequently caged in the Deccan and
in the south of India, sings well, and is an excellent mocking
bird.

We next come to the restricted Larks, with a comparatively
slender bill.

Gen. Alauda, Linnæus (as restricted.)

Char.—Bill moderate, nearly straight, conical or subulate,
slender ; wings long, the first primary exceedingly minute, and
the next four sub-equal, the fifth in some decidedly shorter ; tips
of the lesser quills emarginated ; tail short or moderate, forked ;

tarsus somewhat lengthened; feet large; hind claw very long; coronal feathers elongated, forming a full crest.

766. Alauda triborhyncha, HODGSON.

GRAY, Zool. Misc. p. 84—Alauda dulcivox, HODGSON, apud BLYTH, MSS. Mus. As. Soc.—A. arvensis, Auct., apud BLYTH, Cat. 732—HORSF., Cat. 705—A. cœlipeta, PALLAS?—A. japonica, TEMM., and SCHL. F. J. pl. 47?

THE HIMALAYAN SKY-LARK.

Descr.—Above deep brown, the feathers edged with rufous, broadly so on back of neck : beneath, and eye-brow, pale fulvescent, or earthy white, rufescent on the breast, and with a few brown streaks; tail with the outer feathers nearly all white, and the penultimate with the outer web also white.

Length 7 inches; wing 4 to $4\frac{1}{4}$: tail $2\frac{3}{4}$; bill at front not $\frac{1}{2}$; tarsus 1; hind toe and claw $1\frac{1}{10}$.

This Sky-lark has been found in Nepal by Hodgson. Blyth was latterly induced to separate the Himalayan birds, under Hodgson's name *dulcivox* (under which name he states that he received specimens from Mr. Hodgson), from the European bird, with which he formerly classed *dulcivox*, on the grounds that the form of the wing was distinct, the fourth developed primary in supposed *dulcivox* being barely $\frac{1}{10}$ inch shorter than the third, whereas in *arvensis*, it is at least $\frac{1}{4}$ shorter. The wing of the European Lark is given as $4\frac{1}{2}$ inches, which is longer than in any Indian examples of the present bird. Moreover, the colors of *dulcivox* are said to be brighter, and the contrast more marked. In other respects the two birds are alike, except that the throat and ear-coverts are less spotted in the Himalayan bird, and there is a stronger rufous tinge on the wings.

It is certainly the *A. triborhyncha* of Hodgson, in Horsfield's Catalogue, No. 705, where it is described as follows :—" Very like *A. gulgula ;* differs in being somewhat larger, and the bill smaller; the ferruginous colors brighter, especially on the wings. Length $6\frac{1}{2}$ inches; wing $4\frac{2}{10}$; tail $2\frac{3}{4}$; tarsus $\frac{7}{8}$; hind toe and claw $1\frac{1}{8}$. This Himalayan Lark has been sent from Nepal by Mr. Hodgson, and from Bootan by Mr. Pemberton."

It is most likely the *A. leiopus* of Hodgson, apud Blyth, olim J. A. S., where it is said to be distinguished from *A. gulgula* by its superior size, smaller bill, and longer tail; and from *arvensis* by the shape of its wing. That name however is now given as a synonym of *gulgula*. It is probably also the *triborhyncha* of Gray's Catalogue of the Birds of Nepal, rather than his *dulcivox*, of which no specimens were sent to the British Museum, nor to the Museum of the India House. The name *triborhyncha* should be adopted for this species, under which name it appears to have been sent to the European Museums, and it probably inhabits the higher regions of the Himalayas throughout.

A. dulcivox, Hodgson, apud Gray, may, I think with Horsfield, be considered as *A. arvensis* of Europe and Asia, which we know to be common in Affghanistan, and in the country bordering the Himalayas, and which Hodgson probably saw only as a cage-bird, not having sent any specimens to England.

767. **Alauda gulgula**, FRANKLIN.

P. Z. S., 1831—HORSF., Cat. 706—JERDON, Cat. 184—BLYTH, Cat. 733—A. gracilis, and A. gangetica, BLYTH—A. leiopus, HODGSON (in part)—A. cœlivox, SWINHOE?—A. Malabarica, apud BLYTH, Cat. 734—A. arvensis, apud SUNDEVALL—*Buruta-pitta*, Tel., vulgo *Niala pichiké*, or Ground Sparrow—*Manam-badi* Tam., i. e., Sky-bird—*Bhurut*, H.

THE INDIAN SKY-LARK.

Descr.—Above, the feathers are dark brown, with fulvous margins; beneath fulvescent white, deeper on the breast, and spotted or streaked with dusky; ear-coverts spotted and tipped dusky; a pale eyestreak; the erectile feathers of the head moderately elongated. Some specimens have a rufous tinge on the upper tail-coverts, and also margining the large quills, more especially the secondaries, while the coverts are edged with grey; the tail has the outermost feather almost wholly fulvescent-white, and the penultimate one has its outer web, and sometimes the tip of the inner web of the same tint.

Bill horny brown, pale beneath; legs fleshy brown; irides dark brown; length 6 to 6½ inches; wing 3¼ to 3¾; tail 2 to 2¼; tarsus 1; bill at front ½; hind toe and claw 1¹⁄₁₀.

This species has much the plumage of the Sky-lark of Europe, but is a good deal smaller; the under parts are generally more rufescent, and there is a stronger tinge of this hue both on the upper and under surface of the wings; the outer tail-feathers too are generally tinged with the same. The wing has the fourth large primary barely shorter than the third, and the first three are nearly equal, as in *triborhyncha*.

Hill examples appear to be brighter, and with more strongly contrasting colours than those usually killed in the plains, and these Hodgson sent as *A. leiopus*, but he also appears to have applied this name to the previous species (V. Gray, Cat. Birds of Nepal). Swinhoe has *Al. cœlivox*, which may be the same. He compares it with *A. japonica*, stating it to be a much smaller species than the Japanese bird. Blyth doubtfully puts it as *gulgula.*

The Indian Sky-lark is found throughout the whole of India, frequenting grassy hills, meadows, and fields; the grassy edges of tanks are favorite spots, and also the bunds of rice fields, in which they often breed. It rises into the air singing, but does not perhaps soar so high as the Lavrock of England. It breeds from March to June, making its nest of grass and hair, on the ground under a tuft of grass; and laying three or four greenish-grey eggs, with numerous brown and dusky streaks and spots. In the cold weather they associate more or less in flocks, and are taken in great numbers for the table. It is particularly abundant on the Neilgherries, and also in Wynaad, and in Lower Bengal. I did not procure it at Darjeeling. "The song," says Mr. Blyth, "very closely resembles that of the British Sky-lark."

Comparatively few residents in India are aware that a Sky-lark is common in almost every part of India, and when they go to a hill station, observe this bird, perhaps for the first time, with equal surprise and delight. About February many are brought to the Calcutta market, and sold as Ortolan.

A. cantarella, Bonap., a supposed distinct species that has been
killed occasionally in the South of Europe, and said to be smaller
and duller in colour than *arvensis*, ought to be compared with
A. gulgula.

768. Alauda malabarica, SCOPOLI.

SONNERAT, Voy. aux Indes Or., 2, pl. 113, f. 1—BLYTH, J. A. S.
XXIX., p. 96, not of his Catalogue.

THE CRESTED MALABAR LARK.

Descr.—Very similar to *A. gulgula*, but has a well developed
pointed frontal crest.   It is somewhat smaller, and the general tone
of coloring much more rufous.   It is found in various parts of
Southern India, but I am not able at present to define its geographical distribution.   It is however, a very distinct species, and
follows *Spizalauda deva* very closely.

The wood Larks have been separated by Kaup as *Lullula*, in
which the 1st primary is somewhat larger than in *Alauda arvensis*,
and the 2nd also conspicuously shorter than the next three.

Several African species of *Alauda* are recorded, but some of
them differ slightly from the typical form, and have been named
Calendulauda by Blyth, having stouter bills.

The next form differs from the true Larks in its somewhat longer
bill, crested head (to which, however, we are led by the last
bird), and in the shorter hind claw.

Gen. GALERIDA, Boie.

Char.—Bill lengthened, slightly curved; wings, with the first
primary moderately developed, the next four sub-equal, the second
slightly shorter; toes and hind claw less elongated than in *Alauda*;
an erectile, lengthened and pointed crest on the top of the head.

769. Galerida cristata, LINNÆUS.

Alauda, apud LINNÆUS—GOULD, Birds of Europe, pl. 165—
HORSF., Cat. 703—A. chendula, FRANKLIN,—Gal. chendula,
BLYTH, Cat. 740—A. gulgula, apud SYKES, Cat. 97—A. deva,
apud JERDON, Cat. 186—Certhilauda Boysii, BLYTH (caged
specimen)—A. galerita, PALLAS—*Chendul*, H. also in Tel., but
sometimes called *Jutu-pitta*, *i. e.*, the Crested bird.

THE LARGE CRESTED LARK.

Descr.—Pale earthy or sandy brown, rufescent on the feathers
of the upper parts, with pale dusky mesial streaks; the feathers
of the crest alone, with dark brown centres; wings somewhat
rufescent; upper tail-coverts the same, as are the lower surface of
the wings and tail; outermost tail-feather rufescent white, the
next with a border of the same on its outer web, the four middle
feathers colored like the back, and the rest of the tail blackish;
supercilia and lower parts sullied white, with a few brown
streaks on the breast.

Bill yellowish; feet pale brown; irides dark brown. Length $7\frac{1}{4}$
to $7\frac{1}{2}$ inches; wing 4 to $4\frac{1}{4}$; tail $2\frac{1}{2}$ to $2\frac{3}{4}$; bill at front $\frac{3}{4}$;
tarsus 1.

The crested Lark is widely spread over all the South of Europe,
North Africa, and a great part of Asia; and it is found throughout
all India, most abundant in the North and North-west. It is rare
in the Carnatic, not found in Malabar, more common in the
Deccan, and thence spreading from Behar in the East, to Sindh and
the Punjab, where very common. It is not known in Bengal,
nor in the Himalayas, nor in the countries to the eastwards.
It prefers dry open sandy plains, or ploughed land, to grass,
wet meadows, or cultivation. It rises in the air singing, though
not so high as *A. gulgula*, nor is its song so fine. In winter, it
may be seen in small parties, or sometimes in considerable flocks,
occasionally on roads and barren places. Theobald found the nest
and eggs, the former, a little grass, in a hole in the ground, the
eggs four, yellowish-white, uniformly freckled with greyish-yellow
and neutral-tint. It is frequently caged in all parts of the
country, and the bird is kept in darkness by several layers of
cloth wrapped round the cage; the custom being to wrap an
additional cover round the cage every year. In this state it
sings very sweetly, and learns to imitate most exactly the
notes of various other birds, and of animals, such as the
yelping of a dog, the mewing of a cat, the call of a hen to her
chickens, &c., &c. Examples from different parts of the country
differ somewhat in the depth of colour, some being lighter
than others; and Mr. Blyth, from a small and caged specimen,

considered that there was a second and smaller race in India, which he named *C. Boysii*.

Two or three African species are recorded by Bonaparte and Tristram.

3rd.—Desert Larks.

These have the light aspect and the naked nostrils of the Pipits; typically inhabit desert and sandy places, and are numerous in Africa.

Gen. CERTHILAUDA, Swainson.

Char.—Bill slender, lengthened, more or less curved; nostrils round and naked; wings very long, the 1st quill short, the second a little shorter than the next three, which are nearly equal; tail moderate or rather long, even; tarsus lengthened; toes short; hinder claw variable, typically short and straight.

The only species occuring in India has been separated from *Certhilauda* by several Ornithologists under the name *Alæmon*, Keys and Bl., on account of its peculiar, plain, almost unstreaked coloration, and slightly curved bill. A closely allied race is *C. Salvini*, Tristram, from North Africa; and *C. Duponti*, Vieill., is another of the same group.

770. Certhilauda desertorum, STANLEY.

Alauda, apud STANLEY—BLYTH, Cat. 738—HORSF., Cat. 702—
Al. bifasciata, LICHT.— TEMM. Pl., Col. 393—RÜPPELL, F. Abyss.,
pl. 5--Saxicola pallida, BLYTH, J. A. S. XVI. 130.

THE DESERT-LARK.

Descr.—Light isabella grey above, more fulvescent on the scapulars, tertiaries, and two middle tail-feathers, which are shaded with pale dusky along the middle; lores, superciliary stripe, throat and belly, white; the breast feathers dusky, with broad whitish margins concealing the dark colour within; ear-coverts blackish at the tip; wings deep dusky black; primaries and secondaries pure white at base; the shorter primaries also white tipped, and the small wing-coverts margined with pale fulvescent; tail, except the two middle feathers, deep dusky black, the outermost feathers having its narrow outer web almost wholly white, and the

penultimate with a narrow white edge on the outer web. The
colours of the female are duller.

Length 9 inches; wing 5¼; tail 4½; tarsus 1⅜.

This Desert-lark of Africa and Arabia, and a rare straggler to
the South of Europe, has been found in India only in Sindh,
where observed by the late Dr. Gould; but it will probably
hereafter be found throughout the great desert tracts of the N. W.
Provinces. It is said to run fast, to live on seeds, and to be
a fine songster. An Indian example is much darker than the
figure in Rüppell, generally considered the same bird.

Tristram has an interesting account of this species (Ibis, vol. 1.,
p. 427.) "At first sight it reminded me much of a Plover, in the
manner in which it rose and scudded away. Indeed, there is
nothing of the Lark in its flight, except in early morning, when
I have watched it rise perpendicularly to some elevation, and then
suddenly drop, repeating these gambols uninterruptedly over
exactly the same spot for nearly an hour, accompanying itself by
a loud whistling song. It runs with great rapidity." *Alauda
leautaungensis*, Swinhoe, from the plains of the Peiho, by its long
and somewhat curved bill, may be a *Certhilauda*, but, being
crested, perhaps is more properly a *Galerida*.

Some of the African species are said to inhabit desert, sandy
places, interspersed with brushwood, or wild grassy plains; and,
when not seeking their food, are commonly seen resting upon
small hillocks, or even perched on a low shrub, occasionally uttering a few whistling notes. Several are colored quite as the
typical Larks, striated above and spotted on the breast, and these
are said to affect grassy situations.